Reno,

May this book inspire a
vision for a cosmological
education.

Blessings,

Benjamin Lyda

Advance Praise for
John Senior and the Restoration of Realism

"*John Senior and the Restoration of Realism* is a book that should be in the hands of every educator and parent. It is all about education—and to educate, as Plato already saw twenty-five centuries ago, is a task of such dignity that only the very best are good enough. We must be grateful to Father Francis Bethel for writing a life of this noble Don Quixote whose love of beauty led him to the One Who Is Truth, Beauty, and Goodness."

—Alice von Hildebrand, Dame Grand Cross of the Pontifical Order of St. Gregory the Great and author of *Memoirs of a Happy Failure*

"John Senior's impact on culture has been profound, though largely unsung and unnoticed. His ability to open the eyes of his students to the wonders of the cosmos and the presence of God that it signifies was nothing less than astonishing. It is high time that someone sang his praises and high time that someone introduced his vision of evangelical aesthetics to a new generation. Father Bethel's book is, therefore, to be not only welcomed but celebrated."

—Joseph Pearce, Author of *Beauteous Truth: Faith, Reason, Literature and Culture*

"John Senior said every man was either a cowboy or a sailor. His purpose in saying this was that once people realize *who* they are, they might better realize *where* they are and *what* they should be doing there. Father Bethel's book brings John Senior and his insights back to the world so that a new generation may be born in wonder. Dr. Senior was one of the most important Catholic minds of the past fifty years—a man who taught that, though we cannot restore reality, we can restore our vision of it and vocation to it, and thereby restore realism."

—Sean Fitzpatrick, Headmaster, Gregory the Great Academy

"In our era of cultural degradation, learned people of faith are increasingly discontented with the present and the future. That is all the more reason to read Francis Bethel's account of one of the intellectual and cultural giants of this epoch. Without John Senior and the movements he spawned, there would, in fact, be little hope for the future."

—Kevin D. Roberts, President, Wyoming Catholic College

"John Senior was the teacher modernity desperately needed—and needs. His learning, wisdom, faith, and eloquence supplied the essential corrective to our era's withered soul and imagination. In this intellectual biography, Father Bethel effectively restores Senior to us and makes us see again both the man and the poetic reality he grasped so firmly."

—David M. Whalen, Provost and Professor
of English, Hillsdale College

"John Senior was a gifted professor of classics, a writer, poet, thinker and a student of culture. He was my godfather and, more than anyone else—besides Our Lady and the Holy Spirit, of course—he led me into the Roman Catholic Church. He used to tell his students: "I am simply the janitor. It is my job to open the door and show you the riches and treasures of the best that has been written and said down through the centuries." Dr. Senior loved his students and we loved him. Father Bethel has written a book that unlocks the mystery of the man who was John Senior. His spiritual and intellectual journey is fascinating. Father Bethel has given a synthesis of John Senior's insightful views on education and culture, and has traced how his philosophy and this synthesis grew out of Senior's own life. John Senior was a realist, but he pondered the permanent things in life with a curiosity and childlike wonder. John Senior was well aware that we are all broken creatures, living in a wounded and sinful world. Oscar Wilde once said that, "we are all in the gutter, but some of us are looking up at the stars." John Senior was always looking up at the stars, and he helped all of us to turn our gaze upwards, toward the stars. I highly recommend this book not only as an introduction to John Senior's thought, but also as an important message, especially in our times, about education and culture."

—Most Reverend James D. Conley, Bishop of Lincoln, Nebraska and
Founder of the Newman Institute for Catholic Thought & Culture

JOHN SENIOR
AND THE
RESTORATION
OF REALISM

JOHN SENIOR
AND THE
RESTORATION
OF REALISM

FATHER FRANCIS BETHEL, OSB

a monk of Clear Creek Abbey

Cataloging-in-Publication Data on file with the Library of Congress

ISBN 978-0-9973140-0-7

Published in the United States by
Thomas More College Press
Thomas More College of Liberal Arts
6 Manchester Street
Merrimack, New Hampshire 03054

Thomas More College Press SAN 990-1108

The publisher wishes to thank
Gareth Genner
Frank Hanna III
Charlie McKinney
for their roles in helping to establish
Thomas More College Press

To all the students of John Senior

Contents

There is something destructive—destructive of the human itself—in cutting us off from the earth from whence we come and the stars, the angels, and God himself to whom we go.

—JOHN SENIOR,
The Restoration of Christian Culture

Dictatorial Relativism

JOHN SENIOR and the Restoration of Realism is a book that should be in the hands of every educator and every parent. It is all about education—and to educate, as Plato already saw twenty-five centuries ago, is a task of such dignity that only the very best are good enough. Gardeners treat their flowers with tenderness and wisdom. We cannot set the bar too high for gardeners of the human soul, made to God's image and likeness.

Great things are never easy, Plato tells us and, alas, great educators are rare. Many are mediocre; some are poisonous and if they happen to have rhetorical talents, they are like vampires that suck the blood out of their victims. Nobody better than Chesterton has pinpointed this deadly danger. He writes: ". . . the dangerous criminal is the educated criminal. We say that the most dangerous criminal now is the entirely lawless modern philosopher. Compared to him burglars and bigamists are essentially moral men; my heart goes out to them." [1] The so-called philosopher he is referring to, far from being "a lover of wisdom" is an impostor for he views objective truth as his deadly enemy. He is the man who, knowing that religious and philosophical truths demand obedience, shuns them with dread while trying to convince his hearers that he is offering them a broader view of life, a more "advanced," a more "modern" and "liberating" approach to intellectual problems. His gospel is "all truth is relative." Acceptance of this leaky philosophy should be enthusiastically endorsed in a world of conflicts: for it offers the only possible way to peace and harmony. Tolerance, understanding for "other points of view," they say, testifies to a generous broad-mindedness. After all, is it not arrogant and

pretentious to claim that one has the truth? Any intelligent person should understand that "my" truth need not be "your" truth. The president of a large secular university told me that she had "become a much better person" the day she discovered that "everything is relative." The poison of Relativism is rampant in many societies, but there are historical moments when it conquers schools, colleges and universities and inevitably leads to the demise of those societies.

Born in 1923, John Senior could not escape being influenced by Relativism, for which, in the best of cases, any affirmation can only be "relatively true." Like most people of his generation, he had to struggle and make detours before his gifts were liberated from the nets of confusion and error. Even though the cancer called Relativism was not apparent at the beginning of the twentieth century, the poison was already spreading in schools and universities before its destructive power conquered society at large through the news media.

Richly endowed, deeply longing for truth, moved by beauty and sensitive to goodness, John Senior nevertheless had to struggle long and hard before finding the meaning of life. His sense for beauty attracted him to nature early in life. Aged thirteen, he ran away from home to escape to a ranch in North Dakota, where he shared the lives of cowboys whose stories had fascinated him. When finally found and back with his family, his parents convinced him to pursue his studies, while allowing him to spend his summers in the west, doing hard work on a ranch, and enjoying physical contact with the earth.

As might be expected, the generous young man was attracted to Marxism and the promise of working toward the realization of a better world, a world of peace and justice. He gave it a chance and was disappointed. He seems to have looked also toward Freud for a time, but greater things were awaiting him.

He attended Columbia University in New York, and was fortunate to take the courses of Mark Van Doren, whose eminent teaching talents were universally recognized. English literature was Senior's field, and the young man nurtured and deepened his passion for poetry. In those days, he discovered Plato, who convinced him of the reality of the spiritual.

Married young, he started teaching while still pursuing his graduate studies. His hungry soul was seeking further. Most universities at the time were under the sway of Oriental mysticism; its mysterious poetry was exercising a powerful influence on the young: it emanated a strong perfume that had a note of enchantment, mystery and depth. It had a powerful appeal for starving souls. John Senior indeed flirted with Hinduism but discovered that its glow of spirituality was in fact a *fata morgana*. Oriental mysticism was an escape from the dry scientific approach to life he detested. It was a tempting illusion, but soon the sincere and truth-hungry young man discovered that it actually led to nihilism. Ultimately, being and nonbeing were identical, and he found himself as hungry as before. The Oriental spirituality suffered from a metaphysical "thinness" that left him starving.

He found the intellectual harbor he was seeking in the philosophy of Thomas Aquinas, whose realism and conviction that truth is objective and could be found finally led him into the Catholic Church. At the age of thirty-seven, while teaching at Cornell, he, with his wife and three children, entered the blessed Ark of the Bride of Christ. He was home at last.

Allergic to the noise and increasing industrialization of the East coast, he decided to accept a teaching position in Wyoming. But rightly disappointed upon the appointment of a new president—clearly not made for the job—he moved to the University of Kansas. It is there that his extraordinary talents were to blossom fully.

A teacher—like a doctor—must first and foremost make a right diagnosis of his "patients." The task was both sad and easy: fed on materialism, impregnated by Relativism and blasé, the average student escaped into cheap enjoyments. Not recognizing the deep hunger for truth within themselves, like starving people who are not given healthy food, they gulped down spiritual junk food that made them fall into the illusion that their hunger had been satisfied. Students suffered from a sickness that we might call "spiritual obesity," which prevented them from growing wings, and ascending toward the stars.

Today the task of the educator is arduous: the young plants coming into his hands are often wilted. To quote the psalm: "they have eyes and

do not see; they have ears and do not hear." They must first be purged of the poison on which they have been fed in our anti-culture. To put it differently, let me quote C. S. Lewis: ". . . a hard heart is no infallible protection against a soft head."[2] Lewis further laments the fact that "the task of the modern educator is not to cut down jungles, but to irrigate deserts."[3]

John Senior was fully aware of the immensity of the task to which he was called. A faithful instrument in God's hands, he trusted in His help. The first step was to liberate his students from the world of artificiality in which they lived. Cheap books, vulgar music, loud fun, alcohol and drugs kept their souls and their minds in a state of stupor. Like a talented violinist, he knew how to vibrate the chords of their souls and to attune them to the beauty for which they were yearning.

God brought John Senior to forge a friendship with two other KU professors of like mind: Franklyn Nelick and Dennis Quinn. They, too, knew how serious the educational crisis was. Animated by the same love for "the true, the good and the beautiful," they took the opportunity offered them to start a "college within the college" on the model of Oxford. It was approved by the dean, and a new program was started: the Pearson Integrated Humanities Program. At first, it was limited to some twenty students, but soon the news spread that three professors had enkindled in them enthusiasm for learning and for life. The professors were on fire for "truth, goodness and beauty," and had an extraordinary talent to communicate their love. And the PIHP quickly drew more students.

Starting with great classical works (Homer, the Greek tragedies) the students—for the first time in their lives—discovered that there was beauty, poetry, nobility that were veiled in the gray world in which they had been living. For the first time, they were led out of the "dark den" of Plato's *Republic* (book VII) and into the light. They were encouraged to learn great poems by heart, to watch the stars, to establish a living contact with "the real." They were taught to read the book of nature—as St. Bonaventure put it. They were given real bread. In no time the program, which had started modestly, attracted two hundred students. One would expect that such success would meet with approval. Those who naively

assume that this was the case have little knowledge of university life where mediocrity is honored. Anybody who stands out is a living reproach to his colleagues. One only need recall the world of Shakespeare in *Othello* on "the green eyed monster of jealousy." Jealous people always spy on those of whom they are jealous. Soon, the rumor spread that the three professors were injecting religion into their teaching. They were imposing their ideas upon their gullible students, convincing them of the objectivity of truth. They were therefore sowing narrow-mindedness; they presented their personal ideas as the one and only truth; this was unprofessional and arrogant. Other points of view were anathematized.

Worse was to come; some of the students entered the Roman Catholic Church. This was serious: the separation of church and state was being sinned against. A hypocritical way of stopping this outrage was to deny the program the right to fulfill credit requirements for the students taking the course. Inevitably, the number of students who would have loved to enter the course of the three culprits hesitated to do so. Eager to graduate, they did not want to prolong their student days. When it was discovered that some of John Senior's students had gone to a venerable old Benedictine abbey in Fontgombault, France, and that—horror of horrors—some of them were considering becoming monks, all hell broke loose. The news media expressed their outrage at the brainwashing that was being permitted at KU. The noble work of the three lovers of truth was doomed.

It is noteworthy that when students lose their faith while in college (years ago, the chaplain of the Newman club at Hunter College confided to me that 65 percent of Catholics lose their faith by their senior year), no one objects or even bats an eyelid. After all, the world tells us, colleges should open the minds of their students, and help them to get rid of their childish prejudices. Had students joined an oriental sect, become Buddhists or adepts of New Age, the news media would have remained silent. Had many of them shifted from one Protestant sect to another, it would not have been worth mentioning. But to become Roman Catholic, to enter into this dark fortress that robs people of their freedom and plunges them into a world of darkness and medieval ignorance:

this was scandalous. Such people must be "saved" from intellectual slavery. The work of the three professors—whose crime was to believe in the objectivity of truth and the universal validity of moral values—was destroyed.

Were these three professors surprised? Faithful followers of Christ, they knew that disciples should not be better treated than their Master, who had dared proclaim that He was the Truth. They had sown the good seed; they knew it would blossom in some mysterious way.

But such grief would not be the only one suffered by John Senior in his later days. This ardent Catholic who had a holy love for the Bride of Christ, her holy teaching, her sublime Liturgy, her Sacraments, was to witness the devastation that took place in the wake of Vatican II. Many of us—like him—shed abundant tears over the desecration: the iconoclasm, the irreverence, the hatred of sacred traditions. He suffered and he prayed. The sublimest act on earth, the Holy Sacrifice of the Mass, was too precious of a treasure for him to bear to see defaced.

Before his death, however, he was to experience a great consolation. In April 1999, he learned that a group of his KU students who had become monks in Fontgombault twenty-five years previously were now to establish a monastery in nearby Oklahoma. He passed away to Eternity before this happened, but from Heaven he certainly prays for this foundation, in some ways the fruit of his own labor of love. In their turn, the monks of Clear Creek Abbey pray daily for a man whom God used to bring them into the Holy Ark of the Church.

We must be grateful to Father Francis Bethel for writing the life of this noble Don Quixote whose love of beauty led him to the One Who Is Truth, Beauty and Goodness. The book is strongly recommended. It had to be written, and will benefit all those who—like St. Augustine and John Senior—long for truth.

—*Alice von Hildebrand*

INTRODUCTION

Made for the Stars
but Rooted in the Soil

IN 1999, thirteen Benedictine monks from France arrived at the backlands of Oklahoma to establish a monastery along a remote streamlet, Clear Creek. While they issued from the venerable abbey of Notre Dame de Fontgombault,* one could say that the beginnings of their foundation lay, in fact, in the United States, not so far from Clear Creek, shaped by Providence in the halls of the University of Kansas and set in motion when two of its students knocked at Fontgombault's doors twenty-seven years before. In many ways the monks' foundation was the final outcome of a quest that had begun in the 1970s, when some of the same men, immersed in the anti-culture of the day, entered the university's Integrated Humanities Program (IHP). Designed and conducted by Professors Dennis Quinn, Frank Nelick, and John Senior, the program was built upon a most revolutionary tenet: reality is real. And the means for communicating this fact was quite simply Western culture—prose and poetry, music, architecture and art—bolstered by the book of Nature.

This volume focuses on the life and work of perhaps the most influential of the Kansan professors, John Senior, whose own quest—begun in the occult and ended in the arms of the Catholic Church—impacted the lives not only of the repatriated American monks, but also of hundreds of other IHP students, each one in his or her own way.

---

* The Benedictine abbey of Our Lady at Fontgombault was founded in 1091. After flourishing in the Middle Ages, it suffered decline in the eighteenth century and was closed even before the onslaught of the French Revolution. Monastic life was reestablished there in 1948 by the abbey of Saint Peter of Solesmes. Fontgombault subsequently made four foundations: Randol (1971), Triors (1984), Donezan (1994) in France and Clear Creek (1999) in the United States. All are now abbeys in their own right. In 2013, Fontgombault also took over the monastery of St. Paul of Wisques.

At the time they enrolled in the Integrated Humanities Program, most were typical students of the 1970s, their vision molded by the deconstructionist trends of the day, believing Western ideals and institutions to be outmoded and empty conventions. They knew not where to turn except to what the moment had to offer. Scarcely any realized the immensity of what awaited them; yet very early in the coursework, something awoke in their slumbering souls. Led on by their professors, they discovered, to their surprise, that the old Western tradition was full of treasures, a deep goldmine to be explored. They came to recognize that there are true, good, and beautiful realities which give meaning to life—that indeed there are things greater than self which are worth living for. For a multitude of students, the IHP class was a turning point in their lives. They acquired convictions that continue to guide and stimulate them in their decisions even today.

There are some rather spectacular statistics pointing to the religious effect of this program taught in the context of a secular university. An unofficial count numbers some two hundred among its students who entered the Catholic Church, as well as dozens who returned to the Catholic Faith they had abandoned. Among IHP graduates, as of 2012, there is an archbishop, a bishop, an abbot, a prior and a prioress; two have been religious superiors, another the rector of a seminary; three have been novice masters; one served the Holy See's Congregation of Catholic Bishops for ten years. The secular world has also profited. Former students include a judge, lawyers, school principals, teachers and medical doctors; one alumnus was the head of a U.S. presidential council. Flourishing schools have been inspired by the program; many groups have tried to imitate it. And of course many large, healthy families have sprung up from it.

How did the IHP bring about the extraordinary and unexpected intellectual and spiritual flowering of young lives? Quinn, Nelick and Senior were in agreement regarding the basic needs of education, given the prevailing crisis in learning and culture. In particular, they recognized that Relativism was at the root of the students' disorientation. Most of their generation had fallen into the prevailing philosophy of the times:

the conviction that there is no permanent, universal truth. Each so-called "truth," they assumed, was subjective, restricted to one's own choices. Allan Bloom began his book on university education, *The Closing of the American Mind*, with this attestation:

> There is one thing a professor can be absolutely certain of: almost every student entering the university believes, or says he believes, that truth is relative. If this belief is put to the test, one can count on the students' reaction: they will be uncomprehending. That anyone should regard the proposition as not self-evident astonishes them as though he were calling into question 2+2 = 4. These are things you don't think about.[1]

Given this state of affairs, the three professors knew that the first thing needed was a "conversion" to truth as such, to *reality* itself. Nothing constructive in education could be accomplished until students would accept the fact that there is a difference between truth and error. In fact, the entire IHP project can be summarized as a nurturing of Realism, taking this latter term not in the sense of a particular philosophical system or school, but simply as the conviction that there is an absolute truth, that the exterior world can be known in itself, and that the mind depends on the senses to know it.

At the beginning of the twentieth century, two other movements of religious conversion were likewise set in motion by efforts toward an intellectual return to reality. In France, Henri Bergson worked to show his students that human knowledge is not limited to measurements, that there exists something deeper than quantity. And in Germany, Edmund Husserl longed to escape from centuries of philosophical idealism and "get back to things themselves," as he put it. By breaking down the mental barriers that artificially separated their students from things, Bergson and Husserl enabled them to rediscover the taste for reality and truth. This led many students, through various paths and by God's grace, to accept Christ and enter His Church. It was the case, for example, with Bergson's students Jacques Maritain and Charles Péguy, and

Husserl's Edith Stein (St. Teresa Benedicta of the Cross) and Dietrich von Hildebrand.

Whereas these European conversion movements grew from philosophical studies, the three IHP professors had to operate at a more elementary level. Relativism had been ingrained in their students, not only by their education and by modern culture in general, but also by the artificial world in which they moved. Immersed as they were in an electronic universe of television and rock music, the students were largely cut off from tangible reality. They first had to realize that "stones are hard and water is wet," as the professors liked to say quoting Winston, a character in George Orwell's *1984* (who kept repeating this to himself in order to maintain his sanity under Party propaganda).[2] They had to get a feel for concrete things and thus regain the innate, spontaneous conviction of the existence of reality. They had to rediscover that things are real.

The program took as the means for this rediscovery not philosophy, but the great imaginative literature and poetry of the West, and activities such as song, dance and stargazing. In their teaching, the professors brought out vital human questions present in the readings—what is a home, what is friendship, what is justice, what is healthy work, what is the happy life—dealing with them in concrete ways. They told pertinent stories and quoted literature and poetry, striving to invite their students to taste the mysterious beauty at the heart of these values more than to be able to define them. Above all, they had to instill in this youth the awareness that things are delightful and wonderful, beautiful, good and true.

To understand the IHP adventure, one must delve into John Senior's thought and what led him to help start such an institution. He alone of the three professors elaborated in some detail the theory of this prephilosophical, pre-scientific education.

Senior wrote about culture in general, of which academia is only one aspect. For him, the pre-philosophical need to reconnect to reality extended far beyond the boundaries of the classroom. He recognized that our whole life—in the home, in the community, at work—must return to reality. When

his two books on culture* were first published, in the late '70s and early '80s, some readers thought Senior ranted rather excessively about the woes of our times. However, one can perceive now that he was in fact a prophet of the practical nihilism that has issued from the drastic cultural decline he chronicled. He also provided a radical remedy for it. Although he saw the crisis in contemporary society as one of faith, he had a firm grasp of the principle that grace builds on nature and recognized that natural order and reason are gravely compromised today. He made this comparison: "Faith perfects reason in a manner analogous to the way a sculpture perfects a stone—but if the stone is pulverized, the form is empty air."[3] We need Realism for the good use of our reason and ultimately to provide a healthy ground for faith: "The facts of Christianity," he wrote, "are not real to us because nothing is real to us. We have come to doubt the very existence of reality."[4] And to attain to Realism, we must reconnect sensibly and emotionally with reality. We must restore a healthy imagination.

Similar conclusions had already been drawn by two of the most well-known Catholic converts of the last two centuries. Blessed John Henry Cardinal Newman grasped the importance of imagination and emotion in rendering Christ *real* to modern man, in helping him realize that He is a living person. Senior considered Newman something of a prophet in that the latter foresaw the almost complete absence of Christ from the twentieth-century imagination and the grave danger entailed in this: "It is not so much reason that is against us as imagination," the cardinal wrote 125 years ago, referring to the difficulty of the modern scientific mentality to partake in the world of the Bible.[5] Coming a little later than Newman, G. K. Chesterton, like Senior, had first to devote himself to leading people to the reality of things themselves. Senior quoted Chesterton: "Insanity is not losing your reason, but losing everything else except your reason."[6] A madman may remain quite logical, but he has lost common-sense contact with reality. His mind turns in a disconnection with things.

---

* *The Death of Christian Culture* (New Rochelle, NY: Arlington House, 1978; republished Norfolk, VA: IHS Press, 2008) and *The Restoration of Christian Culture* (San Francisco: Ignatius Press, 1983; republished Norfolk, VA: IHS Press, 2008).

Newman, Chesterton and Senior all agree that we must restore a culture that forms our imagination and emotions in accordance with reality and Christ.

Senior's doctrine is vigorous and clear, simple and practical. Many have recognized that it contains a crucial message for our day. Here are appreciations, not from some local friend, but from two Frenchmen of worldwide renown who knew Senior only through his books. Writing about Senior's *The Death of Christian Culture*, the philosopher Marcel Clément had this to say: "We have here a great book. Each sentence or almost is a lesson of wisdom. . . . It is a most remarkable diagnostic of the intellectual state of the West."[7] And Father R. L. Bruckberger, OP, noted of *The Restoration of Christian Culture*: "I read John Senior's book in one sitting. I was so far from expecting a book of this quality that I am still stupefied. I have my classifications of books, of great books. I put this one in the category of *The Imitation of Christ*. . . . I truly love the United States where I spent eight years that were decisive for me. Never, never could I have imagined that one day an American would write such a book."[8]

John Senior's work has also served as an inspiration to the Spanish writer Natalia Sanmartin Fenollera, whose recent novel *The Awakening of Miss Prim* has become an international bestseller. The novel features a main character who rediscovers the Faith of his childhood and decides to take up residence in a remote European village near a Benedictine abbey— this, after participating in a seminar at the University of Kansas. Fenollera reveals her indebtedness to Senior in an interview: "The reference to the University of Kansas is a discreet homage to John Senior, an exceptional figure who directed a Humanities program outside of the ordinary and whose lucid vision of western culture seems to me absolutely brilliant and finds an echo in my book."[9]

John Senior certainly did not intend to frame a new theory. Quite prudently in our revolutionary and uprooted day, he held that "nobody in his right mind would want to be 'original' or 'innovative' at a time like this."[10] Avoiding novelty was also a matter of conviction: "In the large sense, philosophy and theology have been done; granted there are still

important disputed areas, but the continents are spanned, the lay of the land has been mapped."[11] It often happens, however, that the person who wants only to be a disciple is the one who truly advances doctrine. Senior's deep and ardent assimilation of Western masters enabled him to draw from tradition certain fundamental points that needed to be elaborated and applied to the circumstances of our times.

I was a student of Senior's in the early 1970s. I kept up friendly contact with him all through the years by correspondence, and avidly devoured his writings as soon as I could get my hands on them. I have always reflected on what I received from him and the IHP, especially in the light of my later studies in philosophy. Although Senior regularly laid out philosophical principles in class, he did not teach philosophy *per se* or write a treatise. His writings were, rather, poetic or rhetorical. He modestly considered himself only an amateur philosopher, teaching elementary things presupposed by philosophy: "The ordinary is the province of the schoolmasters like myself who from their low vantage, while in the high and palmy ways of science and theology they know little or nothing, know the things that everybody must do first."[12] Nevertheless, a well thought-out philosophical framework supported his doctrine. The goal of the following pages is to unfold that doctrine.

Senior once said that Shakespeare's plays, in relation to the lyric poetry they contain, are like a Gothic church that exists for its stained-glass windows. Quotations from Senior are certainly the stained-glass windows of the present work. I will proceed mainly by quoting the professor and then providing commentary that will mostly demonstrate how the philosophical synthesis behind his teaching is rooted in Plato, Aristotle, St. Thomas Aquinas and Newman. I will occasionally develop a point on my own, because the ultimate goal of the present work is not simply to understand Senior's thought, but to advance in Realism ourselves. Senior should be less the object than the guide for a study of Realism to encourage our own ascent to the stars.

While this book is not a biography in the strict sense of that term but rather a study of John Senior's thought, it will nevertheless have a biographical character, as his deep convictions and doctrine grew out of his

personal intellectual and spiritual journey: from a Marxist materialism that denied spiritual realities, through an Oriental spiritualism that strove for the spiritual stars by discarding man's roots in sensible realities, to Realism and ultimately to the Catholic Church. The title of this introduction—*Made for the Stars but Rooted in the Soil*—represents the pivotal philosophical point of that pilgrimage as well as the crux of all of Senior's thought. He realized by his own experience that the human plant, in order to tend to the stars, must be nourished in the soil of this world. His turnabout and then his work with students deeply impressed on him that we must ground all intellectual and affective life on the experiential and imaginative level. This concrete way of nourishing Realism underlay everything he taught and the way he taught it. It is the key to entering into a deep understanding of his doctrine.

Part I of our book will follow Senior through the 1950s, from his youth through his first teaching assignments and the completion of his doctorate. His intellectual and spiritual conversions will give us the opportunity to uncover the principles behind the two fundamental positions of human thought: "Realism," and what can be termed "Anti-Realism," the first holding that the real is real, beautiful, good and true, the latter, that it is an illusion. With Senior, we will examine the history of the war between these two spheres, starting with the ancient Greeks but focusing in detail on what has led to our contemporary Anti-Realist climate. Parts II and III will refer especially to the 1960s, when Senior's positions on education and culture matured at the University of Wyoming. Part II considers the theory of Realism itself and how Senior came to it, while Part III covers Senior's ideas for applying the theory in the home, school and general culture. Part IV discusses how Senior, with Professors Quinn and Nelick, implemented his educational ideas in the 1970s at the University of Kansas and describes the fate of the IHP, an episode that so aptly illustrates the perennial war between Realism and Anti-Realism.

The reader already may have noticed that the many references to cited works are provided in endnote form, while notes providing content of more immediate interest are denoted by asterisks and appear as footnotes. This has been done so as not to interrupt or distract the reader.

I want to thank those who looked over all or part of the manuscript at various stages of its development, notably Katie Miller, with whom I discussed ideas as well, Chris Owen, who much encouraged me, and Charles Pendergast, as well as Kelly Boutross, Annie Calovich, and Ken Craven. Also, my special gratitude goes to Kirk Kramer for some zealous research and to Maria Gerber for always being so available to help with editing. I thank William Fahey for shepherding the book to publication, and his wife Amy for the final editing. I also thank Senior's colleagues and students of before my time who told of him in the 1950s and 1960s, and members of his family who gave me views of Senior's life outside the range of a student's experience, especially his daughter Penny Fonfara and his late sister Mary Cornish. Finally, I express my gratitude to Father Abbot and the monks of Clear Creek for bearing with me during these long months.

Let me close this introduction by applying to this present work a poem Senior wrote in conscious imitation of Geoffrey Chaucer's own famous *Retraccioun* to usher in his book of poetry:

Retraction
If any of these rhymes
sownen* into sin,
blame it on the times
that let such notions in.
If it's on the poet's part,
commend him to the Sacred Heart.

---

* The Middle English *sownen*, Senior noted, comes directly from Chaucer's *Retraccioun* and means "lead someone into."

Part I

Two Perennial Philosophies

Because it is rooted in duality, the Christian tradition is opposed to the Oriental. There is nothing and there is something; and they are not the same.
— The Death of Christian Culture

John Senior, circa 1958. *Courtesy of Annunciation Monastery of Clear Creek and Penny Fonfara.*

CHAPTER ONE

The Cowboy and the Scholar

The immediate (practical) purpose of drinking a cup of coffee is to wash the biscuit down. Its proximate (ethical) purpose is the intimate communion of, say, cowboys (they do exist; Will James was right!) standing around the sullen campfire in a drenching rain, water curling off Stetsons, over slickers, splashing on the rowels of spurs, as they draw the bitter liquid down their several throats into the single moral belly of their comradeship. The remote (political) purpose of coffee at the campfire, is the making of Americans—born on the frontier, free, frank, friendly, touchy about honor, despisers of fences, lovers of horses, worshipers of eagles and women. . . . The ultimate purpose is spiritual. For a boy to drink a can of coffee with cowboys in the rain is, as Odysseus said of Alcinous's banquet, something like perfection.

—"The Restoration of Innocence"

ONE day in 1936, a boy in his early teens, tired of the mechanized and comfortable life of Long Island, put together a few things and the little money he had saved, sneaked away from home, and hopped onto a Greyhound bus going west, telling the driver to take him as far as his money would allow. A couple of days later he was wandering

down a road in South Dakota while a storm was brewing. A truck pulled up and the driver pointed in the distance, shouting: "Kid, there's a tornado brewin'. Get in!" Thus began John Senior's first season as a cowboy.

Senior always said he had had a great youth, referring especially to his days in a rugged life out west. The cowboy ideal, with its nobility, chivalry and healthy comradeship, caught his fancy as a boy and never left him. This man, steeped in European culture, would always be proud of nineteenth-century "free, frank, friendly" America. His adventure in the Dakotas is emblematic of Senior's life. Already as a boy he fled from whatever he found artificial in search of reality.

The Boy

Professor Senior's great-grandfather, also called John Senior, had come from England to settle in New York, but traveled several times back and forth between the Old World and the New so that John's grandfather, Frank, spent some time in England during his young years. Frank was inventive, something of a self-made man. The youngest of seven children, he worked his way through medical school, notably by designing jewelry. He was a well-known personality in Brooklyn, an involved Republican who ran for sheriff. When one of his two sons, John's father Roy, began medical school, Frank hoped he would continue his own practice. However, while Roy enjoyed the scientific aspects of his studies, he did not appreciate its practical application and soon withdrew from the school. As an alternative, his father helped him and his brother Harvey set up an automobile dealership, aptly called The Pathfinder.

The Senior line, then, was of English stock, but Frank's wife, Mary, was a Kip—an old New York Dutch family (there is a Kip's Bay in the borough of Manhattan, New York). The Kips were related to other Dutch families in the area, notably the Roosevelts, who were less well known than the Kips before Theodore appeared on the scene. A Dutch ancestor of John Senior's had fought as a general under Washington in the Revolutionary War.

14

Evelyn White, John Senior's mother, was also English on her father's side, while her mother was an Irish Catholic. Though Evelyn was baptized a Catholic, she became an Episcopalian like her father as her mother died when she was only four. Dr. White and his family lived in Manhattan, where he had a dental practice, but would regularly visit the Caribbean for his health and for the culture of the English colonies. The Whites considered themselves English indeed, but the Irish blood received from John's maternal grandmother would always be especially dear to him.

While training as a nurse in Brooklyn, Evelyn White met Harvey Senior, the husband of a fellow nurse trainee, eventually coming to know his brother, Roy. The two, Evelyn and Roy, were married in 1917 and moved in with the hospitable Dr. and Mrs. Frank Senior in Brooklyn. Their first son, Hereward, was born in 1918, followed by a daughter, Catherine Mary, in 1920. When Evelyn's sister Clare came to stay with them, Roy and Evelyn thought it best to find their own home. They sublet a house that Harvey had rented for hunting purposes in Stamford, Connecticut, moving there with the children and Clare. Roy kept his job in Brooklyn, coming home only for the weekends. Thus, John Senior, the New Yorker, was in fact born in Stamford, Connecticut, on February 21, 1923, the third and last child of Roy and Evelyn. When John was still a toddler, the family moved to Hempstead, on Long Island, soon afterward settling in a little fishing village called Christian Hook, about six miles from the ocean.*

John's relatives on the Senior side were quite active; they were well-coordinated and good at sports, sung in key, and liked to joke and have fun. Roy in particular was known for having a great sense of humor. The Whites, on the other hand, were inclined more toward culture and liked to sit around and discuss serious subjects. Roy's business often took him out of town, so Evelyn and her sister Clare managed the household and initiated the children into all aspects of high culture. In particular, the two women read to the children often. They helped them learn nursery rhymes by heart and introduced them early on to nineteenth-century English

---

* For glimpses into Senior's childhood, one could take a look at the poems of *Pale Horse*, part V, "A Second Childhood's Garden." He spoke of Aunt Clare in "Valencia," Grandfather Frank in "Kip's Bay" and Uncle John—his mother's brother—and his wife Tess in "At the Convalescent Home."

classics, such as Charles Dickens, Robert Louis Stevenson and Sir Walter Scott. They took the children on excursions to Shakespeare plays at an outdoor theater near Columbia University. Music, as well, was an integral part of Senior family life, as John would describe: "My father, in an amateur way, had a fine baritone voice and one of the warmest memories of my childhood is of him singing, 'And for Bonn Annie Laurie I would lay me doun and dee' and 'I would die for love of thee, O Mavoureen.' And he would put his arm around my mother's shoulder as she sat at the piano with the children."[1]

All three children were avid readers. Hereward was interested in history and army life; John, in cowboy stories and poetry. He learned to play guitar and sing cowboy songs, some of which he wrote himself, as he had started writing poetry and songs at an early age. Senior characterized his boyhood formation thus: "I was brought up on what was left of nineteenth-century English culture and the popular stuff of cowboy movies and moralizing boys' books."[2] Nevertheless, he was not overly bookish as a boy, nor was he a loner; on the contrary, he was popular and a natural leader. Although he was well coordinated, John was slightly built and somewhat asthmatic, shying away from traditional American sports. He liked to ride bicycles, frequently went swimming in the ocean and would practice lassoing for hours at a time. His love of acting—second only to his thirst for the cowboy's life—landed him several leading roles in high school plays.

One activity missing in the household was religion: none of the adults practiced any faith. Rather on their own initiative, the two older children attended Sunday school at a neighborhood Episcopalian church, but John did not go with them. Mary was baptized at age thirteen, Hereward at a later age, John not at all—although it is obvious that he knew the Episcopalian minister fairly well, because Senior tutored the minister's son and was allowed to ride a horse that belonged to him.*

John and his brother held odd jobs throughout their school years. His sister tells that John was never very successful at his little jobs, but was certainly persistent. On one such assignment, he was to sell ice cream bars.

---

* Senior wrote a poem about this minister: "In the Time of the Healing of the Nations," *Pale Horse*, 39–43.

He strapped an ice chest on his bicycle and armed himself with a little bell to inform children of the ice cream boy's approach. It was a very hot day and things did not go well. At about noon, his parents sought out the young salesman and tried to convince him to come home. But he resolutely persevered to the end. When he finally did return, he was exhausted and beset with bad cramps. The family had to call a doctor.

Working was partly a necessity for the two boys. During the Depression, people did not buy cars. John's father had to forfeit his own car dealership business and take on employment, first as a salesman and then as a civil-service welfare inspector, each position bringing in considerably less pay. The Seniors eventually had to give up their home and rent an apartment.

Perhaps John's flight west was undertaken in part to ease the family's financial burden, something not uncommon in those days. But mostly, John was dismayed at seeing Long Island lose its farms and open spaces because of the economic slump and steady urbanization. His home town even changed its name from Christian Hook to Oceanside in order to attract development. A life close to nature was fading away. He touched on that experience in "A Second Childhood's Garden":

> When I awoke on attic cot
> I looked across a Camelot
> of red and green, steep-slanted roofs
> and heard the milkman's horse's hoofs;
>
> ...
>
> And now the fields conglomerate
> into suburban real estate;
> where the landscape, days and nights,
> is cacophonies of lights;
>
> ...
>
> When the wind no longer whispers
> there will be no Lauds or Vespers;
> when there isn't any dawn,
> chanticleer will not go on.[3]

Thus it was that, at the age of thirteen, the impulsive youngster sought the cowboy life that he had dreamed so much about. In his words:

Having had from childhood an urge for good times lost, I satisfied it first with poetry and then with cowboy stories . . . and at thirteen ran away from home and the encroaching city which by the 1930's had metastasized suburban cells in our rural fields. But by that time fenced farms had pretty much destroyed the open range . . . so it was something of a miracle that as late as 1936 I found a ranch in the Dakota Badlands where cowboys still rode horses on roundups.[4]

It was a Norwegian, Morgan Tinzer, who had picked up the young New Yorker as a tornado formed not far away. At his invitation, John stayed in Tinzer's summer house and for a time assisted him in strip mining coal. He eventually wrote his parents—who were understandably frantic and had authorities looking for their son in several states—but did not tell them where he was. Tinzer finally contacted the Seniors and informed them of the boy's whereabouts. Roy hurriedly flew out to South Dakota, rented a car, and drove across a roadless prairie to retrieve his son. Upon John's return back home, his siblings would not speak to him, being all the angrier that he had not even been punished!

Fearing that their son might run off again, the Seniors consented to his going west every summer, provided he return home afterward to continue his schooling during the winter. Through various connections they found a job for him with another Norwegian, Vic Christensen, on a ranch in the Red River Valley, near Grand Forks, North Dakota. This arrangement proved to be a perfect compromise. John could still live much as his cowboy heroes had, riding horses, drinking coffee at the campfire and sleeping in the bunkhouse with the hands. "In those days it was the real thing," he said. "They had roundups and horses—none of the modern conveniences."[5] He went on cattle drives of more than sixty miles that often lasted two or three weeks. Mr. and Mrs. Christensen had no children except an adopted son and readily accepted the young New Yorker as a

member of the family, letting him lounge about the house and read in the library during his free time.

Senior later recounted some anecdotes from his days in the Dakotas. The hands used a trolley with a grapple hook powered by horses to carry big piles of loose hay into the barn. One day, John was given the task of guiding the hay by a rope. He accidentally pulled on the trip rope and the whole load fell right on the foreman. John heard a muffled voice scream-ing furiously from underneath the hay. The hand next to him cried out, "Get out of here, you little idiot. He's gonna kill you! Get lost for the rest of the day!" John did as he was told and only that evening crept back quietly to the bunkhouse. He concluded the story with: "I learned then that I'm no durn good with machinery!"

Another time he was charged with taking provisions to some workers about five miles away. He was proud to be given such a responsibility and was happily singing to himself as he went along driving the horses, listen-ing to the birds and looking at the flowers. Unexpectedly, he heard a horse wildly galloping and a man yelling, "Can't you see what you're doin'?!" John looked back and had the spectacle of sacks of flour and cans of pork and beans strewn along the road behind him. He had forgotten to close the wagon's clapboard.

Of course, much of the experience was less poetic and romantic than John had dreamed—they did, after all, use trucks!—but he persevered year after year. These five or six summers at the ranch provided him with a rich experience of nature, animals, weather, men and hard work. He once mused that Will James's book *Sand*, about a boy who practically fell out of a train in Montana and became a man among the cowboys, was the story of his own life.

Studies and First Teaching Posts

John had excellent marks in high school and received a scholarship to attend Hofstra, a small but high-level suburban liberal arts college in Long Island. His brother was studying there, and the two Senior boys were on the debating team together. John was a natural orator. His brother

recounted, "He could talk off the top of his head while I always had to prepare my debate." John also continued participating in drama and wrote a play that was performed with some success. He nevertheless focused on his classes in literature and philosophy.

After completing two years at Hofstra College, John served in the army during World War II. He was never sent overseas, but because he knew some German, he helped with the interrogation of prisoners who were being held in the United States. Fortunately, John later reminisced, most of the prisoners knew some English; in fact, he was able to have excellent conversations about English literature on several occasions!

While John was still at Hofstra, before the war began, he had met a high school senior named Priscilla Woods. They had a mutual interest in the outdoor life and animals, especially horses. Priscilla intended to become a veterinarian. Soon after the war, on September 3, 1945, the two were married in the American Episcopal Church, with John's brother serving as best man. After a honeymoon in the mountains of northern New Mexico, John's sister ceded to the newlyweds the apartment she and her husband had in Greenwich Village, a rather Spartan place with no running water in the kitchen—a deprivation that appealed to the adventurous young newlyweds.

Priscilla was a woman with abundant and down-to-earth common sense, always a private and discreet presence in Senior's life. She accompanied him in all his adventures, sometimes entering into them wholeheartedly and sometimes simply putting up with them. Mrs. Senior was the practical and firm woman her husband needed. She helped to keep her husband's feet on the ground, steering the somewhat quixotic intellectual through the concrete realities of life. An anecdote that Senior liked to tell brings out the play between their two temperaments. One evening at table, he was going on and on about the beauty and riches of silence. After a while Mrs. Senior broke in: "If you like silence so much, why don't you be quiet!?" Senior closed the story commenting that she was, of course, right.* In the acknowledgments of one of his books he

---

* He wrote a humorous and affectionate poem for his wife: "Nocturn," in *Pale Horse*, 13.

wrote of "one to whom the debt is measureless: Mulieris fortis beatus vir (Blessed the husband of a valiant woman)."[6]

The couple would be favored with three children: Penelope in 1947, Matthew in 1952 and Andrew in 1953. The grounding of a normal, happy family life played an important role in John's intellectual and spiritual journey. Its affections, natural joys and often accompanying sorrows kept his soul anchored in those days when his studies suggested that reality was an illusion.

John was honorably discharged from the army on September 9, 1944. Perhaps in the summer of 1944, with the forces already in France, the army no longer needed him for the interrogation of prisoners. An accident causing a serious hand wound may have contributed to the decision as well.

He did not return to Hofstra, as he had been disappointed with the education offered there. Taking advantage of the GI Bill, upon his release that fall Senior enrolled at Columbia University, where he continued his studies, eventually obtaining his doctorate. There, he followed various courses in philosophy, both ancient and modern, but mostly focused his attention on literature. Several of his professors were involved in the then rather novel Great Books movement, which had the audacity to put aside manuals in favor of the classical authors themselves being read. Thus, Senior participated in a renowned humanities program in this line, and then continued in an equally renowned graduate comparative literature program. He received a decent formation in classical antiquities, notably from Gilbert Highet, a recognized Greek and Latin scholar. As to literature, Senior gained a first-rate education from three professors in particular, well known in the literary world, each of whom stressed that the aim of literature was truth and love, not merely aesthetics, pleasure, or recreation: Raymond Weaver, known for his studies on Melville; Lionel Trilling, a prominent cultural commentator; and Mark Van Doren. Of the latter, Senior once said he was the greatest man he had ever known, referring to him on another occasion as his "Socrates."[7] As a key figure in Senior's life, he deserves special mention.

Mark Van Doren was an accomplished poet, novelist, short story writer and literary critic who, when Senior began studying under him,

was fifty years of age and had just received a Pulitzer Prize for Poetry. What Van Doren wrote of another applies to himself as well: "He loved [the world] in all its parts, the great, the small. Nothing was small for him, and nothing was great; every person, every thing, deserved to exist."[8] This professor and friend imparted to John Senior a sympathetic understanding of individual concrete things, of animals and people.

"There was something magical about it," Senior once said about Van Doren's teaching. His class was an authentic conversation with the students about the great books they were reading, an adventure where both teacher and students learned. He stayed away from historical and scholarly analysis, and led students to consider what the author himself was trying to express. Thomas Merton, who had attended Columbia a few years earlier, also appreciated Van Doren as one who, "instead of subtly destroying all literature by burying and concealing it under a mass of irrelevancies, really purified and educated the perceptions of [his] students by teaching them how to read a book and how to tell a good book from a bad. . . . He had the gift of communicating to them something of his own vital interest in things."[9] Any student of John Senior's will recognize their teacher in those features. Senior thus found in Van Doren not only a mentor but also a model for his own teaching. In fact, he explicitly said that when he would go into a class, he always wanted to sound like his old Columbia professor.

The two remained in friendly contact throughout the years. Correspondence between them in the 1960s shows Senior, now in his forties and himself an accomplished college professor, with a charming filial veneration and affection for the older man. Still, he does not hesitate to respectfully and humbly let Van Doren know when he does not agree with him on some point. On the occasion of Senior's reception into the Catholic Church, in 1960, Van Doren wrote "Estote Ergo Vos Perfecti" (Be Ye Therefore Perfect; see the epigraph of Chapter Two). This same poem was read at a public lecture given by Van Doren in 1970, when he visited John Senior at the University of Kansas in Lawrence, during which he memorably mentioned that his former student was an inspiration to him. For Christmas in 1968, Senior in his turn wrote a poem to his mentor,

which he largely reworked at Van Doren's death in 1972, naming it at that time "The World's Last Lover." In its closing lines, he refers to Van Doren as "a noble voice," after one of his former teacher's books on poetry, and in an allusion to Shakespeare's *A Midsummer Night's Dream*, speaks of Oberon, king of fairies—the "king of music" as Senior says in a note—who put magical nectar in people's eyes so that they would fall in love:

> now the Noble voice is spent,
> now the festival is over;
> Oberon's enchanted wood
> closes in the world's last lover
> whose music was a murmur
> in the rivers of our Summer,
> and whose eyes,
> disappointed, hurt and wise
> with philosophic fatherhood,
> saw everything (including us) as good.[10]

John Senior was an immediate success at Columbia University, both in and out of class. The 1945–46 school year brought him two poetry prizes and an editor's chair at the *Columbia Review*. He also became a book reviewer for *The Nation*, perhaps through the mediation of Van Doren, who had in preceding years been literary editor of the magazine. After a dozen successful reviews, however, Senior was dismissed because he had found *Up Front*, Mauldin's universally acclaimed book of World War II cartoons, "demeaning and depersonalizing."

In the spring of 1946, Senior received his BA from Columbia. It was also a time of sorrow, for his father had suffered and died from a stroke, having faithfully been cared for by Evelyn. The death marked the young man. Senior later would say that the day one's father dies is the moment one realizes he too will someday die. He wrote and published a poem about his father at the time.

Senior continued to be consumed by dreams of a rustic life where he could leisurely write poetry. One day following his graduation, he and his

wife jumped into their Studebaker, hauling a trailer behind piled high with their belongings, and escaped to the wilderness. They purchased some cheap land in the mountains near Taos, New Mexico, obtained some goats and began settling into their mountain shack. But the adventure was short-lived. As Senior told it, "The indians stole the goats. And the winter came along and we almost died. We had to run down from the mountain. Besides that, our first child was going to be born. I ran all the way back east again and got myself a job."[11]

In 1947, Senior began teaching English in a rather unofficial way at Bard College on the Hudson River, a small, liberal and progressive school; for example, it had no grading system. Concurrently, he studied for his Masters degree, which he received from Columbia in 1948. Senior was not yet resolved on a teacher's life: "At that time I was writing poetry, even novels. . . . I thought of myself as a creative writer."[12] He did write a novel, but his wife found it uninteresting so he discarded it. In 1949 he accepted a teaching position at Hofstra, the small but rapidly growing college he had first attended.

Still trying to find a more romantic, rural life, he at one point investigated the possibility of moving to a Caribbean island, and for years retained the property in New Mexico, just in case. His preference for living in the country was fulfilled when he was fortunate enough to find an old farmhouse on a few acres of ground near Huntington, New York, close to his wife's family.

One of his Hofstra students remembers Professor Senior as being steady, patient and gentle. He recalls that, one day, the young teacher found him reading Dewey and asked him, "Why waste your time on second-class authors? Read the greats!" Writing assignments, which he graded on his train commute, would come back with neatly written comments along the margins. Nevertheless, the same student reports that his teacher "was quite unconventional," remembering how he would sit on two legs of his chair, leaning against the wall and, from time to time, clack a piece of chalk on the blackboard to get his students' attention. A former colleague of John Senior's recalls good memories of stimulating conversations in the teachers' lunchroom, noting that "John was really into James Joyce

at the time."* He and another professor at Hofstra edited *Poems for Study*, an anthology of poems from the sixteenth to the nineteenth centuries intended primarily for their own students. Senior contributed the introduction, biographical notes on the authors of the sixteenth through the eighteenth century, and a study on rhyme, rhythm and imagery.

In 1954, Senior was awarded a scholarship from Columbia University to spend a year in Ireland and England doing research for his doctoral dissertation. He thoroughly enjoyed living in a small village in Ireland, but "[w]hat really brought me home was the awareness that even though I could achieve the life that I wanted over there, it would be wrong for me to do that. . . . You can go off and succeed by yourself, but you become some kind of nut."[13] From that year forward, he fully invested himself in teaching. He passed his comprehensive doctoral exams summa cum laude in 1955 and joined the English Department at Cornell University.

Senior found a pleasant old country house in the tranquil Finger Lakes district of upstate New York, built a barn and bought an old horse he named Sam Bass that he and his daughter often rode. A Cornell professor of the time tells the following story:

> John invited my wife and me to attend a race. The weather had been unusually dry, but I hadn't realized how much dust a group of horses could make, especially if lined up side by side on a dirt track. Almost as soon as the race commenced, the dust so billowed up that the spectators could see nothing of the horses and riders, only the sound of galloping hooves. Upon finishing the race, the riders and their mounts trotted away from the clouds of dust, the one who came in first dust-free, but each horse and rider that followed increasingly covered with it. Maybe ten horses competed; John and his horse came in last, and they were both so shrouded in dust they seemed like ghost-like apparitions—like a modern-day Don Quixote and his beloved but plodding Rocinante.[14]

---

*   Senior's views on Joyce certainly changed, as one can see in Chapter Five of *The Death of Christian Culture*, where Senior demolishes the modern Irish writer who rejected his Catholic faith.

While teaching and writing his dissertation—and riding horses—John maintained an interest in films. He was well acquainted with the principal actors and directors of the time and even produced some home movies himself. For a while he also found time to delve into making pottery and raising bees. Priscilla, meanwhile, earned a degree from Cornell and began raising Afghan hounds, in her turn, which were to be famous members of the Senior household for decades. She and her hounds would be successful at several dog shows.

In 1957, Senior completed his dissertation, receiving his PhD in comparative literature—that is, literature of various languages. Senior was by then a young, vibrant and popular professor at one of the most prestigious universities in the country. Yet during those years he was obviously searching for something more, something of a different order than academic success.

The Quest Begins

There had been a number of intellectual and spiritual waves in Senior's life: "I myself have suffered, since my first intellectual awakening in the late 1930s, shocks of Marxism, split by Stalinism and Trotskyism; Freudianism, split by Jung and Adlerism; varieties of Bloomsbury Positivism and California Hinduism, Taoism, Zen . . ."[15] He was "a follower of Positivism and Agnosticism."[16] Positivists hold that one can only be sure of what one immediately senses and measures, that knowledge terminates in appearances; agnostics assert that certitude about the nature of things, especially of the human soul and of God, is impossible. "My generation," Senior lamented, "which was terribly influenced by the ideas of Marx and Freud, denied the existence of spiritual realities."[17] Marx and Freud explained everything—knowledge and love in particular—by material causes.

The first wave, then, was Marxism. After witnessing the suffering and poverty of the Depression, Senior became aware that "something was not right between the world and [himself]."[18] This awareness, he realized later, was the first step in his eventual conversion. With practically no

religious training and influenced by Positivism and agnosticism, John Senior, together with his brother and many others of their generation, turned to Marxism as a response to social injustice. As far back as his cowboy days, Senior would read Marx in his tent at night, and it is said that he wrote his first published work out on the range—an article on Trotsky for a small Marxist paper in New York.

John, unlike his brother Hereward, never became a member of the American Socialist Party. He coined himself a Trotskyite, and at one point reported to the office of an offshoot of the Communist Party, but the Party did not want him while he was in college. At the beginning of World War II, before Russia was involved, he protested for peace, much as the youth of a later generation would do against the Vietnam War. However, at the assassination of Trotsky by Soviet agents in 1940, the seventeen-year-old Senior began to suspect that politics was suited more for thugs than for intellectuals. Furthermore, when a Trotskyite group tested him by ordering him to steal a book, he reasoned that something was awry with a doctrine that imposed immoral acts. After the war, many leftist intellectuals (John's teacher and friend Professor Trilling among them) were moving away from Marxism, influenced in part by the disillusionment provoked by the Soviet-Nazi pact and the revelations of horrors in Soviet concentration camps. Senior gradually began losing interest and hope in politics.

His drift from Marxism made him more receptive to influences that would bring him out of his materialism. A seed in this direction was planted during his first years at Columbia:

> I vividly remember standing before a fine teacher at college who had done a lot to promote the hundred great books and saying to him, "But I just can't read all those books!" In the middle of *The Critique of Pure Reason* I had despaired. "Of course you can't," Mark Van Doren said. "Nobody can read a hundred books; but here is one—read that." He took a volume from his desk haphazardly and handed it to me; it happened to be a collection of Plato's *Dialogues* that helped to change my life.[19]

The reading of this ancient philosopher began opening to Senior a world of spiritual realities that resonated with his love of beauty and poetry. He would later acknowledge this discovery as having been the second step toward his conversion. "What I learned at Columbia," he said in an interview, "was . . . that there was an end to things. I was not sure what it was, but I was sure it existed."[20] Thus, his reading had sparked a quest for the absolute at about the same age at which St. Augustine—also stimulated by Platonic thought—had begun his own spiritual journey.

Van Doren's influence in helping John Senior become aware of the delight and wonder found in individual, concrete things was an essential catalyst to launching the younger man in his spiritual quest. But his influence did not go much further. Senior received little help in the way of doctrinal direction even from Van Doren who, in the 1950s, described his own spiritual stance in the third person: "He still refused to say that the world had one meaning and no other; he still inclined to take as it came, in numerous guises which he would not question as to the order or their importance and truth. All things continued acceptable to him; he was happy, and he insisted he did not know why; there was no single secret he had discovered."[21]

Rather on his own, then, Senior took off on a divergent path: "However, reading Plato sent me on a long detour. Held back by pseudo-scientific prejudgments, the direct road [to Truth] was blocked and I thus had to try the easy path to the Beautiful, especially in poetry, which had enchanted me since my childhood."[22] Freud was left aside in favor of Karl Jung, who, like Plato, also helped him to look beyond this world.[23] For years Senior wrestled with his positivist prejudices, all the while sensing there was something beyond empirical reality and seeking the path to attain it.

As he turned in a more spiritual direction, Senior was struck by the vital significance of religion and tradition in literature and philosophy. He began studying the history of religions. At Hofstra, he taught a course on comparative religions, which procured for him a denunciation to the administration by a student who accused him of being anti-religious. The affair made some noise and Senior was distressed by it; he had not

intended to offend anyone. Nonetheless, it was true that he did not have any religious attachments. At Cornell, he gave a series of classes on a more specific and defined area: the Occult. A student in one of these classes reports that alchemy, astrology and the Cabala became fascinating as Senior brought to the fore their deeper meanings. He was ahead of his time, speaking already of the upcoming new age, the "Age of Aquarius."

Early into his doctoral research, Senior recognized that modern developments in literature and their relationship to the Occult were rooted in the nineteenth century, particularly in the Symbolist movement. Symbolist writings became the focus of his study, which culminated in his dissertation and his first book, *The Way Down and Out: The Occult in Symbolist Literature*, published in 1959. The book was not meant to be "popular"; for example, it had many lengthy quotations in French without English translation. Although not widely acclaimed, it did see a second printing in 1968. Today some recognize that Senior achieved a breakthrough in the history of modern literature through this work. One scholar states that Occultism as the broadest and most profound source of Modernist literature "was first proposed by John Senior."[24] Another notes that the book received little notice precisely because there was reluctance to admit that our favorite poets, such as T. S. Eliot, were influenced by the Occult, as Senior shows them to be.[25]

Senior was not concerned solely with historical interests. While interpreting a particular aesthetic theory, his goal was to assess its import in our present culture. Most significantly, his research dovetailed with his personal quest for meaning in life. He wanted to see if "the way down" would, indeed, lead to salvation.

Box 786
Lawrence Kansas
66044

2 Oct. '67

Dear Mark,

Esto Ergo was perfect: will always be your best poem, for me — the last line is perfect. It is a great thing as everyone knows to unlock the power in an atom — but in a word!

I remember your telling a wonderful story about Greece: you said you were up early looking out the window of the train at a mountain, & pointing you asked the porter, "Olympus?" & he replied, "Parnassus!" that is a great story for a poet; and now you have discovered a mountain higher even than Ararat. that is the great thing for a man. We'll get somewhere on the shoulders.

Love to you & yours from us all —

John

Letter of John Senior to Mark Van Doren. *Courtesy of Kirk Kramer*

CHAPTER TWO

The Way Down

Be ye therefore perfect.
Be less, and cease to be.
There is no going downward
Save into the great sea
Where things continue falling
Forever and a day;
Except that all is darkness
Down there, o soul of me.
Be ye therefore perfect.
But how will I do that?
Patience, little brother,
And inwardly take thought.
Breathe evenly. Remember
What many have forgot:
The hill to climb is higher
Even than Ararat.

—"Estote Ergo Vos Perfecti"
by Mark Van Doren, dedicated to Senior

JOHN Senior's quest for meaning in life, as we have seen, led him first to an interest in the Occult, which was the stuff of his published dissertation, *The Way Down and Out.* As such, the book is a deposit of Senior's thought before his conversion, or at least the expression of what he was then exploring. It provides us with a means of knowing what it was that Senior later reacted against, and thus can greatly contribute to

an appreciation of his definitive thought. A study of the work will help us obtain a deeper understanding of "the way down" and, ultimately, of what is at the base of modern culture. We will then be prepared to examine, in subsequent chapters, Senior's shift from the "way down" to the "way up," from considering the world as a shadow to looking upon it as real, valuable, and truly pointing to God, its creator.

The Way Down and Out is divided into two sections: the first is an investigation of Occult doctrine, while the second studies its influence on the Symbolists as founders of modern poetry and literature.

Occultism

In his introduction to *The Way Down and Out*, Senior states the thesis of his book: "The problem posed is this: What is the metaphysical foundation of the symbolist movement? And the answer is 'Occultism.'"[1] "Occult" comes from the Latin *occultus*, meaning hidden. For most people "the Occult" evokes the domain of crystal balls, palm-reading, witchcraft and communication with spirits. These shady aspects of the Occult are secret techniques for gaining knowledge and power in ways hidden from ordinary consciousness. Senior investigates such popular expressions of the Occult, but he is primarily seeking its philosophical presuppositions. He considers this deeper Occultism as "worthy of our respect and meditation."[2] When we "try to find the assumptions behind the exteriors . . . we are led to profound and universal ideas."[3] Even forty years later, as a traditional Catholic and a Thomist, Senior would affirm: "There is a serious philosophy behind these foolish phenomena."[4]

Around 1800, the term Occult* was adopted by certain groups in the West who had abandoned Christianity and were attempting to find a religion of sorts through a rediscovery of mystical philosophies of the past. Accordingly, in the first few chapters of *The Way Down and Out*, John Senior traces the many forms these philosophies took throughout the course of human history—"the mysteries of Babylon and Egypt; the

---

* For a clear and authoritative study on Occult orientation, one should read the document issued by the Holy See on the New Age. See the insert in *Osservatore Romano*, English edition, August 3, 2003.

religious and philosophical movements in India, Greece and Alexandria, the alchemy and astrology of the Middle Ages and, in modern times, the Rosicrucians and theosophists of various kinds."[5] He strives to uncover a common spirit in these many expressions of the Occult and presents his findings in the last of these opening chapters.

The basic Occult notion affirms that "the universe is one, single, eternal, ineffable substance."[6] Reality is, for the Occultist, essentially one thing. Everything is god and there is no God, one might say. There is no creation by a God of something other than Himself. In that case, how does Occult philosophy explain the multiple and distinct things we experience? Concerning that point, we find an ambiguity in Occult tendencies. Sometimes the world is presented as an emanation from God, something of an accidental and temporary individuation of the divine substance; at other times it is affirmed to be an illusion, a shifting mirage. Senior paraphrases a scholar who had concluded that Occult groups in the Middle Ages held the following: "1) that this world does not exist; 2) that this world does exist but is the result of a disaster; 3) that there are some things one does not discuss because they are ineffable." Senior declares that these positions are not the opinions of different schools but are held by all. "All three," he continues, "have been maintained at once by the schools we have examined and, of course, from the Occult point of view, the inconsistency is the result of the limitations of modern philosophic method."[7]

Nevertheless, in *The Way Down and Out*, Senior usually affirms that the world is simply the way in which the infinite appears to finite faculties of knowledge: "The essential force of the universe is actually everywhere the same, but it appears to be only as much as can be comprehended by the perceiver."[8] Consequently, "this world is illusion, if by that we mean that it is not completely the way it appears to our perceptions."[9]

Another fundamental Occult notion tells us that since all is ultimately one, everything in the universe corresponds to everything else. Some of the Occult beliefs that seem so strange rely on this idea of a mysterious link between things. Notably, astrology proceeds from the idea that "things above are as they are below"[10]—as the stars go, so goes life on earth, as parts of one whole. Likewise, belief in alchemy is built on the

idea that there is no substantial difference between what appear to be different types of entities. Magic also supposes this deep unity between things—by acting on one we can affect the other.

A further effect of the essential unity of reality concerns man's spiritual quest: "[Man] is capable of becoming God because he is God without 'realizing' it. . . . The task of man is therefore self-realization. To know thyself is to be everything."[11] Every man is divine even if he does not experience himself as such. To "become" God, therefore, consists simply in returning to the real self, that is, in breaking through illusions and thereby perceiving what one really is. Each one of us, according to this doctrine, must strive to move beyond the phenomenal consciousness, the psychological, individual self to "the great discovery that the essential Self and the essential force of the universe are one,"[12] to the "total experience of the identity of God and Man in which both the human creature and the superhuman Creator disappear."[13] As a man enters into his own depths, he discovers the root of all reality. As in all Gnostic types of mysticism, salvation and enlightenment are one and the same thing.

For this quest of deification we need leaders: "Certain supermen, having achieved self-realization, turn back to help their unrealized fellows. These are . . . the founders of religions who veil the ultimate in terms suitable to time and place. Thus all religions are variations on a single transcendent unity."[14] In the Occult view, Moses, Zoroaster, Buddha, Jesus and Mohammad were heroes who attained ultimate illumination; they were also merciful men who desired to help the unenlightened, adapting what they knew to what the common man was capable of receiving. These supermen could express their knowledge of the ineffable reality only through myths, metaphors and figures—symbols—"to communicate something of the higher truths to those not able to understand."[15] Thus, the Occult worldview would be the esoteric, hidden and interior core of all authentic religions and spiritual philosophies; specific doctrines, rites and customs would only be its exoteric clothing: "Religion is symbol and . . . beneath the body of this or that particular ritual and this or that particular theology lies one, single, universal, metaphysical doctrine, the

philosophia perennis."[16] This last term will recur in our study and deserves particular attention.

The idea that there are fundamental truths present in diverse religions and philosophies had already been expressed in ancient thought. Cicero, for example, appealed to the authority of tradition, to the teaching of Greek mysteries and to the "sanction of universal religion" in favor of the immortality of the soul.[17] Christian thinkers have always recognized that elements of Christian truth exist in non-Christian religions and philosophies. In the sixteenth century the expression *philosophia perennis* or "Perennial Philosophy" was coined to represent the idea of the universal nature of much of Christian doctrine. Occultists later adopted the term for the supposed transcendent unity behind all religions, the oldest and highest truth, present throughout history—in fact, according to them, predating history. In the twentieth century Aldous Huxley popularized this use of the term in the English language. He wrote:

> More than twenty-five centuries have passed since the Perennial Philosophy was first committed to writing; and in the course of those centuries it has found expression, now partial, now complete, now in this form, now that, again and again. . . . This final purity can never, of course, be expressed by any verbal statement of the philosophy, however undogmatic that statement may be, however deliberately syncretistic.[18]

The Symbolist Movement

After bringing to light the basic notions of the Occult worldview, Senior demonstrates its influence on the Symbolist movement "exemplified by a few of its greatest practitioners."[19]

What is this Symbolist movement?* Senior, writing for professionals, presupposes his reader's familiarity with it; most of us, however, require

---

* While John Senior did not capitalize the names of philosophical and cultural movements in this early writing, he changed his approach later on. We will follow this later practice.

an introduction. Histories of literature define Symbolism properly as a movement or "school"—with theorists, disciples and journals—beginning shortly after 1870 and reaching an apogee around 1885. They recognize that Symbolism found an initial font of inspiration in French poet Charles Baudelaire a little after the mid-century, who himself drew from American Gothic poet Edgar Allen Poe. These two poets' ideas were taken up, systematized and developed by young French poets in the 1860s and 1870s, notably Paul Verlaine, Stéphane Mallarmé and Arthur Rimbaud. Symbolist ideas remained a dominating force in twentieth-century poetry, through poets such as W. B. Yeats and T. S. Eliot in the British Isles, Paul Valéry in France and Rainer Maria Rilke in Germany. While poetry is its most propitious domain, Symbolism also penetrated other fields in modern literature—James Joyce in the novel and Eugene O'Neill in drama, for example. It spread into art and music as well, where we find artists often known as Symbolists—Vincent van Gogh in painting and Claude Debussy in music, among others. Symbolism was in fact a major inspiration, if not the very source, of Modernist art in general.

John Senior, in *The Way Down and Out,* is not particularly interested in circumscribing the school in a strict sense. For him, Symbolism is first of all a type of literature and art that had always existed, characterized by the consideration of the world of which we have direct knowledge as a set of figures of the hidden spiritual world. Such a vision of reality was common to art in more religious and spiritual cultures. According to Senior, the modern Symbolist movement wanted to rediscover this deeper way of looking at the universe. To explore the foundation of this modern Symbolist effort, Senior returns to the beginning of the nineteenth century (even before Poe and Baudelaire) to two crucial figures: William Blake and Victor Hugo. He then proceeds to cover two recognized forerunners of the Symbolist movement, Baudelaire and Gérard de Nerval, followed by four or five prominent members of the school, finally introducing the twentieth century with Yeats and Eliot.

"Historically, symbolism was an arc within the great curve of romanticism," Senior declares.[20] Romanticism can be characterized as a preference for imagination, emotion, and freedom over reason and rules. It arose

in the middle of the eighteenth century and reached its peak in the first part of the nineteenth. When the Romantic fascination started to wane in the mid-nineteenth century, a "naturalist" or "realist" reaction arose against its sentimentality, seeking a more objective and descriptive, almost scientific representation of reality. This new, naturalistic, artistic movement shunned Romantic idealism, choosing instead to explain human actions scientifically through circumstance, environment, heredity and instinct. A counter-reaction was inevitable, however, because most artists found this materialistic direction stifling. Symbolists returned to the Romantic perspective, but with a twist.

Senior asserts that the Romantics in general, and the Symbolists in particular, were repulsed by modern man's habitual scientific outlook, which rendered the universe a complex chain of drab and colorless forces, with atoms randomly hitting one another as on a billiard table. As Senior writes of this overly scientific view: "A kiss from this point of view is the contiguity of oral mucous membranes."[21] There had to be more to reality than what we can measure and verify in a laboratory: "One of my chief contentions," Senior wrote, "is that the symbolist poets, finding the scientific world view inadequate, embraced another they considered more complete and beautiful."[22]

How, then, would these men of the nineteenth century find a more satisfying reality? Reason seemed to have come to a dead end with experimental sciences and dry, lifeless abstractions in philosophy. But Christianity did not appear to be the answer either, because scientific investigation had seemingly proved that religions based on historical revelation could only be myths: "[The symbolists] had eaten the bitter fruit of Voltaire," Senior writes. "Simple faith is impossible to anyone who has studied science."[23] Because neither reason nor religion could lead to a spiritual world, the only possible escape from the increasingly dominant materialistic view was to seek an experience of the spiritual, that is, to approach the matter in a scientific way by seeking direct evidence of the spiritual world: "The only means remaining is that science based on observations beyond the ordinary senses which reveals religion not as faith, but as fact"[24]—in other words, techniques for procuring secret knowledge,

Occultism. According to Senior, the Romantics generally accepted Occult philosophy, thus reaffirming "the chain of being," meaning that this sensible world is connected to a spiritual one:

> It is most popular to consider romanticism a reaction to the excessively mechanistic world view of the Encyclopedists, a return to the possibility of religion in an age of disbelief. . . . Romantic religions turn out to be . . . forms of Occult tradition. The great chain of being, which snapped after the successive strains of Renaissance science, was re-established.[25]

The Symbolists differed from the Romantics in that, for them, art itself was to be the instrument of enlightenment. Their goal was not to argue doctrine or relate experiences; it was to provoke experience. Art itself would become religion:

> According to its practitioners [symbolism] is a better way of accomplishing what the romantics wanted to achieve. . . . The world views are the same, but the romantic poet tends to write about his ideas or relate his experiences in which these ideas were acted out; the symbolist poet tries to create the experience on the page.[26]

For Romantics, the artist is a prophet, the teacher of humanity; for the Symbolists, he is a priest, a mediator who accomplishes the union between the divine and man: "The poet's function is to communicate vision."[27] Senior quotes William Blake's rendition of this idea:

> I rest not from my great task,
> To open the Eternal Worlds, to open the immortal Eyes
> Of Man inwards into the Worlds of Thought, into Eternity
> Ever expanding in the Bosom of God, the Human Imagination.[28]

How does the artist—the poet in particular—use symbols to "open the immortal Eyes," to awaken them from their slumbering in our soul?

The ordinary man accepts the various forms that he perceives through his senses, he believes in the reality of the distinct things of this world. The Occultist looks on these forms as symbols and recognizes mysterious links between them. Senior quotes Baudelaire:

> Nature is a temple where living columns
> let sometimes go up obscure words.
> Man goes there through forests of symbols
>
> . . .
>
> in a dark and deep unity
>
> . . .
>
> Perfumes, colors and sounds correspond.[29]

The Occult artist brings out correspondences and parallels, and thus gradually works through the illusions of this world, progressing toward the realization that all is one. Imagination provides the key in this contemplation because it can find bonds in that which senses and reason separate. Imagination is thus superior to the natural world we experience; it is more real. The stanza by Blake quoted above presents imagination maneuvering all the way to the divinity, with its "immortal Eyes . . . expanding in the Bosom of God."

By means of various links, the Symbolists made the "attempt to express the simultaneity in time, the identity in space, of many possible forms."[30] Simultaneity in time and identity in space, however, contradict the physical world. Consequently, "the end which the symbolist envisions is the negation of everything we know as the world."[31] This poetic and mystical effort is a sort of "de-creation," a "destruction" of the multiplicity of things, to attain, in a supra-rational intuition, to the one ineffable Substance. "The physical world is an occasion which the poet destroys step by step by a kind of linguistic yoga—until beyond all occasions, we are face to face with the unknown."[32]

In fact, the Symbolist's effort of destruction bears not on reality itself but on how one perceives it. Senior pointed out that "the difficulty is with our perceptions, with the *way* we see, not *what* we see."[33] As we have

indicated, our limiting capability of apprehension "creates" the world of experience by causing the illusion of distinct and limited things: "[The Occultist] maintains that the entire perceived universe of things is a quality of our consciousness."[34] Consequently, the Symbolist wants "to provoke us into this different kind of perception, that is, to present to the ordinary eye an object so dazzling that the scales will fall."[35] The poet uses secret, magical forces to "stretch consciousness." "A symbol, they say, is what the Hindu would call a *yantra*, an image which permits the mind to break through its ordinary limits in order to perceive things not as they seem but are and this is to perceive them as infinite."[36]

The sought destruction of perception aims ultimately at the destruction of the illusory self—the fundamental illusion and barrier—so that one may recognize one's identity with the infinite Substance: "The purpose of human life, according to the Occult doctrine, is to destroy the ordinary self, so that the Self may be discovered."[37] By progressively demolishing the usual ways of viewing the world and of reasoning, one sheds layers of the false self linked to degrees of consciousness, until at last remains only "the naked self stripped of illusions."[38] Indeed, it is the individual consciousness that limits our knowledge. We have "to liberate the Knower in us all from the limitations of the ego"[39] because "the only way to know [the infinite] is to become infinite."[40] We have to awaken the Self slumbering within us.

The way down thus becomes the way up. The title of Baudelaire's epoch-making book of poetry, *Les Fleurs du mal* (Flowers of Evil), was an exact and striking image of the way down, as Senior explains: "Flowers grow out of evil as pearls from sick oysters, butterflies from ugly worms, or the Self from the ordinary self."[41] We go through destruction and death to eternal life, through Hell to Heaven. Referring to a line from Our Lord, often used by Occultists, Senior presents the basic principle of the way down: "The soul is a grain and unless it die, it cannot flower. The way down—into Hell, into mortification, into the abyss of the unconscious—is the way up. The descent into Hell is the way to Heaven."[42] He further elucidates: "The true way down is out, out of the self altogether; and this means genuine pain, genuine self-destruction."[43]

For many Occultists and Symbolists, "the way down" into Hell also takes on the sense of indulging in evil. Senior illustrates this doctrine by paraphrasing Rimbaud:[44] "The way down is the way out. Damn yourself, indulge in evil to arrive at good. The specific means to self-damnation is the deliberate confusion of the senses, by drugs chiefly, and of the moral self, by crime."[45]

But, as we now know, "the truth of higher consciousness is that all the antinomies meditated on in order to achieve that consciousness turn out to be illusions sprung from the fact of lower consciousness."[46] Good and bad, joy and pain, mind and matter are simply inverse symbols of the single, inconceivable, universal Substance. Senior comments on Baudelaire: "The world is a reflection of Heaven and, as in all reflections, things are reversed. Bliss appears as suffering; one day, however, things will be seen not as they are reflected, but as they are. . . . To the enlightened consciousness pain is felt as ecstasy."[47]

We have to work our way through this inverse reflection, as Senior writes: "Baudelaire's Satan, like Blake's and Hugo's, must be lived through; he cannot be denied or jumped over."[48] We go down "until as with John of the Cross or Buddha, Satan Trismegistus* is seen through."[49] Satan is the shadow of God, the fallen God, creator of this world. Even the duality of Satan and God must be transcended. "Ultimately we will see Heaven and Hell as one."[50]

Senior's Views at the Time of The Way Down and Out

We find in *The Way Down and Out* some of the later John Senior we will come to know. Beyond his gifts, such as a penetrating intelligence and brilliant wit, we can often recognize his style, for example, his tongue-in-cheek humor and his way of throwing out something surprising to keep the reader alert: "Metaphysics and theology are often dismissed," he writes, "as if the question of how many angels could sit on the point of a pin were

---

* *Trismegistus* means "thrice great" in Greek. Occult texts of the beginning of our era applied the term to Hermes, the messenger of the gods who reveals the Occult arts. Baudelaire used it for Satan, as the god of this world.

not serious."[51] Even some of the content itself carries the stamp of the future University of Kansas professor. Senior has this to say on the philosophy of art:

> There is a great and disastrous dichotomy in modern thought: the feelings are taken to be separate from the intellect. In religion this takes the form of sentimentalism . . . in literature, and the arts generally, it takes the form of "aestheticism." . . . Though prettiness may charm aesthetically, beauty is the radiance of truth.

One can also recognize the later Senior in the following criticism of modern philosophy:

> Philosophy for some philosophers has been reduced to epistemology, as if the very important question of how we know were the only way of considering what we know. . . . This is simply taking means for ends and may be precisely described as a worshiping of graven images.[52]

However, at the time he wrote *The Way Down and Out,* John Senior's outlook was akin to that of the Symbolists. Like them, he realized that the West must go beyond modern experimental science and get back to some sort of religious, mystical philosophy. Like them, he could not accept Christianity at face value. He and his wife had had their first child baptized, but by this point in time his family did not go to church; his children did not receive instruction in the Christian religion. A passage he wrote years later doubtless described his own perception of Christianity at the time:

> For the greater number of educated people, Christianity is not serious; it will not bear up under critical shock. . . . As for the Christian facts like Christmas, they do not seem real. Something like one's mother, they are embarrassing and nice—but you do not go to your mother with an adult intellectual problem and neither do you seek for truth among pretty stories.[53]

In fact, it is obvious throughout the book that Senior at the time shared with the Symbolists their Occult syncretic attitude toward religion, ranking Christianity with all other religions as a simple figure and veil of the primordial mystery. He writes, for example:

Mysticism is the form Occultism took in Christendom as yoga is the form it took in India.[54]

[The descent into Hell] will be enacted by Osiris and Isis, Atticus and Cybele, Adonis and Aphrodite, and even Jesus and the Virgin Mary.[55]

The juxtaposition of these two principles—that the universe is illusion and is God—is the yang and the yin, as it were, of Western Occultism, from Platonism through Christian mysticism to twentieth-century theosophy.[56]

Far he was from being ready to participate in an organized Christian institution, particularly the Catholic Church. He was convinced that the Church's condemnation of Occult philosophy derived from the error of taking Christian symbols for realities: "Church opposition to Occult doctrine has been chiefly the result of a split between esoteric and exoteric religions."[57] The authors he studied in *The Way Down and Out* contributed to keeping him far from that path, as most were fallen-away Catholics who conflated Christ and Buddha, Sacraments and magic. Though two of them—T. S. Eliot and J. K. Huysmans—had indeed become Christians, Senior took the former's conversion to traditional Christianity only lightly, and found the latter's entry into the Catholic Church sincere but foolish. He wrote of Huysmans that he "fell into the Church because the highly charged equilibrium between the two forces of naturalism and mysticism was too great for him; and, short of the insanity of a Gérard de Nerval, he turned, for whatever consolation he could get, to a kind of Catholicism. In embracing this kind of Church, however, he surely found the Chimera in his arms, if not the succuba herself"[58]—that is, the illusory, if not the demonic.

43

In Senior's judgment, the Symbolists were pioneers trying to rediscover and reopen the path to the spiritual order: "Different cultures are led by different means. We must take ourselves as we are and proceed as we may. The symbolist movement is an attempt to find that way again."[59] In spite of their lax morals, the Symbolists held high spiritual views and were motivated by a transcendent yearning; and they sought to awaken men and women from the complacency of a mediocre, comfortable and meaningless existence. Senior praised them especially for undertaking a serious quest in their art instead of indulging in mere aesthetics or sentimentalism. He knew we must return to an art that helps us learn to look upon the world through spiritual lenses. In those days he even tried his hand at Symbolist-leaning poetry.

Senior recognized, however, the difficulty of a spiritual undertaking in a materialistic and faithless culture: "Modern symbolists have worked almost alone, and against the grain, without teachers or the 'support' of society."[60] Their spiritual effort, having nothing positive in our culture to bolster it, had more than ever to go the "negative" way of eliminating obstacles: "In the West we have split the self off from the Self and declared our self and what it sees to be the whole of being. In a schizoid society, when the Self has no living form to take, the call must be negative."[61]

In other words, the only viable solution is indeed a descent into Hell: "The real beginning of the way down," Senior wrote, "is the realization that the world is in pain. Hell is the realization of how far we are from Heaven."[62] The epilogue of *The Way Down and Out*, entitled "The Destructive Element," predicts that life in the West would have to get worse before it got better, as it counteracted the emptiness of our contemporary culture. Senior himself, one recalls, had begun his spiritual journey with the discovery that "all was not right between [himself] and the world."

The Symbolists had taken the first step by recognizing the vanity of modern society and revolting against it. They had also advanced in "the way down"; they had found correspondences, they had pierced through some of the multiplicity of this world. They had not, however, achieved enlightenment and, consequently, had not accomplished the task of

transmitting it: "The symbolists began the journey; none finished his work; perhaps it is impossible in our time."[63] Senior held some of them to be geniuses, but they were not supermen who, having achieved self-realization, could find symbols appropriate to communicate secret truths to others: "In practice it is probable that a great many symbolist poets were far from being enlightened men and that just as we feel the vague sensation of the 'beyond' in a given symbol, they discovered a given symbol entirely on the basis of their vague sensations."[64] Thus these artists were able to take men down but could not lead them out of the morass: "Symbolist poets have taken us on a profound voyage away from the world of ordinary consciousness into the abysses of ourselves, but they have not got us to the other side. We have descended with Istar into Hell, but have not got out."[65] Senior describes Baudelaire's effort: "The way for Baudelaire, therefore, is down through lust where at the very core of the apple of the self he finds 'Ennui'—*shunyata*, the void. *Les Fleurs du mal* begins with lust and ends, not with love, but the absence of everything which is not love, with ennui, with *le néant.**"[66]

To be led down but not out, according to Senior, leads to one result: "Failure means confusion, terror and despair."[67] In fact, several of the French Symbolists ended in hopeless, even raging, desolation and at least one in insanity and suicide. Senior explains: "The magus invites the infinite into the finite glass of his soul, and unless he is of superhuman stature, he is likely to be destroyed by the experience. To give up, even momentarily, our usual faculties is to invite insanity."[68] He thought that, in spite of the dangers, one must continue the journey begun by the Symbolists: "It is dangerous to peel off the ordinary skin of things-as-they-seem to seek the pulp of things-as-they-are, but if the hero sees it through, he may find at last 'au fond de l'inconnu, le nouveau'"[69]—"in the depths of the unknown, the new," as Baudelaire said.

The Way Down and Out ends at this point, in a somewhat disappointing way, without indicating the next step. Senior, the content family man, realized that the debauchery of so many Symbolists and Occultists was

---

* Nothingness.

not the answer.* He was aware of the error of those who think that "the way out of their troubles is to go down to the bottom and lead a bum's life."[70] Probably at the time of his book he already perceived what he wrote in the early 1960s about "neurotic experimentation by cultists who feed their fantasies on misinformation":

> These desperate persons act out of a mania for power and peace. . . . The arc of this demonic life is plain in Baudelaire or poor Rimbaud and their recent less gifted imitators in the "beatnik" movement—the infantile eroticism, the taking of drugs, the fascination with violence and death.[71]

For John Senior, a deeper, purer path to the Absolute was necessary. He therefore turned to the Eastern masters as the greatest authorities of Occult philosophy. While still writing *The Way Down and Out,* he began to pursue Hinduism. He experimented with the Hindu way of life for about three years, adopting its dietary practices and chanting its prayers with a colleague at Cornell. What Senior later wrote about those who go East can be applied to himself in the 1950s:

> There must be some other way—some other place—something more than cowardice and selfishness, something one can subject himself to without shame, something noble, beautiful, good, and true. It is a terrible but understandable mistake that the inexperienced and bursting heart, turning in disgust against the culture of the Golden Calf, confuses it with Christianity—because Christianity is certainly confused with it. And so we have the reason why some of the best have made the journey to the East. What they discover there at least is spirit.[72]

---

* See the first part of "The Generation of the Leaves," in *Pale Horse,* 29. Concerning this poem, Senior noted that "the beat movement was spawned in the West End Tavern near Columbia." Allen Ginsberg, Jack Kerouac, and the other founders of the "beat" form of Occultism and anti-Western rebellion were Senior's contemporaries at Columbia. Senior playfully mentioned one day that back in his college days as editor of the *Columbia Review* he did not accept Ginsberg's poems for publication.

CHAPTER THREE

The Real Is Really Real

*Oriental doctrine is like a garden gone to seed. The
air is still, late dahlias drop their heads amid the
pungent odor of decay; there is a peace here, certainly, a generosity of dissolution, a beauty so
intense sometimes that it is itself a meditation. . . .
Beautiful, but unreal.*

—The Death of Christian Culture

IT was critical for all that followed in his life that, in the mid-
1950s, Senior should begin to focus on Eastern philosophy rather
than the lesser Western brands of Occult thought, having found in the
former the "primordial philosophy" in its depth and purity. "Yoga," he
wrote in this regard, "is the exact science of what is yet only a parlor game
with us."[1] Two elements of this purer and deeper view would push Senior
to Realism, to the West and ultimately to Christ. First, Eastern philosophy's denial of *being*, and therefore of rationality, ran counter to his
intellect. Second, the absence of a personal relationship with God struck
against his heart. In this chapter, we will trace Senior's intellectual turnabout, leaving his actual religious conversion to the next. Here we shall
delve into philosophy, since this was the path that Senior himself took.
In order to acquire a lucid, vigorous notion of Realism, we must first
understand the fundamental, absolute antagonism between Realism and
Anti-Realism.

A Metaphysics of Nonduality

Chapter Four of *The Death of Christian Culture*, entitled "The Real Absence," was based on a talk Senior gave in the mid-1960s after his conversion to Catholicism. It is a vigorous synthesis and criticism of Eastern religious and philosophical tradition and incidentally presents his own intellectual path out of the way down. Therein he identifies his main sources on this tradition: "The only serious Occidental commentary on Oriental doctrine from the Oriental point of view is the work of René Guénon and A. K. Coomaraswamy."*[2] The "acknowledgments" of *The Way Down and Out* also express Senior's reliance on these two philosophers: "For my indebtedness to published works, I must especially cite those of Coomaraswamy and Guénon, which are responsible for the partial lessening, at least, of my ignorance of traditional thought."[3] Many years later, in the mid-1980s, when a former student quoted Guénon in a letter, Senior acknowledged that he had not read that author in twenty-five years and yet still felt his power of seduction!

Ananda K. Coomaraswamy and René Guénon are associated with the Traditionalist School, also called Perennialism; Guénon, in fact, could rightly be styled its founder. Although the two held that there was one source and secret essence transcending any particular religion, they believed that the seeker should be formed in the customs and rites of one tradition in order to draw near to the common fountain. They emphasized that the West's post-Renaissance materialist and technological culture had progressively lost contact with authentic spiritual traditions and therefore with that essential source. They rejected modern Occult groups as artificial, not in continuity with tradition. According to Coomaraswamy, Senior stated, there were only two authentic spiritual traditions in the West—Catholicism and Freemasonry. Both of these scholars received a Catholic education but turned to the East when they had reached adulthood. Guénon chose the Sufi tradition, a mystic branch of Islam influenced by Hinduism; Coomaraswamy adhered to Hinduism.

---

*   Later, Senior seems to have nuanced his position, saying that Guénon and Coomaraswamy promulgated Occult philosophy as Oriental doctrine. See *Remnants*, 127.

During the first half of the twentieth century, Coomaraswamy and Guénon were generally recognized as the foremost Western interpreters of Eastern thought. Senior would always be convinced that they had grasped the deepest metaphysical principles of Eastern philosophy. Although their doctrine reflects only a portion of Eastern schools, most notably the *Advaita Vedanta*,* Senior saw in it the implicit foundation of Hinduism and even the key to all Eastern philosophy as well as to the Occult worldview. While we may be familiar with its basic doctrine, laying it out in more philosophical terms will help us in understanding what Senior was dealing with precisely. A quotation each from these two philosophers will prepare us for Senior's text.

Guénon explained why, for the absolute point of view, there is only *Brahma*, that is, the one ineffable Substance of the Occult tradition:

> There can be nothing really outside of *Brahma*, since such a supposition would be tantamount to limiting it. It follows immediately that the world . . . is not distinct from *Brahma*, or at least is distinguished from It in illusory fashion only. On the other hand *Brahma* is absolutely distinct from the world, since none of the determinations attributed to the world can be applied to It, the whole of the universal manifestation being strictly nil in relation to Its infinity.[4]

Coomaraswamy indicated how the "world" comes to be by our limiting the infinite reality and thus positing various beings:

> [*Brahma*] is a syzygy of conjoint principles, without composition or duality. These conjoint principles or selves, indistinguishable *ab intra* . . . become contraries only when we envisage the act of self-manifestation implied when we descend from the silent level of the Non-duality to speak in terms of subject and object and to recognize

---

* *Advaita* means nonduality. The term *Vedanta* signifies the final writings of the *Veda*, the *Upanishads*. In the second century of our era, the teachings of the *Upanishads* developed into the philosophical direction envisioned here.

49

the many separate and individual existences that the All or Universe presents to our physical organs of perceptions . . . This finite totality can only be logically and not really divided from its source.[5]

Senior's core philosophical development in "The Real Absence" comes to bear at this point. First, he elucidates how we think of everything—all that our "physical organs" perceive—in terms of *being*,* as things that exist:

> The state . . . that we occupy as rational animals is exactly that state in which reality is conceived according to the Principle of Being, as explained by Aristotle—namely, that the first thing to be said about something is that it is; and its immediate corollary the Law of Contradiction—namely, that since something is, it cannot at the same time and in the same way be what it is not.[6]

From the sense data taken in, we perceive that *something is*, which is the principle of being at the foundation of our perception of the world. This principle lays the basis for the law of contradiction because from the recognition that a dog *is* derives the recognition that it is a dog and *not* a tree, that this dog is not that dog. Fundamentally, then, it is the principle of *being* that establishes distinctions and multiplicity. For Eastern thought, it must therefore proceed from an illusory point of view, since in fact there is only one non-differentiated and infinite substance, *Brahma*. Senior wrote:

> According to Oriental tradition this state that we inhabit is not the state of the universe, but only one of a multiplicity of points of view depending on the state of the viewer. Reality is comprehended only according to the mode of the comprehender. Man, since he operates in the mode of existence, cannot understand anything beyond existence.[7]

---

* I prefer to use the lowercase for the word *being* as closer to St. Thomas's meaning, even though Guénon and Senior do not. Capitalized, the term seems to indicate something vague and abstract if not divine, whereas St. Thomas had in mind something rather concrete.

As we know, according to this school of thought, even if he cannot "understand," man can go beyond this limited, rational mode:

Granted certain gifts, however, given certain initiations and having practiced certain disciplines, a man may, according to Oriental tradition, transcend his physical state of rational animality. . . . From this higher point of view, reality is seen under the aspect of *advaita* or "nonduality." In such a state the rational is transcended and the comprehender sees all things as one.[8]

The goal, then, is "*Moksha*, the Hindu term for 'freedom,' [which] means liberation from the mental habit of duality."[9] The principle of *being* is the essential barrier between us and nonduality because it creates that mental habit. It is the first container where we place the little pieces of reality that we break off. In the journey toward *Brahma*, the distinction between *being* and *nonbeing* is the ultimate duality to be suppressed. If one transcends them, no distinction is possible, there can no longer be any distinct things. If we go beyond the category of *being*—that the dog and cat really exist— there will be no more diversity. We would realize that the dog and the cat are simply temporary mirages of *Brahma*. Senior concludes the passage:

[The principle of Being] is the first manifestation of *maya*, the illusion consequent upon the state of rational animality. To say that something is and that something is not, from the point of view of *advaita*, is to say the same thing. Reduced to the simplest formula: "*Is* is not." . . . All of the hundreds of Oriental schools and their Western imitators . . . are so many ways of *yoga* or "discipline" leading to the achievement of *moksha*—liberation from *maya*, the illusion of "is"—so as to achieve the Supreme Identity "*Is* is not."[10]

It is baffling to see the Hindu study this world, invent machines, meditate on a philosophy of *being*, pray to the gods, love their wives and seemingly consider things we experience as real on one level, yet still view this all as mirages on a higher level, a deceptive manifestation of the only

reality, *Brahma*. More baffling still, however, is the *Advaita* doctrine that one must move beyond not just experienced phenomena, but existence itself. Existence is part of the illusory world, part of our rational, divisive process and must be abandoned to find the infinite, eternal and unique Substance. One cannot even say that *Brahma* itself *is*, because that would be to make of it a *thing*. Guénon explained that perspective:

> Being is not really the most universal of all principles . . . because even if Being is the most primordial of all possible determinations, it is nonetheless clearly a determination and every determination is a limitation at which the metaphysical point of view cannot stop short.[11]
>
> Whereas Being is "one," the Supreme Principle, known as *Brahma*, can only be described as "without duality," because being beyond every determination, even beyond Being which is the first of all determinations, It cannot be characterized by any positive attributes; such is the consequence of Its infinity.[12]

All determinations and therefore all ideas are limited and must be transcended, even those of *one* and *being*. Senior explained how *being* itself is a determination: "The Hindu says that Being itself is a limiting term; 'to be' is 'to be something.'"[13]

Senior was once asked how to advise a student who was venturing into Eastern religion. His suggestion was to push him deeper into the subject: "Have him read Coomaraswamy. That way he will get to the bottom of Hinduism and may be shocked out of it. That's what happened to me. I discovered that for Hinduism there is finally no difference between existence and nothing!" As he said elsewhere, "Oriental doctrine . . . brought me face to face with Nothing."[14] Shocked as he was in the 1950s to read such teachings, Senior could perhaps have continued his mental journey and accepted the East's bewildering goal as a mystery, had he not read St. Thomas Aquinas. This philosopher enabled him to perceive the nihilism and mental destruction intrinsic in Hindu doctrine.

Common Sense and the Metaphysics of Being

Coomaraswamy often quoted Western philosophers, notably St. Thomas Aquinas. Senior himself cited St. Thomas twice in *The Way Down and Out*, giving Coomaraswamy's writings as reference. One day in 1959 Senior began reading the *Summa Theologiae* for himself. As he once told an interviewer: "[Coomaraswamy and Guénon's] poor reading of St. Thomas nevertheless led me to the *Summa Theologiae*."[15] As previously noted, Senior identified his first two steps toward conversion as his readings first of Marx and then of Plato. The discovery of St. Thomas, he said, was the third and final step.

He noted two points in his initial reading of St. Thomas that broke the spell of Eastern thought. First, Senior mentioned more than once in class that during his initiation into St. Thomas he encountered a passage that directly refuted the idea that the "way up" could be identical with the "way down." St. Thomas simply pointed out that although a road is physically one and the same, a man can still travel in opposite directions, each determining a different destination.[16] "By what then seemed merely chance, my angel interfered: Meditating on the famous proposition of Heraclitus that the 'way up and the way down are the same'—which the Gnostics take to mean that, since opposites are one, the law of contradiction is void—I happened (oh happy chance!) to take up St. Thomas who says the way up and down are indeed the same, except as to direction."[17] As Aristotle illustrated, it is not the same thing to go from Athens to Thebes as to go from Thebes to Athens.[18] One has to choose where one wants to go. This insight may seem ridiculously simple to most of us, but Senior said that its discovery had immense import for him, helping him recognize that a duality among things is undeniable, that there really are two ways. Second, in the aforementioned interview Senior stated that in his first reading of St. Thomas he discovered "the notion of truth. Thanks to reading St. Thomas, I understood what is meant by 'common sense' . . . To use the phrase of Hamlet's: 'to be' exists while 'not to be' does not exist."[19] This pithy and allusive statement linking truth, common sense and existence calls for some reflection.

At the beginning of the *Summa*—where Senior doubtless started his reading—*truth* is defined as "conformity of the mind to what is" because "things are the measure and rule of the human mind"; truth consists in "matching the mind to the thing."[20] Concrete reality, not isolated thought or, even less, imagination, is normative. As we tell little children, dreaming or wishing does not make things so. Truth, then, presupposes accepting the existence of concrete reality, as Senior wrote: "Truth follows upon the existence of things."[21] The *common sense* he spoke of in the cited interview consists basically in that acceptance. Any healthy mind recognizes the existence of things; "It is the normal mind's first reaction to the world— to know that it exists,"[22] as he put it in later days. In other words, truth presupposes the principle of *being*.

St. Thomas Aquinas never speaks specifically of common sense with the meaning Senior gives it here, nor did he use the expression "principle of *being*"; but he did teach the doctrine Senior outlines. Right at the opening of the *Summa*, Senior read that *being* is the first thing known and the most evident. "*Being* is the first to fall into the intellect,"[23] writes St. Thomas in a striking way, there and elsewhere, to underline the immediacy and primacy of this knowledge.

Chesterton, the great doctor of common sense, speaking of this doctrine of St. Thomas, illustrates it in this way: "When a child looks out of the nursery window and sees anything, say the green lawn of the garden, what does he actually know; or does he know anything? . . . Long before he knows that grass is grass, or self is self, he knows that something is something. Perhaps it would be best to say very emphatically, 'There *is* an Is.'"[24]

After saying that *being* is what falls first into the intellect, St. Thomas continues by proposing "next, that this *being* is different from that one."[25] Human thought begins with *being* and continues in its light. After the recognition of *being*, we distinguish various things and strive to ascertain what *type* of *being* we are dealing with—a dog, a tree, a rock. In other words, the law of contradiction comes into play: this is not that, a dog is not a tree. St. Thomas speaks very clearly of the reliance of the principle of contradiction on the recognition of *being*: "The first and immediate

principle is that we cannot at once affirm and deny. This principle is founded on the nature of *being* and that of *nonbeing*, and upon this principle all other principles are founded."[26] If one does not distinguish *being* from *nonbeing*, all contradictions are permissible. One might affirm that a particular table at once is and is not. One could refuse and deny; "yes" and "no" would be the same; no truth would be possible.

Although Senior attributed to St. Thomas Aquinas his discovery of these notions of truth and common sense, when he referred to man's fundamental reaction to reality he would more often cite the first source in this domain, namely, Aristotle. Senior, who knew Plato so well, apparently had been largely unfamiliar until then with Plato's most famous disciple, at least with respect to his metaphysical and epistemological doctrine. It was St. Thomas's constant references to Aristotle that led Senior to investigate this Greek philosopher as well. The following passage by Aristotle is his classical statement on the subject of first principles, quoted more than once by Senior in his writings. In fact, as may be noted, both St. Thomas and Senior use terms reminiscent of Aristotle's terms in the texts cited above. Aristotle begins by expressing the law of contradiction, and then establishes it and all judgments on the basis of what Senior called the principle of *being*:

> It is impossible for the same attribute at once to belong and not to belong to the same thing and in the same relation. . . . This is the most certain of all principles, for it is impossible for anyone to suppose that a thing is and is not. . . . Hence all men who are demonstrating anything refer back to this as an ultimate belief; for it is by nature the starting point of all other axioms as well . . . It is obvious that this at any rate is true: that the term "to be" or "not to be" has definite meaning . . . [otherwise] all statements would be true and false.[27]

This text, Senior commented, is "simply common sense raised to philosophical perfection."[28] Aristotle clearly discerned and expressed man's normal, visceral recognition that things really are, and that this recognition is the foundation of all intellectual knowledge.

Thus, by linking truth, common sense and existence, Senior had discovered Realism. For the realist, one's thought goes beyond oneself to exterior reality. The verb "to be" has meaning; it is different from "not to be." When the realist says "the dog exists," he means what he says. For the antirealist, one's thought does not go beyond the self or the Self, one's mind or the Mind. When he says "the dog exists," he does not mean it.

Beyond certain striking passages found in St. Thomas and Aristotle, Senior's discovery of Realism came about more generally through his encounter with these authors' vigorous metaphysics centered on *being*. The two philosophers identified as the object of metaphysics *being* as *being*. Metaphysics, or "first philosophy," analyzes concrete existents in order to discover the laws of *being* as such. It seeks to know why and how things exist. Here was a philosophy that focused on things of our experience, but from a perspective other than that provided by modern science. And certainly for St. Thomas, existence is not only the light of the intellect, but also the heart of reality, the source and summit of all things. He brought before Senior's gaze the riches of *being*, the fact that *being* includes beauty, goodness and all values. The Occultist, the Symbolist and the Hindu thought that one must flee this world and eschew rationality in order to break into the spiritual world. With Aristotle and St. Thomas, Senior discovered a rational study of concrete things of our existence that goes beyond the superficial approach of modern experimental science, beyond simply dealing with what can be measured. Their philosophical analysis of sensible existents rises above this world to spiritual reality, all the way to God, as will be seen in Chapter Four.

Adherence to Being and to the West

Confronted, on the one hand, with such vibrant presentations of a metaphysics of *being* by Aristotle and St. Thomas, and, on the other, with a clear refusal of the very principle of *being* by Coomaraswamy and Guénon, Senior realized that he had an inescapable choice to make. He had either to accept, with common sense, the evidence that the real is really real and follow *being*'s call upward, or to refuse that evidence of *being* and

follow the way down into nothingness. He had to either accept the human mind's normal, innate, activity or refuse it.

In spite of his deviations at the time, Senior had had a healthy experience of reality, cultivated by a poetic and literary formation that had given him a taste for concrete things. This made for a well-disposed soil for sowing Realism when he finally ran into a vibrant and convincing presentation of it. He recognized that there was no possibility of denying the fact that the dog in the backyard really is; that it was impossible to truly think that the dog is the tree or that he himself was both of them. Even if there is a mystery of communion among entities upon which one can focus, one cannot deny the reality of their differences; one cannot obliterate their separate existences. And nothing can be beyond existence.

Senior had written in *The Way Down and Out* about the danger Occult methods posed to our faculties. Afterward he came to realize that yoga and analogous practices aim precisely at hindering or damaging mental processes in order to instigate a delusion of the unity of all reality. His judgment may seem harsh but he had experienced what he was talking about. In fact, as he noted, "Many of my friends and colleagues from this time, driven by the thirst for truth beyond Existence ended in insanity and death from overdoses of drugs and bogus Buddhist meditations."[29] Others have remarked, for example, how certain drugs accomplish a similar reduction of the sense of one's own identity that facilitates confusion of self with other things. Senior described how the techniques operate:

> [Yoga] is the science of hallucination. It is practiced by techniques Huysmans only fooled with, but what Rimbaud, in one of the most influential documents in modern literature called "the deliberate derangement of the senses." Whether by shallow breathing, which cuts off oxygen to the brain, thus causing it to malfunction; or by constrictive postures, which affect the blood and lymph systems; by fasting, drugs and above all, self-hypnosis induced by *mantra*— the repetition of sounds—or *yantra*—the gazing on intricate

geometrical patterns—or by *koan*—the Japanese system of thinking about logical impossibilities—by any and all these devices the yogi is able to break through his own normal experience of the world.[30]

If you succeed in this enterprise, Senior wrote, you "will *know nothing,* that is, have a direct intuition of vacuity."[31] Indeed, blurring the difference between things and ultimately between *being* and *nonbeing*, emptying things of their reality and making everything—even *being* and nothing, even God—a pure symbol, is insanity. In this framework, someone who has attained enlightenment thinks that everyone else errs in thinking they themselves are a reality. Senior wrote that such a one "does not dwell under the delusion that he is Napoleon, or even that he is Buddha. He dwells under the supreme delusion that everything is delusion—that Napoleon was a paranoiac under the delusion that he was Napoleon, God is a paranoiac demon under the delusion that <u>HE</u> is God."[32]

Turning from the way of nihilism and insanity, Senior charged in the direction of *being* and sanity with all his might. Had Hamlet asked him to choose whether to be or not to be, Senior would have cried out: "To be!" He definitively discarded Coomaraswamy, Guénon, Eastern thought, and even in a large measure modern philosophy and twentieth-century literature, so tainted by Occult philosophy and the anti-rational.

Senior's adherence to Realism led him to rediscover the grandeur of traditional Western culture. He recognized that, until modern times, Western culture had been rooted in Realism:

With due respect to its failures—for it seems to be failing now— the triumph of three thousand years of Western civilization has been, from the point of view of ideas, the philosophy vaguely called Realism or the Perennial Philosophy, because it has survived so many seasons. It may be summed up in a sentence: *The real is really real*; or in a word—*is*. The terse scholastic formula defines it: ... truth follows upon the existence of things. According to this view, the principle of all things is "to be."[33]

In *The Way Down and Out*, Senior used the term Perennial Philosophy to denote the "primordial tradition" of Occult doctrine. After his discovery of St. Thomas and Aristotle, as we see here, he applied it to the Realist tradition, according to Catholic practice. Indeed, at about the same time that Occultists adopted the expression "Perennial Philosophy," Catholics began using this same expression for the Church's philosophical patrimony, the natural wisdom of the ages propounded first by the Greeks and then developed and refined by the Church in the light of the supernatural wisdom of Divine Revelation. Pope Pius XII confirmed this usage and affirmed that Realism is the Perennial Philosophy's cornerstone, while declaring St. Thomas Aquinas to be its greatest and best proponent. According to him, the Perennial Philosophy essentially "safeguards the genuine validity of human knowledge . . . and the mind's ability to attain certain and unchangeable truth."[34] Jacques Maritain, prior to Pius XII's text, explained in particular why the philosophy of Aristotle and St. Thomas is perennial, why it endures: it is built on and develops a "prephilosophical instinct"—which Senior identifies as common sense and first principles—present in all men of all time. In Maritain's words:

> This philosophy of Aristotle and St. Thomas . . . can therefore claim to be abiding and permanent (*philosophia perennis*) in the sense that before Aristotle and St. Thomas had given it scientific formulation as a systematic philosophy, it existed from the dawn of humanity in germ and in the pre-philosophic states, as an instinct of the understanding and a natural knowledge of the first principles of reason and ever since its foundation as system has remained firm and progressive, a powerful and living tradition.[35]

After his turnabout, Senior began employing the term Perennial Heresy as an appellation for Occult doctrine, Eastern philosophies and modern idealism—generally, for all Anti-Realist doctrines wherein existence does not hold primacy over thought or imagination. Heresy derives from the Greek word *hairesthai*, meaning to choose. Anti-Realists arbitrarily choose to turn away from the evident reality of things and therefore from

the ground of normal, right reason. Denying the value of "is," refusing, as it were, the world's greeting, constitutes the fundamental philosophical error, a deviation at the point of departure that contradicts both experience and reason. Senior was convinced that he had discovered the great dividing line in human thought: "All questions come down at last to the assertion or denial of a reality independent of the mind which we can know by means of the mind with certainty."[36]

History reveals that this heresy is indeed perennial. It is an enigma that mankind should constantly experience the temptation to renounce common sense and refuse reality. In the case of the Eastern philosopher, it seems that his ardent spiritual quest of the Absolute tended to make him diminish or deny the reality of the physical world. Dazzled by a mysterious communion among things, he was led to refuse the multiple and distinct. Yet presuppositions similar to those of the East have often surfaced in the West as well.

In the early history of Greek philosophy, Heraclitus proposed that reality was like a fire where differences in things are fused as ephemeral parts of the universal process of becoming. All is One in fact. It was he who first said that the way down is the way up.[37] A little later, Parmenides affirmed the Absolute according to the pure requirements of the intellect. For him, Being, as he called it, is eternal, unchanging, without distinction—nonduality, Guénon would say—whereas the world we experience, because it changes and has differences, is illusory; it is nonbeing. A little later, Plato himself, who reflected continually upon sensible experience to ascend to the spiritual, nevertheless considered this changing sensible world to be only a pale reflection of the non-sensible, eternal world of Ideas. The expression "really real," used by Senior in the above quoted passage, comes from Plato, although Plato is referring to the Idea rather than to the concrete reality we experience. Furthermore, Plato proposed that our knowledge proceeds not from our experience of the sensible world but from a "reminiscence" of Ideas seen in a previous life before we fell into our bodies.

Senior would always love and meditate on Plato, while acknowledging that it was, rather, Aristotle who firmly set Western reflection on the right

track by recognizing the solid reality of our tangible experience and properly appreciating the role of sensible knowledge in the formation of our intellectual knowledge. His lucid formulation of the first principle, Senior wrote, was "the moment of truth in this perennial battle" between the Perennial Philosophy and the Perennial Heresy.[38]

Even then all was not yet won in the West. What is termed the "Neoplatonic position," for example, coming well after Aristotle, developed the ambiguity in Plato's overemphasis of man's contact with the spiritual world, by discarding man's humble link to concrete sensible realities so as to directly attain to spiritual ones. Much like the Occultist and the Hindu, this philosophical movement even posed a divine One beyond *being*.

The Realist context of Western thought was, on the other hand, greatly strengthened by Divine Revelation, beginning with the dogma of Creation. As Senior remarked, "If God exists and really acts and if one of His acts is creation, then the world really exists."[39] Things are not simply a mask of the divine; they are realities, distinct from God. The problem of the contingency of our world, so intensely felt by the Hindu, Parmenides and Plato, could be resolved: Things are neither nothing nor an absolute, they are God's works; they have substantial reality but are totally dependent on Him. God's love for human beings, proven by the Incarnation and the Redemption, especially impressed the reality and value of individuals on Western consciousness. Furthermore, the Christian was all the more inclined to trust in his faculties of perception and understanding since they were given to him by this loving God. A strong climate of Realism was thus established in all of Western culture. Realist philosophy also advanced: If Aristotle's philosophy is based on the fact that "the real is really real," St. Thomas was the first to show that "the principle of all things is 'to be.'"

Unfortunately, this climate of Realism has faded in modern times, as Senior well recognized. Even in the later Middle Ages, some schools, such as Nominalism and Voluntarism, by denying the stable essence of things of our experience reduced their reality. This tendency toward reduction became more widespread in the Renaissance. Senior's analysis of the

decline of Realism in modern times, however, will be the subject of a later chapter in our book. For the moment, we will simply quote G. K. Chesterton comparing East and West, pointing to manifestations of Eastern thought again resurfacing in the West: "This [Occidental] world of different and varied beings is especially the world of the Christian Creator, the world of created things, like things made by an artist; as compared with the world of the many ancient religions of Asia and modern German idealism that is only one thing, with a sort of shimmering and shining veil of misleading change."[40]

Following his awakening to Realism, Senior then turned to Greek and Roman civilization, to Homer and Virgil, but most especially to the Christian West, particularly the Middle Ages. He characterized this new phase of his quest as a return to a former love; he had once taken delight in the fresh charm of medieval poetry and literature. While he continued to acknowledge with Coomaraswamy and Guénon that a break in tradition had taken place at the time of the Renaissance, he no longer held medieval culture to be an expression of the Occult view. More and more, Senior realized that all the great works of the Middle Ages—cathedrals, statues, frescoes, poems and sagas—were glorious celebrations of *being*. Medieval art was indeed symbolic. But the symbols were not empty, pointing finally toward nothing; they represented real things as signifying higher realities.

Senior's discovery of Realism and its fundamental place in traditional Western culture was essential to his journey toward religious conversion. Indeed, while reforging his links to the West, Senior not only found intellectual and poetic affinities, but discovered spiritual ones as well. As he read the Western authors, something awoke in him: "Like someone who has studied maps and read descriptions and diaries by travelers to a far country reporting such marvels as to make this place a *terra aliena*, I have awakened to some deep ancestral memory of my native country and its King."[41] That awakening is the subject of our next chapter.

CHAPTER FOUR

The Real Presence
of He-Who-Is

The journey to the East—if undertaken honestly—
will end where it did two thousand years ago, with
the Magi going West to the stable in Bethlehem,
falling on their knees, rapt in adoration before the
real presence of Him who is, born of a Virgin, made
flesh and therefore in the world, to redeem the
world, not annihilate it.

—The Death of Christian Culture

ONE day in 1960, Professor Senior went to tell the Catholic chaplain at Cornell University that he wanted to be received into the Catholic Church. Monsignor Donald M. Cleary asked what his preparation had been. Senior responded that he had read St. Thomas, St. Augustine and Cardinal Newman, among others. The priest leaned back in his chair, reached behind himself and pulled out a volume from some shelving. He put it on his desk and asked, "Have you read this one?" Senior looked at the title, *The Baltimore Catechism*, and replied: "No, I haven't." "Well, go through it and then come back." Senior, in retelling this story, would always conclude with: "You know, that was the best thing I read!"

Senior revealed few details of what led up to his visit with the chaplain. He was a private person, not prone to make disclosures of his interior life. We have no record of the final intellectual or spiritual steps of his conversion. Years after the event, his daughter asked him, "What made you become a Catholic, Dad?" "It was a miracle," he replied. "No one could

have been farther from the Catholic Church than I was." And no more was said.

His journey to the Church was a solo trip. As we just saw, his decision was made before the priest who later instructed and baptized him knew of his intentions. His closest friends at Cornell University happened to be Catholic, and they eventually became his family's baptismal sponsors; but even they had not been aware he was deliberating the matter. Nor did his family know about it until he announced one evening around dinnertime, "Guess what! We need to become Catholic!" He once told a friend that he "read" himself into Catholicism via the great Catholic intellectuals. Senior also related that one day during a talk he was giving on Hinduism, someone in the crowd began to dispute with him. This left him thinking on his way back home, and, "God finally won the argument," he later recalled.

Any conversion involves, above all else, the mystery of God's gift—collaboration of the free will with His grace. Senior would sometimes say that you wake up one morning to discover yourself to be a Catholic, without being able to discern exactly when or even how it happened. Despite the mystery concealed in any conversion and Senior's reluctance to discuss his own, some information drawn from his writings and a few remarks made in conversation reveal a certain rational process in his religious conversion.

A Real Absence

As the epigraph of this chapter indicates, the journey East was for Senior, in various ways, the road back West to Bethlehem. He included himself among those of whom he wrote: "It is certainly true that for many . . . the only way to Christianity is, as Eliot said, 'by the back door.' For them this oriental vision, by antithesis, is a kind of Advent, a season of spiritual preparation."[1]

Senior's experience of Eastern thought contributed to a positive spiritual awakening that eased him away from the influence of materialistic ideology. He learned to look at the world in a spiritual way, to see things

of experience as symbols of invisible realities. This kindled his desire to reach beyond this physical world. He once commented that he knew there was a spiritual world—that there were spirits—even before he knew there was a God.

The East also served as spadework for Senior's conversion in an antithetical way by provoking a reaction, driving him in the opposite direction. Aside from the intellectually destructive forces he discovered in Eastern philosophy, he also experienced true spiritual anguish when immersed in it. As he would later note, underlining the paradox of the Eastern effort: "The Oriental mystic gives up his house, his clothes, his friends, his family, his body, his mind, his soul and God."[2]

The Eastern philosopher or mystic must go beyond not only a philosophy of *being*, thus foregoing all rationality, but beyond the mind itself. He also goes beyond God, who is an illusion if not taken as a symbol. But he then is left with nowhere to go, finding only a "real absence," the title of Senior's lecture on Hinduism referred to in the preceding chapter. Eastern and Occult philosophy is, one can say, a desire to see as God does, but without God. There is no God to know us and love us. And, in any case, there is no self to know and love God, because our individuality, our sensitive and exterior ego, our consciousness, is simply a temporal manifestation, or rather, a mirage, as Senior wrote: "In the state of nonduality, there is no distinction between one's self and any other self, or any other thing, or even nothing."[3] Senior concluded that "perhaps the most disconcerting aspect of Oriental doctrine is its radical impersonalism."[4] Mere knowledge of metaphysical principles cannot fulfill the human soul because, Senior explained, "The final rest of the intellect, as of the will—of thought as of love—is in a person."[5]

One can sympathize with what must have been Senior's interior desolation when he recognized that his efforts led to a void. He wrote:

Once this state of liberation from his "self" and from "the ten thousand things," as the physical universe is called, is achieved, there is discovered—one cannot say "he discovers"—an abyss beyond even emptiness because the masters of this tradition say

that "nothing" is an illusion too. The ultimate irony is that after a lifetime of seeking one discovers that there is literally nothing to have sought; not even "nothing," which is a rational idea.[6]

Senior mentioned an incident that impressed on him the emptiness of his spiritual and Eastern pursuits, finding no one and nothing to believe in. On Ash Wednesday in 1959, while going to get the *New York Times*—his "daily sacrament" in those days, as he said years later—he saw a nun with ashes on her forehead. With a sigh he said, "There goes someone who really believes in something!"

Turning from the Occult and Eastern thought toward a metaphysics of *being*, while opening himself to the West with a hope of finding rest for his soul, Senior had to investigate God, Christ and the Church. In many a conversion the three support one another—discovering Christ supports the belief in God, and the splendor of the Church renders easier a belief in Christ. Senior may have come to all three of them rather simultaneously, but there is nonetheless a certain logical order to his discovery.

He Who Is

Liberated from artificial barriers stemming from prejudice against philosophical Realism, Senior could now look at the world with a normal mind and heart, and recognize that it leads to its Creator. Everything cried out to him that *there is a God*. Senior was helped in this appreciation by Christian texts that began to echo in his soul, such as this passage by St. Augustine:

Consider the beauty of the earth, the beauty of the sea and the beauty of the sky extending above us far and wide. Consider the beauty of the heavens, the order of the stars and the sun illuminating the day with its brilliance. Consider the moon, whose glow softens the shadows at the coming of night. . . . Consider all of these and they will proclaim to you: Behold us and gaze upon us, for we are beautiful. This beauty is their confession.

Who made this ever-changing beauty, unless it is He, whose beauty is changeless?[7]

Some years after his conversion, Senior described in a letter the conclusion to which the mind naturally comes after reflecting on the spectacle of the universe:

The existence of God is best proved in the five ways of St. Thomas, but best seen in the common sense experience of us all negatively, like the taxi driver who said, "Sure I believe in God because the opposite I can't believe—that all this happened by accident." Suppose God does not exist? But then there is nothing. But that is clearly wrong: look <u>there</u> is something!—really you and me and the stars.[8]

In this text, Senior distinguishes proofs from commonsense considerations. A proof, with its abstract principles and rigorous syllogism, is difficult to follow, but anyone can realize intuitively that there has to be Someone behind the order and beauty of the world. The existence of God is seen "negatively," that is, the impossibility of the harmony of the universe resulting from mere chance should make one realize that the positive affirmation of God's existence must be true. Also, Senior indicated that the commonsense inference of God's existence depends on the evidence of *being*: He said "look," pointing, as it were, by emphasizing the word "there." Things really *are*, so their cause really *is*.

Senior, of course, also worked through St. Thomas's proofs. Here is his summary, close to the commonsense experience but expressed in philosophical terms:

Anyone in his right mind can see that all of this around us and including us is not a sufficient reason for its own existence. Either there is an ultimate existent (which we call God) who is sufficient reason for existence or there is no reason for the existence of

anything—which is radical absurdity and radical absurdity is not a reasonable alternative.[9]

This passage determines what was implied in the taxi driver's and St. Augustine's insight: things do not have "sufficient reason" for their existence, so there has to be behind them Someone who does. A detailed and technical argument first would lay out this insufficiency by establishing the fact that things change, come to being, have only limited, participated values and are ordered to a finality. The next step in the argument would show that since things do not exist by themselves they exist by another; that is, they are caused. The third step would explain that there cannot be mere transmitters of existence, which would be like a train having all its cars dragged and yet without a locomotive to produce the movement. The conclusion then imposes itself that there must be Someone who does not receive existence—who exists by Himself—and can therefore be the cause of the existence of things. Thus, philosophical proof points out more clearly the term of the argument: the "ultimate existent," whom we normally call God, as St. Thomas said at the end of his proofs. We must accept God's existence because the only alternative, as Senior told us in the cited text, is absurdity, which the intellect cannot choose. It is, once again, the negative reaction against the impossible that pushes us to affirm the existence of what we do not directly experience.

The Hindu and Occultist will object that to conceive of God as the "ultimate existent" is to make of Him a thing, simply a *being* among others, even if the Supreme Being, the first in the series. Such a God is not absolute, transcendent; He is determinate and limited, like all existents. That is why, at least according to the *Advaita* school, *Brahma* is beyond *being* and existence, and can be characterized only as nonduality. He, or It, is unknowable by the means of our finite ideas, which are always limiting. Senior well knew, however, that St. Thomas's reasoning concluded not exactly in an existent, but in a pure act "*to be*," and that this was the least inadequate philosophical idea of God, and one apposite to resolving the Hindu dilemmas. In order to deepen our dialogue with Eastern

thought—and with the Perennial Heresy more generally—let us further our examination of the matter.

For St. Thomas, anything that *has* existence receives it and so requires a cause. The first cause does not receive existence and therefore must *be* existence. God is an absolute IS, a subsisting *To-Be*, St. Thomas said.[10] Akin to a heart that would love with all its strength, passing all its life into a perfect act of love to such an extent that it would have no possibility of loving more, so has God, as it were, passed everything into His act *to-be*. He has accomplished all the possibilities of *being*. By this metaphysical deepening of the proof of God's existence, St. Thomas seems to have found what Hindus and Occultists are groping for in the dark, while resolving their philosophical impasse.

The Hindu holds that we cannot know the infinite *Brahma* by the means of our finite ideas taken from the illusory finite things of this world. We might note that the Church herself speaks in partly similar terms concerning God's transcendence. She teaches that God is "eternal, immense, incomprehensible, infinite . . . altogether simple and unchangeable."[11] However, for the Church, of course, God is not beyond existence. And the affirmation that He is incomprehensible means that He cannot be completely grasped; it does not, however, exclude some knowledge of Him through creatures. The Church, in fact, teaches that God "can be known with certainty from the created world by the natural light of human reason."[12]

St. Thomas's doctrine does full justice to the legitimate requirements of Hindu teaching. First, this God is not the first of a series. He is of a different order from all other realities. Everything else, even a spiritual reality, is a thing. It is a horse, a tree, a rock, or an angel, of a particular nature, that is, a form or modality, a measure or degree of *being*. It is limited to this or that way of existing, whereas God exists purely, absolutely, infinitely. He is not this or that; He is above modes of *being* and ways of existing. This absolute act *to be* is not a limiting term, but the principle of all things.

It is interesting to note that the Latin *ens*, like its English counterpart *being*, is a participle and so applies well to things that participate in existence. St. Thomas preferred the infinitive *esse*, *to be*, when speaking of God.

Commenting on a Neoplatonic treatise, he remarked that there was some truth in the position that God is indeed above *being*—*supra ens*—understanding the term *being* to mean *something*-that-exists: "The first cause is above *being* because it is the infinite *to-be* itself; *being* is predicated upon what participates in *to-be*."[13]

Furthermore, an absolute *To-Be*, a pure existence, because it has no limits and determinations, constitutes a supreme identity, the nonduality the Hindus demand, "the absolutely simple," as St. Thomas said. For the same reason, it offers no contours that would permit us to grasp it. God is infinite and incomprehensible; He cannot be enclosed in an idea.

St. Thomas's metaphysics also avoids excesses and errors that can be elusive and difficult to refute. Fundamentally, one understands how the supreme identity, while transcending *being* in a way, is not beyond existence and that, consequently, some similarity remains between limited existences and God, the absolute existence. The absolute and pure *To-Be* eminently contains all the various types of *being* as white light contains the colors of the rainbow revealed by refraction. It follows that God is not totally unknowable through ideas. *Beings* speak of and point to the pure existence, even if they do not adequately define Him. Any perfection that does not imply limits is fulfilled in absolute existence, although in a sublime, inconceivable way. God is good, for example; we just do not realize how good He is because He is better than anything we can conceive of. Much of theology consists in seeing how truth, good, beauty, love, knowing and power converge toward and lose their finite modes in God's pure act *To Be*. Again, as colors do for white light, these ideas help us to better appreciate the riches of this absolute existence. God, the absolute *To-Be*, is too bright for our mortal eyes, but *beings* screen His light so we can catch an indirect glimpse of Him "as in a mirror, darkly."*

Through his studies, reflection and prayer, Senior realized that beyond this world there lies, not an empty abyss, but a Real Presence. And he knew

---

* On God as pure *To Be*, see Hyacinthe Paissac, "God Is," in *Theology Library* (A. M. Henry ed., Chicago, Illinois: Fides Publishing, 1955), Vol. II, 21–118. See also Etienne Gilson, *The Christian Philosophy of St. Thomas Aquinas* (New York: Random House, 1956), 84–95; this section was reprinted in *A Gilson Reader* (Anton Regis ed., Garden City, New York: Image Books, 1957), 230–245.

that this absolute *To-Be* accomplishes all the perfections of *being* and, therefore, knows and loves. After having lived in a world of empty symbols, Senior would now allow no compromise with the various ways of diluting God's reality. "God is not an idea," he wrote, "or a theory to be demonstrated, or a symbol to be translated into the latest style, or even an ideal of perfection. He is a person, really existing here and now."[14] He had known both sides of the coin when he wrote that he who follows the way down "imagining the Infinite, sees nothing and panics; it is difficult for him to understand that others do not imagine *what* but *Who* and have not seen emptiness but a warm and loving plenitude."[15] The fact that God is a person, not a concept, was a point of emphasis for him: "I believe in God, not merely that he is."[16]

Henceforth not only his intellect, but Senior's heart as well could be involved in his quest of the Absolute, which was a dialogue, a relationship with a Person. The spiritual life did not consist of the destruction of an illusory self in order to become aware of one's already existing substantial unity with the ultimate reality; nor was it an array of techniques for an isolated exploit on one's own. It was an opening of oneself to another person's love, a relying on someone else.

A living realization of this personal presence, a conversion, requires more than an intellectual turnabout. Senior doubtless experienced himself what he wrote concerning the importance of turning the will toward God so that God may be a living reality for the soul: "As long as doing what we will does not mean doing His will, we simply will not see the fact of God's existence and presence."[17]

This discovery of the possibility of a personal relationship with God would be confirmed and deepened when Senior delved into Christian Revelation. Before his eyes would be unveiled a God who personally acts in this world and has spoken to us in the prophets, and then in His own Son, Who became man in order to save us and open the way to the Father.

Christ

While his embrace of Realism blossomed into a conviction of God's existence as he read St. Thomas and other authors, Senior, of course, looked

toward Christ. As he stated in the epigraph to this chapter, the journey East led not only to God but to "adoration before the real presence of Him who is, born of a Virgin, made flesh." His flight from absurdity and the empty abyss of the Eastern quest took him all the way to Christ. To himself he applied Huysmans's line: "It was either the bullet in the head or the Cross."

Senior continues his argument against absurdity in the letter cited above referring to the taxi driver's common sense:

And does God care about us? To whom should I go? If God does not care, He could not be good, but good is order and conformity to what is. Perhaps as Thomas Hardy says, He is a purblind shooting dice with our lives. But if He is, He must be in conformity with Himself and with us whom He makes. And is He Christ our Lord? Well, who else? If He exists and cares for us, let's look for Him in history and in our lives. "To whom will we go?" Where is the supreme act of love in the whole of history if not on the Cross?[18]

Ultimately, God contradicts Himself if He does not care for His creatures, especially those to whom He gave free will and the capacity to know and love Him. Propelled by this conviction, Senior sought to find God's care at work by examining history. For him, this meant verifying whether Christ was indeed sent by God, whether He is truly His Son. This study brought him to recognize that there was nothing in history comparable to Christ, to His gift of Himself for our sins. As St. Peter said to Christ: "To whom will we go?"

Before looking into Senior's inquiry into the person of Christ, we should mention that as he read Christian authors in their own light, he discovered ever increasingly that traditional Christian views corresponded marvelously to all he was learning about Realism, about God and His creation. He wrote: "The Christian says, 'God really exists.' In this inescapable fact, the whole fabric of pagan and oriental illusionism, and the syncretism of religions that follows from it, is dissolved."[19] As we have indicated, there was no illusionism among Christians, because they knew that this world, made and redeemed by God, is real. Senior also now

72

recognized that even the most enlightened Christian mystics were far from being syncretists. They did not consider Christianity to be a manifestation among others of the primordial Occult tradition. St. John of the Cross did not look on the Christian faith as an exoteric veil for totally ineffable experiences.

Since Christians believe in a real Creator of real things, Senior also realized that he and many others had made a dangerous oversimplification in equating the Occult, the Eastern way down, with Christian asceticism. A certain similarity in words and in some practices disguises what are two opposing philosophies. The point of asceticism, according to adepts of the East, is that this world, including and especially the self, is made up of illusions and barriers and must therefore be "destroyed." In his chapter on Hinduism in *The Death of Christian Culture*, Senior quoted a famous passage from Buddha. After enumerating procedures for "destroying . . . all latent 'I am,'" Buddha concluded: "Herein 'I am' is got rid of, made as palm-tree stump that can come to no further existence." And Senior commented: "Every agent, Aristotle says, acts out of a desire for Being, whereas Buddha teaches 'desirelessness.' For us, all things in the real world naturally desire their own Being. . . . Far from quenching, extinguishing, cutting himself down to a dead stump, [a man] flowers and seeds."[20]

For Christians, even more than for Aristotle, the self and the world are good, and meant to be cultivated. It is evident that Christians are often worldly, but Senior knew now that this is not because they hold things to be real: "Worldliness is to forget that things are creatures—not illusions, but creatures created by God for the purpose of getting us to Heaven."[21] Things and our desires for them are God's gifts to help us come to Him. By making idols out of things, worldliness—or sin—has twisted our relationships with them, so that they no longer lead to God. The Christian "way down" is the discipline of human desires so that we use things in accordance with their and our true relation to God. The effort sometimes feels like a destruction of self, but, in fact, the Christian strives only to destroy his disordered attachments, to purify his knowledge and love. He does not want to annihilate the tree, but prune it in order to concentrate its energy, so that it may grow vigorously straight up and bear fruit.

Senior appreciated this Christian Realism and marveled at the beauty in Christian writings. Yet, how could he be absolutely sure of Christianity's fundamental claims? Realism and St. Thomas had helped him understand that reason can go beyond the horizon of the material world and of experimental science, but there are no philosophical demonstrations that Jesus is the eternal Son of God. One cannot deduce from the tree in the backyard that Christ rose from the dead, as one can that God exists. How then to probe Christian claims about Christ?

While Coomaraswamy and Guénon had contributed the first step in making Senior wary of modern scholarship and critical history, it was Blessed John Henry Cardinal Newman who positively helped him accept the Gospel stories. In Senior's view, Newman's life was a kind of paradigm of conversion in face of the modern scientific mentality, first experienced and then set out in theory by the cardinal. Realizing that old scholastic thought did not touch modern man, Newman had to forge a new path, or rather, he had to show how one, in fact, believes. His *Grammar of Assent* is a theoretical exposition of how one can attain certitudes without the aid of philosophy or experimental science; how one very regularly uses other means, such as converging probabilities, in domains where science has little or no hold. For example, Newman countered John Locke's assertion that the only sure truths are those conclusions drawn from modern experimental science. Newman argued that very little of our knowledge is obtained in this way, most of our certitudes being of a commonsense type, relying on some sort of belief.

We know that England is an island, although we have never sailed around it; we know that our friend will not poison us with this evening's meal, although we have not analyzed the food in a laboratory.

In a talk given only six months after his entry into the Church, Senior stated that he had made the cardinal's views his own. A germane theme of this talk—substantially taken up later in Chapter Nine of *The Death of Christian Culture**—was that abstract arguments are insufficient in apologetics because, in Christianity at least, one believes in a

---

* The chapter is entitled "The Emperor of Ice Cream" and is named for a poem by Wallace Stevens. Senior's idea was that either all is empty symbol and façade, or Christ is real.

person, not an idea. General notions are not adequate for getting to know an individual person. Consequently, Christian apologetics should be more an affair of presenting Christ. As St. Philip did with St. Nathanael in the Gospel according to St. John, one must invite and help people—"come and see"—to have the experience of Christ's person. Senior, following Newman, had a special fondness for the Gospel scene of the Presentation, where Simeon and Anna recognized Christ the Savior in the Babe. "Who else do we expect?" Senior would ask. "Where else to go?"

To demonstrate the need and value of a "Presentation" in dealing with knowledge of a person, Senior referred to David Hume's objection concerning miracles: We have ample experience of violation of truth but none of violation of natural laws; men lie and are mistaken whereas laws of nature are constant. "Hume was right," he said, "as long as he was arguing about abstractions and probabilities; he never faced reality."[22] Senior then stated Newman's retort, which is that generally such a statement is true, but that in this case we are not dealing with generalities. The question does not concern most men but particular witnesses by the name of Peter, Paul and John. Did they lie or were they mistaken? As to Christ Himself, Senior summed up the reason we should believe that He was not lying or crazy, and that, therefore, He is what He said He was:

> A non-Christian has got to believe that Christ—author of the Sermon on the mount, this man Whom we come to know so well in the course of His history in the New Testament and in the figures of the Old—that this man was at the same time either a liar or a lunatic. . . . What is our experience of liars and lunatics? Do they speak sermons on the mount?[23]

One might perhaps protest that Christ's profession of His divinity before the Sanhedrin or His miracles and so forth were inserted in the Gospels at a later date, that they are not historical. Senior would respond, with Newman, that the Gospel's picture of Christ is cohesive; a powerful, personal presence emerges from the various scenes and discourses:

You will discover in the end that the more you tear [the New Testament] down the more it will adhere and that the Christ of the trial is the same one as the Christ of the sermon, that the Christ of the beautiful maxims cannot be torn from the Christ of the miracles and that the maxims you cannot deny as being beautiful and good and sane are of a piece with the harsh maledictions that repel you because to avoid them you would have to change your life. You cannot evade Newman's case by higher criticism.[24]

By reading Scripture and meditating on the writings of saints, through his own prayer, Senior came to know Christ's person. He wrote that Newman had once thought religion consisted mainly of sacred scenes, like figures in a frame that give rise to pious sentiments. Then one day "Newman saw the figures in the frame begin to move."[25] Something similar occurred in Senior's life. Christ began to come alive for him. Things are real, God is real, Christ is real.

The Real Presence of God was thus made flesh; it had a human face and heart. Senior recognized that God's love and care for us were truly manifested in Christ Who came as Savior and Who suffered true pain, shed real blood, truly died for us. Senior's Realism concerning Creation pointing to its Creator now developed into what one can call a supernatural Realism. Following the Symbolists and Eastern philosophers, he had sought a window on eternity, but these poets and mystics thought they had to destroy the world in order to create that window, and in the end saw nothing. Senior found a real window present in this material world, through Whom we go directly to God: "He who has seen Me has seen the Father."

The Church

Christian life could not consist merely of the independent reading of sacred books: there had to be more to it, there had to be a community within which to live it. At a restaurant one Sunday morning before his conversion, as Senior and his wife watched people going to and from

church, they realized that there must be something more meaningful to do on Sunday than simply going out to breakfast. Mrs. Senior suggested they start going to church as well. Many groups claimed to be Christian communities. To which church should they go?

Senior noted how the answer emerged in his mind: "And did [Christ] not pray for Peter that his faith might not fail? And order him: *pasce agnos meos* [feed my lambs]? If not the Church of Peter, 'to whom will we go?'"[26] What could Christ's words mean except that Peter was to lead the other Apostles? And it is the Catholic Church that claimed Peter as her head. Furthermore, this church was at the heart of the Western culture Senior was rediscovering in new depth and joy. Which church to turn to if not that of St. Augustine, St. Thomas, Dante, Chaucer and Newman? The more he delved into Catholic tradition, the more Senior discovered its riches.

Senior and his wife probably first went to an Episcopalian church when they decided to start attending Sunday services again. When he announced his impending conversion and his daughter asked why Catholic and not Protestant, he answered that he had "checked out the Protestant ministers." Yet, it does not seem that he had ever been tempted by Protestantism. Guénon and Coomaraswamy had rather directed him to Catholic mysticism, if not to the hierarchical Church. For them, Protestantism—the Episcopalian denomination included—was an invention of the post-Renaissance modern world, a splitting off from the great spiritual tradition of the West.

Moreover, Senior was repelled by the lack of Realism that was more or less pervasive in the various forms of Protestantism. They upheld the basic Christian Realism mentioned above; they professed no syncretism or illusionism. However, in principle, they heavily emphasized the corruption of the natural order by sin. Hence, a distrust of any analogy between creatures and their Creator prevailed among them. In most denominations, the Sacraments are drained of reality and are simply symbols useful for provoking acts of faith. Many Protestant churches resemble stark lecture halls, devoid of signs or images of the invisible. In classical Protestantism, grace loses its reality. It is nothing within man, but

only God's merciful gaze upon him. Earthbound man is incapable of being lifted up to a participation in divine life.

In the traditional Church, Senior found a vigorous Realism. He recognized that the Catholic Church was and always had been the great defender of philosophical Realism, in particular by proclaiming the capacity of the human mind to know God. St. Thomas was officially the Common Doctor of the Church, that is, the regular reference and guide for her philosophy and theology. And for Catholics, grace was an objective reality that intrinsically transformed the Christian. More generally, this Church believed in the inherent goodness of the sensible world, its natural orientation to God, its aptitude to signify the spiritual and to help people climb to the invisible and transcendent. Thus, for the Catholic Church, the Sacraments, which make use of real, natural things—water, oil, bread, wine—are not mere symbols; they really confer grace. The Church also envelops the celebration of the Sacraments in sensible signs—candles, incense, architecture, vestments, stained glass windows, chant, ceremonies and so forth—to direct the gaze of the worshiper toward Christ and His mysteries.

Catholic Realism, as it permeated the life of the faithful, was also a point of attraction for Senior. We have mentioned already how Senior discovered the Realism of the intensely Catholic medieval art and literature. He had already experienced some Catholic culture in the 1950s, while studying French in Quebec and again during his year in Ireland. Now, as he actively investigated the Catholic Church, he encountered a thoroughly Catholic environment. Perhaps partially under the influence of Huysmans, the erstwhile Symbolist who frequented Benedictine monasteries, Senior made a retreat at Mount Savior Monastery, not far from his home near Ithaca. The liturgy, the Gregorian chant and the artwork certainly moved him. However, in an interview, he referred to only one aspect of his retreat as having been decisive in his conversion: his reading of *The Rule of St. Benedict*. He explained the reason for this in one phrase: *Ora et labora*, "Pray and work," commonly considered to be the Benedictine motto. "Everything I have learned in literature and philosophy can be summed up by *ora et labora*."[27] He expanded on this thought elsewhere:

"Truth, St. Thomas says, is a relation of the mind and thing. Founded on work and prayer, [the monastic life] is proportioned to the dual nature of man in his mind and body. Both work and prayer are intellectual habits relating the mind to thing."[28] Senior had found a deep and healthy Realism in Benedictine life, rooted in the soil and pointing to the stars. This insight helped him recognize the realistic wisdom of the Catholic Church. During the retreat he bought a medal of St. Benedict which he always wore from that day forward. We will come back to Senior's appreciation for the Benedictine life at a later point.

For his scrutiny of the tenets of the Catholic Church, Senior went through a process akin to his reasoning concerning Christ. Blessed Newman's *Grammar of Assent* had a role in Senior's belief in Christ; the cardinal's *Essay on the Development of Christian Doctrine* assuredly had a hand in his accepting the mystery of the Church. Senior considered the *Essay* to be one of the greatest books ever written and highly recommended it to those interested in the Catholic Church. It was all the more convincing that Newman wrote it before becoming Catholic; he converted in the course of writing the work. Senior explained that, at the outset, Cardinal Newman began his work with the notion that the Roman Church had diverted from the Church of the Fathers at the time of St. Gregory the Great, while others had thought that the Constantinian Church had spoiled the Apostolic Church. Senior continued:

Newman began to examine, stage by stage, the actual life history of Christendom in order to prove just where and when and under what circumstances the original primitive Church had gone wrong. He concluded that "to be deep in history is to cease to be Protestant." Newman did not argue this proposition; he discovered it against his own best will.[29]

In a similar approach to that used in *Grammar of Assent*, where Newman invited the reader to get to know Christ, *Essay* was not about working through a hundredfold difficulties and arguments, but rather about coming to know the Church. As always, Newman said: "Come and see!"

Alluding to Newman's autobiography, *Apologia pro Vita Sua*, which likewise was a presentation rather than a detailed argumentation, Senior encapsulated the thought:

> You say the Church said such and such in 325, such and such to the contrary in 1845. Newman's reply is his greatest work, *An Essay on the Development of Christian Doctrine*, a kind of biography of the Church, an *Apologia pro Ecclesia Sua*. You offer such and such arguments against the Church, but this is she, "bright as the sun, terrible as an army in battle array." Her proof is history.[30]

Newman's *Essay* expertly lays before the reader the fact that the Church has remained essentially the same throughout her development, from the Church of the Apostles to that of Pius IX, the pope of his day. When one reads history without prejudices, a general but clear and definite picture of the Church emerges. Concentrating on the Church's flaws would be committing the proverbial error of not seeing the forest for the trees. Senior wrote concerning this singular entity in history: "Take it all in from Adam until now. The Church . . . has been the light of the world; and without the Church, broken as she is, the darkness would be unbearable."[31] Presented with such continuity over the centuries, one realizes that the Church is not so much an idea to be discussed as a living reality to be recognized; a face begins to form. There must be more here than a human institution. Christ is present.

The secret of what unfolded in the depths of Senior's soul remains hidden between him and his Lord, but it is possible to trace the elements that came into play in his conversion, as we have attempted to do in this chapter. Most especially, the fact that the real world points to its real Creator, the testimony of the many beautiful and healthy aspects of Christianity and of the Church, and Newman's reasoning on historical facts and witnesses—all these played their role in leading him to fall on his knees, not before an empty symbolic idol, but before the real presence of "Him who is, made flesh," and Who lives and acts in His Church.

Msgr. Cleary instructed Senior, his wife and, separately, their children, who also attended a religious class taught by a nun. Mrs. Senior, who hailed from a rather staunch Protestant background, had been confused at first by the outcome of her husband's investigations. She had not followed him in his Hindu experimentation, letting him do his own thing, as it were, but his new convictions were obviously of a different nature. By the grace of God, Mrs. Senior was soon won over and remained a devout and solid Catholic to the end. On April 13, Holy Thursday, 1960, all five members of the family professed God, Christ, and the Catholic Church, were baptized—Mrs. Senior and Penny conditionally—and received the Holy Eucharist. As newborn Catholics, they experienced their first Easter Triduum and the sacramental and liturgical celebration of the great mysteries of our salvation.

Senior's reserve continued: only the godparents were present at the ceremony. That Easter Sunday, one of his fellow young professors at Cornell, seeing him receive Holy Communion, said to himself, "There goes Senior after a new high!" Soon afterwards Senior would be off to teach at another university and begin a new life.

Senior was thirty-seven years old at the time of his conversion, almost exactly at the midway point of his life. Summing up the first half of his life, he compared his journey East to his search for an idyllic life in the Caribbean:

> I was looking for some kind of life which I am now absolutely convinced can never be found except in heaven. . . . After several years of studying Hinduism, Buddhism and many other philosophies, I had the tremendous experience of getting to the bottom of that and discovering that was just another form of trying to find the island paradise. I realized that all these ideas and all these experiments of mind really led to something very old and traditional, namely the Catholic faith, and concluded that little half of my life.[32]

After a period of darkness and discouragement, with only nothingness at the end of the tunnel, Senior had now found the great, essential truths.

Now he had beautiful objects worth contemplating and loving, mysteries into which he yearned to enter more and more deeply: the Blessed Trinity, the Incarnation, the Redemption, the Eucharist, the Church, Our Lady. He was not in Heaven yet, but he was on a sure path leading there. And he was not alone in the journey. Someone was watching out for him, helping him along the way, drawing him to Himself. There was also a whole community around him, leading the same life and loving the same truths. He had found the living, inexhaustible, divinely guaranteed tradition from which he could draw all wisdom. A new life was beginning for him; he wanted to be "faithful to the celestial vision," to all he had received from the Lord. He wanted to bear fruit for God and His Church.

The Contemporary Form of the Perennial Heresy

O Artificial Paradise,
My dream-god's Kingdom of the False!
I hate this seething enterprise,
this vile, insulting IS—it galls!
—From "Il Miglior Tessitore," Pale Horse, Easy Rider

A FTER Senior's discovery of the authentic Western tradition and his entry into the Catholic Church, he literally moved west. In 1960 he left Cornell University to accept a position at the University of Wyoming, thus withdrawing from the Ivy League world. As he explained, "I found myself in one of the top ten American universities, led by an intellectual elite that had been perverted by Existentialism and Phenomenology.... In the 1960s the new intelligentsia of the Left made thought subservient to power by rejecting the existence of all reality. I responded by fleeing to the American West, where people's minds were not as corrupted."[1] Existentialism affirmed that "existence precedes essence"; that is, reality is a formless mass until man puts order into it. Phenomenology, as Senior uses the term here, adopted a similar perspective: that human consciousness gives meaning to what, in fact, are random and fragmented phenomena. Because of their denial of intrinsic nature, both of these worldviews are open to manipulation by propaganda. Senior was saying that, by returning to the land of his dear cowboys, he hoped to find both students and an environment less influenced by Modernism, the contemporary "resurgence of this perennial heresy that has worn so many different faces."[2]

For purposes of concluding our examination of two perennial philosophies, it is useful here to examine Senior's analysis of Modernism as the foundation of our contemporary culture, so that we may understand more in depth the milieu in which Senior was—and we still are—operating. Indeed, for Senior, Modernism permeates the ways we spontaneously think, feel, desire and act in all domains, because, as he writes, "culture is integral. As an organic growth, all its parts—music, painting, literature, science, politics, philosophy, religion—move and work as one."[3]

Here, we will consider the intellectual and artistic arenas, leaving the religious sphere for a later chapter.

While at the University of Wyoming in the 1960s, Senior gave three brilliant lectures that together form something of a post-conversion rethinking of his book *The Way Down and Out*. These are now found as three chapters in *The Death of Christian Culture*. Chapter Two, "The Perennial Heresy," and Chapter Three, "Eastward Ho!-Hum," both analyze the writings of the Symbolists and other founders of Modernist literature, leading to Chapter Four, "The Real Absence," a study of Eastern thought as a logical outcome of Modernist orientation. It is said that Senior wished to add another final chapter to the second edition of *The Way Down and Out*, but was refused by the publisher. If that is the case, we presumably find much of that material here.

We have already perused Chapter Four, "The Real Absence";* we will now investigate Chapters Two and Three of *The Death of Christian Culture*. This will bring our rather hefty metaphysical considerations to a conclusion, providing a foundation for what follows in our book, that is, for the study of Senior's theory of education and its application at the University of Kansas.

Modernism's Historical Roots

We have already noted how Senior recognized that the Perennial Philosophy was failing in today's West. He never produced a comprehensive historical study of this demise, but here and there sketched parts of

---

* See our Chapter Three.

the progressive course of Modernism in the past centuries. We can piece these parts together to trace in general lines how the West reached its present stage. An examination of the historical roots of Modernism will enable us to better understand its nature.

Senior regularly identifies the Renaissance as the turning point that eventually led to the current domination of the Perennial Heresy over Western culture. What surfaced in the Renaissance, of course, was not *ex nihilo* but had its roots in developments of the late Middle Ages. Nevertheless, there was a shift in mindset during the Renaissance, expressed especially by the term *Humanism*.

It is common knowledge that, as Senior explains, "in general, [Renaissance] Humanists . . . centered their philosophy on man and the things of man."[4] He affirms that this focus isolated man from both sensible and spiritual reality: "The Renaissance cut the human off from its roots in the humus and its flowering among the stars."[5] Historians acknowledge that, to a certain extent, attention was averted from God, from the supernatural and the world to come. But how was it that the Humanists separated man from the "humus" of this world?

We have already mentioned that the Renaissance introduced a less symbolic manner of considering reality, dwelling mostly on the material aspect of things. Many Renaissance Humanists thoroughly scrutinized the world, but did so in a novel way, by means of empirical and mathematical sciences. Senior observes: "It is commonly agreed that at the Renaissance, science shifted from the study of things first known by heart to the construction of mathematical models tested by instruments that quantify things."[6] These means limited the object of man's gaze to only a superficial aspect of reality. The foundation was laid, Senior writes, for what would one day become "the wholly unexamined assumption that the real is the quantitative; that is, the real is what can be measured. [This assumption] affirmed the evidence of appearances divorced from substance. By considering the truth to be only what is sensed, science lays itself open to the psychologizing of knowledge."[7] Several points in this passage reflect how Modernist developments are rooted in perspectives that arose in the Renaissance.

First, there is the "assumption that the real is quantitative." Instead of dealing with substantial things, the new sciences centered attention on measurable attributes—weight, mass, force, size, and so on—that could be controlled and verified by observation in a laboratory. This prescinding, as it were, of a portion of reality may at first have been intended to be only practical and methodological. However, with the many discoveries that ensued, it led to the notion that by taking the quantitative as the heart of reality one could unlock the secrets of the universe. These sciences were deemed superior to Aristotle's complicated and seemingly sterile theory of knowledge concerning the supposed essence of things. As Senior writes, "The new observation of nature— with the invention of the telescope and the dissection of anatomists— rendered, they said, obsolete [Aristotle's theories]."[8]

Thus, this materialist gaze on reality in the Renaissance limited the object of human knowledge. The new scientific method tended to be extrapolated into a general philosophical view: we only know quantity, and quantity is all there is. In other words, the success of the experimental scientific view stimulated the prejudice that one could know with certitude only "appearances divorced from substance." The focus on measures brought about, according to a line Senior borrows from the Spanish philosopher José Ortega y Gasset, "the progressive disrealization of the world, which began in the philosophy of the Renaissance."[9] In man's sight, "things" of ordinary experience were losing their reality, their distinctive essence. Man began viewing this world as made up of empty boxes, as it were, of geometrical figures and not of trees, rivers, horses—made up of what we can measure rather than the substance of things.

This "disrealization" opened men to a "psychologizing of knowledge," Senior affirms, that is, to making knowledge a purely mental event. The new sciences dealt with what can be observed, not with what is, and so tended to hold onto only one term of the relationship that constitutes truth, as Senior explains: "If truth is only what is sensed, truth is in the mind . . . and not, as Aristotle said, a real relation of the mind to things."[10] Since concrete things of experience appeared less real, since the focus was on perceptions within, one could begin to believe that knowledge was

simply a psychological process. Science, methodically restricting its study to sensation, produced a mentality which tended to consider that everything takes place within us.

Thus we see that the Renaissance scientist, by considering the world in such a limited way, severed man's roots from the fullness of their real, rich humus. He was left with only barren clay that no longer nourished growth toward the stars. An unforeseen consequence arose from this cutting off of humanity from the humus and the stars: Man's new knowledge and his swelling domination over the world's material forces seemed to liberate him from God and earth; but, now having only himself to rely upon, he began losing confidence. Senior again quotes Ortega y Gasset, who spoke of "four centuries of criticism, of doubt, of suspicion"[11] begun in the Renaissance. It appeared ever increasingly that, not only Aristotle's philosophy, but everything that depended on the previous "unscientific" ways—in religion, in Scripture itself, in tradition, in politics, society, history—was doubtful and needed to be critically scrutinized. Skepticism eventually infiltrated many domains that until then had been taken for granted: man's ability to know, the moral good, Christian faith, the existence of God, reality itself. Humanity was losing any humus from which to draw.

Senior illustrates the ambiguity of the Humanistic glorification and isolation of man, which ultimately leads to doubt or despair, by quoting Shakespeare's tragic character Hamlet, a type of the Renaissance and of modern man in general: "What a piece of work is man! . . . how noble in reason! how in action like an angel! In apprehension, like a god! the beauty of the world . . . Yet to me what is the quintessence of dust? Man delights me not, no nor woman neither."[12] Having discovered that his mother is not virtuous, Hamlet begins doubting everything, and this doubt then paralyzes his will until, finally, nothing matters to him. His questioning of whether life is worth living would become for future generations a question about the existence of reality; as Senior writes: "For the five hundred years since Hamlet pushed it over the brink, Western Civilization has been on the downward path of doubt, where 'to be' becomes a question."[13]

In this "disrealization" of the world and the "psychologizing of knowledge" that emerged in the Renaissance, both converging into doubt, we have all of Modernism in germ. The germ then proceeded to unfold in the course of history. In the seventeenth century, disrealization, psychologizing and doubt were decisively engaged in the thinking of René Descartes. Admiring the clarity and success that mathematics lent physics, Descartes longed to do something similar in philosophy. He therefore sought a precise method for organizing a new and unassailable objective system of thought. In his desire to refute skepticism, he looked first for an indisputable truth to use as the foundation of the entire edifice of human knowledge. Everything, he reasoned—sensible experience, even the very existence of outside things—was doubtful, but he could not doubt that he was doubting. From the unshakable truth of his consciousness he concluded that he existed: *Cogito ergo sum* ("I think, therefore I am"). From there he deduced his system.

After Descartes's formal rejection of man's innate and spontaneous confidence in the senses, which severed the natural relationship between the mind and exterior reality, two opposed habits of thought now developed and came to dominate in the West. Senior explains: "The divorce from Realism gives us two possibilities to exploit. First, the piling up of empirical evidence without regard to intelligence at all. . . . The second possibility . . . argues that we know nothing but what is in our minds."[14] Empiricism denied universal ideas, as if all knowledge consisted in sensible experience; any affirmation that cannot be reduced to experience is illegitimate. Consequently, knowledge consists simply in measuring, counting and organizing sensible data. On the other hand, Rationalism under its various forms strove, in the wake of Descartes, to work everything out from the interior of the *cogito*, of isolated thought. Both Empiricism and Rationalism, Senior concludes, fought Realism, for neither held onto both sides of the relationship of truth. Neither understood knowledge as the mind's drawing out of universal ideas from sensible experience.

To explain the more immediate preamble to Modernism, Senior refers to the dialectical development of the two cultural periods preceding it—the Enlightenment or the Age of Reason on one hand, and Romanticism

on the other. Beginning with the close of the seventeenth century, there was a determination to exclude from philosophy, science, and politics, from art and religion, whatever could not be rationally manipulated. In this way, it was believed, one could at last get on with the positive work of mastering nature and solving all of mankind's problems. This tidy scientific world of the Age of Reason, however, imprisoned the human spirit. In the late eighteenth century, the rising generation realized it needed a connection to the infinite, something beyond the bounds of reason and a dreary mechanical universe. People wanted to feel free again. A general tendency to reclaim the emotional and spiritual aspects of life emerged in the Romantic period.

The Romantics believed that although—or because—emotions and imagination resist all clear conceptualization, they give access to life and beauty, to a deeper level of reality than reason and science lead to. The material world could be abandoned to science; the spiritual domains— religion, metaphysics, art and morality—depended on man's interior world. "The Romantic thought of himself," Senior writes, "as a sensitive instrument tuned to unseen presences in himself."[15] Thus, after excessive belief in the powers of reason, the pendulum swung in the opposite direction and there came about an exaggerated interest in feelings: "I feel, therefore I am," as Kenneth Clark aptly put it in his BBC television series, *Civilisation*.

Yet, by the mid-nineteenth century, many Romantics were tiring of their unfulfilled dreams and falling back into a weary and disillusioned pessimism. Furthermore, the supposed riches of man's interior world were beginning to be undermined, it seemed, by materialist science. Darwin's theory that humans accidentally evolved from other animals took a foothold in education. Soon psychologists and sociologists would explain that aspirations and emotions toward the good and the beautiful merely reflect animal instincts or socially imposed group habits. Physicists seemed to reduce man to "a physiochemical reactor, a confused and wretched vibration in a universe of particles and waves."[16] Reason had already been jettisoned by the Romantics as unapt for the spiritual world, but now emotions and even morality were taken to be merely subjective. With the

failure of excessive reason and of excessive emotion, the Modernist era was ushered in, "repudiating both reason and affection, repudiating the idea of significance itself."[17]

A Blossoming of Renaissance Tendencies

Contrasting Modernists with their predecessors, the Rationalists and Romantics, Senior observes: "The [Rationalists] believed that significance derived from reason. The Romantics attacked them, declaring that significance derived from affections. Modernists attacked them both, repudiating both reason and affection, repudiating the idea of significance itself."[18] He quotes Robert Frost, who described the Modernist gaze on a seemingly meaningless world:

A blanker whiteness of benighted snow
With no expression, nothing to express.[19]

Prior to these lines, Frost had referred to Pascal's fear in the face of the infinity of outer space; here he remarks that this empty earth is equally frightening.

Senior explains that the Modernist, lacking any trust in ideas or affections, is left with what he "can immediately observe,"[20] that is, with sensations or imagination, which then, pointing nowhere, have no meaning or significance. He also notes, still referring to the preceding cultural periods: "Ideas have permanence; emotions, durability. But sensations are instantaneous"[21]—that is, they are always changing. Consequently, a life of sensations is a life void of permanent truth. Senior's insight corresponds to what St. Pius X presented as the philosophical basis of Modernism: "[According to the Modernist,] reason is confined entirely within the field of phenomena, that is to say, to things that are perceptible to the senses and in the manner in which they are perceptible: it has neither the right nor the power to overstep these limits."[22] All we know are appearances.

Senior places the beginning of cultural Modernism in France at the mid-nineteenth century: "[Modernism] describes that period in our

cultural history beginning in 1857.... The particular choice of year is somewhat arbitrary of course—Marx published in 1848 and Darwin in 1859—but from the literary point of view the birth of *Les Fleurs du mal* and *Madame Bovary* takes precedence."[23] Senior always considered Baudelaire's *Les Fleurs du mal* to be the first Symbolist work, and saw the Modernist movement in art as being rooted in the Symbolist school. We have noted that in *The Way Down and Out* he distinguishes the Symbolists from the Romantics by the latter's effort to provoke the intuitive experience of something beyond reason through their art. In *The Death of Christian Culture*, he shows how Symbolists took yet another step away from reality, identifying a second aspect that set them apart from Romantics: their rejection of emotions. He writes: "Baudelaire is, as the Modernist jazz musicians say, 'cool.' 'All mastery is cold,' said Mallarmé; and he speaks in his letters of having climbed 'pure glaciers of aesthetic.'"[24] As the product of pure intellectual calculation, the pure aestheticism of the Symbolists became entirely detached from any emotion.

Gustave Flaubert, author of *Madame Bovary*, represented the "naturalist" or "realist" movement in art. As we have seen, this group reacted against Romantic idealism, considering the scientific view of the world to be the only valid form of knowledge; they went so far as to deem material phenomena to be the only reality. Affection and emotions, notably, are illusions. As an example, Senior points out: "And as for love, Flaubert proposed it thus: 'We wretched little grains of dust, paltry vibrations of an immense movement, lost atoms!—Let us join together our nothingnesses in a common tremor.'"[25] At nearly the same time, Marx and Darwin set to work controverting human ideals and repudiating objective knowledge, with the exception of empirical science. For them, reality is simply evolution, in which man and his supposed values are puppets. Flaubert, Marx and Darwin are thus even less Romantic than Baudelaire! All four of these men rejected the Realist validity of normal human reason and emotions.

According to Senior, Modernism attained "majority" by the turn of the century and "prowled about the world at will."[26] Pablo Picasso launched Cubist distortion; his ideas became the reference for future generations of painters and sculptors. James Joyce's novels presented his characters' stream

of consciousness in an attempt to lend coherence to an otherwise meaningless world. In the human sciences, Freud's theories reduced all ideals to animal instincts or to socially imposed group habits. The great French philosopher of the period, Henri Bergson, proclaimed a philosophy of pure movement or evolution; phenomenology, with its denial of intrinsic nature, also began making inroads in the academy. Although already present in Protestantism, Modernist theology—in an effort to adapt dogma to current sentiments—began to surface in Catholic thought, proposing that religious doctrine is nothing but the temporary and circumstantial projections of our desire for the divine. Religion, in other words, is only a symbol.

Modernism reached "the full extension of middle age ripeness in the 1920s,"[27] as Senior observes. Existentialism, with its emphasis on the primacy of the individual consciousness and the absurdity of the external world, was born in those years. Soviet Communism and then Nazism came to prominence, as political systems of force and will in a world without truth. Senior also explains that in the beginning of the twentieth century American "expatriates" like T. S. Eliot, Ezra Pound and Ernest Hemingway caught a "virulent and more advanced form of the disease in Paris, which spread through their literary sects," and that Modernist culture took over in this country after World War I.[28] In the wake of that devastating conflict, Eliot published the classic Modernist text *The Waste Land*, in which, through the ruined myths of the past, he tried to find water for the desert of a faithless Western world.

Modernism has dominated, Senior tells us, "with increasing vigor since World War II."[29] Senior points to a growing androgyny and mob rule as evidence of this state of affairs. In the 1960s and 1970s, Modernism finally entered "old age" in the Western world as a whole, "where evident signs of senility appear in the latest cinematic shocks and the graffiti novels."[30] The contemporary quest of novelty for novelty's sake and absurdity for absurdity's sake can be considered part and parcel of this cultural senility. Belief in the mind's power accompanied by a hope of imposing order on the world has given place to total skepticism; even man's thought and communication are absurd and incoherent. Everything is absurd, even the judgment of absurdity.

Man is a monster vainly seeking meaning in a monstrous world. Senior remarks that we have come a long way from the Symbolists: "[Modernism's] best effort was a vain attempt by men of considerable genius to make art into religion and its worst has been beneath contempt."[31]

Thus, today there is a general and spontaneous conviction that we have no grasp of the nature of reality, or, in fact, that there is nothing to grasp, no real nature at all. All is subjective opinion, relative to the given situation. This Relativism, or Anti-Realism, is omnipresent as an unquestionable presupposition, a dogma to be upheld. Senior writes: "Relativism is the religion of the mass-media, including not only newspapers, magazines, books, radio, records, television, but alas, schools, colleges and universities as well."[32]

Relativism is what is behind that common phenomenon of our day— the tendency to reject former ideas and ways of doing things. Because, according to the Modernist, we cannot know anything with certainty, tradition, customs, institutions and laws are to be considered simply as mere conventions. No exterior, independent reality or nature imposes itself; there are no absolute rules. In the 1960s, the "straight" was he who still took these formalities for realities. The "hip" saw through these structures. Since each person had his own consciousness and truth, and could but "do his own thing," the only universal good was freedom.

The seeds of disrealization and the psychologizing of knowledge sown in the Renaissance have thus come to full blossom. Doubt has also reached a summit because the verb *to be* has no definite meaning and indeed becomes a question. Senior quotes the nineteenth-century author Thomas Carlyle, whom he considered something of a prophet: "We quietly believe this universe to be intrinsically a great unintelligible Perhaps."[33]

Artificiality, Sensationalism, and Fantasy

In his unique analysis of Modernism, Senior discerns a number of special characteristics that constitute this current form of the Perennial Heresy. In Chapter Two of *The Death of Christian Culture*, he reflects on two of Modernism's essential traits, "intertwined and reciprocally

causative—*artificiality* and *sensationalism*."[34] In its basic definition, "artificial" refers to something man-made. By including the suffix "-ity," Senior emphasizes the unnatural aspect, a human intervention that tries to cut man off from and to replace nature, an intervention opposed to a collaboration with the world God created. "Sensationalism," likewise through its suffix "-ism," evokes the idea of the pursuit of sensations for themselves, the more striking the better.

First, let us consider artificiality. If we know no objective reality, nor the nature of things, it would be rather a relief to escape from what we previously thought was natural. Senior indeed consistently finds a predilection for the artificial among the builders of our culture. Huysmans, for example, seriously preferred the beauty of machines to that of women: "Does there exist anywhere on this earth a being born in the throes of motherhood, who is more dazzlingly, more outstandingly beautiful than the two locomotives recently put into service on the Northern Railways?"[35] Senior suggests that much of our modern culture is, in fact, at war against nature. For example, in reference to science and technology, he writes: "It was Bertrand Russell who summed up the arrogance of his technocratic clique in saying the function of science is 'to make nature sit up and beg.'"[36] Senior regularly spoke of the artificiality of his time, with its electric lights and television.

In Chapter Two of *The Death of Christian Culture,* Senior concerns himself primarily with literature. He again quotes Huysmans: "There can be no shadow of doubt that with her never-ending platitudes the old Crone [Nature] has by now exhausted the good-humored admiration of all true artists and the time has surely come for artifice to take her place wherever possible."[37] The idea that art is superior to nature underlies the Modernist approach, which holds art as its own object and end, without need of meaning or reference to anything outside itself—art for art's sake, that is, pure artificiality. Bringing into play the dialectic between Enlightenment and Romanticism, Senior explains that Modernist artists intend to go beyond reason and emotion—confuting the normal view of this world in the process—in order to produce an autonomous object, liberated from nature. He elaborates: "The function of the Modernist poem is to rid ourselves first of thought and next of emotion. . . . And then, at the

second stage, the poet, as magician, creates upon this absence of idea and emotion the pure artifice of the work of art as a thing in itself."[38]

The Modernist is a sensationalist because, as we have seen, sensation or immediate consciousness is all he has. The frenzy for sensations is intimately linked to modern artificiality. One has only to walk down a city street at night to realize how much the electronic world of flashing lights and blasting speaker music feeds the desire for sensations. Sensationalism itself is essentially artificial, to the extent that it cuts sensation off from its natural connection to reality. As a literary example, Senior refers to a scene in a Huysmans novel where the protagonist, instead of going on a real trip, simply gives himself the various sensations of one, thinking it equivalent to—or better than—reality.[39]

The third chapter of *The Death of Christian Culture* dealt especially with the outcome of this artificial sensationalism. Senior explained that as the Modernist sets out on this path toward separating himself from reality, he runs into a problem: severed from its natural, intrinsic relation to exterior and substantial reality, sensation has no depth and quickly grows stale. The Modernist is therefore driven to abandon familiar surroundings, to seek novelties: "In order to renew the instantaneous sensation, [the Modernist] must flee whatever it is that he has—the bourgeois, the conventional—and he must flee the known and conventional past."[40] Baudelaire strikingly expressed the fact that in traveling it is not the object in itself that counts:

O Death, old Captain, it is time, weigh anchor.
This country is a bore. O death set sail . . .
Plunge to the bottom of the gulf—hell or heaven, who cares,
Just so we find the *new* in the depths of the unknown.[41]

But the new and unknown eventually become familiar. Hence the unavoidable and meaningless wandering, travel for travel's sake:

At the very start of the Modernist arc we find this restlessness without purpose, as near the end it survives in the jargon of the beatnik motorcyclist: "let's go, man, go"—nowhere in particular

95

but just go. *Part pour partir* is the theme of all true voyagers, Baudelaire says; or, as he said in another poem, quoting Poe, it is to go "anywhere out of this world."[42]

Many go East, but the title of Senior's third chapter, "Eastward Ho!-Hum," suggests that that exotic land will likewise eventually lead to boredom. "Ennui," Senior writes, "is the hell of the Modernist."[43] The French word *ennui* means not only boredom but also disgust or annoyance. This common use of the word in France corresponds to its etymology, as Senior explains: "Monsieur Ennui is not his Neoclassic or Romantic brothers Messrs. Skeptic and Despair. The word 'ennui' derives from the Latin *in odium* from a root meaning at once 'to hate' and 'to stink.'"[44] Sooner or later, an overabundance of sensations nauseates. Seeking only sensation but finding no genuine satisfaction in fleeting pleasures, the Modernist becomes sick of reality.

Confronted with a world that seems empty of truth, goodness and beauty, the disillusioned Modernist feels cheated. He revolts against reality:

Modernistic boredom is not the exhaustion that follows upon excess like Byron's; it is a positive disgust and finally a hatred of existence itself. To Modernists the world is not an accident, as science led the men of the Enlightenment to believe and the men of the Romantic age to despair. The world is rather a deliberate, malicious, and very dirty trick. Everything that is, is wrong, and the only salvation is destruction.[45]

The poets and novelists brood like suicidal Hamlets on the great cheat of their existence—Hardy, Hemingway, Camus, the list is famous, tedious and long; or they comically deride and satirize, singing canticles of absurdity—Flaubert, Joyce, Nabokov.[46]

Since he does not know the exterior reality but only appearances, since all is subjective, the Modernist easily turns away from that absurd objective world toward his own interior. Senior again quotes Huysmans: "The imagination will provide a more than adequate substitute for the vulgar

reality of actual experience."[47] The Modernist thus turns to fantasy, to an artificial imagination, to the image separated from its reference to reality—where, as Senior writes, "the image . . . substitutes for Being."[48] It is especially in their belief that imagination is superior to things we experience, as well as in their techniques to liberate imagination from experience, that Symbolists are *de facto* founders of modern art. As Senior comments on Huysmans: "Huysmans has suggested that we concentrate by a kind of artistic yoga on a single detail—what is usually called the symbol—in order to annihilate reality. And then he goes one crucial stage further: after the achievement of unconsciousness, he reconstructs his own false consciousness, a deliberate, self-induced hallucination."[49]

Fantasy, understood by Senior as total artificiality and pure sensationalism, is perhaps the most characteristic note of Modernism, in a summit of unreality. Senior explains how this dialectic of history discerned by him finds a sort of Hegelian synthesis: "The original bifurcation of Rationalism and Empiricism has reached its end at last in fantasy."[50] Mind and thing have been rejoined because for the Modernist the mental image is the thing; it is reality. Pointing to the pretension of some artists, Senior summarizes: "Since reality is nothing but sensation, art can create reality by means of invoking sensations. . . . The artist [is] the fabricator of illusions . . . the magician who hallucinates sensations."[51]

Living in one's own fantasy world is not simply the whim of a handful of avant-garde artists, drug-popping adolescents or enthusiasts of Eastern religions and the Occult. There are many today who create "alternative worlds" in one way or another. Modern "intelligentsia" take seriously the acceptance of hallucination as reality. Senior quotes Ortega y Gasset, who considered the question of what philosophy can do when humans inhabit a purely interior world of imagination:

There may be no corresponding reality to what our ideas project . . . but this does not make them purely subjective. A world of hallucination would not be real, but neither would it fail to be a world, an objective universe, full of sense and perfection. . . . The imaginary centaur . . . is a virtual object, or as the most recent

philosophy expresses it, an ideal object. This is the type of phenomena which the thinker of our time considers most adequate as a basis of his universal system.[52]

Apart from Senior's works, a comment by the well-known art critic Herbert Read is apropos: "We have now reached a stage of relativism in philosophy where it is possible to affirm that reality is in fact subjectivity, which means that the individual has no choice but to construct his own reality, however arbitrary and even 'absurd' that may seem."[53] Everyone—philosopher, artist, scientist, politician, the ordinary man in the street—must create his own world.

A Spiritual Option against Being

While these chapters of *The Death of Christian Culture* focus on an intellectual and artistic elite, what Senior describes in them corresponds directly to the state of our culture. We see everywhere the ebb and flow between, on the one hand, a feverish quest for artificial sensations, going from novelty to novelty, finding initially exciting experiences in travel and new sights, or in sex and wild music, in fantasy, and then, on the other hand, a falling back on drab reality, in boredom, disgust, despair, and revolt. Thus, it is not surprising that in our nihilistic culture children commit mass murder in school. Instances of a vengeful, raging pleasure in destroying and degrading are sadly not uncommon. Senior quotes John Ruskin to describe what happens when one seeks sensations for themselves: "It is constant and universal that the pursuit of pleasure leads to desire of horror and delight in death."[54]

The voyage that began at the Renaissance has led to our being trapped in a labyrinth of subjectivity. Yet, Senior writes, "as Aristotle said, and as over two thousand years of Western civilization have affirmed, according to the common consent of the vast majority, according to what is justly called the philosophy of common sense—there is no reason to go on the voyage in the first place."[55]

To conclude Part I and our examination of the debate between the two perennial philosophies, let us draw from Senior and a few other sources a reflection on Descartes's *cogito*, that veritable paradigm of a lucid attack against common sense. This will take us back to Senior's own personal rejection of the Occult to embrace Realism.

Descartes wanted nothing as the foundation of his system aside from his own consciousness. Senior pinpoints the philosophical revolution this entails: "[Descartes's] metaphysics begins, opposite to Aristotle's, not with Being, but with . . . thought."[56] Descartes's decision is a refusal of *being*, a turning away from the evidence of existence, both of the other and of self. As St. Thomas has told us, the first thing to fall into the mind is *being*. As Senior expresses it: "Something exists and I know it and therefore I know that I exist and think."[57] G. K. Chesterton declared that, although *being* is indeed a mystery, its presence transcends doubts that might arise from our inability to encompass it:

> There is at the back of all our lives an abyss of light, more blinding and unfathomable than any abyss of darkness; and it is the abyss of actuality, of existence, of that fact that things truly are and that we ourselves are incredibly and sometimes incredulously real. It is the fundamental fact of being, as against not being; it is unthinkable, yet we cannot unthink it, though we may be sometimes unthinking about it . . . For he who has realized this reality knows that it does outweigh, literally to infinity, all lesser regrets or arguments for negation.[58]

The existence of things cannot be proved because one cannot put at the conclusion of a syllogism that which is at the beginning. One cannot reason to the principle of *being* because all reasoning depends on it. If someone tries to deny or question the obvious *being*, all we can do is point to it, underline its presence by a striking and redundant expression: "'To be' exists while 'not to be' does not exist," in Senior's words, similar to those of Aristotle and St. Thomas.

Descartes's rejection of the evidence of *being* enclosed modern thought in the mind. The Modernists, having refused to accept existence as a given at the beginning of their thought, cannot find it in any other way. As Senior writes: "Doubt that the world exists and you have not begun to think philosophically for the first time, as Descartes imagined; you have rather entered the labyrinth of self from which there can be no escape except on the waxen wings of a viewless poesy,"[59] that is, fantasy. "Wings of a viewless poesy" is an allusion to Keats's "Ode to a Nightingale," wherein the poet wishes to fly away with the bird. Descartes and his followers are trapped in themselves; they are no longer connected with reality. Solipsism, which recognizes one's own subject person as the only certain reality, is a logical conclusion of the *cogito*, its *reductio ad absurdum*.

Philosophy begins not when one excludes the presence of the world, as modern philosophy after Descartes purports to do, but when one takes a deeper view of it. Before one reflects in a philosophical way, one is already in relationship to the world, posing questions about it. These questions are of all types: Why has this or that happened? What is this thing? Where did it come from? In the process of questioning one might also reflect on how and to what extent one knows, but this subsequent reflection cannot negate the first evidence of a value for the verb *to be*. Senior writes: "Before he reflects, that is, 'bends back' his attention to his own mental and sensory processes, a man first simply looks, smells, tastes, touches, and affirms existence. . . . Thinking follows from existence."[60] Philosophy, or at least metaphysics, begins when one takes up the universal question, when one looks on reality from the absolute point of view of *being*, when one aims at the mystery of existence itself in things.

In fact, Descartes artificially constructed his doubt in order to base science on what he considered to be ideal conditions for an absolute certitude. But neither he nor anyone else really, practically, doubts the existence of the world. Senior often quotes Aristotle's obvious refutation of the *cogito*: "It is quite evident that no one . . . is really in this position. Otherwise why does he not walk early one morning into a well . . . instead of clearly guarding against doing so?"[61] Professors, who from their ivory towers declaim idealism, solipsism, or subjectivism, do not in fact live as

if there were no world. Outside of their noetic exercise in office and class, they conduct themselves like everyone else—eating, sleeping, making money, getting married, going swimming when it is hot, fearing death.

If no one denies *being* in practice, why do some choose this intellectual position? Why do they jump intellectually, if not physically, into the well? In fact, Senior responds, "nowhere does [anyone] in this position ever find an answer to Aristotle within the terms of reason. It is not that they have committed an error; they have abandoned the intelligence."[62] Turning away from reality and from reason is an act of the will—indeed an arbitrary choice, a heresy: "No intelligent being can act in such a way as to deny its own intelligence; such an act can occur only by a deliberate act of the will darkening the intelligence, a perverse choice."[63]

The original refusal of reality in Descartes was reinforced by a sick hatred of reality in the Modernist. For Senior, Modernism ultimately "is an assault on the verb to be."[64] He discerns a strange perversity in the modern fascination with destruction and fantasy: "It is Being itself that the Modern wishes to destroy."[65] An even deeper hatred of *being* lies in the replacement of reality with fantasy: "The opposite of Being is not just nothing—the mere absence of Being, like empty space, which has a kind of ablative reality, a potential for being filled. Pure non-Being, anti-being, is the *faking of reality.*"[66]

Jacques Maritain commented on Descartes in his essay "The Incarnation of the Angel." He perceived in Descartes the pride of someone who wants to think as a pure spirit, without reference to the sensible, material world. This may be true of Descartes, but the Modernist goes a step further. The requirement that all truth come from the mind alone resembles demonic pride itself. Senior recognizes behind this ultimate artificiality the angel who wanted to be like God, producing a new artificial paradise, a creation of his own: "Behind the shifting mask of Modernism," he writes, "is the diabolic. The perfection of nonbeing is the lie. . . . *Satan, the Prince of Lies, is called the Ape of God. The perfection of nonbeing is parody.*"[67]

We of course do not intend to judge individuals here, but there is a bit of the devil in each one of us, and today's individualist haven is propitious to fallen man's deep pride. Like Satan, the Modernist as such wants to be fully

autonomous. He does not want to receive anything; he wants to dominate everything. Senior sometimes alludes to the following passage from Milton's *Paradise Lost* in which the devil proclaims, as he falls into Hell:

Infernal world and thou profoundest Hell
Receive thy new possessor: one who brings
A mind not to be chang'd by place or time.
The mind is its own place, and in itself
Can make a heav'n of Hell, a Hell of heav'n.

Satan in this text is the perfect Modernist. He is saying that the way up to Heaven is also the way down to Hell. All is one, because the mind makes reality. Slightly changing Descartes's line, one could say: *Cogito ergo sunt*—I think, therefore they are. Let us eat the fruit of the tree of knowledge, decide for ourselves what is good and evil, true and false, and declare that *is* is not.

Senior quotes a line from Lewis Carroll's *Alice in Wonderland*: "'Words mean what I want them to,' said the Mad Hatter to Alice."[68] As we saw when reviewing Eastern thought, *moksha* consists essentially in liberation from the verb *to be*. In the terms of the epigraph of this chapter, the Modernist looks down on the vile and vulgar "is" as insulting because it affirms something outside the mind to which he must submit. Once *being* has been denied, one would be free. For Senior, the refusal of being is linked to the refusal of God. The real history of the world is that of the "yes" or "no" to reality, to God. After Satan, the first Modernists, he says, were Adam and Eve. Thus, in the very roots of Modernism we find a disordered desire for freedom—*non serviam*—begun at the Renaissance, developed by the Rationalists and the Romantics into Liberalism, that is, freedom of thought, and, with the Modernists, culminating in the desire to create what we wish.

A creation according to our desires, however, does not make us happy. Gustave Thibon once said: "Better a real hell than an artificial paradise." He would have agreed with Senior's conviction that an artificial paradise is itself hell. As Senior writes: "Beyond the hell of ennui . . . is the deep

hell of hallucination."[69] Senior explains why hallucination is worse than ennui: "Insofar as one is cut off from Being, he is cut off from good. There is what we may call a law of gravity of artificiality. The universe of hallucination cannot be pleasant for long. It is inevitably hell that the artificer constructs. That is why in the pantheon of idols the hideous predominates."[70] Truth, goodness and beauty are aspects of *being* and consequently the Modernist, who puts aside *being*, necessarily creates and seeks the false, the evil and the ugly.

One's desires, fervent as they may be, cannot make a Heaven out of Hell. Even an angel cannot create truth, goodness, beauty and *being*. God alone creates; He alone can bring *being* out of nothingness. Man must submit to what is—or rather, he is made in such a way that he might respond with a yes to God's gift of being. To know something, to accept a meaning for *to be*, does not entail mere submission to something imposed from the outside, a capitulation, so to speak. Rather, it entails conformity to something inherent in man. Although reality is not produced by the mind, neither is it completely foreign to the mind. The intellect is essentially a capacity for objectivity, for relationship to an outside reality. The existence of the world calls out to us and touches our souls in a mysterious correspondence because we share in its mystery. In docility, through a receptive attention to the other, to *being* itself, the intellect finds itself and blossoms.

Man can say no; he can refuse God's gift; but he cannot make God's gift other than what it is. He can twist, lie and destroy, but in so doing he destroys himself. The Modernist has turned away from the evidence of *being* and has seen only nothingness. He has refused the only light— that of the first principles in the natural order—and is surprised to find only darkness. He has closed himself up in his isolated self—a self made to know and love by reaching outside of itself—and finds emptiness and anguish.

We are now prepared to examine John Senior's thoughts on education and culture, understanding them primarily as efforts to revive and foster Realism. Having experienced the nihilism of the Perennial Heresy himself,

he was able to perceive how modern education and culture were permeated by it, and discern what was needed to redeem them:

> The long way out of the radical diseducation of our time will be found, I think, only by those who get to the bottom of the [labyrinth] . . . and there distinguish, as Dante said of the bottom of Inferno, "through a round opening, the beauteous things which Heaven bears and thence again to see the stars."[71]

Long before his intellectual and religious conversion, Senior had learned that one could not go to the stars if the desire to know and love was frustrated at the level of the barren top soil provided by empirical science. After his philosophical turnabout, he further recognized that one could not bypass this world and leap directly to the stars as the East would have us believe. The ungrounded ideas of the Rationalists, the liberated emotions of the Romantics, or the isolated consciousness of the Modernists were not the answer either. Senior therefore would strive in his teaching to unite what the movements of the previous centuries had divided—reality, senses, emotions, imagination, will and intellect—in a delightful, wondering, loving, commonsense consent to reality, an opening of the whole man to all that reality might have to say. Thus his students would be rooted in the rich soil of reality that nourishes and directs man's quest for the stars.

Part II

Nurturing Realism

In the life of the mind, as in all things, there is an order, having a beginning, a middle, and an end. Poetry begins in delight and ends in wonder; philosophy begins in wonder and ends in wisdom.
—The Death of Christian Culture

John Senior, circa early 1970s, at the University of Kansas.

Courtesy of Monica Sercer

The Man and the Teacher

*The first quality of the teacher is his own freedom,
his moral rectitude, his character. We want a good
man—strong, temperate, prudent, just. Second, he
must have a knack for teaching his subject. He must
have a certain fire, a certain spirit, a certain personality. . . . A competence in the communication of
the subject must be there.*

—The Death of Christian Culture

S ENIOR would always denounce the flagrant moral aberrations
of our time—infanticide, euthanasia, pornography—but he
stayed aloof from active involvement in politics. His main activity in that
domain consisted of a few pro-life talks. He believed that the most effective way of healing these social ills was to attack them at their root, which,
in the intellectual order, is Modernist Relativism. If there is no objective
substantial reality guiding society's decisions, but only empirical science
and our whims, then human life is meaningless, freedom is the only good,
and there is ultimately no reason, for example, not to murder babies and
old folks when they bother us.

Although Senior was a redoubtable debater, he did not immerse
himself in controversies. It was through education that he would work at
leading souls from the Perennial Heresy to the Perennial Philosophy and
on to Christ. He followed his own advice to a fellow teacher: "Say the

best, most beautiful, most true things you can, and swallow the polemic, the contingent and the unfriendly." He was not afraid to counter errors, but he knew his essential role was a positive one: forming young souls, helping them see the good, beautiful and true.

Part II of our book deals with Senior's ideas on education. Before we probe those ideas, however, it would be apropos to present him as a teacher, the subject of this chapter. We have arrived at the period of Senior's life when, after his assimilation of St. Thomas Aquinas and his conversion, he was fully himself. His providential experience and formation as well as his outstanding natural gifts contributed to the extraordinary success of his teaching. But something beyond these was necessary in order to ignite a spark in his students for truth and beauty, for high ideals and Christ. Senior's noble soul imbued his experiences, gifts and methods with incredible dynamism. To come to know him as a teacher, therefore, necessitates a few preliminary remarks about the man behind the teaching.

A Dynamic Balance

There is almost too much to grasp when one tries to describe John Senior. His was a profound soul, larger than our conventional categories. One of his students wrote: "To many of his students Senior seemed a bundle of contradictions: here was an East Coast intellectual who spoke with knowing ardor of the life of the cowboys; here was a professional scholar who nevertheless did not worship scholarship."[1] One could continue: Senior was an idealist who was fascinated by concrete, individual things; he was reserved and yet outgoing in social events; he preached about and loved the contemplative life but continuously gave himself over to teaching initiatives. In the same vein, his daughter, Penny Fonfara, remembered her father's emotional contrasts: "At Dad's funeral and reception following, I listened to all the things his students and friends said and felt that all those things were true, but that I had known another person also. He was our

sometimes forgetful, angry, worried, disgusted, sad, happy, gleeful, perplexed and beloved Dad."[2]

These contrasting emotions worked together in Senior to form a moral rectitude—"a good man" like the one described in the epigraph above. In fact, his virtuous character seemed so simple and ingrained that one might assume that it had always been the same. However, he, like everyone else, had to put his tendencies in order. By viewing Senior in the light of the four traditional temperaments—sanguine, choleric, melancholic, and phlegmatic—we might be able to grasp a couple of reasons for his success.

One can define "temperament" as a person's pattern of inclinations and reactions. It is the foundation or the raw material, as it were, of one's personality and moral character. Senior noted a few elements of the classical types:

> Phlegmatic is slow, choleric angry, sanguine companionable, melancholy reserved. Temperaments are natural dispositions, not moral habits; one is not better than another nor is anyone responsible for them. Each has its virtues and its difficulties and each participates to some extent in all so that while one may be predominately phlegmatic and find joy in systems (like St. Thomas), he still is capable (like St. Thomas) of righteous indignation, good cheer and contemplative prayer. A temperament is something like a station in life; it is our job to realize the best in it and a disaster if we try to change.[3]

Senior was not of the dominating, live-wire, active choleric type, and even less was he the dispassionate phlegmatic or the optimistic and carefree sanguine. He regularly mentioned that he was melancholic, the temperament characterized by a thoughtful introversion.

Senior markedly possessed the typical melancholic trait of pensiveness. His daughter observed: "Dad was always thinking and analyzing things, even when apparently doing nothing but enjoying scenery. By analyzing

I mean more of a pondering attitude, not a scientific dissecting."[4] Indeed, on campus, when he was not surrounded by students or teachers, Senior was sure to be lost in his thoughts. The melancholic seeks out and enjoys solitude, quiet time for reflection. Senior thus described himself to a reporter: "I'm kind of a loner by nature, an introvert; certainly not a one-of-the-boys type."[5] Though he led a rich interior life, Senior remained reserved about manifesting the private sphere and his intimate sentiments—witness the secrecy of his conversion. He did tell stories of his youth and even took a few individuals into confidence now and then, but one always felt an interior life that was the King's secret.

Because the melancholic type thinks things over so closely, he easily perceives possible difficulties and is often pessimistic and anxious about the future. As an example of Senior's melancholic tendencies, he once wryly said about himself that when the phone rang, he would think, "Oh no! Who died?" The hallmark of the melancholic is this type of pessimism and anxiety, the tendency to dwell on the sad side of things. Someone of this temperament suffers more than most people from errors, faults and imperfections he sees around and in himself.

Anyone who knew Senior for a period of time perceived how much he grieved over the crisis in the Church, the decline of civilization, the pettiness and sensuality of our society, and the ugliness, the monotony and the impersonal character of the mechanical world.

Yet Senior did not allow his melancholic tendencies to go to excess. He tempered and channeled the various energies at his disposal into a fertile, vibrant harmony. Thus, his pensiveness and reserve did not keep him closed up in himself; they did not render him withdrawn and brooding over his pains. He was interested in people and enjoyed conversation. Though he did not display his fondness for someone as the stereotypical Midwesterner might—with a pat on the back or even a warm handshake—he was, nonetheless, an affectionate man. His pessimism did not paralyze him or make him irresolute in his goals. Rather, he was enterprising, even adventurous, full of zest. Nor did his tendency to sadness make him glum; he had a vivacious side and was easily the life of the

party. He enjoyed telling amusing stories and his unaffected laughter was contagious.*

Senior's various activities throughout his years—his life as a cowboy, his interest in literature and poetry, his acting and debating, his friendships, his teaching, his family life—all this drew him out of himself and helped him to avoid the melancholic's negative pitfalls. Yet the cornerstone of his moral edifice was the blossoming of his melancholic pensiveness into contemplation, in a loving, intent and simple gaze upon high and beautiful truths. Senior's fascination for the true, good and beautiful unified his natural energies by drawing them together toward the summits. We can illustrate the influence of his lofty views and desires through the four cardinal virtues: fortitude, temperance, prudence and justice.

As for fortitude, we have seen that already as a boy Senior was tenacious. As an adult, he drew his moral strength from his love of truth. Some who knew him say he had problems with anger in his youth. Students at the University of Kansas, however, never saw any outbursts of irritation, but they did appreciate in him a controlled, righteous indignation that lent zest and tenacity to his long battles for the truth. He was unshakable and intrepid when standing up for his convictions. One can only admire his calm cheer during the years of painful battle for the very existence of the Integrated Humanities Program at the University of Kansas. He was also constant and persevering in the day-to-day service of truth, patiently teaching basics—notably beginner's Latin—to underclassmen year after year.

Senior was temperate, most likely because his attraction for high ideals kept the domain of the senses in its rightful place. Although he upheld great purity and spontaneously turned away from anything morally staining, he was no Jansenist or Puritan. He indeed felt and respected the goodness of the sensible, but looked upon and treated material things most of all as signs of and support for the spiritual. He liked to compare the moral life to taming a wild horse. One should not strive to crush the energies of one's sensible side, but rather firmly and gently train and direct

---

* Today, one can observe Senior's humor and wit most especially in his poetry. See, for example, "On a Gift of Betjeman's Poems from R.W.," *Pale Horse*, 30.

them so they readily follow the intellect's lead. This metaphor provides an apt description of Senior himself: he rode a lively horse. His was a rich and sensitive humanity, beautifully used in the service of the spiritual.

St. Thomas links humility to temperance. Senior had the forgetfulness of self one finds in a person deeply interested in high ideals, in truly learned and spiritual men who are accustomed to gazing on what is above them. His upward gaze helped Senior develop this forgetfulness into simple, magnanimous nobility. He was far above any self-centered calculations—little jealousies or vanities, trying to attract attention to himself, or speaking poorly of others. His great successes did not touch his character; when one of them came up in conversation, he explained it in ways that pointed beyond himself.

Senior was prudent, although a grain of impulsiveness remained in the same fellow who as a youth had run off to the Dakotas and New Mexico. He had long learned to reflect carefully before doing or speaking, as his youthful impetuosity for adventure developed into a love of high truths. Though he was never a master organizer, his decisions and plans were always made with man's nature and final end firmly in sight. He never got lost in details or in a quest for an immediate or earthly goal. This may be reflected in his radical remedies for school, family and society, which some believe were not practical, but certainly had in view man's real end.

Finally, Senior was a just man, above all because he kept in view the real value of men and things. His upward gaze also helped him avoid being diverted from justice by pettiness, egoism, greed or sensuality. He was attentive to those forms of justice that deal with superiors toward whom we can never adequately pay our debt. Thus, he was imbued with great care for God's honor. And this man, who knew the history of great civilizations, who so esteemed European culture and was well aware of his country's weaknesses, never spoke disdainfully of the United States. He loved the old America, her values, her authentic heroes, her great men with their courageous exploits like Valley Forge and Pickett's Charge.

Senior thus excellently practiced the four cardinal virtues. But he was not a moralist who, for example, might regard temperance as an absolute.

He was a lover, a man of the theological virtues. His gaze was focused on things of the Faith, directed toward the infinitely rich and real mysteries of the Trinity, of Christ, of the Redemption, of Mary and of the Church; he looked upon all else in their light. Supernatural hope was particularly vital for this melancholy man.

There had to be something more substantial than good and beautiful ideas to save him ultimately from sadness and despair. He was animated by the reality that behind the world is a loving Person—or three Persons—knowing that no activity accomplished for Him, even here below, is in vain. Particularly in his last years, it was predominantly supernatural hope that sustained him.

And without supernatural charity Senior's natural goodness and affection could not have blossomed as they did. This comment from *The Death of Christian Culture* illustrates the depth of his sensitivity toward others: "A cripple, a tiny [child with Down syndrome] that lives if only for a day, an old toothless crone, driveling with death but still alive, respond if only with a flicker in the eyes—and that flicker is infinite in value, worth the universe."[6] It was from his love of God that he drew the strength for so much devoted service: "If you are generous," he wrote, "Christ says you must not just give something of yourself, but everything."[7]

A Cheerful, Melancholic Contemplative

Senior's contemplative outlook unified the most striking contrast in his character, namely, his sadness and his joy. In him, neither emotion sprung simply from temperament or feelings; both, rather, corresponded to a deep and realistic Christian view.

Senior held that sadness was "dominant" in this life.[8] All cheer, fun and beauty have an underlying sadness.* He quoted Jessica from *The Merchant of Venice*: "I am always sad when I hear sweet music," and commented:

---

* Senior wrote a poem to this effect: "Robert Herrick," in *Pale Horse*, 14.

A strange response, perhaps. But then it is true, isn't it. Music is deeper than having fun; there is something sad even about the merriest music. Everyone has noted how, for example, in the lightest songs of Mozart, in the comic operas or in his marvelously bright pieces like the Clarinet Concerto, there is an almost unbearable weight, a sadness impossible to hear without tears.[9]

Using the scholastic definition of sadness, he explained: "Sadness is the sensible response to unavoidable evil—on earth, the fact of sad mortality, the *lacrimae rerum*, subject of so much poetry."[10] He often quoted this expression of Virgil: "the tears of things," that is, suffering and the thought of death permeate everything. Indeed, the sweeter and happier the event, the greater its measure of sadness, in a way, because it is not perfect and like everything else will come to an end: "Your marriage day is the saddest day of your life," Senior paradoxically remarked once, "because you say 'until death do us part.' Luckily, newlyweds don't really believe they are going to die and separate." Everything around us, including we ourselves, are doomed.

This mournful view of life, however, was not divorced from the light of Christian Revelation, from the certitude that death is not final. In his definition of sadness, Senior said it is a "*sensible* response." Such an emotion is inevitable here below where one is constantly faced with evil and pain, whereas the life of the world to come is still invisible, largely inexperienced. In any case, one should not brush aside the real miseries of this life as if they did not exist. No one can see a loved one die of a terminal disease without carrying an abiding sadness in his heart. Padre Pio, for instance, was so shattered by the death of his parents that he was unable to celebrate Mass for days!

In some ways, Christian Revelation is cause for more pain; once aware of the beauty of Heaven, the limitations of this life become more evident. Also, Holy Scripture tells us that we must suffer much to attain God's Kingdom. We see in the trials of the saints, both interior and exterior, that Christ's demands go far. Senior writes in *The Restoration of Christian Culture*:

I think, though life is funny, it is not for fun; and we have blurred the distinction between being happy and being blessed, confusing the strong and sometimes bitter Catholic wine with the juice of the Liberal protestant grape. Anyone who says that Christ will make you happy hasn't tried him much, hasn't got even on to the *Camino Real*, let alone very far along it, because the Royal Way is the Way of the Cross.[11]

Yet, since evil does not have the last word, good cheer is appropriate. Senior's gaze on high showed him that one should not be too dramatic about personal pain because we are so little in the whole scheme of things. Humor therefore proceeds from a realistic view. Senior tells us: "*Humus* is the root of 'human,' 'humility' and 'humor,' because, knowing our humble origins, we can never take ourselves too seriously. Fanatics never laugh because they are exclusive; they think they are the only ones and, losing their sense of place, lose their sense of proportion."[12] Without mirth this life would be difficult to bear. We need it to get through the pain on our road back to the Father, as Senior explains: "Chaucer, who certainly had a sense of humor and whom no one ever accused of being gloomy, said we should 'counterfeite cheer,' we should 'make merry,' especially because we know that this life is a vale of tears."[13]

Here it is helpful to quote one of Senior's poems, "Wassail," almost in its entirety, as it portrays so well his view on cheerful moments within the dominating sadness. He begins by evoking Christmas cheer, with the realization, however, that temptation to despair is not far:

Raise the Wassail high, good cheer,
because the end of night is near,
and the Winter of our year!
If you find that that bastard Glee
peeking through the jalousie
blame it on the Muse not me.

Ah, true Penelope, Despair
to know that you are always there!

The next part assures us that this sad life does have wonderful moments, "something like perfection," as when Johnny Senior drank coffee with the cowboys or Telemachus feasted with Alcinous:

Life is restless, short and sad,
were it merry I'd go mad.
Oh there's merriment and cheer
but you will not find them here—
except those moments rich and rare
that charge the startled atmosphere
when things converge upon a sign
and music thrums (as guests recline)
the heroic or the lyric line,
friendship sparkles with the wine
and unassuming grace intrudes
upon our fallen solitudes.

In the last part of the poem, Senior evokes St. Bede's story in his *Ecclesiastical History* of a druid priest who compares our life on earth to the flight of a bird suddenly bursting into the bright feast and then returning to the dark night outside. St. Paulinus explains to the druid that, to the contrary, the real merry feast is for the next life. It is this life that is the dark wintry passage of which we are celebrating the approaching end:

And Saint Paulinus answering:
Here is Winter, *there* is Spring,
if you have the needful thing.[14]

Senior recognizes that merry moments are figures of the celestial banquet, as he writes in "The Restoration of Innocence": "Is this life a momentary fireside in an endless winter night? So the godless say. We

116

know the opposite is true, that here is not our home, because, as Revelation tells us, the home we have is a sign of what we seek."[15] Happy episodes in our life teach us in an experiential way that joy is real and that we are made for it. If we did not have some happy moments, we would have no idea of what joy is and therefore would not be able to desire the eternal and infinite merriment of Heaven.

Cheerfulness is therefore useful, but so is suffering, Senior argues:

> The saints all say that every human act, performed in grace, is a participation in the intimate, infinite life and love of the Blessed Trinity; it is sacramental, mysterious. And in this life, that life can only be understood, like the pattern from the underside of an Oriental rug, not as joy but suffering, as Christ's action on the Cross, as sacrifice. Every work and every prayer on earth is a participation in the joys of Heaven by means of suffering.[16]

In this passage, Senior remembers an intuition of Baudelaire's mentioned in *The Way Down and Out*. The French poet looked on suffering as the inverse mirror of the joys of Heaven, according to the principle that the way down is the way up.[17] Even before his conversion, Senior recognized that the first step toward Heaven is to realize that one is not there yet, that this life is an exile. We need to feel the misery of our condition in order to desire Heaven. After his conversion, he better understood that one must work his way to Heaven in an unceasing, painful war against evil in and around self. The underside of the rug—with its knots and ugly imperfections—is necessary for the top side's beauty.

Through all these writings there emerges something deeper in Senior than his sadness, namely, his trust in God and his hope in the beatitude to come. He knew there was a joy—something, he might say, even stronger than joy—in suffering for love, in being faithful in the midst of pain. For Senior, "a recognition of the tears of things is the condition of hope" and of mirth.[18] We have said that he was inclined toward the sad side of things because of his sensitivity, his high ideals, his Realism. In his teaching, he insisted on that aspect of reality in order to keep the superficial at bay. I believe that Senior's

view corresponds well to a couple of lines from Whittaker Chambers: "True wisdom comes from the overcoming of suffering and sin. All true wisdom is therefore touched with sadness."[19] Nevertheless, he radiated a joy and peace born of his deeply held convictions, especially his belief in Christ's love. "A sad saint is a sorry saint," St. Francis de Sales reminds us.

Bonum Est Diffusivum Sui[*]

In order to understand Senior as a teacher, we should first recall some elements of his intellectual and spiritual formation. His sister recalls that after his conversion, "John completely changed, except his sense of humor!" Nevertheless, the authors he had studied in the years prior to his conversion had marked him for life. Someone who converts at thirty-seven years of age is already somewhat of a made man. Thus, the Symbolists developed in him the habit of never stopping at the material, and therefore meaningless, aspect of things. They helped train his mind for analogies and correspondences, which after his conversion he could recognize in the context of the Christian tradition of creation and the analogy of *being*. Coomaraswamy and Guénon, with their strong, principled, crystal-clear expression, contributed in rendering his thought deep and incisive. The two led him to recognize more clearly and philosophically that the level of knowledge in modern science is superficial and that its growing domination, beginning at the Renaissance, has crushed man's more metaphysical dimensions. They also taught him to participate in the views of past cultures without considering them to be simply steps toward the modern world. Senior was especially indebted to Coomaraswamy's philosophy of art. Senior, like Coomaraswamy, spurned humanistic, naturalistic art for freezing our attention on the image rather than leading us to the spiritual. When Michaelangelo's Pietà was damaged by an attacker wielding a hammer, Senior, as usual, had a surprising point of view. He remarked in class that he was on the side of the assailant—"That statue was treated mostly like an idol!" he said.

---

[*]   Goodness naturally communicates itself.

Given the distinguished professors Senior had at Columbia, we can scarcely wonder at his mastery of English literature and poetry. He was also familiar with French literature, which he read in the original language, and had substantial knowledge of the major Greek and Latin classics. In addition, he was well read in the outstanding works of medieval and modern Western literature of all languages, from Dante to Cervantes to Goethe, many of which he taught at one time or another. In the literary world Senior was unquestionably well qualified.

Senior possessed a philosophical frame of mind, always looking toward first causes with penetrating intuitions. Thus, along with his literary pursuits in college and graduate school, Senior studied particularly Plato, the Pre-Socratics and modern philosophies. At the moment of his conversion he delved into an intense and systematic study of Aristotle and St. Thomas, becoming largely autodidactic in both. St. Augustine soon became a constant meditation and reference for him. Newman was a formative influence—as we have seen and will see more of—in ways that concern the importance of experience for *real* knowledge. He had read Gilson and Maritain, of course, but did not particularly use their works. He did, however, find Maritain's views on the poetic use of knowledge of interest, as we shall see later. Senior's Thomist acquaintances were mostly formed in the school of Charles de Konink, which insists on the preparation for philosophy through sciences and logic, and focuses on Aristotle. Senior also studied and recommended Father Henri Renard, SJ, a disciple of the well-known Charles Boyer, SJ, and his formal style of argumentation. Whatever might have been Senior's preferences for a type of Thomism, they are not obvious in his writings, where he adhered to principles of epistemology and metaphysics common to all these Realists, and where his penetrating intuitions rather transcended schools.

As for theology, Senior was even more of an autodidact. He studied St. Thomas, as we know, and Newman. Over the years he would immerse himself into one or another of the greats—St. Bernard at one point, St. Bonaventure, and St. Isidore of Seville. He read Garrigou-Lagrange and other contemporaries. He knew the solemn teachings of the Magisterium and had habitual recourse to the *Catechism of the Council of Trent*.

Nonetheless, he himself would have been the first to admit that he lacked a basic theological formation, methodically pursued in Scripture, Tradition, the Magisterium and speculative theology. Because of this deficiency, he rarely ventured into properly theological domains when teaching or writing.

Senior was well read in the important conservative Catholic writers of the recent past, especially those of the twentieth-century English Catholic revival who wrote on subjects as varied as apologetics, history and economics. G. K. Chesterton and Hilaire Belloc in particular were somewhat his initiators into Catholic culture. He appreciated their Catholicism grounded in human soil—in songs and stories and mirth, in customs and manners. We have quoted Chesterton on Realism, but this author did not have a formative influence on Senior. His writings were more a confirmation of Senior's ideas on the importance of common sense, and on wonder.

Belloc had more influence on him as a source of Catholic social doctrine. Senior esteemed his picture of European Christendom and seems to have in a measure adopted his basic political and economic orientations. He wrote that Belloc's "pamphlet *The Restoration of Property* is the best Catholic economic and social manifesto in English."[20] Senior preferred Belloc as historian to the other great twentieth-century Catholic reference in the field, Christopher Dawson, because Belloc recognized a beauty proper to the Middle Ages. "Christopher Dawson," he argues in *The Death of Christian Culture*, "who tried to prove that medieval Christianity was responsible for the whole idea of progress, achieved an academic respectability denied to the cantankerous old Romantic, anti-Modern, and greater historian, Belloc."[21]

Senior carefully studied the great spiritual classics, notably St. Catherine of Siena, St. Teresa of Avila, St. John of the Cross, St. Francis de Sales, and St. Thérèse of the Child Jesus. He read these authors themselves rather than books about them. He was also familiar with some basic psychology, referring favorably to Jean Piaget and Conrad Baars.

And he retained what he read. You could ask him on the spur of the moment about a novel and he would reflect, "Gee, I haven't read that in twenty years." Then he would proceed to lay out the plot and details, helping one recognize its underlying theme. Or someone would mention

Aristotle's *Poetics*, and he would go to the blackboard and show the organization of the whole work. This extraordinary memory of course served him in all his teaching and writing; he would frequently allude to and even quote directly lines from a poem or classical author.

After attaining his master's and doctoral degrees, Senior did not continue scholarly pursuit into secondary sources. He admitted in a letter: "I am not a scholar: whatever studies I have done have been, by way of learning, to convince myself of something and, having been convinced, go on to something new."[22] Although historical research and literary criticism can be useful, he contended, they can also distract one from knowing and loving the great, meaningful and permanent truths. He wrote rather scornfully in *The Restoration of Christian Culture*: "Research . . . is subalternate to learning; it may function in an intrinsic ancillary role supplying illustrations and examples for classroom and extrinsically might furnish some idea or object of marginal utility, as a carpenter sells sawdust or shavings to an iceman."[23]

It was not at all his method to scribble information on note cards in order to classify and compile material for a class or article. He rarely took notes on his readings, but occasionally jotted down a few remarks in the margin, to be later perused. Most of all, he let himself be penetrated by the author's thought; then his own thought and expression could flow from his heart. He placed himself like a disciple at the feet of the great authors; he listened to them, striving humbly to discern the true, the good and the beautiful under their guidance.

Senior's meditative type of reading was obviously fruitful. We have seen how he mastered the principles of Aristotle's and St. Thomas's metaphysics and epistemology, those of the Occult and of Eastern thought, of Modernism, the Symbolist movement, Descartes's *cogito,* and Newman.

With striking perception, he found deep insights not only in philosophers and great works such as *The Iliad* or *Crime and Punishment* but also in less significant works, like *Ivanhoe* and *Hard Times*, and in poetry such as *The Canterbury Tales* or "Ode to a Nightingale."

Key to Senior's teaching success was his habit of reading and thinking for himself first, for his own quest. Referring to the old adage *bonum est diffusivum sui,* he wrote that "learning is a self-diffusive good."[24] For him,

to read, to meditate, to teach, to write, was one. There was no separation between his private meditations and his teaching; that, indeed, was his advice for all teachers:

> This cliché happens to be true: if you want to teach something, you must have that something yourself. If poetry is not a part of your life, no method in the classroom will create *ex nihilo* the love of poetry in your students. Recall the famous dictum of St. Augustine: Love God and do what you will. It is open to grave misunderstanding but the essential truth of its stands. . . . The same maxim applies to what we call English: Love literature and do what you will.[25]

Consequently Senior's teaching was a *contemplata aliis tradere*—a transmitting to others what he himself had contemplated. One felt that what he said was an expression of a reality he was viewing interiorly. It came from something in his soul that words could scarcely express. Listening to him teach, one spontaneously thought of what the Epistle to the Hebrews said of Moses: "He seemed to see the invisible."

Because Senior's words came from the profound depths of his own heart, he was able to touch the hearts of others—according to another axiom: *Cor ad cor loquitur*, originally from St. Francis de Sales, taken as Newman's motto as cardinal. Senior's convictions and his love of and attention to the objects of his meditation effected a similar love and attention in his listeners. Like Socrates, he revealed to his students their own deepest aspirations.

God's Instrument and Representative

Senior's focus was on teaching rather than on writing or giving public lectures. In fact, he wrote and lectured comparatively little. What mattered most to him, what he considered to be most important and worthwhile, was the living, face-to-face formation of students. Writing itself is simply an aide-mémoire, he remarked once. Even recorded talks could not replace the direct encounter.

He was already a popular teacher at Hofstra and Cornell—"even when I was teaching junk," he said. After his conversion, his talents, experience and formation blossomed in the service of great, worthy objectives. Senior's sense of the greatness of truth convinced him that this communication could not be a material transmission. He wrote: "The teacher is not the author of the truth or even the agent of its discovery but an interlocutor and listener, an auxiliary, like the physician who does not cause health but prudently assists nature to its own perfection."[26] The teacher is a servant in the dialogue between students and reality. He must first discern what the students are ready for, what their needs are and how reality is speaking to them, and then assist accordingly.

For Senior, the teacher must be a discreet helper especially because there is a third Person at work, one who is not simply an auxiliary but actually the first agent of discovery, who provides the intellectual light itself. This Person is even the author of truth, in fact Truth Himself. Senior had long meditated on and taught St. Augustine's *De Magistro* and fully realized that the human teacher is the instrument of the real Master: "The ultimate teacher," Senior wrote, "is Christ residing in the soul."[27] Senior's rich soul, his goodness, his ability to help others participate in his vision and love—all this drew students to him. In truth, he became a sort of pied piper, with young folk always following him, yet his ultimate desire was to lead them to Christ.

Thus, he had reverence for the souls of students entrusted to his care, as he wrote concerning teaching high school pupils: "Children must be trained, but with a sense of awe before such marvelously constructed creatures given over to our charge. Interfere we must, but with a startled eye, a skip of the heart, a catch in the throat."[28] He knew that students did not belong to him; he respected their secrets, their level of understanding, their efforts and the sanctuary of their souls. He considered each as unique. A former student writes:

It was many years ago, over thirty, while a student at Casper College when I first met him. He had been invited there to deliver a lecture on Dante's *Divine Comedy*. . . . At lunch, surrounded by college

123

dignitaries, whom John pretty much ignored, he turned his attention to me, an insignificant student, and engaged me in artful conversation about Plato's *Apology* and Socrates' search for truth.[29]

Senior's attention had its usual effect. The student concluded: "The spark that John struck ignited a fire in me, a desire of the truth that persists to this day. Upon returning home that night, I announced to my wife I had found my Teacher."*[30] He indeed followed Senior to Kansas and studied under him as a graduate student for years.

Senior believed that the teacher was engaged in a common quest with his students. He even affirmed that the goal of the university is friendship. He wrote: "Teaching, Plato says, is a species of friendship, in which persons see each other as integral parts of something greater than themselves."[31] Van Doren had provided him the model for this friendship around beautiful truths. It was with that in view that he made himself quite accessible to students. This distinguished New York intellectual wore his learning lightly, looked down on no one and was a regular, unpretentious fellow with those around him. His unaffected affability made him easy to talk to. And students indeed flocked to him in droves outside of class.

While Senior was a friend of his students, he also recognized the nobility of his profession in collaborating with God in that sublime work of guiding and forming a human soul. The teacher is God's instrument:

> The relation of student to teacher is not one of equality, nor even of quantitative inequality as between those advanced and less advanced on the same plane. It is the relation of disciple to master in which docility is an analogy of the love of man and God, from Whom all paternity in Heaven and on earth derives. . . . The student must . . . become assimilated to the spiritual, intellectual and moral model of the teacher.[32]

---

* See "The Other Window," in *Pale Horse*, 34, for a poem expressing how the individual student is incomparably more important than worldly success.

The teacher is thus God's intermediary and has a fatherly dignity and responsibility. Senior wrote elsewhere that the teacher acts not only *in loco parentis* but also *in loco Christi* and that "students imitating them are indirectly imitating Christ, as St. Paul said: 'Be ye followers (*imitatores*) of me, as I also am of Christ.'"[33]

Elements of Style

Senior's own gaze on truth was paramount and fundamental; but to effectively help others see and taste reality with him, to communicate his vision, he also needed skill in the art of teaching. An ensemble of elements came together in Senior, blending into that unique perfection which students, and occasional listeners, had the joy of experiencing. Here is a description of Senior's teaching by someone who was not his student, Father Joseph Fessio, SJ. "I only spent time with him on two or three occasions, but each one was memorable. Especially the first, at a summer program at a cabin in Powell, Wyoming. When I first saw and heard him I wondered, 'Is *this* the John Senior I've heard so much about?'" Father Fessio describes Senior's appearance as "the archetype of the disconnected professor." But, "then [Senior] began to speak about Newman's essay on St. Benedict and education. He'd quote a line of verse from memory here and there. The listeners were drawn into another world, a world of beauty and reverence and awe. It was amazing. I realized why he had such an influence on people. He was mesmerizing. But it was *real*."[34] Senior indeed held his listeners spellbound, so much so that one critic literally accused him of hypnotism and warned potential listeners not to look into his eyes! A better metaphor, perhaps, would be to say that his teaching was like music that enveloped the listeners' whole being, charmed them and swept them away in a rapt attention that did not wane. His hearers were fascinated, with their imagination, emotion, will and intellect all involved.

We might mention his personal appearance. Senior recognized its importance as part of the respect due to the teaching profession as well as to the subject being treated: "Einstein at Princeton pioneered the ruin

of formation in his dirty sweat shirt, flaunting sloppiness as the prerogative of genius. Remember, in contrast, Socrates whose homely beauty stunned his handsome student Alcibiades."[35] Senior indeed presented himself well, as the Wyoming University chaplain, Father Charles Taylor, noted: "The way of his dress, in and out of the classroom, was always that of Newman's gentleman." Senior was a tall, good-looking man, with blue eyes and a full head of black hair combed to the side. His deportment was calm, simple and steady, without gestures when he spoke. His demeanor was modest and unassuming.

At the University of Kansas, Senior never used notes in class. He occasionally wrote out a public lecture, but usually would have with him only a couple of references or quotations on a scrap of paper, having thought out his talks ahead of time. Father Taylor told of a radio program Senior participated in with a few other professors. Senior was quite upset because they had been sloppy about it. He had himself spoken without a paper and one of the participants congratulated him on having fallen on his feet. Senior replied: "Fallen on my feet! I re-wrote my intervention five times!"

In a typical class, Senior first read a selection from the currently assigned book. He read slowly to allow time for comprehension and to underline the value of the text. Without ostentation, his veneration and docility for the teaching of the great authors naturally came through. Already by participating in Senior's reading, students learned to listen with the heart, to open up to the deeper meaning of the text. Then Senior would simply talk, commenting on the passage or taking up some particular theme present in it. There was little give-and-take, no real discussion in Senior's classes, although a question was occasionally posed.

Faced with a question, Senior turned to principles to guide his reflection. Because he had well assimilated the doctrine himself, he could lay out its essential structures in clear and simple ways. Through fitting anecdotes and examples, meditating with literature and poets, he helped his students understand the principles and developments he might want to make. Indeed, he had a keen sense of analogy with a genius for embodying ideas in homely images. Thus his talks were colorful, resembling a tableau based on ideas; but there was no excessive use of metaphors, no

ornamentation for its own sake. The sensible was used to point to the spiritual, to something higher that drew one in. He did not hesitate to follow a poetic, even a rather mystical, insight not too concerned with Cartesian clarity.

Senior's talks thus unfolded gradually and without hurry so that all could leisurely follow the ascension. Yet, as we see in his books, even his prepared lectures had only a subtle and loose order, progressing like a conversation in which ideas truly guide the exposition but without a detailed framework. He possessed a remarkable power of concentration that enabled him to keep everything in place—the idea he was developing, the image he was using, the immediate principles that governed the subject, as well as the central and final truths around which the particular subjects turned. Senior was totally present to the subject at hand and committed to getting his points across, without any distracting vanity. Even in apparent digressions, even in the often tongue-in-cheek, sometimes uproarious, humor, he never lost the thread; all was converging upon a goal he was aiming for. He nearly always came to some summit where the minds of his students were lifted into a wondering gaze.

Senior was always very focused. It is told how one day a young lady in the back of the classroom became visibly and noisily sick to her stomach. Senior was so fully absorbed by his subject that he did not realize what was happening until she had staggered halfway across the room to the door. Only then did Senior stop to exclaim, "Oh my!" On another occasion he was teaching a small class when, while gesturing, he knocked his glasses off, launching them about ten feet across the room. A student picked them up and handed them to him. Apparently not having noticed anything, Senior slipped the glasses back on quite mechanically, without the least interruption to his delivery. His concentration, though intense, was nevertheless calm and relaxed. He was, in fact, sensitive to student response: "You can feel when they begin to catch fire," he said.

A few constant features of his teaching style are worth noting. He frequently made use of literary reminiscences and allusions that sprang up spontaneously. Senior's head was full of lines he loved and meditated on; he was habitually in dialogue, as it were, with great authors. This allusive style

was useful as a way of stimulating the reader or listener to greater reflection. He often did not provide the source of his allusions, especially in his pre- pared talks. Senior likely learned this omission of author's names or works from Mark Van Doren, who was known for deliberately presenting poems without mentioning the author, perhaps so students would not be influenced by prestige but would instead consider the poem for its own merit. Senior, like Van Doren, is emphasizing that it is the idea that counts more than who said it. Senior has been criticized for these anonymous allusions in his writings, but in times past educated people would have recognized allusions to Chaucer, Dante, Shakespeare and others without difficulty.

Concerning his own allusive poetry Senior commented: "It is certainly true that the Great Anthology we once had in common is lost. . . . This collection [of poems] is not private but perhaps it has no public."[36]

Care for language was another feature of his style. He wrote: "The first rule for a teacher, then, as for any person, is to be somebody worthy of his calling. . . . And for the teacher of English or the classics this means a high seriousness about language and literature in the presence of which slovenliness and disrespect do not occur, simply as a matter of courtesy."[37] He often reflected on etymologies during his talks, seeking the real and exact meaning of words as a key to penetrating reality.

We must mention another element, which could be considered a defect: Senior's tendency to overstate. He taught by hyperbole, one might say, easily going to extremes or beyond. He used exaggeration as a rhe- torical and pedagogical tool with the view of stressing important points. It was part of his fondness for surprising, extreme statements to spark the listener's attention and thought. Also, the tendency to exaggerate was linked to his poetic Romanticism as well as to his passion for great truths, which prompted him, notably, to an idealization and exaltation of the past where spiritual and human ideals were more obvious. Thus, he read history as a poet and philosopher might, concerned with principles, ideas and types rather than concrete details, which made him sometimes careless in practical historical accuracy. And his vigorous rejection of Relativism pushed him, by reaction, to take this or that contingent conclusion as an absolute. We will see examples of Senior's exaggerations later on, but we

should note now that they were often fruitful in winning over to beautiful ideals young students who were thirsty for absolutes.

The exactitude of the statement usually mattered less than the beauty of the ideal itself, so well put into relief. Also, discerning the nature of his comments usually posed little difficulty to students as they became acquainted with his pedagogy and penchant for extremes.

Senior was, quite simply, a good man with a gift for communicating his subject. Senior's natural abilities, formation and experiences proved to be a choice and fruitful combination. This contemplative—at once a clear-thinking philosopher and an intuitive poet—knew how to train students' minds and hearts on the trajectory of his own gaze. He spoke of real and vital things that touched on the meaning of life and made his listeners feel their reality and depth, and glimpse their beauty. Just as Senior had emulated his mentor Mark Van Doren, a legion of Senior's students who took up teaching did so with a profound desire to imitate their master.

CHAPTER SEVEN

A Gradual Education

Socrates sat down with Phaedrus by a charming
river, the Ilissos, to discuss the Good, the True and
the Beautiful, and the One who is the cause of
everything. If Phaedrus had thought, like Heracli-
tus, that all rivers only flow and that all things
from rock to man are only perpetual movement,
what could have been for Socrates the first founda-
tions of the discussion?

—Interview in La Nef

WE are now ready to consider Senior's positive work on the
restoration of Realism. It is remarkable how quickly Senior
elaborated his philosophy of education following his conversion. Subsequent reflection on his part would only lead to some fine-tuning and
development of details. This rapidity was facilitated by the fact that the
general structure of his philosophy was built on the traditional steps in
education that he had long known and appreciated, thanks especially to
Plato and Mark Van Doren.* Senior's contribution consisted particularly
in his grasping with a new depth the Realist foundation of that doctrine.
This enabled him to develop a unique synthesis of the steps of education
by situating pre-scientific formation in the dynamism of the whole movement, as well as by providing insights on how to implement those steps

---

* For Plato on the steps of education, see especially *The Republic*; for Van Doren, see *Liberal Educa-*
  tion (Boston: Henry Holt and Co., 1943).

in our own time. In order to reconnect with Senior's story, we will first take a look at his life in Wyoming.

Out on the Range

Senior's years in Wyoming were peaceful and happy ones. He at first lived in the university town of Laramie. His mother came out west, moved in next door and was reconciled with the Catholic Church. However, she longed for home and soon returned to New York, eventually leaving this life in 1963. Senior observed: "My parents died in their own beds at home and are buried a few miles from their birthplace."[1] After his mother's departure from Wyoming, Senior bought a wide-open, tumbledown 750-acre ranch—a small tract for that prairie state. "It is sensationally beautiful here," he wrote, "physically, frightingly [*sic*] so."[2] He soon possessed a milk cow or two, some chickens and geese, and an old horse for his daughter to ride—his own horseback days were pretty much over. His wife continued to raise and show Afghan hounds. Economic prospect came from raising alfalfa for hay and leasing land for cattle grazing.

When he moved to the ranch, Senior was an energetic forty-year-old man. Up at the crack of dawn, he would check and feed the animals, break ice on the creek for them if necessary, milk the cow, drive the children into town for school and continue on to the university. In the late afternoon and on Saturdays he would complete the necessary and often rugged chores on the ranch. Senior, quixotic intellectual that he was, could not of course keep up with professional ranchers. Like the knight of La Mancha, his knowledge came from books and, although he was physically hearty, he was not very handy. He would come home in the evening lamenting—and laughing—about his difficulties digging post holes in a straight line or repairing fences. When a neighbor cut off his irrigation, he had no idea how to appeal for his water rights, unfamiliar as he was with the "law of the land."

Meanwhile, his teaching was a solid success. He was controversial as always, but with a devoted body of students and friends. He even obtained national recognition. In the summer of 1966, he reported to Father Taylor: "Guess what, Father. I have good news and bad news. The good

news is that I have been selected as one of the fifty best teachers in the United States. The bad news is that *Esquire Magazine* did the choosing!"

Besides his official university teaching, Senior gave religious instruction at the campus Catholic center, which was well animated by Father Taylor. The university chaplain described his first meeting with Senior, in the fall of 1960:

> Dr. Senior introduced himself as a new member of the faculty at the University and offered to assist with the programs for the Catholic students at the University. I had only been there for a year myself and was just getting the feel of the programming. Not knowing Dr. Senior's background or intellectual greatness and thinking that an operation named after the famous English cardinal should include a presentation of some of Cardinal Newman's works, [I] naively said to Dr. Senior: "Do you think you could handle Newman's *Grammar of Assent?*" His simple [response was]—with what I came to know as his gentle and inimitable style—"Yes, I think I can." That was my introduction and beginning of a most precious friendship with a great man and his family—Priscilla, Penny, Matthew, Andrew and their canine crew.[3]

And thus began seven years during which Senior read, reread and taught four of Newman's major books in this framework—the *Apologia, Development of Doctrine, Grammar of Assent* and *The Idea of a University*—imbuing himself with Newman's thought. In the summer, the center hosted "The Newman School of Catholic Thought," to which Catholic intellectuals came to speak and discuss current topics; these sessions provided Senior the opportunity to discuss questions with visiting priests and scholars. Some of them were surprised to find such a bright light in this little university in Wyoming. The religious services in the Catholic chapel were also to Senior's liking. He greatly enjoyed the Latin liturgy and the Gregorian chant, and sang in the choir.

It is worth mentioning that Senior and Father Taylor quickly became very good friends. The poet from New York and the priest in a Roman

collar and cowboy boots were a complementary pair in their ardent enthusiasm for the Faith and their playful humor. It was beneficial for the newly converted intellectual to have a cordial relationship with a solid, very practical Irish priest. The priest, on his side, wrote about Professor Senior's impact on him—the testimony is all the more weighty because it comes not from a freckle-faced freshman but a priest already fully formed when he had met Senior: "I have had many good and some great teachers in my college, seminary and graduate schools, but I must rate Dr. Senior as having the greatest influence in my life. The depth and clarity of his teaching is indelible."[4] Father Taylor also befriended Senior's family, notably the boys; because he was a sports fan and Senior was not, it was he who took them to ball games.

As for Senior's home life, a major part of his children's memory is of their father always reading and meditating, absorbed in his thoughts. His daughter said that the best time to ask for Senior's permission was when he was thus engrossed! Another memory they have is of visitors to their home. Over the years there was an endless stream of students coming by in the evening. Nonetheless, Senior did not allow his professorial duties to damage his family life. He once proposed that a father spend five and a half hours daily with the family, so one can assume this was the goal he held for himself. His daughter provides a glimpse of the professor in his home:

> We teased him unmercifully about being an absent-minded professor and about being so "retro." He took it all in good humor. Dad was, in fact, a very humorous man. Extremely witty, he had an assortment of names and faces he used to depict our so-called heroes—Bob Dylan and the Beatles for example. He loved comedians like Laurel and Hardy. He laughed uproariously at some Lenny Bruce monologues, although he couldn't abide by some of the nastier stuff Bruce did. He and my mother howled over *Mad Magazine*.[5]

The Senior family never had a television; the long winter evenings on the Wyoming ranch were conducive to reading aloud to the children.

Senior introduced them to the classics he had been brought up on—*Oliver Twist, Ivanhoe, The Last of the Mohicans, Treasure Island*. His daughter also remembers: "We grew up with music. Long before Ravi Shankar was a guru for the sixties' generation, we heard him on our old player of the fifties. We listened to Beethoven, Mozart, Haydn and some earlier opera singers."[6] Sometimes, Senior would play the guitar and sing, and occasionally his two sons would join in, one on the clarinet and the other on the tuba.

We must add that Senior certainly prayed a lot. His interior life is the King's secret, but in the same talk in which he proposed five and a half hours with the family, he recommended that one-tenth of the day—about two hours and a half—be spent in prayer. One can assume that amount was at least what he tried to accomplish himself, through daily Holy Mass, the rosary, the Little Office of Our Lady or part of the Benedictine Office,* some mental prayer, and spiritual reading.

A Growing Realization

With fervor, perhaps even a sense of mission, Senior began teaching at Wyoming in 1960. He wanted to lead his students into the truths and the classical culture of Western tradition, and eventually to Christ Himself. Initially he set out to present St. Thomas's doctrine in direct form. This approach, however, did not work well because most students were incapable of even the most basic philosophical discussions. This shortcoming was not something to be easily remedied, for it did not proceed from a simple lack of formation in logic or similar preparatory subjects. Senior discovered that its source lay much deeper; as he put it, referring to his efforts at the time: "The *Summa Theologiae* contains clear refutations of reasonable heresies but scarcely touches anyone who disbelieves in the very difference between truth and error."[7] Senior's philosophical arguments were disarmed, as it were, when confronted with students who disbelieved in truth, that is, who were immersed in the Perennial Heresy. They did not recognize the absolute difference between "is" and "is not."

---

* Senior had a predilection for the Benedictine Office, though he never became a Benedictine oblate.

This confusion between truth and error, between yes and no, this rejection of the principle of contradiction, was not a "reasonable heresy," because it denied reason at its very roots. Since Senior could scarcely reason with such students, what should he do?

Several factors converged to bring about Senior's discovery of the remedy for the impasse. He knew how critical the healthy experiences of his own youth—swimming in the ocean, playing on a Long Island that still retained some nature, his hard work on the ranch in South Dakota, riding horses—had been for all his education. They had given him interest in reality and material for life reflection. Thanks to them, the books he read found echoes in his soul. Before he came to Wyoming, he had already recognized that a lack of basic experience among his students hindered their ability to appreciate and enjoy literature in which animals, plants, rocks, sky, meadows and brooks played such an important part:

> In my own direct experience teaching literature at universities, I have found a large plurality of students who find, say, *Treasure Island* what they call hard reading. . . . To cope somewhat with this, I tried to get college students at the age of twenty to fill in children's books . . . and discovered deeper still that the problem isn't only books; it isn't only language; it is things: It is experience itself that has been missed. . . . Wordsworth is right when he says, "Come out into the light of *things.*"[8]

And then there were his studies of Newman. Newman is often interpreted as opposing St. Thomas and the scholastics, as a sort of pragmatist rejecting abstract argument. Senior understood that, in fact, the cardinal was simply recognizing why St. Thomas had little influence on minds of his day: abstract arguments presuppose certain dispositions largely lacking in modern times. Senior liked to say that St. Thomas has the arguments capable of winning the case—the lawyer's brief is excellent—but there is no longer a jury of men tried and true, capable of judging. In Hume's dispute with Newman,* the former reasoned with abstractions without

---

* See Chapter Four.

facing reality; he contented himself with *notional* knowledge, as Newman termed it. Newman replies: "Look at the Church, get to know Christ." In order to gain *real* knowledge, ideas alone will not do. We need a living experience of the thing itself, a grasp of things in our imagination, memory and emotions; then we can have a hold on reality through our concepts and arguments.

St. Thomas and Aristotle provided Senior with a precise, philosophical view of the necessity and importance of sensible knowledge that enlightened what he found in Newman concerning *real* knowledge. Let's consider a few texts of St. Thomas on the subject.

For St. Thomas, as for Aristotle, man is not a pure mind or spirit imprisoned in the body that must escape in order to know truth, as Neo-Platonists claim. The two philosophers explained that because the human soul and body are corresponding principles, there is a natural and necessary collaboration between senses and intellect. The intellect needs the senses in order to play its own role. St. Thomas, following Aristotle, delineates the basis of their collaboration: "Our intellect understands material things by abstracting [the idea] from sense images."[9] In fact, the intellect cannot reflect without constantly referring to the sensible, as St. Thomas also teaches: "If someone attempts to understand anything, he will form sense images for himself as examples in which he can, as it were, look at what he is attempting to understand.... The intellect must turn to sense images in order to look at universal natures existing in particular things."[10] It is indeed obvious that one must have experience of *men* in order to form an idea of *humanity*, and even with this idea already formed, one must consider sensible images of men to think about that idea.

This necessity of sensible experience and images is also true for more abstract and spiritual areas of knowledge. To think of beauty, goodness and justice, one must first have the experience and image of a particular thing—the beauty of a rainbow, the goodness of a mother, the justice of a father. To mentally dwell on spiritual realities—angels or God—one also needs to make use of images and concrete things as analogies. St. Thomas writes: "The intellect rises to the limited knowledge it has of invisible things by way of the nature of visible ones.... We know incorporeal realities, which

have no sense images, by analogy with sensible bodies, which do have images, just as we understand truth in the abstract by a consideration of things in which we see truth."[11]

By reflecting on Newman, on his students' difficulties, on his own experience, and on such texts of St. Thomas, Senior developed a vivid sense of man's dependence on sensible experience: "We are a rooted species," he writes, "rooted through our senses in the air, water, earth and fire of elemental experience."[12] The following passage from "The Restoration of Innocence" provides an excellent example of his Realism:

> A child can't honestly admire the Maker until he first honestly admires the things He made. It's an insult to ignore the artist's work while praising him on hearsay, as if "by the invisible things of God we come to know the visible things of earth"! *Vae fideismus!* Taste and see. This thing is good; it couldn't make itself; therefore we know He Who made it is good. Metaphysically speaking, things are good because the good God made them. But we are not metaphysical creatures; we don't think like angels; everything we know is known in things.[13]

Senior here paraphrases St. Thomas who, to help the reader understand man's need to abstract from the sensible, contrasted the human way of knowing with the angelic way, explaining that the angel knows the material through the invisible, whereas man knows the invisible through the sensible.[14] Senior's expression "by the invisible things . . . we come to know the visible" is a deliberate and ironic reversal of St. Paul's statement in the Epistle to the Romans, where man comes to know the invisible by the visible. According to Senior, this reversal is a sort of Fideism, that is, a belief that faith is the only source of all knowledge of divine mysteries. Descartes and the seventeenth-century Rationalists, as well as the Neo-Platonists and the Occult and Hindu tradition of all times, professed to do something similar by knowing God first and then, through Him, the world. According to them all, that is, according to this manifestation of the

Perennial Heresy, the chronological order in learning and the hierarchy of reality are the same. Man's knowledge would begin with the highest forms of *being*; he would receive his knowledge directly from the spiritual world.

For Aristotle, St. Thomas and the Realist tradition, human learning begins with lower, material degrees of *being*, thereby ascending to the higher and spiritual. When Senior says that "we are not metaphysical creatures," he is taking the term "metaphysical" in its etymological sense of "beyond the physical," to point out that human knowledge is not situated immediately in the spiritual domain. Man does not have innate ideas or direct knowledge of the spiritual; he has only an intellectual light. That light is indeed spiritual and caused from above, but in order to bear fruit it needs something to shine upon. It works through our sensible knowledge to disengage meaning, to abstract essences, to draw out ideas.

The practical conclusion of this realist doctrine of knowing "in things" is that a rich and healthy experience of the sensible world is needed for one to know God well. Senior thus affirms in the text that to know God's goodness, we must first be acquainted with the goodness of the things He made. We have to "taste" the goodness of things, Senior says. That requires time and leisure. "If you jump from rocks to God," he writes, "without a long, sensible, emotional, willful, thoughtful intercourse with them, your understanding and love of His goodness and greatness will be proportioned to the meager experience."[15] The need for experience exists, of course, not only for knowing God. We must also experience, know and love beautiful things to form an authentic idea of beauty, and be familiar with individual men, flowers, horses and wood for real and rich notions of them.

Senior also brings out the other side of the coin: "If [feelings and senses are] poorly ordered, the intellect can result only in error."[16] Not only do we need appropriate images for good ideas, but bad images easily result in bad ideas. Drawing distorted material from the imagination distorts intellectual knowledge. Senior recognized that this was largely the case in our time: "Conceptual truth is extracted by the intellect from the

ground of the imagination. But the modern world suffers from a disease of the imagination."[17] Today, not only are experience and imagination lacking; beyond that, they are perverted through contemporary popular music, licentious movies, and the like.

Senior gradually perceived, then, the extent to which philosophy itself depends on a healthy imagination: "The direct study of philosophy and theology will not cure a diseased imagination, because anyone with a diseased imagination is incapable of studying philosophy and theology."[18] He mentions the difficulty of attaining to spiritual ideas today: "Surrounded as we are by a hedonistic and even demonic imaginative ground, it is not impossible, of course, but very difficult for the intellect to grasp ideas like 'spirit,' 'soul,' 'God.'"[19] Someone so attached to the sensual can rise only with great difficulty to this spiritual level and therefore to philosophy.

However, Senior recognized an obstacle to philosophy even more basic than the hindrance posed by a sensual and hedonistic imagination to our thinking about spiritual realities. Earlier in this chapter we cited a passage in which Senior confesses the difficulty in teaching philosophy today because of students' lack of belief in differences between truth and error. In one of his final essays, Senior lays the blame for the difficulty on the new generation's deficient experiential knowledge: "I realized that the scholastic philosophical system, so effective in refuting the rational skepticism of my generation, had had no impact on students whose minds were disconnected from tangible and emotional realities."[20] Senior's writings as a whole conclude that disbelief in truth and first principles arose at least partly from the fact that students were disconnected from reality on the experiential level. Our literature, our art, indeed our whole society today, does not cultivate experience but rather fosters a disconnection with reality.

For Senior, modern man's basic correspondence to *being*, as well as to the true, the good and the beautiful—the primary reaction to reality upon which the intellectual, moral and spiritual life is built—has been dulled by an impoverished and even abnormal experience. Senior came to see

that modern man, by the very milieu in which he lives, is predisposed toward Anti-Realism.

This abnormal experience, this sensible and emotional disconnection, stems largely from modern technology, which Senior consequently considered to be a basic hindrance to philosophy. He wrote: "The first impediment to the study of St. Thomas today is industrialized society."[21] In fact, if what Senior said about experience is true, industrialized society causes problems for all learning. The problem is not only that television, for example, stimulates sensuality and hedonism by its content. The precise point here is that its inherent artificiality weakens our grasp on reality. This position of Senior's necessitates a special examination, being an important as well as problematic element of his thought both in theory and implementation.

Technology, Modern Science and Realism

As noted previously, already as a child Senior suffered from that distance, even separation, from the natural world characteristic of an artificial, industrialized society. Literature, much of which celebrated nature and some of which in modern times expressed great nostalgia for it, had made his perception of this separation still more acute. One could quote Wordsworth, that poetic chronicler of man's lost harmony with nature at the beginning of the industrial age:

This Sea that bares her bosom to the moon;
The winds that will be howling at all hours,
And are up-gathered now like sleeping flowers;
For this, for everything, we are out of tune.[22]

In Senior's own poetry there rarely are verses that rejoice in the beauty of nature because, unfortunately, his experience at the time was rather of an artificial world; thus, he mainly expressed regrets. For example, here are a few stanzas from "The Appalachian Trail." Note the "prelapsarianly clean"—no stains in our artificial paradise!

citizens of Earth, not Nations,
up the blazing trail—but nervous,
under safety regulations
of the Park and (now) Health Service.
. . .
ecumenically super, prelapsarianly clean,
self-composting
toilet paper
UPS from L.L. Bean.
"Oh, for camps without the counselors,
trails without the guides,
birds without binoculars
and uninstructed brides!
. . .
If only we were virgins still
this great, green forest, you and I,
a wilderness, a boy, a girl
and no technology!"[23]

Coomaraswamy, Guénon and other authors such as Ruskin and Father Vincent McNabb provided Senior with reasons to support his wistful desire for earlier times. They showed him why industrial society has in many ways degraded human life and how superficial the materialist scientific view of reality is. But Senior went farther in precisely expressing that our artificial world turns us from the recognition of *being*.

We have no systematic development from Senior on the reason why deficiencies in the domain of learning result from modern technology, but he touched on the question here and there under various aspects. Our reflections can focus on the following passage from Senior's "History and the School":

Cut off from direct experience of the book of nature by city, suburban and rural life (farms are "factories in the field"), we learn to love

false images of God through the distortion of his works on television and the science fiction that passes for science in textbooks.[24]

Christian tradition speaks of two books in which God teaches us about Himself: the Bible and the world He made. In some measure, the "book of nature" is the more fundamental of the two because the Bible itself uses images and ideas that come to us only through nature.

In modern society, then, we are "cut off" from the world that God made to lead us to Himself.

We have already studied the artificiality of Modernist art. Here we are dealing with our being immersed in an artificial world. Senior often strove to help his audiences become more aware of the degree to which this fact alienates us from nature. We have almost no direct contact with God's creation:

> Generations brought up in centrally heated and air-conditioned homes and schools, going from place to place encapsulated in culturally sealed-off buses, swim in heated, chlorinated pools devoid of current, swirl or tide, where even the build-up from one's own pushing of the water is suctioned off by vacuums so as not to spoil the pure experience of sport-for-sport's sake; they play summer games like shooting balls through hoops, but reinvented as "basketball" and on winter nights, dressed in short pants; they play football under air-conditioned geodesic domes in heavy jerseys and ski on artificial snow in July.[25]

We might illustrate the damage caused by this separation from the world of nature with another passage that directly concerns Realism: "Poor little rich suburban children who have all these delights, and living in constant fluorescent glare, have never seen the stars, which St. Thomas, following Aristotle and all the ancients, says are the first begetters of that primary experience of reality formulated as the first of all principles in metaphysics: that *something is.*"[26] Among the many experiences of nature

that modern man is deprived of, Senior underlines here that of gazing at the stars. In their fundamental texts on the beginning of philosophy, Plato, Aristotle, and St. Thomas spoke of the order of the stars soaring over the entire sky as provoking wonder and launching the intellectual quest for the cause of all things, of the very universe.[27] These passages do not explicitly mention the awakening of consciousness to the fact that "something is," that the real is really real. Yet, Senior well understands what was present in their doctrine; ultimately, it was indeed the mystery of the stars' existence that launched the first philosophers in their quest.

The very fact that something exists is wonderful, and the stars, with all their seemingly gratuitous beauty, are a striking example of this. They spark the realization that there is mystery in the fact that something is, that the universe is, that there are untold riches in *being*.

The passage we are studying specifies that we are not only cut off from the book of nature but are confronted with "false images of God." The world God made bears his trace and leads to Him, but if we bend it out of shape it is no longer a good path to God. The first of the two false images, Senior explains, consists in a "certain distortion of [God's] works." Senior was especially thinking of television. In *The Restoration of Christian Culture*, he provides a striking example of such a distortion: "A sixty foot whale splashing across nineteen inches of your living-room while you sip your Coca Cola is not reality."[28]

Moreover, the whale hunt on television, like many electronic representations of things, has an "insidious irreality."[29] Senior writes about records and CDs: "Electronic reconstitutions of disintegrated sounds are not real sounds any more than reconstituted sterilized lactates are milk"[30]—but we easily take them for real. Indeed, television, CDs, iPods and other devices aim at producing an illusion. They are not like a painting that signifies; they are intended to replace reality. They provide, as it were, a counterfeit experience. For Senior, our technological world "where the magician-intellect invents gigantic global systems of relativist science [and] develops virtual realities"[31] is similar to the Modernist dream of confusing fantasy and reality. One understands that when children unplug from their iPod or put aside their video game, they have trouble distinguishing between

real things and virtual reality. And, as Senior so aptly says in *The Restoration of Christian Culture*, "we learn to love these false images." We become attached—even addicted—to these virtual simulations, to this artificial sensationalism. Both the imagination and emotions are forcibly cut off from reality and applied to something else.

The second false image Senior mentions is the "science fiction" of textbooks. Another passage from "The Restoration of Innocence" helps us understand what he was referring to:

> When I was a child, the fifth grade teacher taught us that atoms were miniature solar systems—electrons like planets orbiting a nucleus like the sun. We drew atomic maps and memorized charts of weights, not having a single rock in front of us. We were taught to believe that atoms were real and rocks illusions. Brought up on mathematical models, we took them for reality.[32]

Whatever may be the value, speculative or practical, of such mathematical models, they reduce much of our knowledge of the world to quantitative description. Furthermore, here again one experiences an "insidious irreality." Modern man, accustomed to such models and impressed by science's success, takes them for reality—as the really real—and develops a prejudice against the value of sensible experience. His pseudoscientific imagination replaces God's creation with a false image. In the grip of an artificial substitute, he rejects the immediate, intuitive, sensible and emotional experience of reality. He believes "that atoms are real and rocks illusions," that H_2O is more real than the cool, slightly muddy creek he swims in. Senior writes that students who believe that the world consists of hollow mathematical structures have "minds lost in abstraction through the science of an 'empty universe,' to use the expression of Charles Konink."[33] We have here a strong "disrealization," of course, and also an opening to the "psychologizing" of knowledge previously discussed.

Thus, by both virtual simulation and mathematical schemas, the imagination and emotions are cut off from reality only to be connected

to distortions. Modern man's very experience and imagination incline him toward a mental disconnection from reality. The world seems less real to him and this predisposes him to Modernism, to consider imagination— or rather fantasy—as real as, or even more real than, anything else.

One is not obliged to accept all the details of Senior's thought on the relationship between the modern apparatus and Relativism, but it is certain that man today often has an imagination and emotions disconnected from reality, and that modern science and technology have much to do with that. Our devices make us distant from real things. Watching the whale hunt on television imparts next to nothing of the real adventure and danger, of the smells, of the feeling of the air, nor the skill, strength, endurance and patience required. Also, pushing buttons on computers cannot connect one's mind, sense, emotion and imagination to reality as can guiding a horse, hammering nails into boards and maneuvering a sail on a ship. Driving through our neighborhood in a car does not familiarize us with the lay of the land, the trees and lawns, as walking does. Anyone can recognize that modern man needs to reconnect with the world God made, so that healthy experience and imagination may nurture his intellectual and spiritual life. Such recognition suffices substantially for one to understand Senior's goal of restoring a healthy imagination.

Nothing can replace experience: "No serious restitution of society or the Church can occur without a return to the first principles, yes, but before principles we must return to the ordinary reality which feeds the first principles."[34]

Steps in Education

As the importance of experience impressed itself upon his mind, Senior began to reflect on the appropriate stages of education. Traditional educators consider the ancient Greeks to have achieved the most adequate form of the complete education. Greek boys, of course, did learn the "three Rs," but at the elementary level the focus was on *gymnastic* and *music*. What the Greeks called gymnastic was a physical education, including both athletic exercise and military training, primarily through track and

field, wrestling and boxing. Its aim was to develop strength, endurance, courage, coordination and grace. What was called music embraced all that belonged to the domain of the nine Muses: epic and lyric poetry, song, tragedy and comedy, dance, playing of musical instruments, observation of the stars and history (i.e., basically, stories of heroes). The goal of this musical formation was to develop, refine and control the imagination and emotions, render the pupil intellectually alert and form him in aesthetic taste, patriotism, ethics and religion. Plato believed that good music, working alongside healthy gymnastic, harmonizes the senses with the rational part of our being, in particular by providing decorous images for the mind and lofty orientation for the emotions. He wrote: "The blending of music and gymnastic will render [the body and soul] concordant, intensifying and fostering [reason] with noble words and teachings, and moderating and soothing and making gentle [the wildness of passion] by harmony and rhythm."[35]

At about age sixteen, Greek youth who continued their education were taught to analyze, reason, argue and speak, and were initiated into mathematics and sciences. Shortly before the Christian era, such studies were arranged into the system of the seven liberal arts. The term "liberal" was originally used to distinguish the arts of a free man from the "manual" arts of the servile class.

One could also take it to mean that these arts "liberate" one by providing mastery over the specifically human faculties of thinking and speaking. Plato saw initiation in mathematics and sciences especially as an exercise in abstraction, "for facilitating the conversion of the soul from the world of change to essence and truth"[36]—for passing from images to reason.

By this gradual training, the Greeks aimed at educating the whole man, body and mind. The accomplished Greek was healthy, graceful and eloquent, had good judgment and could conform himself to a moral ideal. After this discipline, the young Greek man could begin professional training by specializing in philosophy, law, medicine, or simply by entering a career or beginning a trade.

Over the centuries, in different places and epochs, the Greek educational ideal has waxed and waned. Instructors often lost sight of the idea

of an integral human formation before specialization. The Romans, for example, arguably overemphasized physical education as preparation for war, or the art of expression in view of public office. For the Middle Ages—to the extent that one can generalize about such an immense period—the Greek ideal of elementary education was transposed to the courts, with songs, knightly exercises, riding jousting, singing and making verse, whereas the more purely bookish clerical cathedral schools concentrated on grammar and rhetoric, and the universities on logic, philosophy and theology, with the higher mathematics having all but disappeared. In the Renaissance, burgeoning modern sciences became more and more severed from letters, arts and philosophy and increasingly ordered to technical progress and use of the world for power, pleasure and comfort. In modern times gymnastic and some forms of music still exist in our schools, but they have largely lost their orientation toward moral and spiritual formation. In addition, we see the world of science and specialized technological studies encroaching ever more, not only at the college level, but even as early as in the elementary years.

Senior thus considers the steps of education very lucidly in the light of the Perennial Philosophy. He recognizes that the Greek model of a gradual education of the whole man must be involved in a return to Realism. Here is a general presentation of the steps, which Senior provided to a Kansas reporter in 1974:

> The ideal educational system would comprise the development of the whole human being. The first stage is the gymnastic stage, in which the student studies how his body moves and functions, and practices the use of his body to help his mind develop. Midway between the body and the mind is the memory or imagination. This area is essential . . . because intelligence is based on only those images that come from the senses and are stored in the memory. . . . This improvement of the memory and imagination is very important to handle the third stage of education, the more factual, scientific part of education. . . . The first two stages of education allow the mind to become awake.[37]

Senior did not use the term "music" in this newspaper article because the old use of the term would have been misunderstood by modern readers habituated to its more restricted meaning. The traditional, broader content of the word is obviously presupposed in this "improvement of memory and imagination" to awaken the mind and prepare images for it.

Senior underlines in *The Restoration of Christian Culture* why this progressive education is natural and normal: "The structuring of learning must follow the order of nature and of the learner from sensible to imaginative to intelligible knowledge."[38] Since teaching assists nature, it should indeed correspond to the way and order in which people naturally learn. We first receive sensible data and then process it in our imagination to prepare its assimilation at the intellectual level. It follows, therefore, that the first focus in education should be on the sensible intake through gymnastic, the second, on the culture of this sensible data in the imagination and memory through music, and the third, on understanding through the liberal arts and sciences.

In the two preceding passages, Senior speaks only of perception and knowing, but, by joining together some famous lines, he devises a formula that conveys the emotional import of the fundamental stages of learning. Robert Frost wrote that poetry "begins in delight and ends in wisdom."[39] For Senior, poetry lifts us up not to wisdom itself but rather to wonder, or to a *desire* for wisdom. This correction of Frost's statement links it to Plato's and Aristotle's affirmation that philosophy begins in wonder.[40] Thus drawing from a poet and a philosopher, Senior teaches us that gymnastic begins in experience and ends in delight; poetry or music begins in delight and ends in wonder; philosophy begins in wonder and ends in wisdom.[41]

There is, of course, no question of isolating any of the levels, the mind, the imagination and the senses working together in all of them, as Senior explains: "Modes [of knowledge] . . . like the colors of the spectrum or notes on a musical scale, are stages of a gradual act. As relative contraries, each is dependent on the other. . . . Though as modes, all are present in each and each in all, there is a natural progression of dominance from sense, emotion, instrument and intellect to practice."[42]

Senior thus subdivides the intellectual level into three—instrument, intellect and practice—which correspond to liberal arts, sciences or philosophy, and professional training. He describes the liberal arts as "instrumental knowledge forming habits of abstracting concepts and constructing syllogisms."[43] Science is "intellectual knowledge by analysis and synthesis in which the mind becomes the thing known by making abstract models of it."[44] One no longer only "feels" reality as in gymnastic and music, but using tools formed in the liberal arts, science draws out hidden roots, the intelligible structures of reality. Professional training or practical science is "the application of [the abstract models of things produced by science] to particulars, changing them to suit our purposes."[45] After his bookish studies, a man exercises his theoretical knowledge against reality in the practice of his profession or trade. The goal of all the steps, Senior reminds us, is wisdom: the knowledge of the first cause, of first truth, in such a way that one recognizes the multiplicity of things as harmonious parts of the whole and then savors this harmony.

First Things First

A noteworthy reaction emerged, in the mid-twentieth century, to the modern stance that would promote early technical specialization in education. It was spearheaded by the founders of the Great Books program: Van Doren himself, Mortimer Adler, Robert Hutchins and others.

Experience of the value of an education gained directly from the masters led them to recognize the need there was to rehabilitate undergraduate formation in general knowledge before professional, more specific training could be provided. These teachers turned to the Middle Ages and to the Greeks for light on how to do this. They decided to restore the liberal arts and sciences through great literature, such as Homer, Shakespeare and Tolstoy, and through foundational scientific texts such as Euclid, Galileo and Newton, with an initiation into philosophical reflection through, for example, Plato, Descartes and Kant.

Senior appreciated the Great Books effort from which he himself had greatly profited at Columbia University, but he acknowledged that it did

not bear the hoped-for fruits. He writes: "The 'Great Books' movement of the last generation has not failed as much as fizzled, not because of any defects in the books . . . but like good champagne in plastic bottles, they went flat"[46]—the recipients were not prepared for such rich fare. He more often used a different metaphor, comparing today's educational situation to the erosion of the 1930s when farmers had to sow common plants in order to nourish the barren land and render it capable of growing food crops. Similarly, teachers today have to enrich their students' memories and stimulate their delight in reality and their wonder at its mysteries through gymnastic and music before they can undertake more elevated studies like the liberal arts and philosophy. Learning is gradual and first things must come first.

One tends to neglect the elementary level partly because deficiency in that domain is a rather recent thing. Training in gymnastic and music has often been taken for granted without too much detriment because in other times and places they were largely assured by ordinary activity, as one walked, rode horses, hunted, worked with hand tools, sang and read together. Today, however, the remnants of gymnastic and music that subsist in home and school are so disordered that a special and deliberate effort must be made to restore them. The scant and warped experience of students and their consequently disconnected and even diseased imaginations were for Senior the most fundamental problem in education.

Gymnastic and music are all the more important in that they are not merely a preparation for the next stages, and ultimately for the scientific. Each educational level has its own inherent value. Mastering reasoning and expression while reflecting on great human questions in the liberal arts is worthwhile regardless of what one does afterward, even if one does not specialize in a science. Likewise, it is not necessary for everyone to study logic, abstract grammar and high mathematics, yet everyone needs to cultivate, through gymnastic and music, the primordial engagement with reality. Gymnastic and music—the culture of senses and delight, of imagination and wonder—are a necessary basis for a man's full life. Wordsworth reflects this idea in well-known verses:

My heart leaps up when I behold
A rainbow in the sky:
So was it when my life began;
So is it now I am a man;
So be it when I will grow old
Or let me die!
The Child is father of the Man.[47]

We have now established Senior's basic educational discovery and considered the reason why the promotion of what the Greeks called gymnastic and music was a leitmotiv of his teaching. We have defined and situated these two disciplines in the whole movement of education. In what follows, we will explore their nature and the principles of their exercise.

CHAPTER EIGHT

Learning How to Gaze on Reality

*The restoration of reason presupposes the restoration
of love and we can only love what we know because
we have first touched, tasted, smelled, heard and
seen. From that encounter with exterior reality,
interior responses naturally arise, movements moti-
vating, urging, releasing energies, infinitely greater
than atoms, of intelligence and will.*
—The Restoration of Christian Culture

IN this chapter we intend to focus on the first stages in education.
However, we will provide only a few remarks on some principles
of gymnastic and its practice, as our real work will be to consider the
musical stage in some depth, as it is more properly Senior's domain and
raises significant questions.

Exercising the Exterior Senses
for Delight in Existence

Senior was far from dismissing the qualities of courage, self-control and
grace admired by the Greeks, but he thought of gymnastic primarily as an
exercise of the exterior senses to initiate contact with the world. He describes
this first level of education as "a vigorous training of the body, the purpose
of which [is] not just health and recreation but the acuity of sensing, as sight
is sharpened and coordinated by archery."[1] It is "the art of right sensation."[2]
The delight Senior speaks of as the goal for this first step is not the sensual

pleasure of artificial sensationalism; it is a sort of relish in one's connection with reality, feeling the immediate appeal of things. In the preceding chapter we read that Senior, like Plato, argues that this training serves to awaken the mind. Indeed, the senses themselves have first to be alert to reality. Inattentive, blunt senses produce dull minds and hearts, whereas keen, attentive senses and proper delight in reality stir the soul.

We are little aware of how much our senses are capable of growing in attention and intensity. Those who learn to draw or play an instrument acquire a precision in sight or hearing beyond the ordinary. Likewise, some doctors are capable of making internal medicine diagnoses by simply palpating the patient a few times. A gourmet cook has cultivated taste buds, and the gardener has acquired a keen sense of smell in distinguishing flower perfumes. Everyone can learn to observe and listen better.

The senses, then, need exercise. They also must have wholesome things to experience. Gymnastic, Senior points out, is derived from the word *gymnos*, "naked," because the Greeks typically conducted their physical exercise unclothed. He intends this reference to evoke the immediate contact with concrete, natural things, which are best for exercising the senses and for moving to delight. As he comments: "The first necessity is getting ourselves and our children into 'naked' contact with the world God made, not just in school as study but habitually in our whole way of life."[3] This delight indeed proceeds spontaneously from a normal experience of God's creation. Senior writes of the Modernist disgust with reality: "But why should anyone get into such a state of mind? The natural response to sunlight and darkness alike is first and immediately delight."[4] And he quotes Shakespeare:

When daisies pied and violets blue,
And lady-smocks all silver white,
And cuckoo-buds of yellow hue
Do paint the meadows with delight.[5]

Largely because of his separation from nature, modern man's ability to perceive sensibly and to take delight in his surroundings has deteriorated.

His entire environment compels him to gaze vaguely and listen idly; he is both overwhelmed with too much to see and hear, and deprived of anything genuinely interesting to look at or listen to. His senses are restless and distracted with background music everywhere and images flying by as he rushes about in a vehicle. Senior writes about television: "Watching it, we fail to exercise the eye, selecting and focusing detail."[6] And it is easy enough to realize that the industrial world of fluorescent lights and chlorinated pools attracts our attention and stirs our emotions far less than stars, ponds, candles or fountains. An airplane is not as beautiful and graceful as a bird, nor can cars measure up to horses from the aesthetic point of view.

Gymnastic does not consist simply in a few exercises now and then. Our homes, schools, work sites and places of recreation should provide an habitual contact with natural things. In that way the senses are spontaneously sharpened and coordinated and can ripen into a lively sensible and emotional connection with reality. We know that Senior always lived in the country while teaching. He had noticed the profit that came to Mark Van Doren from growing up on a farm and, as a teacher, living and working part of the year in a rustic context.

Thus, regardless of age, every human being needs regular activity in contact with God's creation, but this is most important for a child so that he may be formed in a sound relationship to reality by receiving good things in his fresh soul. "Children," writes Senior, "need direct, everyday experience of fields, forests, streams, lakes, oceans, grass and ground."[7] The child needs to discover reality in its manifold and harmonious riches, to be introduced to it through delight.

Sensation is his primary mode of learning as he explores the world through his body. We shall later see how Senior insists on the fact that the child should not be prematurely pushed beyond that natural level. Mark Van Doren insists on this as well: "Whatever we do for the child, he is doing one very important thing by himself: he is growing up. This is not to say that he lacks reason, but to suggest that reason in him had better not be hurried; for it prefers to lie in wait for its proper moment.... It desires cultivation even now, but simply and with ample attention to the senses, which are the suit it wears."[8]

Exercising the Interior Senses

Senior explains that "the food of music is delight in existence."[9] After some gymnastic training of perception comes musical education of the memory, imagination, and emotions. Daily experiences pass, but they are inscribed in the interior faculties and thus naturally continue in an imaginative and emotional life. What has been received through the senses needs to be developed and refined by the interior faculties to prepare nourishing food for the intellect and to stimulate and orientate the will. Consequently, our sensible connection with reality should be strengthened and deepened at this interior level as well. To understand Senior's thought we need first to become more familiar with the interior sensible faculties of memory, imagination and emotions.* He uses these terms according to their scholastic meaning.

The memory as the storehouse of our experiences is the fundamental interior sensible faculty because our interior activity depends on it. Mark Van Doren explains why exercise of the memory is crucial, using a quotation from Emerson:

> Memory is the mother of the imagination, reason, and skill. "We estimate a man by how much he remembers," says Emerson. "We like signs of richness in an individual, and most of all we like a great memory. Memory performs the impossible for man; holds together past and present, gives continuity and dignity to life. This is the companion, this the tutor, the poet, the library, with which you travel. Any piece of knowledge I acquire today has a value at this moment exactly proportioned to my skill to deal with it."[10]

The memory should be fed in an orderly way with real, good and beautiful things. One can therefore only lament the vulgar television shows, the artificial music and the generally ugly, anti-human environment that clutter up our modern memories.

---

* Senior also included "common sense" and "estimative" among the interior sensible faculties. Here only the three mentioned will be dealt with.

156

One must train the memory to recall with precision; it is like a muscle and modern man's is flabby. It needs exercise. Memorization of dates, poetry and mathematical tables was a standard part of American education until the mid-1900s, only to have all but completely disappeared in our day. In an interview, Senior complained:

> [Improvement of the memory] is something we have, by and large, lost track of in modern education. There is very little attention paid to the memory anymore. We think that because we have books, notebooks, computers or tape recorders, we don't have to use our memories anymore. . . . [Students] have shrunken memories. They can't hold anything in their memory.[11]

We are astounded by what seems to have been the prodigious memory of people in less mechanized eras. In the Middle Ages, monks routinely memorized all the psalms and much or all of the New Testament. Missionaries to the Native Americans relate how their illiterate catechumens could recite the Catechism perfectly after only one hearing. Fervent Muslims still memorize the Qur'an. People in less developed areas of Europe know by heart a seemingly endless number of songs and stories.

The imagination is the faculty that recalls stored sense data—not just visual images, but vestiges of all the senses—and can consider them outside their historical context. A text from Senior on "images" of nonvisual senses gives us a feel for how strong and rich our imagination is: "We can imagine the taste of tabasco sauce, the touch of burlap, the sound of a fingernail on slate and what the psychologists call the 'kinesthetic' sense of muscular tension in imagining how heavy fifty pounds is."[12] The imagination can splice and rearrange parts of images into new wholes. It is thus an inventive faculty, able to form images of things never experienced, for example, of countrysides never seen but described in a book. A good imagination is needed to invent practical solutions to problems. Its splicing ability also allows for comparison of various images, thus preparing an intellect apt at dealing with analogies, as Senior elucidates: "Aristotle says intelligence is seen in one's ability to make metaphors—not

fancying, not making up imaginary things, but seeing real similitudes."[13] We need imagination to have real, affective, familiar knowledge of people and things. It is one thing to receive information and statistics about a place and another to have it in our imagination.

As we know, there is remedial work to do here as well, because when our imagination is cut off from reality, it easily spins off into idle fantasy. Its ardor has also faded in our times. Medieval historian Jean Leclerq's explanation of why the ardor of our imagination has faded describes in contrast the so-active medieval imagination:

> Exuberant as this faculty is [among medievals], it nevertheless possesses a vigor and a precision which we find difficult to understand. We are used to seeing, almost without looking at them unless with a distracted eye, printed or moving pictures. We are fond of abstract ideas. Our imagination, having become lazy, seldom allows us to do anything but dream. But in the men of the Middle Ages it was vigorous and active. It permitted them to picture, to "make present," to see beings with all the details provided by the texts: the colors and dimensions of things, the clothing, bearing and actions of the people, the complex environment in which they move. They liked to describe them and, so to speak, re-create them, giving very sharp relief to images and feelings. The words of the sacred text never failed to produce a strong impression on the mind.[14]

Emotions, the third of the interior faculties we are considering, are affections on the sensible level. They consist in attractions or repulsions concerning sensory objects. They are an integral part of human love that is not purely spiritual. Benedict XVI wrote in his first encyclical: "It is neither the spirit alone nor the body alone that loves: it is man, the person, a unified creature, composed of body and soul, who loves. Only when both dimensions are truly united does man attain his full status."[15] As the intellect is dependent on images, the will similarly relies on sensible affections for warmth and zest. A generous will imbued with high ideals and vigor

in fighting weakness and corruption presupposes healthy emotions, whereas disordered and hedonistic affections are a great obstacle to the will's adherence to spiritual values. We quoted Allan Bloom in our introduction. Though Bloom was not an influence on Senior, who read him late in life, his insights into the importance of attuning one's emotions to the spiritual, drawn from his reading of Plato, are consonant with Senior's own views:

> Civilization or, to say the same thing, education is the taming or domestication of the soul's raw passions—not suppressing or excising them, which would deprive the soul of its energy—but forming and informing them as art. The goal of harmonizing the enthusiastic part of the soul with . . . the rational part, is perhaps impossible to attain. But without it, man can never be whole.[16]

The three faculties of course collaborate in this harmonization. Emotions deal with the concrete individual and therefore depend on data from the memory and imagination. If one has good, healthy experiences in the memory, and if the imagination is trained to discern the elements in them, high aspirations should follow because, as their name indicates, emotions are mainly moved. Senior writes that they are "things we do and things done to us . . . like falling in love, wondering, fearing."[17]

Certainly one needs to develop and discipline a variety of emotions—even anger and fear have their place—but Senior tells us that the goal of musical education is wonder. He also affirms that "the purpose of propaedeutic [that is, gymnastic and music] is not knowledge but love."[18] We need to consider more closely these two emotions, love and wonder. They are at the heart of education and culture; they are essential for harmonizing "the enthusiastic part of the soul with . . . the rational part."

Love and Wonder

The epigraph to this chapter tells us that "the restoration of reason presupposes the restoration of love." Senior learned especially through

Plato and medieval authors that love is necessary for profound knowledge: "Science cannot see without the light of love," he wrote. "Love first, then seek to understand,"[19] because "the lover is the only one who really sees the truth about the person or the thing he loves."[20] The cold, apathetic or utilitarian gaze will remain superficial, usually vague and distracted, whereas true affection renders the mind attentive to the beloved and his deeper values. If we do not love something, we will not recognize its goodness. Senior even claimed that love is itself a mode of knowledge because, by uniting the lover to the beloved, it initiates a sympathetic apprehension; one "feels" with the other, as it were. A boy knows his dog and a girl her horse in ways others cannot. A woman sees possibilities in her man that escape everyone else.

This affection must nevertheless be properly ordered if it is to be an aid to knowledge. Aristotle explains that a man judges according to his affections.[21] What one likes, one judges to be good. The glutton will tend to exaggerate the goodness of roast beef; his disordered and egotistical love distorts his judgment. Affections that disengage from the good and engage in evil darken the intellect, whereas upright affections open the mind to light, to what really is. That is especially true for high, vital truths. Plato remarks that although we can simply turn our head to change the direction of our physical gaze, when we are dealing with a new direction for our spiritual view, the entire being—sensibility, emotions, will and intellect—must turn around.[22] If a person loves truth and goodness, he gladly looks for them and is quick to recognize them. If he does not love them, he will turn away from reality lest he perceive what might contradict his desires.

Among the emotions that help us turn toward the great and mysterious truths is wonder. Wonder is something deeper and more dynamic than delight, more linked to the intellectual order. Senior defines it as "the reverent fear that beauty strikes in us."*[23] He explains that a reverent fear is "the response, not to evil in the object, but to limitations in ourselves. It means respect for persons in piety . . . and for things in wonder."[24] This

---

* Dennis Quinn deposited a life's meditation into a book on wonder: *Iris Exiled: A Synoptical History of Wonder* (Lanham, Maryland: University Press of America, 2002).

type of fear is not fright. It is a reaction not to evil, as when we flee a wild beast, but rather to our own inadequacy with regard to an object. St. Thomas teaches that we wonder specifically because we become aware that something exceeds the capacity of our faculty to know clearly.[25] Even material things—a rock, a tree—although to a lesser degree than a human person, contain and point to a mystery. There is something wonderful in them, beyond our reckoning powers.

It is traditional to associate wonder with beauty, as Senior does. Plato writes in his foundational text on wonder as the source of philosophy: "The sense of wonder is the mark of the philosopher. Philosophy has no other origin and he was a good genealogist who made Iris the daughter of Thauma."[26] Iris is the mysterious and stirring rainbow, the messenger of the gods; Thauma is wonder. The gods awaken us through this radiant apparition of beautiful form and color, striking us with reverential fear, stirring a wonder in our souls about heavenly mysteries. Elsewhere Plato compared wonder sparked by beauty to spiritual wings that begin to grow on our shoulders; that is, beauty reminds us of our higher calling.[27] Beauty arouses the soul's sense of greatness, making it realize that the shadows of this world—riches, power, fame, sensual pleasures—are not what really matter, they are not what we are made for.[28] Beauty invokes in us the sense that we are in the presence of something beyond the material world. Something higher is shining through the sensible.

Wonder is a complex of emotions, reverential fear being only one of its aspects. St. Thomas writes that wonder includes a desire to know the cause of what we experience, a desire that holds hope of knowing and even a joy in that hope.[29] Senior would explain in class that when confronted with something majestically beautiful, we are drawn to lower our eyes in reverence, while at the same time feeling the impulse to lift them up so as to gaze, in desire and hope, upon the striking beauty that also attracts us. We are fascinated. One can therefore say that wonder is a type of love, the most proper for education because it is a desire that includes a deep respect for something greater than oneself, for something mysterious. The desire draws us deeper into reality and the respect stimulates an attentive and humble docility. We realize that we must listen in order to

learn. He who studies biology must wonder at life, the mathematician, at numbers, if they are going to aspire to a deep and real knowledge of their subject. "It is only to the just," Senior writes, "gazing in rapt silence, like a lover on his beloved, at the art or the thing, it is only to the patient, silent, receptive listener, that the meaning of the poem, or the mystery of the number, star, chemical, plant—whatever subject the science sits at the feet of—is revealed."[30]

All this explains why the goal of music is an orderly love of the beautiful, as Plato writes: "Is not right love a sober and harmonious love of the beautiful? . . . The end and consummation of [musical culture] is the love of beauty."[31] How then does music cultivate the proper appreciation of beautiful mysteries, an appreciation full of wonder, of a harmonious, reverential love?

Under the Guidance of the Muses

Music—again in the large sense of all the spheres of the Muses—is the major means of exercising the interior senses and emotions, as Senior had long known both on his own and through the teaching of Van Doren and others. The memory is more at ease with stories, songs and poetry than with lists. Likewise, poetry and imaginative literature are the foremost exercise for the imagination, notably since one is obliged to visualize and even hear, smell, touch and taste what is therein described. And the arts are able to move the emotions in a way that an abstract idea cannot. Senior liked to quote Newman: "The heart is commonly reached, not through reason, but through the imagination."[32] A definition of courage does not excite the emotions as a story about a hero does.

The Muses also refine the interior senses and emotions in order to aid the intellect in functioning well and fruitfully. As Senior writes: "Without the rectitude of sense, emotion and will which poetry aligns, the higher mental faculties collapse."[33] Plato similarly explains that music is necessary for the intellect to see clearly: "What if [one] . . . has no contact with the Muses in any way? . . . [The soul] becomes feeble, deaf and blind, because it is not aroused or fed, nor are its perceptions purified and quickened."[34]

How exactly does music rectify senses, emotions and will? How does it arouse and feed the intellect? This is a rich subject that Senior did not develop in his writings. Without pretending to provide an exhaustive answer to this question, we can trace, to an extent, the way in which art prepares food for the intellect and will.

First, the Muses function on the experiential level, as Senior had explained already while still a young instructor at Hofstra:

> We have been careful to make a distinction between art and science.... It is chiefly the difference between thinking about experience and having the experience itself. It is the business of the poet to communicate "experience" to the reader—to present things as they are, not as they can be explained. The scientist talks about a tree in terms of the function of its parts; he can describe, but he cannot present directly. The poet, by instigating the imagination of the reader can present the tree itself, as it were, in all its palpable, living growing, green being.[35]

Art serves to help us experience reality. Senior said that it operates like oil, which makes leather more flexible and receptive; that is, art lets reality better accomplish its work in us. It intensifies experience by developing our attention and spontaneous reactions. He writes:

> Just as we can enlarge our capacity to think by exercise in the various scientific disciplines . . . we can enlarge our capacity to feel by participation in the experience of art. The poet is the man who says "Look! Look! You never saw that before." And if you follow him, you will see much more than you would have seen by yourself. In doing so, you have enlarged your capacity to experience the world, which is another way of saying to live.[36]

Of course, art in itself is not a direct experience of the thing in view, but a representation or imitation of that thing. It is a vicarious experience, but not photographically so. Since art is an experience lived out in the

imagination, an expression of that experience, it can accentuate particular facets of an event or object, singling out certain meaningful aspects as intended. Senior writes of a poet whom he considered to be the best of the twentieth century: "[Thomas] Hardy believed the essential poetic act is precisely to notice—not *any* things, the way the naturalist writers do, piling up insignificant and especially ugly detail, but *such* things, the significant ones that point, like signs."[37]

In this vein, Aristotle distinguishes history from poetry, even when written in verse: "Poetry is something more philosophical and of graver import than history, since its statements are of the nature of universals, whereas those of history are singulars."[38] The inference is that philosophy deals with the universal as universal. History simply tells and explains what happened at a specific point in time, whereas poetry deals with universals as seen and expressed in particulars.

Senior, paraphrasing Aristotle, writes, "[Poetry is] a way of knowing universals in *particulars*."[39] And elsewhere: "Literature by definition is that paradoxical thing—the 'concrete universal.'"[40] The artist is someone who knows how to speak on the experiential level—about a passing, singular event—while giving us an impression of something beyond the individual, suggesting a meaning of permanent and universal value. A poem about a loving father should give us insight on what it is to be a father. A story of a faithful wife teaches us about fidelity and even about the mystery of womanhood.

Art's special contribution, then, lies precisely in the fact that it presents a universal in embodied form. This does not mean that art is simply allegorical, pointing directly to this or that idea, or filled with actors who have speeches where they discuss universals. The story, or the poem or the statue, takes us inside a singular experience, inside a particular human heart, while also leading us beyond, toward a mystery of universal significance. Art reveals a value as it really exists. The sensible and emotional are in this way ordered, ennobled, lifted up to spiritual realms. Inversely, such art guides the mind in perceiving and loving spiritual values present in our sensible experience. Thus, the Muses help the interior sensible faculties and emotions fulfill their role

as intermediaries between a man's exterior senses and his mind. They indeed awaken and nourish the intellect.

To stimulate the proper respect and attraction for these spiritual values, art works through their beauty as incarnated in some singular. When Senior says that before his conversion he had sought beauty rather than truth, he alludes to Baudelaire's affirmation that beauty alone is the goal of art, beauty for beauty's sake, an aspect of art for art's sake. Thus, pure aestheticism boils down to sensations, to feelings. After his conversion, Senior defines beauty in a traditional, realist way that points beyond senses: "Formal beauty is a certain *splendor*, a shining forth of form indirectly visible in matter."[41] In viewing a horse, for example, one does not see its "form," that is, its essence, its properties; one sees the proportion and grace that manifest its essence.

Consequently, art should not be aimed at presenting beauty cut off from *being* and truth—which would be like offering flavoring without food, sauce without the meat. Rather, art should resemble seasoning that brings forth the food's natural flavor. Good art emphasizes beautiful features with the purpose of teaching us to perceive and savor more intensely the riches of reality. It cultivates the proper love of beauty as manifesting real values.

Renewing our vision of reality in order to fully partake of what "really is" is the underlying theme behind G. K. Chesterton's writings. In the following, he explains how fantasy stimulates a craving for the marvelous and the new, whereas a healthy imagination—and therefore good art—highlights beautiful mysteries in our experience; it helps one recognize the extraordinary in the ordinary:

> By the cheap revolutionary it is commonly supposed that imagination is a merely rebellious thing that has its chief function in devising new and fantastic republics. But imagination has its highest use in retrospective realization. . . . The function of the imagination is not to make strange things settled, so much as to make settled things strange, not so much to make wonders facts as to make facts wonders.[42]

Real marvels found in this world and the art that reveals them point beyond this visible world. Senior liked the idea that the word "music" comes from the same root as do mystery and mute, namely from the Indo-European *mu*, meaning silence. He writes in this vein that "music . . . is the song of things whose voices articulate the silent work of angels."[43] There is, as it were, a silence behind the world, something not less than human words but more so; something continually, but never totally, expressed that musical education brings out and helps us hear. Music, or poetry, thus leads us to wonder about the depths of reality. It teaches us to be silent so that we may listen to reality's deeper voice and receive its message. "[Poetry's] zeal is an alert idleness, such as lovers who watch and wait, listening for the footsteps of the beloved."[44] Music can form in us the healthy gaze on this world that Senior describes in his poem "Contemptus Mundi," one that recognizes the value of the world but always in relation to what transcends it and is alone adequate to man's dignity and calling:

> Two ways to make contemptible
> the world: the first is not to look;
> the second and more sensible,
> to read it like a book,
> to learn the grammar and the word,
> loving not the less but more,
> contemning it as music heard
> supersedes the score.

The Muses and Teenagers

The culture of the imagination and emotions is necessary to all as a condition and exercise for an ordered love. As Senior puts it: "No matter what our expertise, no matter what we are by vocation or trade, we are all lovers; and while only the experts in each field must know mathematics and the sciences and other arts, everyone must be a poet."[45] Teenagers especially should be lovers and poets. Musical education should normally be the focus for the teenage years.

Indeed, something new happens in the early teens. Young teenagers should already have a store of memories and be capable of a disciplined exercise of the imagination, but the striking and most characteristic feature of these years is the new array of emotions arising around the attraction to the opposite sex. New desires and hopes spring up; new joys, often new sadness and fears, appear. One becomes more self-conscious, more interior, more sensitive. It is crucial to attune these bubbling passions to authentic values. Plato and Aristotle both conclude that because young people live almost totally on the level of their imagination and emotions, education should attract them to the true and the good through sensible beauty. Music, Plato writes, will "insensibly guide youth to likeness, to friendship, to harmony with beautiful reason."[46]

A sort of love is obviously involved in these youthful emotions, but if wonder is the proper goal of music, how does it fit in? Senior indicates in a poem entitled "Know Thyself" that somehow wonder, in the case of a boy, is linked to the thirteen-year-old's novel perception of girls:

When you're twelve you never wonder,
then one Summer, turn thirteen.
The blue-eyed girls get blonder
and the brown ones keen.[47]

Senior does not develop this theme, but we can turn again to Allan Bloom for some assistance. First, Bloom identifies an obvious difference between men and animals that points to the proper path for education:

In all species other than man, when an animal reaches puberty, it is all that it will ever be. . . . Only in man is puberty just the beginning. The greater and more interesting part of his learning, moral and intellectual, comes afterward. . . . We properly sense that there is a long road to adulthood, the condition in which [human beings] are able to govern themselves and be true mothers and fathers.

This road is the serious part of education, where animal sexuality becomes human sexuality, where instinct gives way in man to

167

choice with regard to the true, the good and the beautiful. . . . This means that the animal part of his sexuality is intertwined in the most complex way with the higher reaches of his soul, which must inform the desires with its insight.[48]

How is sexuality "intertwined" with the spiritual faculties? Bloom explains why awakening attraction to girls generates wonder: "[*Eros*] is the proof, subjective but incontrovertible, of man's relatedness, imperfect though it may be, to others and to the whole of nature. Wonder, the source of both poetry and philosophy, is its characteristic expression. . . . This longing for completeness is the longing for education."[49] *Eros* is not merely the sexual instinct; it is the "longing for completeness," a desire for fulfillment. It is indeed stimulated by the sexual instinct because the strange new yearnings in a youth's soul impress on him the awareness of his relatedness. Wonder, "its characteristic expression," arises as he discovers how much girls and many other things correspond to him and he to them, and how much he needs them. Not only do "the brown ones" become "keen" with this awakening sensitivity, so do personal relationships in general; so does "the whole of nature"—the stars, the rainbows, the sunrise, the very fact of existence. The adolescent wants to learn and to enter more deeply into relation with these realities that mysteriously call to him. Thus, his sexuality should transcend itself and lead him to wonder.

Senior indeed proposes not only delight but also *eros* as the end of gymnastic and thus as the preparation for wonder.[50] The task of music therefore is to cultivate delight and *eros* so they blossom into wonder at mysteries and an appropriate love of beauty. Music should channel these passions toward the true and the good—"to harmony with beautiful reason," as Plato says—so they become what Senior calls "a virtuous energy."[51] Thus, a boy who reads *Ivanhoe* will, hopefully, desire to be courageous, generous, respectful and chivalrous. His instinctive drives become educated as he is attuned to the beauty of these virtues. He discovers resources in his soul that enable him to respond to high callings.

It is usually during the teen years that the spiritual first knocks at the door of the heart. Yet, the sensual domain is especially noisy and absorbing

at that time as well. Those who immerse themselves in sensuality and fantasy—sex, drugs, electronic music—experience a premature, superficial ecstasy and can scarcely hear the calmer, deeper attractions of the spiritual world or of true love above the clamor of artificiality. If this immersion lasts a long time, these young minds might forfeit the capacity to wonder. Among so many youth who should be filled with enthusiasm, hope and desire, one finds already the Modernist *ennui*, made up of restlessness, disgust and despair. The consequence is an epidemic of listlessness among today's teenagers.

As Senior understood, it is vital that both gymnastic and music be restored if we are to capture again the reverential, loving gaze to which reality's secrets are revealed. We all must learn to love the true, the good and the beautiful; and music—built on healthy gymnastic, on *eros* and delight in existence—is the language and exercise of this love. Before going on to Senior's advice on practical applications of gymnastic and music today, it would be profitable to elaborate a point of a more speculative nature on which he often touched, namely, the type of knowledge particularly involved at the musical or poetic level. This study will help us grasp in some depth the importance of gymnastic and music for the restoration of Realism.

CHAPTER NINE

The Poetic Mode
of Knowledge

Oh, poetry is pretty stuff, they say, but in this des-
perate war, idle pleasure must be sacrificed for the
survival of civilization and the Church. Well, sol-
diers without poetry are gangsters, hired guns, blind
means with neither love nor knowledge of the end,
who never will achieve the end because the End is
Truth, not a concept but three Persons only known
in beauty both on earth and as it is in Heaven.

—"The Restoration of Innocence"

IN the preceding chapter we recognized that modern man must
first relearn how to look at the world in a musical or poetic
manner in order to renew his wonder about existence. In the present
chapter, we will consider more closely the type of knowledge engaged
in that look, which Senior calls the "poetic mode." He could have used
the term "musical mode" to designate the very same thing, since the
second step in education operates according to this type. But the matter of knowledge at this level is usually discussed by St. Thomas and
others in the context of poetry as figurative speech, in contrast to
straightforward prose; and so it is called the poetic mode. When he
uses this expression, however, Senior is not referring primarily to an
ability to write poems or even to understand them. Nor does he have
in mind a knowledge that is distinctive to artists or aesthetes. As he
uses the term, the poetic mode describes an ordinary way of knowing,

exercised by all men, although cultivated especially in poetry and art. He classifies the poetic mode as one of the main forms of human knowledge. By the habit of this mode of knowledge, one will not be glued to the surface with the Empiricists, nor fixed more deeply to theoretical ideas with the Rationalists, nor, in an effort to penetrate further, focused on emotions apart from the intellect with the Romantics. One needs the poetic mode in order to go beyond all that and reach a full Realism. For Senior, the restoration of Realism consists especially in the restoration of the poetic mode.

From his youth, Senior knew the value of insights gained through literature, poetry, music and art. His teachers at Columbia refined and developed this awareness. He read the Romantics who, in face of Rationalism, had begun some reflection on the need for using the imagination and emotions to penetrate the mysteries of this world. He was familiar with the Symbolists' theories and with other modern ideas on artistic types of knowledge. Newman's considerations on nonscientific, nonphilosophic knowledge that can neither be proved nor clearly understood impressed on Senior the importance of using different modes of thinking in different domains, as well as the possibility of a poetic type of certitude. His growing awareness of the importance of gymnastic and music led Senior to investigate more precisely the ways by which one knows in the first steps of education. For this he turned to Plato, Aristotle and St. Thomas. He also made use of the work of a modern who had preceded him on this path of investigation, Jacques Maritain. Senior thus collected from various authors, but the result of his work was a unique synthesis of the types of knowledge and a unique view on the characteristics and importance of the poetic mode.

Although Senior taught continually and marvelously in this mode and often spoke about it, he never thoroughly elucidated it. He provided a few simple ideas, principles that sufficed for his immediate purposes. Using the few texts of his that we have, we will try to better understand what this mode is and what is its pertinence to Realism, education and culture.*

---

* See a book issued from the doctoral dissertation of a former student of Senior: James Taylor, *Poetic Mode of Knowledge: The Recovery of Education* (Albany, NY: State University of New York Press, 1998).

The Four Modes of Knowledge

Senior classifies the poetic mode as one of four degrees or types of knowledge, the others being science, dialectic and rhetoric.* He says that "the ancients distinguished" these types.[1] Among "the ancients," however, one does not find a strong, clear doctrine of the four modes as Senior presents them.† Senior takes the names of the four modes from Aristotle, who writes abundantly about science, dialectic and rhetoric but primarily as three types of arguments rather than directly as modes of knowledge. Aristotle also deals with poetics or drama, musical education and experiential knowledge, all of which concern our subject. St. Thomas was perhaps the first to use the expression "poetic knowledge," a mode that he mentioned a few times, as we will see. In the introduction to his commentary on Aristotle's *Posterior Analytics*, St. Thomas organizes several of Aristotle's treatises around four degrees of certitude, which have become classical in scholastic manuals and which may have been Senior's immediate source in this classification of four types of knowledge. In any case, Senior organizes the four types of knowledge into a whole in a way that had not been done before, most notably adding his own development on the poetic mode. In order to better situate the poetic mode we will first examine all four modes of knowledge.

Like St. Thomas and others in the scholastic tradition, Senior follows the Aristotelian definition of *science* as "the grasp by the intellect of absolutely certain truths understood in their causes."[2] Arguments on that level lead "to perfect, absolute knowledge . . . beyond not only reasonable but any doubt."[3] One rarely achieves such a clear possession of facts and truths. Ordinary life consists largely of probabilities and presentiments, or of certitudes that cannot be reduced to evidence. Aristotle recognizes that there must be different modes to be used in different domains: "It is the

---

* For Senior's presentation of the modes, see *Restoration of CC*, 194–195, "The Restoration of Innocence," 28; and "History and the School," 2. "Apologia Poetica," 10, gives a version of the *Restoration of Innocence* text.

† Plato distinguished four degrees of knowledge, which correspond roughly to Senior's four modes. His first degree penetrated to the very principles of things—we would call it metaphysics. His second degree accepted its principles without judging them, which coincides with other philosophical and scientific domains, and especially mathematics. His third degree concerned this world always in movement, about which, according to Plato, we can only have opinions. We will quote him on the fourth degree, which Senior called the poetic mode (*The Republic* VI, 511).

mark of an educated man to look for precision in each class of things just so far as the nature of the subject admits; it is equally foolish to accept probable reasoning from a mathematician and to demand from a rhetorician scientific proof."[4]

In the Aristotelian tradition, *dialectic* is understood primarily as an argument based on principles that are not absolutely sure, where one investigates the truth of opinions or one tests a hypothesis. But the term also aptly applies to a particular mode of knowledge. Although dialectic does not, strictly speaking, exclude another possible solution, it can nevertheless provide sufficient reason or objective evidence to allow for a conclusion beyond reasonable doubt. We may not understand all the details and the causes, but evidence and arguments are enough, testimonies converge sufficiently, for one to form a convinced and prudent judgment. To exemplify this, Senior refers to courts of law and laboratories, where science, in the strong, Aristotelian sense, is usually not possible. "In some cases," he writes, "we can marshal evidence by rigorous control sufficient to execute a criminal or certify a drug."[5] Senior and others considered that conclusions arrived at by modern experimental science are usually dialectic rather than scientific in the ancient sense of the word.[6] Newman's notion of converging probabilities—such as several witnesses none of which is alone a compelling proof but as a group elicits conviction—fits into this category.

Rhetoric is the art of persuasion. Of the four types distinguished by Senior, rhetoric emerges the least in Aristotle as a particular mode of knowledge. The Greek philosopher envisions it as an art that uses dialectic and poetry, logic and emotion. Nevertheless, the term can apply well to cases where, Senior explains, "evidence can't be exercised under rigorously controlled circumstances, so decisions must include doubts."[7] For Senior, rhetoric *as knowledge* applies "to what is characteristically or generally true."[8] Here one is squarely in the realm of opinions. This is the mode of knowledge we must turn to notably in political or business decisions when we are not sure which candidate will be best for the country or which possible venture will provide the most profit. Senior writes that "we think a candidate or policy is good, admitting that, because there

are so many variables, we may be wrong."[9] Since ideas and evidence are insufficient to impose a conclusion in the particular case, the goal of the *art* of rhetoric is to win the listener over.

In these three modes—science, dialectic and rhetoric—evidence and ideas are used to reach a conclusion. In the poetic mode, by contrast, it is images that come into play—stories, songs, dance, sculpture—as the means of knowing. Plato calls the fourth mode "picture-thinking."[10] One forms a sort of judgment by putting together images rather than reasoning with ideas. Senior illustrated this way of knowing as follows:

> The essence of poetic reasoning is *metaphor*, a knowledge by comparison, a moving from the known to the unknown by likeness.
> My love is like a red, red rose
> That's newly sprung in June . . .
> If you have seen June roses spring up, you can imagine (and therefore know) something of what my beloved is like.[11]

St. Thomas explains that this type of knowledge inclines a person to one side of the argument, not by an idea, but by its manner of representation.[12] He uses the example of a man who turns away from certain foods if they are described in disgusting terms. He, like Plato and Aristotle, claims that the poet's special task is to lead people to virtue by attractive descriptions of the moral good.

Nevertheless, the intellect is obviously still involved in poetry and the arts, even if in this case it works through images and emotions rather than by outlining clear ideas or explanations. Plato told stories and myths to get across deep philosophical points. Aristotle discourses on the universal present in poetic narrations. We will soon see how St. Thomas speaks of the need for images in theology, which can make something known even if obscurely. We have here a very human type of knowledge in that it integrates senses, emotions, will and intellect.

By way of summary, we can use the concept of "courage" to illustrate and contrast the four modes of knowledge. The philosopher—the "scientist" for Aristotle—would perhaps define courage and compare it to other

virtues; a dialectician would probably discuss and investigate some controversial point—for example, what the greatest form of courage is; the rhetorician might try to persuade others to embrace his opinion on what courage normally requires in a given situation; and a poet would most likely tell a story of a courageous man to instill in his listeners a sense of what courage is and to inspire them to emulation.

This distinction between modes is of fundamental importance to Senior. He uses them here, in tracing the demise of modern culture:

> The revolution in thought at the Renaissance was an attack on science in the ancient sense. Principles were reduced to "assumptions." . . . Experimental scientists limited knowledge to dialectic. Enlightenment philosophers elevated rhetorical opinion to the status of absolute truth and absolute truth to relative (that is rhetorical) opinion. Romantic poets claimed poetic truth as absolute, and finally, modernistic phenomenologists denying man can know at all, reduced all four modes of knowledge to sensation. Tranquility among these wrangling partisans can only be restored by order.[13]

As described, in each instance one of the modes has been selectively hypertrophied and universalized, whereas all four are complementary and mutually enlightening, even while each has its own domain. Science works with absolute evidence, dialectic with enough evidence, rhetoric with some, and poetry rather with indirect glimpses without evidence. All these modes have to be restored to their proper domain and order, so that their complementarity can operate. The poetic mode, functioning closely to experience, forms the ground necessary for the other modes. As first things come first, what, more precisely, is the poetic mode?

Characteristics of the Poetic Mode

Senior has various ways of characterizing the poetic mode. It is an experiential, emotional, intuitive and connatural knowledge.

It is, first, a "knowledge of experience"[14] because it operates at the level of the singular rather than of the universal. Senior applies Aristotle's description of the type of knowledge gained by accumulated experience, as opposed to science or technical knowledge.[15] Aristotle explains that through repetition of experiences, a person acquires the habit of a particular domain. That person's memory renders him capable of an instinctive judgment in that domain but without necessarily understanding general laws. A carpenter, for example, has a very accurate sense of different types of wood, or a baseball player knows by savvy how to hit a curve ball.

Nevertheless, perhaps neither one is able to explain his skill to others for lack of a universal concept. He can only show how to work the wood or swing the bat so that others can imitate him. These are men of experience, not of science or of even technical understanding.

Such knowledge is quite genuine, even if it unfolds on the level of images and is thus difficult to articulate. Senior liked to illustrate that point by discussing a scene in Dickens's *Hard Times* in which Sissy Jupe, daughter of a horse-trainer, is asked in school to explain what a horse is.[16]

She does not know what to say. Billy Bitzer, who had rarely seen a horse, proclaims, "Quadruped. Graminivorous. Forty teeth, namely, twenty-four grinders, four eye teeth and twelve incisors. Sheds coat in spring, in marshy countries sheds hoofs too." Professor Gradgrind turns back to Sissy: "Now, student number twenty, you know what a horse is." Of course it is Sissy who truly knows horses and in a way that theoretical knowledge was unable to replace.

Bitzer's definition, though technically true, cannot help him with the task of training a horse.

The poetic mode is also "knowledge by emotion."[17] Sissy's affection for horses is presented by Dickens as a crucial part of her experiential link with them. Senior often gave the example of the instinctive fear a lamb has when it sees a wolf and thus recognizes its enemy. We should indeed experience fear, delight or desire when confronted by certain objects; our reaction is part of an experiential understanding of them. Particularly

through a certain affective union with another, one begins to think and feel like the other, one knows the other from inside.

In poetic knowledge, "truths are grasped intuitively."[18] That is, one directly recognizes something. The carpenter, the baseball player and Sissy do not arrive at conclusions through pro and con arguments; rather, they know by an acquired feel for their object. This is exemplified, as Senior points out, "when you trust another's love."[19] By instinct, a man knows his beloved's heart, although he cannot prove she will be faithful, nor can he perhaps even explain in clear terms why he trusts her. This recognition can be intuitive because, Senior wrote, it is a "connatural knowledge . . . where one participates in the being of another."[20] Stemming from one's having a like nature with the object, this knowledge consists in "feeling like the object (in sympathy with it) as if it were ourselves."[21] Senior proposes an apt example from common experience: "Poetic knowledge [that is, connatural knowledge] can be seen in play when a child imitates, for example, the movements and sounds of a horse in such a way that he becomes the horse through his imagination. . . . From a scientific point of view, this knowledge of the horse is not very precise; but from the poetic position it is a knowledge more real than the scientific due to its vicarious experience of the object."[22]

Senior draws upon St. Thomas and Aristotle for this notion of connaturality. For St. Thomas the term *connatural* alludes first of all to anything proportioned to a given nature. Thus the connatural object of human knowledge is not the purely spiritual but the essence of sensible things. St. Thomas also writes of an acquired connaturality, used notably in prudential judgments where one has gained a certain sense of what is the proper moral action. He explains that "correct judgment can come about in two ways: through the perfect use of reason or through a certain connaturality with the thing. For example, in matters of chastity . . . whoever possesses the virtue of chastity can judge correctly through a kind of connaturality."[23] A chaste person can judge by instinct the appropriate chaste action in a particular case without having recourse to detailed reasoning. He has a certain sympathetic, intimate knowledge of things chaste.

Maritain was the first to transpose into a philosophy of art what St. Thomas says concerning intuitive, prudential judgments. Maritain defines "[the artist's] intuition, the creative intuition or emotion" as "an obscure grasping of the self and things together in a knowledge by union or by connaturality."[24] Especially by our affections we are united to the other and so find the other in ourselves. It is thus knowledge "by mode of resonance,"[25] he writes, where one feels the echo of the other in one's sensitivity and emotions. Because of this union, we come to the other from the inside, as it were, in an "intercommunication between the inner being of things and the inner being of the human self which is a kind of divination."[26]

Senior recommended reading Maritain on this subject as the only modern philosopher to have understood poetic knowledge. We should, however, note two differences. Maritain insists on the subjectivity of this knowledge, on its being a self-expression, which led him in some measure to esteem Modernist art, which Senior, being more objective, does not. More important for our purposes, Maritain affirms that such an intuitive experience is reserved to the artist because it is essentially operative. It needs to bear fruit in some sort of imaged or symbolic reproduction or metaphor, because it cannot be appropriately grasped in concepts. Senior, on the contrary, does not even mention poetry, strictly speaking, in any of the above descriptions of the poetic mode; in fact, he mentioned no specific form of art at all. For him, the poetic mode of knowledge is quite extensive, ranging from a knowledge of the gymnastic order—as was Sissy Jupe's and the carpenter's experiential habits of horses and wood—to a lover's intuition of the beloved.

Through accumulated experience as well as through their affection, the chaste man, Sissy Jupe, the lover, the baseball player and the carpenter have become akin to their object and have a feel for it that is second nature to them.

Although connatural intuition through the sensible is fundamentally the same for all types of people, it is, no doubt, especially intense with artists. Moreover, artists are the best able to express it, to communicate it to others. The artist is someone who knows how to stimulate in us the

same view he has: "Poems are instruments by which the art in the artist becomes art in the reader so that he sees as the poet did."[27] Senior explains the mechanism: "Through signs, suggestions and sensuous intimates, connatural knowledge is achieved where one participates in the being of another, 'becomes' the other, in representation, metaphor and play."[28] The picture, metaphor, or some other form of imitation, leads to a connaturality with the object, bringing about an experiential, emotional, sympathetic and intuitive knowledge. In reading *Ivanhoe*, one imaginatively and emotionally lives the knight's adventure as if it were one's own. Music and the arts only resonate when there is prior intuitive experience. When Wordsworth tells us his heart leaps up at the rainbow's beauty, he recalls an experience we all have had; he stimulates a correspondence to beauty each one of us finds in himself, without which the poem or a work of art could not have its effect. The arts nourish connaturality and underline beauty, and thus can assist us in perceiving or feeling the mystery.

The Poetic Mode and Mysteries

Senior arranges the four modes of knowledge—poetic, rhetoric, dialectic, and science—in pyramid fashion, placing science at the top as the clearest and having the fewest objects. He places the poetic mode at the base because, firstly, it is the most frequently used and contains the broadest number of objects; secondly, it is the least clear and has the weakest grip on its object; thirdly, since it operates on the individual level and provides contact with concrete reality, it is a prerequisite for the abstract thought inherent in the other modes: "Rhetoric, dialectic and science, like the upper sections of a pyramid, depend upon the base."[29] These three draw from the experiential, intuitive mode for their universal ideas.

At the same time, Senior also affirms that from another point of view the poetic mode soars higher than the other three. He writes: "St. Thomas calls poetry *scientia infima* because it is lowest in the scale of abstraction, furthest from the intellect and therefore from angels and God. Per se it is *infima*, but *quoad nos* . . . poetry is higher than science."[30] St. Thomas is in agreement with Plato and the whole classical tradition that poetry is

scientia infima—"the lowest knowledge"—because it uses images instead of ideas.*[31] But the great theologian recognizes the importance of the sensible *quoad nos*—"in relation to us." Although spiritual realities are of themselves more intelligible than sensible things, the sensible world is more present to us so that we know the spiritual in and through the sensible.[32] Senior wants to underline that, although the invisible is higher in itself and more intelligible, we incarnate spirits must approach it through the visible, and that poetry is a proper means for this.

Senior affirms that the poetic mode is not only a necessary instrument for us, but precisely because it operates on the experiential level, it is somehow higher than the other three modes. A difficult passage elucidates how this may be: "Obvious fact has no argument because all arguments are based on it (and the principles of reason which can't be argued either). That's why poets who present reality are better than lawyers at expressing mysteries."[33] By "lawyer" Senior refers to the dialectic and probably rhetorical modes, but his words can be applied to the scientific or philosophical mode as well. He affirms that poetry deals with the obvious and for this reason expresses mysteries better than the other modes do. That is a deliberately paradoxical statement because it would seem rather that something is mysterious for the very reason that it is not obvious, that it is hidden and out of the reach of experience.

To begin to understand why mysteries are better expressed by the obvious, we need to distinguish *mysteries* from *problems*. We can say that a problem is something that can be resolved, as when one finds a solution for an algebra equation or for why the earth has become hotter since the last ice age. Something is at first hidden, then the argument brings it into the open, unfolds what was implicit. One sees clearly and finds the solution—the explanation—so that the problem no longer exists.

Senior sometimes would quote a passage by Blessed Cardinal Newman contrasting modern science and poetry, which included these words specifically on problem resolution: "Reason investigates, analyzes, numbers, weighs, measures, ascertains, locates the objects of its contemplation

---

* The exact expression concerning poetry was *infima doctrina* but St. Thomas did of course refer to theology as *scientia*.

181

and thus gains a scientific knowledge of them. . . . The aim of science is to get a hold of things, to grasp them, to handle them, to comprehend them; that is (to use the familiar term), to *master* them, to be superior to them."[34] This scientific attitude also encompasses the dialectic and even the rhetoric mode as Senior presents them: they too deal with reason to analyze and try to grasp.

Such an effort at clarity, solution and mastery is useful in many domains, but all knowledge cannot be reduced to clear ideas and problem resolution; reality cannot be reduced to something reason can fully comprehend. Senior writes that "to most of life's grave issues, science, dialectic and rhetoric are blind; their reasons cannot penetrate to mysteries like love and war, or why a sinner hopes for his redemption."[35] Mystery can be described as those aspects or depths of reality that can never be brought completely out into the open and done away with as with a resolved problem. We will never get to the bottom of a mystery, never figure it out completely.

Yet, Senior observes that the mystery was in the "obvious fact"; love, defending our country, and hope are part of ordinary life. G. K. Chesterton marks the paradox: "I think there is a mystical mission in human history and experience which is at once too obscure to be explained and too obvious to be explained away, like the sun."[36] A mystery is something at once obscure and obvious, like the sun, which is obviously present but upon which our eyes cannot focus. Chesterton was doubtless thinking of a well-known image that Aristotle and St. Thomas use: before the highest truths, they said, men are like owls or bats looking at the sun.[37] There are great truths present in ordinary and obvious things, but which are too bright for our weak eyes.

This is not to say that reasonings proper to the first three modes of knowledge cannot be used in reference to a mystery, but, in this case, they rather serve to investigate problems involved in the mystery. The scientist asks how much upbringing influences a person's activity but his findings do not explain why a human being finds joy in giving himself in love, why a soldier dies willingly for his friends in war, why someone trusts in God. The scientist studies how the stars emit light, or why light refracts in the rainbow, but scientific considerations leave intact the stars' and the rainbow's beauty

as such, and the reason they appeal to us. Mysteries cannot be closed up in a finite idea, packed neatly away into some scientific box.

Philosophy deals more directly with mysteries such as love and beauty than experimental science is capable of. It tries to understand what they are, bringing into clarity what is possible through analysis, concepts and arguments. It presupposes the base of the pyramid; it must accept some sort of intuition, an obvious although obscure knowledge, before it operates on its level to resolve problems. One must first recognize that the rainbow is beautiful before being in a position to ask how and why it is so, and what beauty is. St. Thomas's definition of beauty as "what, when seen, pleases"[38] means nothing to us unless we have had the experience of a rainbow, of a mountain or of a river.

How then is the poetic mode apt for this knowledge of mysteries? First, it remains at the experiential level, with the "obvious fact," wherein is found the mystery that cannot be drawn out in an idea. The reality of beauty is in a rainbow, and the reality of love, in the relation between a particular man and his particular wife. Senior writes: "Short of intellect, which by abstraction isolates the intelligible content of reality, imagination is a way of knowing universals in particulars, at once a prerequisite to intellection and a great, subsisting good in itself as the only way mysteries can be intimately known, not as abstracted universals but particular things."[39]

Second, the poetic mode differs from the other three modes in its stance toward the object. Of itself, it does not seek the cause, it does not search for clarity. The poetic approach is satisfied with a sure presence even if it cannot prove it. It realistically accepts a certitude that it cannot comprehend, as Chesterton illustrates: "Poetry is sane because it floats easily in an infinite sea, reason seeks to cross the infinite sea and so make it finite . . . The poet only desires exaltation and expansion, a world to stretch himself in. The poet only asks to get his head into the heavens. It is the logician who seeks to get the heavens into his head."[40] In the continuation of his text on science, Newman tells us that this humble, accepting attitude is indeed more appropriate than the analytic and dominating scientific approach for gazing toward things higher and greater than oneself:

[Poetry] demands, as its primary condition, that we should not put ourselves above the objects in which it resides, but at their feet; that we should feel them to be above and beyond us, that we should look up to them and that, instead of fancying that we can comprehend them, we should take for granted that we are surrounded and comprehended by them ourselves.... It implies that we understand them to be vast, immeasurable, impenetrable, inscrutable, mysterious.[41]

Third and finally, it can give us our fundamental, experiential knowledge of mysteries because it is based, not on ideas, but on connaturality, on sympathy, on a feeling of correspondence. Chesterton says that man has a "mystical mission" for obvious and obscure values. A dog that enters a beautiful church experiences no wonder, no reverent fear and desire, not because it is above the beauty and sacredness of the place but because it is so distant from them that it has no relationship to them. A human being, on the contrary, is normally respectful when he enters a church because he attains to something the dog does not. Likewise, the man, but not the dog, on seeing a beautiful sunset, hearing of a courageous deed or witnessing an attestation of love, wonders in reverence; the spiritual world shining through the material speaks to his soul and beckons him. He has a poetic—experiential, emotional and connatural—intuition. He is awakened to a deeper part of his soul and obscurely perceives that he is part of a whole. He recognizes the mystery and is drawn to it because he participates in it. That is why uncultivated but upright folk often have a more authentic sense of great truths than many scholars do. Their habitual response to the primal call of truth, goodness and beauty has attuned them to these values.

The great mysteries—the true, the good and the beautiful, as well as our personal response to them in knowing and loving—are simply aspects, different faces of *being*. *Being* is the fundamental mystery for all philosophy. Here it will be helpful to apply the poetic mode of knowledge to our recognition of *being*. This consideration will bring us back to the foundations of Realism.

*The Poetic Mode and Being**

Senior told one of his students: "Our most immediate brush with metaphysical knowledge is that of *being*, where we intuitively know that something *is* due to our experience of *being*. This certitude continues as it is seen that other things share in this being—trees, dogs, cats—and that the cat and ourselves are alike in that both participate in being."[42] We see that the qualities of the poetic mode which Senior champions apply to this recognition of *being*. He speaks of an intuitive experience. We have already seen how the recognition of the existent is the very first principle, preceding any reasoning. One instinctively and immediately knows that the reality one experiences exists, that it is really real. Senior also implies here that our awareness of *being* is connatural. We recognize our common participation in *being* with cats and dogs and trees. It is by means of an awareness of our own existence that we have a sense of another's existence.

What about emotion? *Being* as such does not strike us in the same way as beauty does. We are not moved to write a poem about *being* as such. Yet, if *being* is truly a mystery, it should awaken reverence and awe in us. As we have pointed out, it does have the traits of mystery: *being* is obvious, the most obvious, but is also obscure. In fact, all of the monumental effort undertaken by philosophy is ultimately directed to simply knowing what *being* is. We will never fully understand *being* before we see God Himself, absolute and pure Being. But we also participate in *being*, Senior says. We know it as something greater than ourselves and we are a part that needs relation to that whole; we are drawn to a greater participation. Consequently, *being* should touch us; that things exist should strike us more than anything else in the natural order. We are so accustomed to things, however, and so utilitarian in our approach to them, that we do not marvel at the fact that they exist. Existence is taken for granted, without our paying much attention to it until some aspect of being, such as beauty, awakens us to wonder anew at it.

---

* A student of Senior's wrote his dissertation on Chesterton's Realism as a preparation for philosophy and emphasized a theme very pertinent to this matter, that of wonder and the primary experience of being. See Randall Paine, *The Universe and Mr. Chesterton* (Peru, Illinois: Sherwood Sugden and Company, 1999).

Behind the beautiful, it is indeed *being* that is beckoning to us. Beauty, the splendor of the form, strikes us because it is a manifestation of a deeper reality: the riches of *being*. The function of gymnastic, and particularly music, building on it is to cultivate delight in things and a wonder at their beauty, and thus awaken us to the mystery of *being*, refreshing our gaze. Poems, songs and stories do not formally speak of *being*, but through individual existents, through aspects of beauty, love and goodness, they stimulate and nourish our amazement at existence itself.

We have mentioned that science presupposes poetry. The highest natural science, metaphysics or the study of *being* as such, clarifies and develops elements that are implicitly present in the poetic recognition of *being*. Philosophers presume insight into *being* at the basis of their study, without, of course, formally mentioning the poetic mode. Discussing the philosophy of St. Thomas, Etienne Gilson expresses the paradox of knowing and talking about something that is perceived in our experience but is beyond concepts and cannot be objectified in an abstract idea: "What characterizes Thomism is the decision to locate actual existence in the heart of reality as an act transcending any kind of quiddative concept and, at the same time, avoiding the double error of remaining dumb before its transcendence or of denaturing it in objectifying it."[43]

Likewise, Joseph Rassam insists that the philosopher must put aside the tendency to abstract in order to listen to the mystery of *being*: "To attune ourselves to *being*, thought must renounce its power of separation, its ways of abstracting, dividing and simplifying. Metaphysical reflection must deliberately accept this defeat of a kind of thought that hurries to define and prove, because the metaphysical sense proceeds from an attention which is docility to what things suggest by their presence."[44] Basing himself on this primordial and obscure poetic view, the philosopher pursues in a scientific manner the meaning of existence, the secrets of *being*.

The Poetic Mode and the Supernatural

In his works, Senior often points to a relationship between the poetic mode and the supernatural life. He writes, for example, "Poetic knowledge

isn't admissible evidence in laboratories and law courts . . . but is prerequisite for Heaven."[45] In other words, poetic intuition is insufficient if used in the place of dialectic reasoning to convict a criminal or verify the safety of a drug, but it is required as a condition, or is even the basis, for the supernatural life. Senior summarizes the principle: "Since grace perfects nature, Revelation presupposes poetry."[46] The supernatural builds on nature. However, fallen human nature requires the aid of the poetic mode of knowledge to be malleable to the supernatural. There are different aspects to this operation, which we will briefly examine.

As we have noted, knowledge and love of the true, the good, the beautiful and of *being* stem from a poetic recognition. We also know that these values direct us toward knowledge and love of the First Truth, Supreme Goodness, Pure Beauty and Absolute Being. Thus, the first élan toward God in the natural order is in the poetic mode. Senior teaches that when beauty stirs up reverential fear and desire in us, it is God Himself who touches us: "Through wonder, Christ teaches us at the center of the soul."[47] The world is a poem wherein not only *being* but He-Who-Is beckons to us behind and through the great values. A person who has begun to read these values through this poem of reality is moving in the right direction. Supernatural grace raises this natural dynamism to aid the soul in reaching God Himself.

The humble and reverential poetic attitude Newman describes is all the more necessary when probing Christian mysteries because these are further above our comprehension, further beyond anything that we can directly know. The scientific mindset of our day, with its requirements of clarity and analysis, makes it difficult for many people to repose in the obscure certitude of faith. A man habituated to a poetic gaze is more easily at home in a simple and confident acceptance of the dazzling truths of our faith. In the supernatural order, more than any other, we need wonder: "The beginning of wisdom is the fear of the Lord."

In fact, faith itself is rather of the poetic mode. First, faith is intuitive—not that we see God, but the gaze of faith goes directly toward its object. Reasoning helps one arrive at faith, but the virtue of faith is not a product of rhetorical, dialectic or scientific reasoning. It is an infused habit,

a gift from God, which becomes a first principle in the supernatural order. Second, faith presupposes emotions, because, as St. Thomas teaches, adherence to something so high and obscure requires affection; we must be drawn to the object.[48] Newman insists on this importance of affection. One comes to the faith, he writes, "not on an examination of the evidence, but from a spontaneous movement of the heart towards it."[49] To illustrate this, he uses a most apt example of poetic knowledge applied in analogy to belief in Christ: "Does a child trust his parents because he has proved to himself . . . that they are able and desirous to do him good or from the instinct of affection?"[50] Third, faith is even experiential to the extent that its object is not an abstract universal but a singular, a Person, Whom we need to know in ways other than through general ideas and reasoning. Finally, faith is connatural because it depends on God lifting us to a participation in His own knowledge and life.

This poetic facet of faith is especially pronounced when it blossoms into contemplation— the simple, fixed gaze on God and His mysteries. In fact, St. Thomas uses the term connaturality especially in reference to this intuitive, though obscure, knowledge of divine things, a knowledge gained through charity and the gifts of the Holy Spirit.[51] Like the chaste man knows things chaste, so too can one know divine things by a spontaneous affective inclination—medieval spiritual writers especially insisted upon this point. As one grows in faith and charity, the original participation in the divine life by grace develops into an experience, an awareness of this life, based on a greater union with God through love. A stanza from the *Spiritual Canticle* of St. John of the Cross illustrates this interior participation:

> O spring like crystal!
> if only, on your silvered-over face,
> you would suddenly form
> the eyes I have desired,
> which I bear sketched deep within my heart.

The silver face of the fountain reflecting the light, St. John comments, represents the articles of our faith, ideas we can formulate about God.

These ideas at once point to and veil the substance of the water, that is, the divine realities. St. John has a sense of God and His mysteries; his heart already obscurely participated in these beautiful realities. The articles of the Creed stimulated his desire to achieve that participation through the Beatific Vision of the Divine Face.

The essential role that the poetic mode of knowledge plays in the supernatural realm gives an indication of the importance of good art; as Senior writes: "Poems are the food of faith"[52]—alluding to Duke Orsino's comment in Shakespeare's *Twelfth Night* that music is the food of love. The arts—sculpture, painting, poetry, music—nurture our faith through all the aspects of the poetic mode we have just examined. They operate on the level of the intuitive, experiential, loving and connatural, communicating the true, good and beautiful, and thus launching us toward God. Frequenting them habituates us to peacefully gaze at mysteries without pretentions of clarity. Senior indicates poetry's experiential way of leading to faith in contrast to the rhetorical mode: "Poetry disposes to faith not by persuasions but participation . . . having to do with the beginning of religious life in the consciousness of sin and helplessness and the end in bliss."[53]

Reading Francis Thompson's "The Hound of Heaven," for example, we feel our misery and, consequently, our need for help; we also can have a glimpse of the merciful love that is beckoning us, and therefore, of the joy to which we are called.

Metaphors, signs, and symbols are particularly necessary when articulating the supernatural. In the passage of the *Summa* referred to above, in which St. Thomas speaks of poetry as an inferior knowledge (*infima scientia*), one of the objections states that poetry is unworthy of theology. In reply, St. Thomas explains that poetry is useful and necessary precisely because of the sublimity of theology's objects. We can scarcely conceive of them, and must have recourse to metaphors in order to envision them. Plato regularly resorted to a picture or a myth to direct his companions' gaze to the mystery that is beyond our conceptualization, beyond science. Senior explains how poetry is a means for this: "By the fact of something seen you can infer the mystery of things unseen,

seeing likenesses in unlike things, poetry's essential exercise."[54] I know my mother's goodness and so I can know, in a way, something of God's own. Furthermore, these sensible images, in their likeness to the invisible, also attune the soul's sensibility and affectivity to the faith, so that spiritual realities become living and attractive to us. Senior writes: "Beatitude insofar as it is known and expressed in this life is sensational—witness the Song of Songs."[55]

God, who created man as an incarnate spirit, has confirmed the necessity of the poetic mode and of art by His own action. He has spoken of Himself through sensible things, using stories, songs and figurative language. He gave us parables in the call of Abraham, in the Exodus from Egypt, in the journey to the Promised Land, the Exile— parables that really happened, as J.R.R. Tolkien liked to say.[56] God even became man partly to give us a sensible and emotional grasp of Him and His mysteries.

Thus, Scripture is largely poetic rather than philosophical, dialectic or rhetorical. It presents, it conveys an experience, more so than it argues a point. Consequently, Scripture should not be approached simply as a source of abstract ideas, moral precepts and dogma. As one contemporary author writes: "In the face of God's Word in Scripture, the most efficient 'method' to begin understanding what God is saying to us is the same befitting our confrontation with a great poem or a masterpiece of painting or music, or sculpture: the 'method' of wonderment, of admiration, rather than the disincarnate reductivism of a purely analytical or historicist view."[57] One should often read God's Word as one does good literature or poetry, listening rather than analyzing, letting the music sink in, becoming personally involved in the story or song, approaching it with all one's being—sensitivity, emotions, will and intellect. Even a man who knows his theology must meditate on Scripture in order to impress upon his imagination and affections the reality and beauty of its scenes, people and values. He must learn a more intuitive perspective and follow Scripture's holy signs.

The Church, as well, addresses the whole man. In the liturgy, that special means for nourishing faith and arousing the supernatural life, the

Church uses the sensible and the beautiful to lift our hearts toward the invisible. Holy Mass in particular is a work of art—poetry, song, drama—in which mysteries are reenacted and signified through the sensible, directing the senses, affections, will and intellect to Christ's true offering of Himself to the Father. Sight and sound, touch, taste and even fragrance combine to make Holy Mass meaningful and beautiful. These sensible experiences help the invisible mysteries take hold of the imagination and stimulate the affections, step by step, through that great work of art, the liturgical year. Gymnastic and music, delight and wonder, are elevated to their pinnacle in the liturgy, blossoming into praise of the Creator and Redeemer.

Finally, in the supernatural realm as well, the poetic mode is at the base of the pyramid of types of knowledge. Christians long believed, in a poetic way—with an intuitive, connatural knowledge—the great truths of faith that only centuries later were rendered in defined, conceptual form. A modern author writes: "The theologian reasons, makes deductions and expresses concepts in precise terms; the contemplative scrutinizes the living depths of the truth."[58] To be living and fruitful, theology's scientific, abstract analysis must be directly supported on the experiential level by a faithful and loving contact with Christian realities. Without the intuitive, obscure awareness of the Divine Face sketched in our hearts, there is a danger of placing all our attention on clear determinations to express the divine reality—on formulas, arguments and logic—while forgetting the reality beyond them. It is inside the living and poetic habit of those spiritual realities that we can patiently, humbly and fruitfully proceed to analyze, for example, how Christ is present in the Blessed Sacrament, how we participate in the divine life, or how there are three Persons in one God. The intellectual quest to resolve problems can then be safely and effectively guided by St. Thomas's precise and often austere definitions and syllogisms. One can say that St. Thomas's hymn "Adoro Te" is the principle and end of his scientific work in the *Summa Theologiae*.

Thus, poetry is not merely the "silly stuff" or "idle pleasure" referred to in the objection that opens the epigraph to this chapter. On the contrary, as the epigraph continues, we are blind, we cannot know the End—which is "not a concept but three Persons known in beauty"—unless we

have the insights provided by the poetic mode. We do not see God, but we can recognize and be attracted by the beauty that shines from Him, and the Muses can contribute in manifesting that beauty.

We have now completed our speculative reflection on gymnastic, particularly on music built upon healthy gymnastic. This leads us to the other contribution of Senior's in this domain, namely, the incarnation of the poetic mode in culture. After having soared somewhat in the realm of speculation, it is now time to come back to the ground and consider Senior's practical advice on how to restore gymnastic and music, which will be our intention in the following chapters.

PART III

The Gymnastic and Music of Christian Culture

Our Lord explains in the Parable of the Sower that the seed of his love will only grow in a certain soil—and that is the soil of Christian Culture, which is the work of music in the wide sense, including as well as tunes that are sung, art, literature, games, architecture—all so many instruments in the orchestra which plays day and night the music of lovers; and if it is disordered, then the love of Christ will not grow.

—The Restoration of Christian Culture

John Senior, circa early 1970s, at the University of Kansas.

Courtesy of Monica Sercer

The Death of Christian Culture

*If truth is nothing but opinion, right springs from
the barrel of a gun. Liberalism is the smiling face of
Modernism. Behind it lies the grinning skull. As
everybody says, we have arrived again at something
like the end of ancient Rome, but worse—because
after two thousand years of Christianity we are
capable of a perverse and theologically exact apostasy no pagan ever knew.*

—The Death of Christian Culture

IN the next few chapters we will examine how Senior proposed to
educate the senses, imagination and emotions in various domains,
both inside and outside the classroom. Here we will begin by presenting
his idea of culture, which stresses the need for good gymnastic and music.
We will then proceed to gauge how poorly today's culture measures up
to that idea.

Having already studied the philosophical principles at the base of our
present-day miseries as Senior outlined them, as well as the artificial
milieu that nourishes those principles, we will now turn our attention to
the Christian side of things. We will consider how that heretical philosophy has extracted Christ from our experience, and how this elimination
of Christ's sensible presence has undermined our culture and thus contributed to ushering in those miseries. This will prepare us for subsequent
chapters, including our exploration of Senior's recommendations for the
restoration of Christian culture.

A Christian Environment of Truth

The word "culture" is habitually used today in a rather sociological manner, referring to specific threads of social life, the style of some society—its festivals, customs and tastes. One is most often dealing with diversity, with "subcultures" rather than something commonly shared. We speak of French, Spanish, or Chinese culture, or even drug and rock culture—often without value judgment, without discrimination made between good and bad, better and worse. The term culture, however, traditionally connotes development of the faculties, at least to some extent, notably in aesthetic or intellectual refinement. Senior discusses its fundamental meaning:

> The word culture is generally taken to mean any arranged environment to facilitate growth. . . .
>
> Culture as in "agriculture," the cultivation of fields, derives from the Latin *cultus*, which means essentially anything subjugated. . . . So culture is anything subjugated, put under a rule . . . and made tame. A cultivated field is subjugated to the rule of the farmer to facilitate the growth of crops; it is no longer wild.[1]

Some people, confronted with the ugliness of the mechanized world, prefer simply to let the wild grass grow. Aldous Huxley, for example, in *The Brave New World*, presents a choice between brutal, uncultivated nature on the one hand, and artificiality, in the sense of something imposed violently on nature, on the other. The protagonist chooses what appears to be the only escape from a world controlled by social scientists, namely, returning to savagery. Senior believes that genuine culture is not artificial. In contrast to the Modernist ideal—destruction to recreate upon a void— Senior knows, rather, that culture organizes and disciplines so as to help nature be what it should be. By way of example, he points out:

> Cities and suburbs are beneath [sensible measure and beauty] because they don't have natures; they are irrational monstrosities constructed against nature to substitute for it, unlike the classic human city which complements and perfects its people and

place—like the towers of Siena or Assisi along their hilltops lifting the landscape up into themselves and riding off with banners![2]

To help human nature blossom, culture must be, Senior writes, "the physical, moral and spiritual soil in which human beings grow."[3] Man, with his load of sin and disorder, certainly needs a subjugating and taming influence to attain to human fullness. What Senior thus expresses in his own way is now classical doctrine. St. Pope John Paul II has said:

Culture is that through which man, as man, becomes more man, "is" more, has access to more being.... All man's "having" is impor- tant for culture, is a factor of culture, only to the extent to which man, through his having, can at the same time "be" more fully a man, become more fully man in all the diversity of his existence, in everything that characterizes his humanity.[4]

Cardinal Ratzinger explains that culture is "an attempt to understand the world and the existence of man within it.... This understanding is meant to show us how to go about being human."[5]

Before studying how culture humanizes, we should determine what it is to be human and how one goes about it. It can be said that man as such is characterized by a relationship to truth. Whereas an animal simply follows sensitive impressions and instincts, man is made to judge accord- ing to what is. Senior thus maintains that culture is "the environment of truth, assisted by art,"[6] so that culture helps us adhere to truth. Senior is not speaking of mere theoretical truth.

For him, as for John Paul II and Cardinal Ratzinger, "being human" means not only knowing truth, but also loving it, freely conforming one- self to what is, to the good and the beautiful. One grows in being human by developing an appropriate response to these values.

By defining culture as an "environment," Senior resonates with the doctrine that points at man as an incarnated spirit who draws even his spiritual sustenance through the senses. He held in robust balance the fact of man's spiritual dimension alongside man's dependency on his sensible

surroundings. His books on culture deal largely with education, literature, arts and philosophy, but also with the types of tools we use, our ways of eating and dressing, because everything a person does and experiences enters his imagination and thus influences him and his relationship to truth. Nothing is indifferent, Senior explains: "There is a cause-effect relation between the work we do, the clothes we wear or do not wear, the houses we live in, the walls or lack of walls, the landscape, the semiconscious sights, sounds, smells, tastes and touches of our ordinary lives—a close connection between these and the moral and spiritual development of souls."[7]

It follows that a man should integrate his surroundings and his ways of carrying out even material activities into his quest for truth and the authentic human good. Senior adds that, to dispose humans toward growth in truth, the environment must be "assisted by art." This "art" is, first of all, what we usually understand the term to be: songs, paintings, architecture and so forth; they all should cultivate truth. Senior likens this aspect of culture to wine, "a literary, musical, artistic and intellectual drink."[8] He likewise recognizes that man also needs "bread," that is, the more ordinary areas of our life, all of which should be deliberately arranged to help the environment point to truth. Nothing should be purely functional and nothing should be purely aesthetic, that is, aimed only at pleasing the senses. Everything we make and use should have meaning and be a support for contemplation, a means of spiritual development, like the handle of the crusader's sword, made in the form of a Cross to indicate whom he was serving and from where he hoped to draw his strength.

Among the many authors who speak of such things, Senior first drew his basic orientation on the subject from Coomaraswamy in particular. Once this author's syncretism is put aside, one finds much of interest in his writings on the alliance between the spiritual and the material, which he insists was a reality spontaneously recognized up to the Renaissance. His book *Christian and Oriental Philosophy of Art*, from which Senior quotes several times in *The Way Down and Out* has the following apropos passage:

Industry without art is brutality. Art is specifically human. . . . From the stone age onwards, everything made by man, under

whatever conditions of hardship or poverty, has been made by art to serve a double purpose, at once utilitarian and ideological. It is we who, collectively speaking at least, command amply sufficient resources, and who do not shrink from wasting those resources, who have first proposed to make a division of art, one sort to be barely utilitarian, the other luxurious, and altogether omitting what was the highest function of art, to express and communicate ideas.[9]

This call for meaning in art is pertinent to things we make, but also to all our life, to all our activity and our manners. As a human being wears clothes because he is not a beast, so every aspect of his life should be "dressed up," so to speak. His environment should not be fabricated purely for comfort or immediate efficiency, but conformed to his spiritual dimension, indicating that he has an end beyond the material use of this world. Thus, for example, it is not appropriate that a man jump on raw meat or tear it apart with his fingernails. He should cook and handsomely prepare his food, and then calmly sit, use knives, forks, spoons and napkins. Beyond that, he should not reduce eating to the utilitarian minimum, solely for health purposes as if he were merely a body. A meal is a time for communion and conversation among friends, in a celebration of God's gifts. Senior goes to an extreme to affirm that disorder in the sensible will echo with disorder in the spiritual: "It is ridiculous but nonetheless true that a generation which has given up the distinction between fingers and forks will find it difficult to keep the distinction between affection and sex or between the right to one's body and the murder of one's child. If you eat ketchup-smeared French fries with your fingers day after day, you are well on your way to the Cyclops."[10]

To grow in our humanity, we require an environment that most of all cultivates our relationship to the great, fundamental truths, truths that ultimately give meaning to life, truths that pertain to God, Truth in Person. Man's intellect and will cannot be satisfied with anything less than a personal relationship with God. In other words, culture should mostly help men grow in their humanity by submitting them to God's rule. Sanctity consists in a man's full growth, his complete response to truth. It is, therefore, the goal of culture. Senior writes:

Culture, as in agriculture, is the cultivation of the soil from which men grow. To determine methods, we must have a clear idea of the crop. "What is man?" the Penny Catechism asks and answers: "A creature made in the image and likeness of God, to know, love and serve Him." Culture, therefore, clearly has this simple end, no matter how complex or difficult the means. . . . All the paraphernalia of our lives, intellectual, moral, social, psychological and physical, has this end: Christian culture is the cultivation of saints.[11]

If such is its purpose, the entire environment should be ordered to cultivate our knowledge, love and service of Christ. Senior completes his definition of culture by stating that the environment should be "ordered intrinsically—that is, from within—to the praise, reverence and service of God our Lord."[12]

Because an individual's Christian life cannot be isolated from social influence, this ordering of culture to God cannot be restricted to a personal, or even family, environment. Man is a social animal, part of a whole, so his religion must have a social dimension—he needs others for his religion—and his society should be religious. Therefore, it is a matter of coherence that public life, as well as one's private life, should revolve around religious truth. As Senior expresses it, "religion is the first determinant of culture."[13] Cardinal Ratzinger recognized that "the very heart of the great cultures is that they interpret the world by setting in order their relationship to the Divinity."[14] Consequently, Christian culture is, according to Senior, "not just pious practices and doctrine, but the 'thing,' faith incarnate, Christendom,"[15] by which one normally means a society that recognizes Christ as king, where the community as such serves Christ, or at least where Christian faith and principles govern the whole environment—laws, institutions, art and social life. Chesterton and Belloc have elaborated these themes, Chesterton most notably in his book-length study of Christianity entitled *The Thing*. But it was especially Newman who impressed upon Senior the necessity to restore Christ back into our lives, to ground our senses and emotions in a Christian environment.

This ideal of the social incarnation of the Faith was concretely realized, especially in medieval Europe. As Senior recognizes, "the spirit of Christ informed all aspects of life down to the smallest detail."[16] Christian moral and spiritual values were the explicit references for all standards in the Middle Ages; public life revolved around Christian feasts. The culture of that period formed the imagination and emotion in harmony with faith, and so provided fertile soil for the intellect and will, for the supernatural life. Newman describes, in the nineteenth century, the fruits of an environment where one is immersed in Christian imagery:

> As to Catholic populations, such as those of medieval Europe, or the Spain of this day, or quasi-Catholic as those of Russia, among them assent to religious objects is real, not notional. To them the Supreme Being, our Lord, the Blessed Virgin, Angels and Saints, heaven and hell are as present as if they were objects of sight.[17]

The Middle Ages were often brutal and war-torn, but one must admit to the greatness of its art, of its philosophy, of its holy men. Perhaps, in fact, our culture has declined to such an extent that we are no longer capable of appreciating that greatness of our own past. Senior writes in *The Restoration of Christian Culture*: "There is no possibility in the general loss of Christian Culture that we could build a cathedral like Chartres or write a text like the *Summa Theologiae*—or even, except for a few, understand them."[18]

Putting Christ Aside

According to Senior, Christendom lasted approximately a thousand years, "from the fifth to the fifteenth century,"[19] that is, from about the time of St. Benedict to the Renaissance. Seeds of a pure and rich Christian culture were sown in the fifth century by monks, and the weeds of humanism began destroying that culture in the Renaissance. That is a very general statement, of course; Senior sometimes referred to the French Revolution as finishing off Christendom. Following that view, one could,

perhaps, put the thousand years from the eighth to the eighteenth, from Charlemagne and the establishment of the Christian empire to the French Revolution and the destruction of Christian structures. In any case, we are now well beyond those thousand years, in a general culture that is no longer Christian. In *The Death of Christian Culture*, Senior quotes Matthew Arnold, writing some 150 years ago:

> The Sea of Faith
> Was once, too, at the full, and round earth's shore
> Lay like the folds of a bright girdle furl'd.
> But now I only hear
> Its melancholy, long, withdrawing roar,
> Retreating, to the breath
> Of the night wind, down the vast edges drear
> And naked shingles of the world.[20]

Faith is not just retreating now; it no longer roars at all. As Senior soberly notes: "We have become victims in our public life of a mass agnosticism unknown anywhere in history."[21]

Various factors contributed to the demise of Christendom—the Plague, the Great Schism, the Protestant revolution. From the philosophical point of view, the West's progressive evacuation of Christian culture was based on the centuries-long process of the growing skepticism we have already examined. "Steadily step by step," Senior writes, "over the last few hundred years since the triumph of Rationalism and Liberalism and now Modernism, the person of Christ has been withdrawn from our experience. Generations now grow up in a religious vacuum, in an atmosphere charged, as it were, with His absence."[22] We need to reflect on this passage to understand how the Presence that once penetrated everything has all but vanished, how Christ no longer has a hold on our imagination.

We have seen that Rationalism blocked off man from experience in favor of ideas; Romanticism, from ideas in favor of emotions; and Modernism from both ideas and emotions in favor of pure consciousness. Applying the same scheme to religion, we can say that for the Rationalist,

religion is an idea, for the Romantic an emotion and for the Modernist a metaphor, a symbol. Coming after Rationalism, to which ideas are not drawn from the sensible world, both the Liberal and the Romantic tended to conclude that there are only opinions: "Whatever you think, you may be wrong," Senior writes in their person, "because the ground of all reality has been rejected and there is nothing to measure the intellect against."[23] As that orientation grew, Christianity became increasingly confined to the private domain, where personal preferences and tastes belong. The Enlightenment, which developed from this trend, tried to organize public society without God, or at least without any particular religion, which, in practical terms, meant without Christianity.

In spite of this effort, official references and ideals in the West remained basically Christian until the French Revolution. Even after the Revolution, some public Christian manifestations escaped the wreckage; many Christian sentiments, moral presuppositions and customs were still largely and publicly acknowledged. Indeed, up to the very recent past, the West maintained, generally speaking, a Christian perspective. Senior writes concerning the United States: "Despite its heresy and all the strains of massive immigration and, though severe, nonetheless accidental injustices, America was essentially a Christian commonwealth from Plymouth rock to Pearl Harbor."[24] Some public Christian vestiges lingered even after World War II: stores were still closed on Sunday; classes at public schools prayed the Our Father and put up Nativity scenes. Since the mid-1960s, however, there has been an ever stronger and vociferous pressure to eradicate even such practices. References to Christian traditions have mostly disappeared from politics and education. One rarely, if ever, hears church bells.

There is a logic of Liberalism at work in this total suppression of Christ's presence, but a new spirit has now entered the arena. Liberalism has gone beyond the right to opinions to an attack on convictions as such. Senior writes:

Now we hear, not that whatever we think *may* be wrong—which was the agnostic position of a hundred years ago—but absolutely,

according to the doctrine of a dogmatic Liberalism, that it *must* be wrong. There is no truth and every belief is an error. . . . There is abroad today a dogmatic and inquisitorial Liberalism that insists on the positive establishment of disbelief, that proposes an infidelity at the point of the sword.[25]

Elsewhere, he further elucidates:

It is as if you took the famous scholastic statement that the intellect in its very nature tends toward truth, and negated it to say that the intellect in its very nature does not tend toward truth; or perhaps to negate it more perfectly, the intellect tends toward non-truth, or falsity. In the 20th century the second view has taken over. Liberalism has changed its name to Modernism, and it is the perfection of the tendency that began as far back as the 18th century.[26]

Contemporary Liberalism, as Senior reminds us, is only the "smiling face of Modernism," which reacts against the Christian religion for its pretension of being an absolute and exclusive expression of truth. Senior foresees a new type of persecution, which has indeed begun: "Christians look fearfully toward a second age of martyrdom, this time without the lions, under the reign of a sophisticated terror by lobotomy and drugs to create international, nondenominational, multiracial moral and political imbecility."[27]

Be that as it may, our civilization now places religion and public life in separate spheres. A Christian today is obliged to live in two worlds. Weekly church services cannot compete with an educational system, an entertainment industry and a public environment that are completely secular, divested of signs of Christianity or of spiritual things, without reference to an existence beyond this world. The average person, though he may believe in Christ and know the tenets of his religion, is all too easily swayed by his secular surroundings. When Christ is far from experience and therefore from the imagination, He will be far from the mind and heart as well.

Relegated to the private life of the individual, Christ is perceived as more and more remote from the real world. He seems unreal, an object of wishful thinking. Blessed Paul VI writes that "the split between Gospel and culture is undoubtedly the drama of our time."[28]

The Agony of Civilization

As would be expected, not only has religion been struck by the dichotomy brought on by secularism, but, concomitantly, the very foundation of civilization has been severely rattled. Senior often cited Matthew Arnold in his role as poetic chronicler of the turning point toward Modernism. His father was the famous Thomas Arnold, founder of Rugby School, who, in fact, invented the game of rugby. Thomas was a liberal in what concerns Christian dogma, if not in Christian morals. Matthew takes a further step. In "Dover Beach," he describes the consequences of the recession of Christianity:

For the world, which seems
To lie before us like a land of dreams,
So various, so beautiful, so new,
Hath really neither joy, nor love, nor light,
Nor certitude, nor peace, nor help for pain.

Absent Christian certitude, only utter despair remains.

Many have spoken of the crisis of our civilization. Here we will reflect on a few statements of Senior's describing how the putting aside of Christ has brought us to this state of crisis. According to Senior, by choosing to be non-Christian, Western man has become subhuman as well; the "death of Christian culture" is equivalent in the West to the death of civilization. We have recognized the deadly results springing from the retreat of truth in Modernism; beyond this, secularism has reinforced Relativism.

Like any firmly established civilization, the West had commonly accepted bases—an unquestioned, solid ground for all to walk on, as Senior explains: "In politics and ethics . . . the given is what in general we

call civilization or culture, opposed to which is savagery. Civilization is a complex web of givens."[29] A civilization, an authentic culture, lives by a certain number of presuppositions, a consensus about certain fundamental truths and ways of behaving.

In the moral order the "given" consists substantially in the Ten Commandments—honor God, honor your parents, keep the sacredness of the marriage bond, do not lie or steal. Because these commandments can be known through natural means, they are also called natural or moral law. Due to Original Sin, however, we need supernatural Revelation to fully and correctly know that law, and grace to obey it accordingly. One can easily recognize that over the last couple of centuries Western civilization, having turned its back on grace and Revelation, is falling away from the natural law both morally and intellectually.

In the Enlightenment period, when a religious Liberalism, if not a political one, began to dominate, the masters of the time wanted to exclude Christ from public life while retaining the moral law. The Ten Commandments continued to regulate life; the first three commandments were even observed for a while, as homage to a distant Supreme Being. But people could not long be held by an abstract cult, and even a vague deity soon became too absolute for Liberalism.

The religious commandments (or the three commandments referring to God) were therefore soon discarded, although some countries maintained a nominal official mention of the divinity. The last seven commandments still were generally acknowledged, since they were concerned with visible objects and human relationships. Likewise, moral ideals continued to be fed by vestiges of Christian perspectives in the arts, music, literature and popular traditions.

In the twentieth century, consensus on the remaining seven commandments began to fade away. The tendency to Relativism at the basis of Modernism, refusing any absolute moral norm, was reinforced by the prevailing secularist environment; the dominant secular culture impressed upon "the man in the street" the view that there was no final meaning to anything, no definitive measure for true and false, for good and evil. Within this context, it became evident that the commandments could

not be absolute, but simply conventional. Marriage, for example, became only a piece of paper, because without God nothing can be sacred.

Further, since Modernism does not accept Christianity even as an opinion and sees in Christianity's proclamation of one truth a mortal enemy—almost the only enemy in the West—it attacks any Christian vestiges still to be found in our culture. Senior notes in particular that the elimination of Scripture from our lives has cut us off from vital contact with our heritage: "The one book all men have read, whose imagery, ideas and very language were the sun that held the planetary system of Christendom in order, is not now read; and one of the secondary consequences is that nothing else in English literature before 1920 can be read without copious footnotes."[30] Senior mentions our inability to understand Chartres and the *Summa*; but even more recent monuments—and not only deeply religious ones such as those of Bach and Rembrandt, but most of the great Western works of thought and art—are largely lost to modern comprehension as well, because of our lack of understanding of Christian things. As Senior writes: "Anyone can see for himself that we are really the 'hollow men,' in Eliot's poem and in De Chirico's paintings, like stuffed, stitched dolls, walking mindless among the broken statues of a devastated civilization."[31]

Beyond the open rejection of Christianity, this rupture with our Christian-based cultural past in itself has had its obvious moral impact. Senior comments: "So many are shocked today to find their children lacking religious motivations, lacking patriotism, lacking even a very clear sense of moral responsibility. They fail to realize that these virtues are in great part culturally determined. We have lived on cultural capital from a past generation, having failed to counteract depletion."[32] There is in fact a positive, resolute rejection of moral law as historically linked to Christianity. Chastity and marriage, fidelity, courage, love of country, the whole idea of natural law, are often considered to be specifically Christian and so to be thrown away as part of the past.

Once such doors are open, anything goes. Indeed, not only moral law, but all givens of civilization, even the most commonsense ones, rapidly disappear. Good manners, courtesy in public discourse and modesty in

dress are largely lost, formally rejected, blatantly mocked. Previously unspeakable things that have always existed but were kept underground have passed to the broad light of day. More and more individuals and groups, even governmental laws, officially accept and advocate activities previously considered abominations: "We have raised the abnormal and aberrant to the condition of human rights," Senior laments.[33] In an article written at the time of the anti–Vietnam War riots, he pointed as an example of this to a "subcultural creature" blowing his nose publicly on an American flag.[34]

Modern man is thus arguably more corrupt than pagans who never knew Revelation. Pagan—even barbarian and savage—societies usually observed some of the natural law. They strove to honor a deity, respected parents and recognized the inviolability of the marriage bond, all things falling away in the modern West. And it is not only the *practice* of moral law that, in important ways, is worse today. All societies have had difficulty obeying the moral law, but in the past that law was at least recognized. Today, by the converging influence of Relativism and secularism, disobeying the moral law is no longer a crime; breaches have even received legal recognition and support. As Senior notes:

> Eighteenth-century indifferentism led to nineteenth-century liberal toleration, which has led to Modernistic infidelity, to that state so common now in which each of the Ten Commandments is systematically and with malice disobeyed, not out of weakness but by political design. . . . Dishonored parents are consigned to antiseptic bedlams known as rest homes at the first slight cardiac tremor; the termination of unwanted life—murder—is a matter of medical discretion . . . Marriage in fact has become a legal form of prostitution . . . and theft is property, legitimated by tax accountants; and truth is managed news.[35]

With no absolute law, with the rejection of even the social seven commandments, we are given over to the law of the jungle. Pius XII warned us long ago:

The synthesis of religion and life . . . is the indispensable cornerstone for any civilization, the soul by which any culture must live,
lest it destroy itself with its own hands and fall into the abyss of
human malice which opens under its feet when it begins, by apostasy, to turn away from God.[36]

And John Paul II explains that in "a social and cultural climate dominated by secularism . . . the sense of God is lost" and therefore also "of
man, of his dignity and his life."[37] This "leads to *a practical materialism,*
which breeds individualism, utilitarianism and hedonism."[38] The heated
quest for pleasure cannot but provoke violence, brutal or subtle, instigated
by individuals or groups, in what he called "a war of the powerful against
the weak."[39] The only law is the law of the jungle, as he so often said.

For Senior, we are "in between crisis and catastrophe."[40] Comparing
our period to that of the disintegration of the Roman Empire, he writes:
"Today we are, I think, in times like those of St. Jerome, moving rapidly
toward those of St. Benedict. Barbarians have destroyed our cultural
institutions, this time mostly from within."[41] A Western culture without
Christ will spin on faster and faster into the night, like a planet that has
lost its sun, to borrow Nietzsche's image. Yet, although Senior entitled one
of his books *The Death of Christian Culture*, he was not without hope. He
named his next book *The Restoration of Christian Culture*. And we recall
that, for Senior, the times of St. Benedict were in fact the beginning of
Christendom. Here and now, we must work for restoration, leaving the
results to the Lord, as he writes: "The question is what can be done—what
can and must be done, because there isn't any choice."[42]

The Restoration of Elemental Things

If we are to restore an authentic . . . Christian cul-
ture, we will have to think not just about fighting
infanticide, sex education and pornography—by all
means fight them to death—but for the positive
work of the restoration of culture which lies wrecked
in the wake of the humanist assault: we will have
to think about simpler, larger, elemental things
which, losing their original strength, gave access to
the enemy in the first place—elemental things
which are the foundation and the principle of the
superstructures we must rebuild.

—The Restoration of Christian Culture

WE are caught in a never-ending spiral of pursuit of satisfaction through things that can never fulfill, but rather bankrupt the individual soul and create the unhappy and restive society of our day. The forces behind this, we have noted, are Relativism and secularism. For a return to civilization, we must therefore restore Realism and Christian culture, and come back to reality and to Christ. But where to begin? What can we do today to nurture our society—education, the media, the arts, philosophy—in truth, both natural and supernatural? Senior held little hope of directly achieving anything in the political arena: "If, as I think, America is down and out," he writes, "any political action is vain."[1] In any case, restoration of truth cannot be accomplished by decrees or by some concocted program that would engineer results: "Philosophical realists

have never advocated sweeping change; nothing serious or deep is accomplished by techniques."[2] Rebuilding culture calls for quiet and hidden work in more human and personal areas; foundations must be restored: "Restorations never start in the collapsing tops but always in the dull low places of simple hearts."*[3] Thus, rather than having recourse to noisy and spectacular public action, one must patiently dispose the soil, sow seeds and put our trust in the Lord for growth: "If we have any time at all, let us plant such seed and sleep. Christian culture imitates the Kingdom: 'So is the Kingdom of God as if a man should cast seed into earth, and should sleep, and rise, night and day, and the seed should spring and grow whilst he knoweth not.'"[4]

For Senior, planting seeds meant most especially cultivating gymnastic and music. Regarding gymnastic, he knew how fundamental his own experience of real things had been toward bringing about his conversion. He writes: "The first necessity is getting ourselves and our children into 'naked' contact with the world God made, not just in school, as study, but habitually in our whole way of life."[5] As to music—songs, stories—it is the lifeblood of culture. Good music in the broader sense, as Bloom explained, unites our enthusiastic side to the rational. Senior writes, echoing Shakespeare: "Music is the food of love . . . which gentles the rebellious, rude, savage, sinful heart. You see what it means—that civilization is the work of music."[6] He observes, in a similar vein: "I believe the breaking up of families and nations is due in great part to the recession of poetic habit."[7]

It must be recalled here that Senior does not, in any way, underestimate the importance of the other modes of knowledge. Fallen man cannot live by poetry alone. In fact, the masters of poetry are often wayward, whatever might have been their brilliant intuitions on a given point. "Poets as poets are reckless and dangerous," Senior writes. "If they were legislators as [Shelley] said, we would have anarchy."[8] Culture must be guided by

---

* Senior sometimes referred to lines from "In Time of the Breaking of Nations" by Thomas Hardy that evoke these "dull low places": "Only thin smoke without flame / From the heaps of couch-grass; / Yet this will go onward the same, / Though Dynasties pass. / Yonder a maid and her wight / Come whispering by; / War's annals will fade into night, / Ere their story die."

philosophy and theology: "Unless the mind achieves its perfection in the making of conceptual judgments, religion and philosophy cannot be understood; and with religion and philosophy gone, all human activity is rudderless."[9] It remains clear, nonetheless, that rational arguments are of little avail if souls are not well disposed, thus "to put the intellect first, we must have restored the imagination."[10] Senior was supportive of Leo XIII's project to reinstate the study of St. Thomas Aquinas in seminaries, but he realized that St. Pius X's aim to restore *all things* in Christ took precedence, being more fundamental—for our spiritual life, as well as for an authentic understanding of St. Thomas.

Consequently, in the light of Christian faith and the Perennial Philosophy, we must work to rehabilitate the imagination by a return to reality on the natural level, and to Christ, on the supernatural sphere. The next two chapters will focus on the natural level, while the final chapter in Part III will treat of supernatural sources from which the natural must draw. Here we will consider Senior's recommendations on gymnastic and music in some of those "dull low places," namely, the home, the neighborhood and the workshop. He does not propose techniques for this, but simply provides a few principles, aware that culture must develop naturally.

Home and Community

First of all, it is necessary to cultivate home life. It is in the home that one discovers love and joy, that one learns manners, discipline, responsibility, respect, generosity, and how to relate to others. More than half the battle of life is already won when someone comes from a good family milieu. And it is only through renewed families that a general restoration of culture can be possible. Senior writes: "If even a fraction of the next generation" should practice this home life, the restoration, if it comes, "will come because of them, far from the madding crowd, far from the protests, bull horns, klieg lights and cameras, in that quiet place at home by the fire which in the meantime, little as it is, is of immediate and lasting worth."[11]

Yet, today the home is often little more than a dreary place of transit where one sleeps and sometimes eats, devoid of common life. To remedy

this state of affairs, Senior provides some fundamental directions for the restoration of home life using gymnastic and music. While children's education at home will be dealt with in the next chapter, here we will examine how gymnastic and music play a role in their formation.

Starting with gymnastic, it is around the home that we acquire basic habits of sensation; it is here that we receive the first good or bad impressions that form our soul. For Senior it would be best to live, work and play in a rural or semi-rural area so that sharpening the senses and tying them to reality would become part of daily life. In fact, he suggests northern Canada for those who dared to go far from the web of technology: "For young and more adventurous souls, there is the vast, still-virgin wilderness to the north waiting for saints."[12]

Though Senior scarcely elaborates on the theme of home gymnastic, it can be deduced that if one cannot live in a rural region, it would be desirable to have regular experiences in nature through camping trips, or visits with family and friends in the country. Even in town, some neighborhoods are closer to nature and more delightful than others. The home itself should be of natural materials, simple and attractive, with harmonious wood furnishings and handmade objects. It would be good to live among animals: domestic ones—cats, dogs, chickens, pigs, horses; and wild ones not far away—ducks, squirrels, rabbits, blue jays. Recreation should likewise be close to nature, and active rather than passive. Walking in the countryside or across parks, drawing, juggling, horseback riding, golfing and hunting are far superior to video games and watching television. Senior writes:

My football game! the old man cries. . . . The armchair quarterback, puffing his gut on insipid American beer and potato chips, gapes like Nero at his gladiators hacking each other up, while his neglected children take up punk rock on their car-cassettes. If you really like football, get out on Saturdays and play it with the boys.[13]

By engaging gymnastic roots to grow from, wonderful music can be cultivated, forming a healthy imagination and deep emotions. Literature, poetry, songs and conversation in the home are the normal basis for culture,

for a thriving human and Christian life. Senior observes: "Parents are the primary educators and no school, no matter how advanced or clever the curriculum, can do anything more than develop as it were the film that has been taken in the home."[14] Systematic school education cannot replace music in the home: "Twelve years of formal instruction in reading and composition given in modern schools are ineffective substitutes for the habit of poetry and prose which can be acquired only by reading the best aloud night after night. . . . The best instruction in writing is good reading and good talk."[15] Lack of music in the family milieu has its consequences in the classroom, as Senior testifies from his own experience:

> Why are students coming down from high schools and colleges . . . so appallingly deficient they cannot read a normal paragraph in Matthew Arnold, a popular writer of less than one hundred years ago? . . . If there were music, poetry and art at home, they would have learned despite bad teaching—teaching has always been mostly bad.[16]

More generally, poor taste and an impoverished culture can also be attributed to a deficient family setting. Senior describes an instance of this: "Catholics have accepted some of the worst distortions of their Faith in the order of art, music and literature without a shiver of discontent because they never really heard the 'Tantum Ergo' or the 'Ave Maris Stella'—not for lack of faith, but because there had never been ordinary music in the home to have created the habit of good sound and sense."[17]

The common musical life—family conversation around good reading, poetry and song—is necessary not only for the children's schooling and discernment, but for every aspect of their existence, for their souls. Senior writes: "What I suggest, not as the answer to all our problems, but as the condition of the answer, is something at once simple and difficult: to put 'the touches of sweet harmony' back in the home so that boys and girls will grow up better than we did, with songs in their hearts."[18] This is important, as well, for the family as a whole, for the union of its members:

215

Then families will be together at home of an evening and love will grow again without thinking about it, because they are moving in harmony together. There is nothing more disintegrating of love than artificial attempts to foster it at encounter groups and the like: Love only grows; it cannot be manufactured or forced; and it only grows on the sweet sounds of music.[19]

Senior, then, urges leisurely reading, singing and conversation together of an evening: "Read, preferably aloud, the good English books from Mother Goose to the works of Jane Austen. . . . And sing some songs from the golden treasury around the piano."[20] The prospect may seem idealized and romantic, but it is what Senior experienced as a boy growing up and accomplished in some measure as a father. Keeping everyone around the piano is more difficult today than in the 1920s when he was a child, and the city is more distracting than his Wyoming ranch. There are so many activities today that lure one to go out somewhere, so much communication with the world that plucks the attention outside; home life is interrupted in so many ways. Senior's advice is to begin with one evening a week using simple material at first, like "the songs of Stephen Foster, Robert Burns, the Irish and Italian airs."[21]

There are two prerequisites that Senior proposes for music in the home. The first of these does not come as a surprise, after all we have heard from him: "If you measure the hi-fi against a piano, for example, you can see that families don't gather around the stereo and sing. Families don't draw their chairs up closer to the central heating duct. No one sings while attending to the automatic dishwasher."[22] Television and videos are so attractive and easy—we have supposedly the best entertainment in the world there in our living room at the push of a button—but, among the already mentioned negative consequences, these machines take away interaction among family members, and ultimately destroy family life. With such gadgets on, there is no reading, singing or conversation. Senior concludes that we must put the modern conveniences aside, at least some of the time: "Smash the television set, turn out the lights, build a fire in the fireplace, move the family into

the living room, put a pot on to boil some tea and toddy and have an experiment in merriment."[23]

Another condition for drawing the family back together and fostering music and love is that the heart of the home be habitually present there:

If women stayed home . . . food would taste like meat and vegetables again because it would be cooked, not just defrosted; life would be wholesome, good and full of love again because she would be home; pianos would shake old music from the scores, children, parents and grandparents would sing together of an evening and tell stories by the fire. Someone would even be home to love and care for the crippled, sick and dying.[24]

The culture of the home—homemaking—is the foundation of all culture, and is the special role of the woman. Senior knows there is no family life without the woman to animate it, no authentic home without her to put love into it and make it a place where people like to be. Referring to the etymology of the Anglo-Saxon word "lady," he comments: "All those feminists who want to free women from the drudgery of making a home don't know what a home is . . . The lady—maker of bread, the bread of life, even the bread of angels. [The] home, [the] living room, [is] a holy place."[25]

Senior was a chivalrous man, having great respect and love for women: "Men's perfections are mediated to themselves by women."[26] He appreciated the differences and complementariness between the two sexes: "Woman was created for man, she is his helpmate, made from his rib and finds her happiness only in serving him; and man is a beast until he fully becomes himself in loving her."[27] As such, society is deprived when women take on roles counter to their nature. About the news of a woman in the Armed Forces having been wounded, he wrote:

The worst is not that the Soviets are firing laser beams at us, but that girls are out there fighting them. . . . What does this do to the imagination, the heart, the soul, of the next generation? What becomes of girls made by God in their nature to be their husband's

helpmates and to bear and raise their children, whose influence, stronger than the moon's on the tide, attracts man's rougher self to all the gentle, tender, soft, sweet, loving moments that make love possible.[28]

He described an instance of this "influence, stronger than the moon's" in a letter to his professor, Mark Van Doren, pointing to Mrs. Van Doren's discreet presence and impact: "Her influence over so many lives, secret, working through things you have said and written and through the way she looks and talks and is, is incalculable."[29]

Senior grieves that our economy compels women to find jobs outside the home: "The worst fact in the present crisis is the creation of an economic system in which women must work to make ends meet. In the worst of the '30s depression the vast majority of women were housewives."[30] Explaining further: "It is against the natural law for women to engage in socially productive industry unless necessity demands it. According to the law of nature a woman's place is in the home because by nature she is nurse and nurturer of children."[31] Let us at least say, with the Church, that society should cultivate esteem for the beautiful role of the housewife and mother, which is intimately concerned with what really counts in life—forming human souls. John Paul II writes about the mother:

> It will redound to the credit of society to make it possible for a mother—without inhibiting her freedom, without psychological or practical discrimination, and without penalizing her as compared with other women—to devote herself to taking care of her children and educating them in accordance with their needs, which vary with age. Having to abandon these tasks in order to take up paid work outside the home is wrong when it contradicts or hinders these primary goals of the mission of a mother.[32]

A family cannot avoid influences from the outside, for good or for bad. In fact, it cannot be all it should if kept isolated, enclosed within itself;

it needs other families for a full life. The natural milieu for it is a family of families. In the climate of our day, many have come to realize that there is a need to form local communities where intellectual, moral and religious life can be sustained and cultivated, where friendships are made possible. Senior, with his colleagues Drs. Quinn and Nelick, taught a course on "The Village," painting a charming picture of what a healthy community could be. He insisted on the advantage of living on a human scale "where," he wrote, "we can walk at a normal human speed, shop in friendly stores where the butcher and the grocer know their customers, send our child off to school where the parents know the teacher and the teacher loves his subject and his students."[33] A community such as this—where people know each other, where the common interest is more manifest—will foster in each person a better sense of cooperation, of responsibility, of the common good. Only in such a community can there be sympathy and affection for individual members and the whole, and young and old relate regardless of age; only there can stability nurture local experience and memories, and imagination take hold. Small towns on this level still exist, and neighborhoods of this kind were a familiar thing in larger cities as late as in the 1960s.

To convey a sense of this normal and humane community life, Senior cites Oliver Goldsmith's poem "The Deserted Village," which laments the passing of the village of the poet's youth in the early eighteenth century. Here are some lines describing its common musical life:

Dear lovely bowers of innocence and ease,
Seats of my youth, when every sport could please,
. . .
How often have I bless'd the coming day,
When toil, remitting, lent its turn to play,
And all the village train, from labour free,
Let up their sports beneath the spreading tree;
. . .
These gentle hours that plenty bade to bloom,

Those calm desires that ask'd but little room,
Those healthful sports that grac'd the peaceful scene,
These, far departing, seek a kinder shore,
And rural mirth and manners are no more.[34]

There have been instances where some have drawn detailed plans to manufacture such a place, but in the end the outcome is an artificial utopia. Senior himself at one time dreamed of starting a village. As time went on, however, he recognized that a community needs to develop naturally. In *The Restoration of Christian Culture*, he simply indicates that some like-minded families could group together in the country, in a village or in a neighborhood, and little by little a community life would come to be: "The cornerstone will come back again, the barbershop and the convivial bar . . . and more important still, the tearoom will reopen."[35] And, as in Goldsmith's lost village, families would come together for gymnastic and music, for play and conversation.

We have mentioned Natalia Sanmartin Fenollera's novel *The Awakening of Miss Prim*. Much of the book's vision of a healthy village was inspired by Senior and can contribute to our discussion of healthy village life. She presents the village at the outset of the book:

To visitors, San Ireneo de Arnois looked like a place that was firmly rooted in the past. Old stone houses with gardens full of roses stood proudly along a handful of streets that led to a bustling square full of small shops and businesses, buying and selling at the steady pace of a healthy heart. The outskirts of the village were dotted with tiny farms and workshops that supplied the local shops. It was a small community comprising an industrious group of farmers, craftsmen, shopkeepers, and professionals, a retiring, select circle of academics and the sober brotherhood of the monks who lived at the abbey of San Ireneo. Their interlocking lives formed an entire world. They were the cogs of a human machine that was proud of being self-sufficient through trade and the

small-scale production of goods and services, and of its neighborly courtesy.[36]

With Miss Prudencia Prim we discover the village: its shops, its ways of educating children, the friendships, the discreet influence of the abbey. One of the characters comments, in a line that Senior could have written:

It would be utopian to imagine that the present-day world could go into reverse and completely reorganize itself. But there's nothing utopian about this village, Prudencia. What we are is hugely privileged. Nowadays, to live quietly and simply you have to take refuge in a small community, a village or hamlet where the din and aggression of the overgrown cities can't reach.[37]

Beginnings of a Musical Culture

Given a family or community that would like to start up musical culture anew, where to turn? Unfortunately, the Muses—if one can call them that—have gone astray. We have examined the artificiality and sensationalism in Modernist "art for art's sake," and chronicled how the fine arts have become a major factor in the diseased imagination of our society. Whether through popular art, with its electronic sounds and sights, or through high-brow abstract art, there is an attack on right sensation, based on illusion rather than reality. By rejecting *being* and Christ, Modernist art forms attune us to the ugly and evil. Concerning these, Senior observes that "it is an obvious fact that here in the United States now, the Devil has seized these instruments to play a *dance macabre*, a dance of death, especially through what we call the media."[38]

We are all, to a greater or lesser extent, infected by this omnipresent, sick art. Our senses and sensitivity were shaped by it. The best remedy for someone who is ill is to follow a good diet combined with healthy exercise; Senior applies this same principle analogically to all arts, especially literature:

The cure is to put ourselves under the causes of health. In the particular case of literature, these are primarily the Greek and Latin classics and the classics of various national literatures of Europe written in imitation of them—which, indeed, make little sense in their absence—for English-speaking people, the Oxford Standard Authors.[39]

As to how to best start, Senior's counsel to beginners in poetry can be applied to other arts:

> Knowledge is a habit of mind. And habits must be practiced. First imperfectly on easy everyday examples, proceeding with increasing difficulty up to the level of second nature. The only way to support the lost habit of poetry is to make small effort in ordinary material, learning by continual use the anthology of English verse and the daily playfulness of whatever power we have ourselves in writing our own Valentines and Christmas cards.[40]

One should, then, begin with easy classic works. In this way, a person will cultivate good habits of taste in general. Senior remarks that a return to the classics "is not to disparage all contemporary artists any more than the tradition itself denies experiment; quite the contrary, one of the fruits of such reading should be encouragement of good writing and drawing by the reader. A standard is not a strait jacket but a teacher of norms and a model for imitation."[41]

In the area of literature, Senior compiled a list of "the thousand good books" especially apt for gymnastic and music, which should be playful, in contrast to "the one hundred great books" appropriate to liberal arts study. He explains: "Great books call for philosophical reflection; whereas good books are popular, appealing especially to the imagination. But obviously some authors are both great and good, and their works may be read more than once from the different points of view—this is true of Shakespeare and Cervantes for example."[42] So as to ensure an "ordered, connected sensibility," he stops the list at World War I, "before which cars

and the electric light had not yet come to dominate our lives and the experience of nature had not been distorted by speed and the destruction of shadows."[43]

The vast majority of the books he chooses for his list were originals in English (as opposed to translated works) because "our language is English and if we are to learn it, we must absorb its own peculiar genius."[44] Senior has a great esteem for this heritage: "English literature has been done and can't be done again, the best since Greece and Rome, full of beauty, good and truth."[45] But, he admits a difficulty: the few English Catholic writings "are all second-rate"[46] and translations from foreign languages are rarely of high quality. That places us in a dilemma: "the thousand good books which are the indispensable soil of the understanding of the Catholic Faith and indirectly requisite to the Kingdom of Heaven, are not Catholic but Protestant."[47] "The heart, indeed, the very delicate viscera, the physical constitution and emotional dispositions as well as the imaginations, of children will be formed by authors who are off the Catholic center and some very far off; and yet, not to read them is not to develop these essential aptitudes and faculties."[48]

Nevertheless, the situation is not dramatic. The English classics "are 'good,' artistically, morally and spiritually, though they are incomplete."[49] In what concerns the spiritual, they are "Biblical and Christian; the existence of God, the divinity of Christ, the necessity of prayer and obedience to the commandments is very strong stuff for the most part."[50] Furthermore, "there is little anywhere in direct violation of the Catholic Faith" in this literature.[51] The misunderstandings can easily be corrected by parents and teachers, and the omissions compensated for by a rich Catholic life.

Senior also describes how "good books" should be read. Musical reading does not consist in character analysis or moral study of motivations, which are approaches fit rather for the liberal arts level. Senior writes that reading on the musical or poetical level should be "something simple, direct, enjoyable, unreflective, uncritical, spontaneous, free, romantic, if you will, with the full understanding that such experience is not sufficient . . . for science and philosophy, but indispensable as the cultural soil of moral, intellectual, and spiritual growth."[52] One mainly takes delight

in the story, poem, song, painting, sculpture, in order to open oneself to wonder and love.

Work

Work is a significant part of the environment in which we live and is therefore a factor of culture: "We become the work we do," Senior writes.[53] Of course, we have a duty to accomplish our work well, but first we must have good work to be accomplished, one that is, as Senior explains, "really necessary for the common good." He continues:

> A large amount of work in the bureaucratic state consists in what is called management but is really manipulation of labor, supplies and markets.... Managers take pride in facilitating and expediting, but how many useless products and needless services are multiplied just for the sake of being facilitated and expedited?[54]

In this instance, the goal, the object in view, is profit, rather than what is useful, truly needed, and worthwhile.

We also need work that is morally and spiritually invigorating. Senior enumerates some occupations that do not provide support for faith because they are particularly ungymnastic, that is, removed from natural reality, and unmusical, having little or nothing that inspires or leads to personal, interior growth: "[Christians] who work in factories, banks, insurance companies, government agencies and fast-food shops have to rely on faith alone."[55] Less hours, good wages, job security and benefits do not adequately compensate for the better part of a day spent in inhuman, frustrating, meaningless work. There was a time when one could scarcely tear a man—the smith, the cobbler, the joiner, the farmer—away from his work, which he took pleasure in doing well and was for him more of a vocation than a "job."

Senior insists on the importance and value of working with one's hands: "Manual labor, accomplished at the hands of the artisan . . . constitutes a path toward spiritual perfection. Machines turn by themselves

and give a result without effort from us; they lead the mind and the body to idleness and fantasy."[56] The "blows" require effort and discipline. Work is a "support for contemplation" because in it the person encounters resistance to which he must adapt, and the mystery of anotherness that calls for an appropriate response. He applies his mind to reality—a type of wood, the soil, climate, plants—and thus discovers new facets of God's creation, acquiring a poetic, participating, sympathetic knowledge of the thing in hand. Such work tests, purifies and enlightens thought and heart. As Douglas van Steere writes in *Work and Contemplation*: "[The mind of man] requires a certain manual expression to keep its balance. Robbed of this manual expression, the mind goes askew and we get the shallow, rootless quality of thought that has so largely marked our time."[57] While Senior eschewed machinery, it is true that hand-operated machines, at least, still retain much of the benefits just mentioned. However, in most cases they do, to a degree, separate the worker from physical reality. This is especially true of factory work, with its dominating mechanical gear at which one can grind away while day-dreaming, mentally cut off from reality.

A return to the land is encouraged by Senior, who considers farming and ranching to be the normal type of work for most men. He envisions a model order in society, which indeed had some reality in the not too distant past: "sixty per cent farmers; twenty, craftsmen; ten, clerks; five, soldiers; and finally, the 'zero' status (not a class) of outlaws (beggars, criminals, cripples and clowns)."[58] While carpentry, gardening, and crafts put us into relationship with the physical world, agriculture involves a greater immersion into, and requires a more all-encompassing adaptation to, God's creation. Senior quotes a beautiful passage from Pius XII on the physical, moral and spiritual benefit of regular agricultural work:

> It cannot be too often repeated how much the work of the land generates physical and moral health, for nothing does more to brace the system than this beneficent contact with nature which proceeds directly from the hand of the Creator. The land is not a betrayer, it is not subject to the fickleness, the false appearances,

the artificial and unhealthy attractions of the grasping city. Its stability, its wide and regular course, the enduring majesty of the rhythm of the seasons are so many reflections of Divine attributes.[59]

It is possible to have natural work even in town. If one's job does not revolve around natural reality, there are always chores and maintenance to be done around the house. One can still have a regular second occupation, or at least a useful hobby, such as raising a few animals, gardening, or perhaps cutting hay or making wooden objects or pottery. Senior advises: "If you would dig up your front and back yard by hand and plant them full of flowers and vegetables, you would replenish the table, beautify your lives, lose weight, and gain physical and emotional strength and cheer sufficient to cancel the trip to the mountains and quit the absurd and unhealthy exhibitionism of jogging."[60]

We know that Senior usually had some type of manual hobby going on, and more than a hobby at the ranch in Wyoming. We can suppose that he was able to use this as a "support of contemplation." Father Taylor tells of a day when he went to see the professor, and not finding him at home walked around to the back to see if he was in the barn. Sure enough, there he was milking the cow. When Senior saw him, he exclaimed, "Father, this is a holy place! Our Lord was born in a place like this!" Father Taylor closes the story: "*That* is John Senior."

In his directives, Senior has in mind primarily the individual and the individual's immediate circle. "The question here," he writes, "is not the reform of the social and economic system however important that may be, but the particular moral choice each one of us must make in the meantime."[61] Still, he has comments at a more general level regarding a social ideal. He opines that "unless the determinate number [of people in a society] are land owning farmers, the virtues necessary to citizenship atrophy, and the vices destructive of the human race flourish."[62] A "determinate number" is a very useful notion elaborated by Belloc, signifying not necessarily the majority, but a number that sets the tone of a society, provides its character. According to Senior, we need enough farmers

working their own land to establish a whole, stable society that is well rooted in the soil, in harmony with God's creation. There, care for the land arises spontaneously, as well as a natural sympathy for neighbors and even the animals that share that space with us.

Otherwise, society tends to lose the foundations of civilization, built on adherence to natural law and basic human values, resulting in a greater tendency toward individualism and, thus, a quest for profit above all other considerations.

This of course would be a revolution in these our times of a distant, "remote control" economy that works with statistics instead of real things, run by financiers. Senior speaks of "voodoo economics," which, like magic, multiplies signs and appearances cut off from reality, "where money itself, cut free from the gold (or any) standard [is] no longer a means of exchange but of manipulating value."[63] For his ideal, he has in mind the still largely self-sufficient villages with surrounding farms of the latter part of the nineteenth century.* There we would find the model human-sized communities, where the worker was familiar with the supplier and the user of his product, and where each knew his place and that his role for the common good was well established. For Senior, after that period—which is when Modernism emerged—Western man left behind "the golden mean of ordinary life."[64]

Senior believes that Catholic teaching supports his views. He writes that "Catholic social teaching, against both socialism and capitalism proposes an essentially agrarian economy of family farms and the workshops needed to support them as the normal basis of society."†[65] In his view, the pope's social encyclicals "teach essentially that . . . the political and social power of the faithful must be used in favor of what economists call a distributist rather than a capitalist or socialist society, that is, one in which the tax and other public instruments work to favor independent, small, free enterprise and especially the family farm."[66] Some comment on such affirmations are in order.

---

*   For a delightful description of such a village by William Allen White, see "The Restoration of Innocence," 74–75.

†   It is only fair to note that this quotation from Senior was written in a non-published document, although one well thought out and carefully written. Senior habitually spoke in this vein.

According to the theory of Socialism, the community as a whole—that is, in practical terms, the state—would own the means of production and would control exchange. In contrast to this, Capitalism is the economic system in which chiefly individuals or private corporations would own the means, and the market would be free. By Capitalism, however, Senior is thinking, in particular, of a society in which big business and accumulation of wealth dominate, with the result that the means of production are in the hands of only a few, who in turn pay others to do the work. Distributism proposes to distribute ownership, to decentralize. Its immediate goal is to keep the common man from being treated like another cog in the machine, to render him satisfaction in his work, to stimulate initiative, generosity, responsibility and independence. The attendant benefits are the strengthening of family bonds, the placing of relationships on a more local and personal level, and the cultivation of personal growth through work. In short, Distributism facilitates all the humane values we would like to find through our labor.

The Church has constantly and definitively condemned Socialism, especially for denying the right to private property,[67] but her position toward Capitalism is much more nuanced, partly because of the ambivalence of the term. The Church promotes economic initiative and a substantially free market; she even accepts the means of production in the hands of a few and the accompanying wage system as not unjust in themselves. Nevertheless, against what can be called an unbridled Capitalism, where competition and personal profit are the only rules, she recognizes the need for some control, some protection, some harmonization through public institutions for the common good.[68]

Popes have never used the term Distributism. Nevertheless, Belloc, who won over Chesterton, among others, to his views, was inspired to develop the Distributist theory by the thrust of much of Leo XIII's encyclical *Rerum Novarum*. Leo XIII, Pius XII and John XXIII encouraged fostering the family farm and small businesses. More deeply, the goals of Distributism correspond to principles that guide Catholic doctrine in the domain of economics, notably, that man is the subject and end of work,

that there must be solidarity, subsidiarity, and moral responsibility. The popes remind us of the human dimension of work and economy.

Nevertheless, the Church takes into account the contingencies of human history and recognizes in our day that matters of economy have greatly evolved in the last few decades. We do not see the popes today setting an essentially agrarian society before us as a point of reference. It is misleading, then, to affirm, as Senior does, that the popes favor a Distributist framework and an agrarian economy.

Still, Senior's economic views form a beautiful ideal; favoring small businesses and family farms is quite reasonable, and proposing an agrarian economy as being most suited to man's nature a perfectly legitimate thing. He is not too concerned with financial progress, for example: "'Philosophical happiness,' said Edmund Burke, 'is to want little'—that is, less of things and therefore more truth, beauty, mirth, merriment and friendship."[69] He would have agreed with John Ruskin, who observed:

> There is no wealth but life. Life including all its powers of love, of joy, and of admiration. That country is the richest which nourishes the greatest number of noble and happy human beings. . . . The final outcome and consummation of all wealth is in the producing as many as possible full-breathed, bright-eyed, and happy-hearted human creatures.[70]

Within the framework of Church doctrine, always our guiding light, Senior's call for a return to reality is very compelling. "Work itself must be in harmony with God's plan, which is nature's plan too because God is the author of nature. We will never find economic, domestic or political and social security *contra naturam*, in a society contraceptive of children and of everything natural and real."[71]

What do we do with machines, then, since they are a major factor in man's separation from nature? We need to take a last look at this subject of machinery to see what Senior proposes in practice.

Senior's Practical Position on Modern Technology

Father Joseph Fessio had this story to tell:

> I invited him to give a lecture at the St. Ignatius Institute. Mother Angelica was just starting her TV empire and she had sent her new mobile studio to San Francisco so that we could broadcast the great John Senior live. We were excited about being able to use modern media to make people like John Senior accessible to thousands instead of dozens. How did he start his talk? "I understand this is being televised. Well, I'm telling you to turn off the TV. Smash it to bits. Throw it out or burn it." The Queen was not pleased![72]

At every turn, Senior has struck out against machines. They blunt our senses, cut us off from reality and lead the imagination to fantasy; they breach family life and relationships; they weaken our mindfulness in work. In Chapter Two of *The Restoration of Christian Culture*, "The Air-Conditioned Holocaust," which is a diatribe seemingly against technology as such, affirmations such as this are common: "Technology—the new or the old; there isn't any difference whatsoever in the philosophical basis; a computer is a complicated abacus—technology is the inevitable consequence of Epicureanism; it is the dedication of our lives to the pursuit of happiness defined as pleasure."[73] Authors Senior read in his formative years, whom we have mentioned previously—Coomaraswamy, Guénon, Carlyle, Ruskin, Karl Marx—criticized Western man's use of machines, especially as the main component of factory labor, but none of them proscribed machines to the extent that Senior does.

It would seem that Senior would have us imitate the Amish and abandon machines altogether. Here, however, is a slightly more nuanced position: "Machines (as opposed to tools) are, if not intrinsically, at least commonly, evil, to be tolerated only because in a machine society there is no viable option short of heroic virtue (which God counsels but does not command)."[74] "Intrinsically" means essentially, necessarily; "commonly" denotes that the evil is accidentally, but usually, attached to something because of

circumstances.* Senior is thus proclaiming that the use of machines generally harms us and, thus, should only be "tolerated." In his opinion, those who
have the courage and opportunity should put machines aside, which would
imply living apart from ordinary society to some measure, since mechanization is part of the fabric of our world. Senior indeed admired the Amish
from this point of view: "Virtuous people such as the Amish are trapped
by a narrow theology but not by their honest way of life."[75]

By no means was Senior the distant intellectual sitting at the comfort
of his desk, asserting on his blog that all should plow their fields with
horses, while himself having never touched a tractor. On the contrary, he
had known labor in tough, primitive conditions. And he was indeed
speaking about real and important problems. Industrialism, that is, a
highly mechanized society, has in fact brought on ruinous effects upon
community life, in replacing beauty with ugliness, by polluting the land,
air and water. With its colossal means of production, industrialism practically demands that these be property of the state or the rich, thus making it more difficult for small businesses and the family farm to exist.

While we must at least recognize that technological progress brings
challenges, often dangers, and even some losses, there are obvious difficulties with Senior's views. He used to give lectures against the use of cars.
They went well until the day someone asked: "How did you get here
tonight?" The professor, of course, had driven there like everyone else. For
a while he rode a bicycle instead of driving to town, but at last admitted
this just took too much time—which is precisely the point! Machines do
bring possibilities of real good. They can take away what is most burden-
some in toil. John Paul II wrote that of itself the machine is "man's ally"
because "it facilitates his work, perfects, accelerates and augments it."[76]

Senior seemed to think that the very notion of machines was
linked to the germs of materialism in the Renaissance and the Positivism of that age; he saw them as a disorder produced by the perversion

---

* Fifteen years earlier Senior had written that television was "intrinsically evil" (*The Restoration of
Christian Culture*, 27), and the reason given was its dulling of exterior and interior senses. Senior
could not have meant by this expression, as one does in moral theology, that it is always a sin to use
television. He did want to say that use of television is always in some ways damaging.

of thought of that time. However, even without the help of modern materialist orientations, machinery would doubtless have eventually emerged, although in a more orderly fashion. Benedict XVI criticized those who "deny *in toto* the very idea of [technological] development" because that view proceeds from "a lack of trust in man and in God." As to the lack of trust in man: "It is . . . a serious mistake to undervalue human capacity to exercise control over the deviations of development or to overlook the fact that man is continually oriented towards 'being more.'" Refusing technological development is also a lack of trust in God and His Providence because "technology . . . is a response to God's command to till and to keep the land that he has entrusted to human beings."[77]

We cannot hold man back from learning and from wanting to progress in instrumentation. Mankind is always advancing in knowledge and mastery of the world. Cultural dynamism is habitually accompanied by some technological progress. While it is true that our powerful instruments have become a threat, even fallen man can use them properly; he can critique what he has done and ameliorate the situation. For that, however, we must first step back a moment, slow down and take stock of things, to avoid being caught in the mad, downhill rush of technology.

Senior's reflections certainly remain a helpful starting point for a thoughtful discussion of modern technology. First, they impress on us the importance of such an analysis. Although Senior's romantic idealism and his habit of rhetorical exaggeration color his bold statements, a book review of *The Restoration of Christian Culture* remarked that his affirmations awaken us and make us sensitive toward the degree to which technology affects our lives:

Even if you find [Senior's] contempt for modern technology somewhat extreme, I would recommend reading his ideas in order to make yourself aware of how significantly our lives are impacted by technology today. Although it's not often talked about, I think it's vitally important for parents to understand that problems with

television for children go beyond simple concerns with regard to morally offensive content. People were not designed to sit in front of a box (be it a computer or a television).[78]

Second, he provides the basic principle of order for the analysis. Even in that hard-hitting chapter, "The Air-Conditioned Holocaust," one can find at one point the essential nuance to his position: "Technology must be regeared to the proper dimensions of the human good."[79] This substantially puts all of Senior's sweeping affirmations in right order. Technology is a means, not an end; it should serve man's authentic good. We make ends out of means when, for example, "industries are organized for the efficiency of their administration and not the product or the job to be done, where we are served tasteless meals under conditions beneath the level of the feeding-trough in fast-food shops because they can get us in and out faster with a greater cash return and fewer dirty dishes."[80] We must give primacy to human values, to all that Senior argued for: beauty, relationships with other human beings, groundedness in reality, and, in work, quality and excellence rather than quantity, speed and money.

Third, he shows that this refocus requires a profound and extensive transformation of our approach to nature. The proper attitude toward nature should fundamentally be that poetic gaze Senior so advocates—seeing the visible world as a clothing, as it were, of the spiritual world, and thus approaching it with a contemplative reverence. Then we would no longer consider sensible reality as a simple source of pleasure, power and comfort. We would seek to collaborate with nature rather than crush it. We would strive to cultivate its beauty and worth.

If Senior were to have it his way, we would all be riding horses. But it must be admitted that, in practice, he did endeavor to simplify and discipline the use of technology in his immediate milieu and family. As we know, his house had no television. He lived in the country. He walked, rather than drove, or rode, when he could. He exhorted others to practice simplicity. We have examined some of his practical suggestions. Indeed, each person should reflect for himself on how best to use

technology without becoming a slave to it, how to compensate for losses. He should judge what is the best means for the human good in the circumstances at hand. We are to use machines according to God's will, for His glory and man's good. I would add that, if we use them, we ought not to curse them but give thanks to God for them.

A former student of Senior's wrote a book about his experience of a year in an Amish type of society. Its concluding passage reads:

> There really is no end to the possible uses of technology, nor are there limits to finding a way around it; but in all cases it must serve our needs, not the reverse, and we must determine these needs before considering the needs for technology. The willingness and the wisdom to do so may be the hardest ingredients to come by in this frenetic age. Perhaps what is needed most of all, then, are conditions favorable to them: quiet around us, quiet inside us, quiet born of sustained meditation and introspection. We must set a time aside for it, in our churches, in our studies, in our hearts. Only when we have met this last requisite, I suspect, will technology yield its power and become a helpful hand servant. Mary and I still turn on the kerosene lamp and read by the fire on a cold winter's eve. By switching off the electric light, I think we see a bit better.[81]

Senior has no secret, magical solution for reestablishing an environment of truth, or initiating the restoration of Realism through gymnastic and music. What he does in his writing is mainly describe the healthy, natural bases from which culture would grow. He encourages a return to normal family and community life in a natural setting, with poetry, stories, songs and conversation; he proposes the taking up of inspiring, honest work, preferably close to nature and with some use of the hands. In the domain in which he specialized, however—education—Senior has more practical details to provide. Education, then, is where we must now turn our attention.

CHAPTER TWELVE

The Restoration
of Innocence

College teachers faced with freshmen who hate lit-
erature, think their job is somehow to convert
them—by cajolery, finding something in a text (or
selecting lesser texts) relating to their sick, impov-
erished wants. But the fault was back in high school
where they should have loved Shakespeare. But, the
high school teacher found his freshmen coming up
from elementary school with no desire to read
Shakespeare because they had not first loved Ste-
venson. And the grade school teacher found his stu-
dents coming up from home without Mother Goose.
And more important still, the love of literature at
any stage supposes love of life—grounded in acute
sensation and deep emotion.

—"History and the School"

IN this chapter we will present in some detail the ways in which
Senior proposed to apply gymnastic and music in the school. Most
of Senior's recommendations on this subject are recorded in "The Restoration of Innocence: An Idea of a School." This unpublished book
provides a concrete plan drawn specifically for a boys' high school, but
also considers the preschool and grade school levels. We will examine
each of these three pre-college stages in succession. However, before
proceeding, three points are to be kept in mind.

First, Senior writes for boys' schools and has boys in mind in all the various dispositions he foresaw. He admits that "for girls we need another book beyond my competence about domestic arts, technical or liberal—strong, sweet, pliant and subdominant."[1] A reflection on boys' education is very timely in our day when boys are habitually constricted to the model of well-behaved little girls, often by the use of calming drugs. As Senior notes: "Girls win all the stars because boys spend half the time resisting itchy collars."[2] Nevertheless, most of the principles he provides, and even much of their application, can be used in girls' education. Both boys and girls need to accomplish what he set as the goal of pre-college education: "The final cause of schools is feeling in the knowledge of things the throb and thrill of them."[3]

Second, we shall see throughout this chapter that, since education assists nature, teaching should cultivate and discipline the pupils' natural path to learning. Senior describes a swimming lesson as a paradigm of this approach:

Education is benevolent neglect—provided that right order has been established. Of course we don't pitch children in the sea to sink or swim. . . . Give them the rules: Don't go in till half hour after meals. Scissor. Don't kick. Don't bend your knees. And then let them be! Don't force rules beyond their due. You can't swim for them. Swimming is remembrance of amniotic bliss.[4]

This collaboration with nature is a governing principle in Senior's proposals about the education of boys: "[A school's] work," he writes, "is not to do but to be, not to make boys into special kinds of men, but realize the rich potential of their age, which is to know and love the Maker and the things He made with all their mind, heart, strength and souls *as boys*."[5] In other words, we must let the boys be boys.

Third, the focus of Senior's program is literature, but not simply because it was his domain. Literature is of essential importance, as he explains: "Since language is the distinguishing property of reason, the formal principle of the human species, learning to listen, talk, read and

write is the chief work of schools from the nursery to college. Reading is the horse of culture, carrying the burden of 'the best that has been thought and said.'"[6]

Nursery

"A child before the age of reason . . . in the nursery, explores his consciousness and gains control of his body."[7] The infant first discovers, with delight, his faculty of movement. He learns to sit up, crawl and walk. As a toddler, he begins distinguishing between his imagination and the real, exterior world. His exploration of reality, however, is piecemeal. Senior writes: "Nursery school is pre-knowledge; experimental and experiential, it is tentative, not integral (not a unity of parts)."[8]

The little child is closed up in himself because he manifests only an immediate sensitive reaction rather than reason or deep emotion: "Before the age of seven," Senior writes, "reason and emotion are dormant and learning solitary. Though children seem to converse, as Piaget puts it, they engage in 'collective monologues.'"[9] The child's instinctive desires are not yet under enough control for conversation and life in common in grade school. He is a young plant, to be protected and cared for.

Consequently, Senior insists, the first level of education must be in the home: "Day care centers, kindergartens and the first two grades of modern elementary school are products of the oligarchic, materialist mind that, denying the spiritual nature of children, thinks in terms of social engineering."[10] The mentality that pushes toward production and accomplishments—as if one were dealing with animals or robots, as if learning were mechanical and could be measured quantitatively—this mentality wants a child to be in school as soon as possible. For Senior, on the contrary, we must respect the child's nature, leaving him in the proper habitat for his age. Traditionally, a child began school indeed only around the age of seven.

In the nursery, the principle of education according to nature would indicate that the parent should lay out the essential rules, provide a healthy framework, and then let the child go forward with only a measure

of guidance. In Chapter Eleven, we mentioned the benefit of rural surroundings for the home. The child must also move in a wholesome human milieu where he can learn spontaneously through a flexible schedule and light supervision. He will instinctively imitate those around him, pick up good habits and manners, and be instructed in little childhood tasks and arts:

> Under the guidance of parents, uncles, aunts, older brothers and sisters, boys learn to tie their shoes, make their beds, do chores, count and read. From five or six on they can be given the care of plants and animals from whom they learn the love of creatures. . . . There are no subjects or fixed horarium except the household's—we get up in the morning, eat, work, play and go to bed at night. Little boys . . . spend most of the time living the best part of a boy's life in play and, in the evening, listen to their elders read aloud the classic children's books, looking at the pictures and print until they start to read themselves.[11]

These little chores foster the desired sensible and emotional connection to reality. Senior notes a singular benefit in the care of animals: "As the love of God is learned in love of neighbor, love of neighbor is learned in love of animals."[12]

He values the reading aloud to children partly because personal contact is essential to learning: "The gift to us of life and understanding . . . can only be handed down. . . . It cannot be done in print or on records or the television screen; the child must have the direct experience of a warm and loving person. . . . It is in the tone of voice, the touch, the kiss upon the forehead."[13] In this way the preschooler already begins learning to read by "following the pictures and print and then silently reading what [he] heard."[14] Senior is against "phonics, 'look-see' and the like [that] teach words as signals ('this' means 'that') as if language were a set of counters for exchange."[15] According to him, "letters . . . are a song you have to guess the meaning of."[16] Senior wants the child to recognize that words are not used in a one-dimensional way, but have deep and rich meanings, often

with mysterious resonances. The child needs to appreciate reading in context and learn to delightfully explore language.

Pictures are an important part of this education since, writes Senior, "classical children's books must be read with all our senses, heart and mind."[17] "Because sight is the first of the senses and especially powerful in the earliest years, it is important to secure editions illustrated by artists working in the cultural tradition we are restoring, both as introduction to art and as part of the imaginative experience of the book."[18] He has his own thoughts on specific illustrators, in this case, making a nuanced comparison between two famous ones, likening one to Shakespeare and the other to Robert Herrick:

> If you compare Bewick's Stag gazing at his image in the pool to Caldecott's (otherwise the best), the difference is something like that between Herrick and Shakespeare. Both meet Dr. Johnson's test as having life; and both are merry. But one is—well, Shakespeare. Caldecott is full of wit and worldly wisdom, with a boisterous love of Merry England's countryside before the industrial blight. See his troop of hunters galloping behind their sniffing dogs of which the narcissistic stag is quite oblivious! But Bewick, having all of that, has something else precisely named in "illustration": He cleanses the scene in a laver of light.[19]

Little children respond to a genre of literature appropriate to their age: "[They] are dreamy creatures, apt for Mother Goose and fairy tales."[20] Senior knew from his own childhood experiences the importance of nursery rhymes: "Without the habit of these rhymes in earliest childhood, Shakespeare's or anyone's poetry will always be a learned thing, known as if in translation."[21] This early exposure to poetry sets the ground for potential budding poetic talents:

> Rhyme is nowhere better learned than in the opening song:
> Old Mother Goose, when
> She wanted to wander,

> Would ride through the air
> On a very fine gander.

Anyone who has that soft sound "wander/gander" in his head will have the right receptors.[22]

It is readily seen that Mother Goose will help the child acquire a sense of rhyme; but are not nursery rhymes and, even more so, fairy tales and fables rather unrealistic? Do they not perhaps prevent the restoration of Realism, that reconnection to reality which Senior so emphatically advocated and labored for?

We must differentiate the old tales from modern fantasy stories such as the Harry Potter and Twilight series, or even *The Wizard of Oz*, *Peter Pan*, *Alice in Wonderland*, and Dr. Seuss books, which are fabrications with only a distant reference to the world we know. Fantasies create a strange and dreamy atmosphere, a make-believe universe in which the marvelous makes up the fabric and context of the story. Through this quest for the curious and the new, such stories tend to teach children that the real world is not very interesting, and thus instigate a sort of childhood Modernism. In fact, it was in the 1920s when, according to Senior, Modernism began to flourish in the United States that an outbreak of children's fantasy literature occurred. Today we see a flurry of movies, toys, dolls and games with strange, twisted and grotesque forms—all of which develop diseased imaginations.

Old fairy tales and fables, by contrast, are always well rooted in the world of our experience. Actual preternatural marvels or moments of enchantment are exceptional, outside interventions into what is otherwise rather ordinary life. Even talking animals retain their familiar characteristics, though a certain playful liberty is taken. Senior explains: "Mice don't happen to eat with forks and spoons, but eat they certainly do. Animals don't talk but have consciousness; they respond to tone of voice if not the rational content of words."[23] Indeed, we talk to them, and they communicate among themselves. It does not take much, therefore, to imagine them speaking. Thus, the tales show a healthy imaginative invention, not fantasy: "Play and fantasy seem alike but play is the combination of two or more things which could go together in real life and just don't happen to."[24] Providing an apt

illustration of this, Senior comments that "a flying horse is play, a flying elephant fantasy. When horses run with manes and tails loose in the wind, they really seem to fly; an elephant with wings is an absurdity."[25] Pegasus is beautiful and meaningful, while Dumbo is grotesque and unreal.

That is all very well, but what good are these stories other than for relaxation and amusement? G. K. Chesterton suggests that fairy tales "say that apples were golden only to refresh the forgotten moment when we found they were green" and that "rivers run with wine, so we remark, for a wild moment, that they run with water."[26] Hearing of other possibilities, we come to realize that green apples and water are not a mechanical necessity, but objects of a mysterious and wonderful choice by their Maker. We are restored in the freshness of delight, surprised anew by the fact of trees laden with green apples and of rivers flowing with beautiful, sweet water.

These tales can prompt all ages to delight in existence, but they are especially appropriate for children. They help the child discover, in ways that he is apt to assimilate, the mystery and dignity of living things, a sense of good and evil, spiritual presences. That is to say, they foster—in beauty, delight and wonder—the child's budding connection with the real world that God created.

Yet, Senior affirms that fairy tales take place in another world: "The setting is the Other World, a preternatural place, no less real than this one, inhabited by creatures intermediate between the natural and supernatural, such as fairies, elves, sprites, flying horses and unicorns."[27] Elsewhere he indicates what he meant by "Other World":

> [When you read such tales to him] the child's eyes grow glazed as he listens and seems to see some world—that world, more real than this, not fantasy, not whimsy, not the stuff of the Walt Disney movies, Grimm's Fairy Tales are very real and very grim sometimes. . . . You tell it again until your eyes begin to glaze and you too begin to see again that there is more to this world than meets the eye.[28]

Thus, the old tales lead to a deeper look into things, as Senior writes concerning nursery rhymes: "Though it may sound pretentious to say

so, there is a mystery in all these cats, dogs, horses, cattle, pigs, trees, grass, crooked walls, jolly boys, nasty old men and saucy girls. Lyrics lift us up beyond our ken; defying gravity, they show us things *sub specie æternitatis*."[29] This childhood initiation into gazing upon the world "from the perspective of eternity," may be the very reason why these tales prepare the child for subsequent education, even the study of philosophy and theology, as he comments: "The seminal ideas of Plato, Aristotle, St. Augustine, St. Thomas, only properly grow in an imaginative ground saturated with fables, fairy tales, stories, rhymes, romances, adventures."[30]

Gymnasium

At the age of seven or so, reason begins to manifest itself. The child begins to realize that the world is not centered around himself. He becomes morally conscious, capable of being sensible to other peoples' needs. He can converse and grasp some nuances and wordplay, and catches an absurdity brought out by a joke. He is able to master his feelings enough to be attentive and sit still for a while. Thus, he has ripened sufficiently for the next stage, gymnastic discipline with classmates in grade school.

Although many of Senior's former students chose to implement his education model by homeschooling their children, Senior himself did not consider this type of education to be the ideal, even for preteens. Because the child is ready to explore the world and is eager to socialize with other children, he needs to leave of the nest, though not for very long, nor far away. Normally, grade school should take place in a "neighborhood schoolhouse."[31] For Senior, this small school should not be co-educational, because even when very little, boys and girls are not the same and require distinct approaches in education from the start, "suited to the different ways the sexes understand."[32] Otherwise, Senior writes, "sexes get confused."[33]

The principal mode of learning in grade school is of course gymnastic. Senior comments on the fact that boys learn through doing and playing:

Six to twelve year olds . . . think by sight, sound, touch, smell and taste, in a word in things. You can pry them loose by teaching methods but in so doing deprive them of the natural strength in child learning. Tom Sawyer on his island spending hours watching insects or alert for shooting stars at night is far from wasting time. It is the work of schools to discipline such learning, not to subvert it.[34]

Accordingly, one should let the boys carry out real and natural activities, without abstractions or artificial intermediaries being placed between them and reality: "Writing [is learned] by writing of real events; counting by counting real things; swimming by swimming in rivers, lakes, mud holes or surf; riding by riding with someplace to go; shooting by shooting at rabbits and squirrels."[35] For example, regarding mathematics, here is how the gymnastic principle is applied: "Let children know what chickens are by seeing, hearing, chasing, being chased and pecked before they count their eggs! The education expert says, 'It makes no difference if it's eggs, peanuts or stars! Two and two of anything is four'—a mode of discourse college youth can handle, but abuse to six- to twelve-year-olds."[36]

The minimum a Catholic boy should learn in grade school, according to Senior, would be "sufficient Latin for comprehending and serving Mass, Gregorian Chant sufficient for singing the Ordinary, Catechism, Reading, Writing, Arithmetic and Calisthenics."[37] In his writings, he does not elaborate on how these subjects should be handled in grade school, but much of what he said in the context of high school education can be applied at that more elementary level. One specific area, however, does receive some attention: reading. Grade school boys should hear and read literature that deals with direct experience because eventually "boys turn away from fairy tales to things that count."[38] The dreamer of fairytale worlds has awakened and entered into the concrete visible world. He suddenly feels that there is much to experience and figure out. He is drawn to adventure stories, extraordinary experiences of the ordinary world, such as are to be found in *Treasure Island, Huckleberry Finn, Robin Hood, Call of the Wild, Robinson Crusoe*:

[Grade school boys] want facts about horses and ships. . . . In schoolbooks [they] learn about lives they hope to lead with all the gear, tackle, and trim. Place takes precedence over character and plot. The hero gets into a scrape, finds a map, runs off to an island, gets lost in a cave, rafts down a river, sets off to sea, rides up the Chisholm trail —whatever it is that puts him outside society—and off we go on serial adventure.[39]

In "The Restoration of Innocence," Senior comments on a number of classical books for boys. He notes, for example, that *Huckleberry Finn* points to a mystery of boyhood prior to the experience of sin, or at least before the cold clamp of vice:

All the while the river flows, teeming with natural and human life by day, past lonely village lights at night beneath a swarm of stars. As everybody says, despite the unsentimentalism down to the stink of dirty men, Mark Twain describes lost paradise. Huck is now about fourteen and Nigger Jim, with a wife and several children, perhaps eighteen or twenty; but both still keep their nakedness intact. Somehow, unlike the rest of us, they have survived the sins of puberty as savage innocents invincibly ignorant. They don't grow up like us and go to school. On the raft, there are no girls and therefore neither culture nor temptation nor the *lachrymae rerum* that only come to those who learn by suffering and sin.[40]

Such books escort the boy through to the early teens and eighth grade. After "curing" the wood in the gymnasium, it is time to "carve" it in high school, according to a metaphor Senior uses.[41]

Risks and Protection in High School

Senior advocates boarding school as the best setting for high school lest "boys stay tied to apron strings."[42] During "adolescence, the first spring of the independent state of manhood,"[43] they need to acquire some

self-reliance and judgment and be with other boys and men, "leaving mom for *alma mater* [to] practice the male culture of barracks."[44] A boarding school has the advantage of taking the boy away from the nest while still protecting him from our so turbulent world. School, deriving from the Greek word meaning leisure, is an appropriate term for this escape from agitation: "The most important integral accident of a school is its 'quiet.' A school is a place for leisure. Not business, war or politics, a sanctuary, a refuge. . . . In the glare of publicity and the din of battle, it is difficult to see and hear the world God made rather than the one we did."[45]

Furthermore, it is propitious that high school boys reside at their place of study because, not only classes, but everything—Holy Mass and prayer, sport, manual labor, recreation and friendship—should work together in an organic gymnastic and musical whole: "High school learning is integral, which means that all its parts cohere; it is, therefore, best achieved at boarding school where the education and the life of the place are unified."[46] This allows for an integral formation affecting their conduct of life as well. Teachers act in *loco parentis* and should, for example, form the boys in fitting personal beauty—this too has its importance:

A good student is good-looking. . . . Grooming, dress, deportment, tone of voice—these must be taught because, without the habits and bearing of the artist, the art can't be learned. . . . Teachers, having polished the boys' rough edges [should] also make them beautiful . . . not pretty, which comes from a root meaning "coy," "tricky," "deceitful," but beautiful of soul, handsome, decent, manly and pleasant.[47]

The teen years, as we know, need to be under the special tutelage of the Nine Muses. "Boys in high school," Senior writes, "exercise their newly discovered powers of emotion as they grow in strength and grace."[48] This is the time to focus on music. Nevertheless, a good portion of teaching in gymnastic mode is still required because young adolescent boys continue learning very much through their bodies. Beyond this fact, Senior recognizes that, in our day, gymnastic is necessary as a remedial measure:

"Teaching the five external senses in gymnastic should be the work of elementary schools, but they have been so badly mechanized, their graduates are totally deprived, or, at best, know 'nature' pasteurized at summer camps."[49] He expands further, therefore, on gymnastic in high school.

Senior also has something to say about the rooms, buildings and grounds of the school, as these pertain to the gymnastic environment. The site itself should be natural and handsome, pleasing to all the senses:

The campus . . . must be well proportioned with pleasing shapes and colors . . . cascades of flowers and striped awning with a lace of vine and cloud and under starry skies at night, away from the indecent glare of city lights; . . . sounds must be beautiful too . . . there is rest and peace in the sough of winds and the shouts of boys at play . . . [for odors] there will be lilacs in spring, dahlias in fall, wood smoke in winter with animal manures and human sweat all year long![50]

High school gymnastic is not childish. Senior champions a school with a quasi-military discipline:

A modified rule is the best way to file the rough edges off ill-mannered rubes and roughen suburbanite fops who are used to getting up, eating, playing and going to bed pretty much as they want. Our boys jump out of bed at the blast of a horn at five-thirty in the morning, get their britches on in ten seconds and dash to the latrine for a splash of icy water in the face. First erudition is gymnastic![51]

He does take the idea of close contact with nature to an extreme: "no electricity, plumbing, central heat or air conditioning, hot in summer, cold in winter, bright on bright days, dim on dim ones, black on black nights, no running water, no inside sinks and toilets—all of which . . . is part of education."[52] A former student of Senior's commented: "Such children will have a fond familiarity all their lives of living with the seasons and

the changes of weather, for the memory of light and shadow as given by the sun and the clouds. . . . These are important details of sensory and emotional growth, grounded in the real, and reverberating the beautiful, true, and good."[53] One might at least advise, in our times, that boys be temporarily denied some of the comforts they are so accustomed to and unplugged for a while from their computers, smartphones, video games and iPods. Divested of these things, they can then be more connected with creation and acquire healthy memories, and will also learn not to be so dependent on luxury and artificial entertainment. They will better develop who they are and, in fact, have much more fun.

Senior also recommends a rough camping trip:

> Beyond the day to day physical encounters with nature in study and each other in sports, the boys must go for a couple of weeks each year on a wilderness survival trek. . . . Boys have got to face real hardship and danger, even to the chance of injury and death. If they don't learn how to cry and pray for help sometime in adolescence, they fail their rites of passage and remain emotionally prepubescent for the rest of their lives. This is a harsh, hard school. One hopes the accidents will not be too severe—of course that they won't be fatal; but what can't happen can't be faced; they have to swim out beyond the ropes or there isn't any test.[54]

Senior is not advocating intense hardship, but simply realistic experiences. Such suggestions can be shocking, however, to us moderns who flee in terror from the idea of injury or pain. Yet, modern preoccupations with "pasteurizing" nature and avoiding risks are opposed to a real experience of reality. Authentic emotions need real challenges in order to be developed and disciplined. If boys do not find adventure in healthy settings, they might well seek it in fantasy, drugs, sex, violence and crime.

Senior offers these elucidating words regarding the adolescent's new perspective on music in relation to that of the two preceding age levels: "Though the fact is abused when taken as unalterable, there is a dialectical movement to life. Infants yearn for the Other World; schoolboys scorn

any place but this one; adolescents recoup the loss in the higher synthesis of romance."[55] Thus, the high school adolescent's proper genre of reading is the romance—*Ivanhoe, Tale of Two Cities, Gawain and the Green Knight, A Midsummer Night's Dream*—where, Senior writes, "rounded characters, many-sided and interior, are sent on impossible quests, confronting uncontrollable reality that only women can mediate."[56] These three features of romances—the interior life of the characters, heroic deeds and girls—are especially appropriate for teenagers. Senior underlines the feminine presence as a major distinguishing feature: "In boys' adventure books if girls appear at all, they are extrinsic to the story, whereas in adolescent romance they are the origin, progress and consummation of everything men do."[57]

We have already described how the newly risen attraction to girls draws the boy out of himself, leading him to discover the beauty of the world and to aspire to high ideals. For Senior, girls have an important role in the proper development of affections, preparing the way for friendship with God: "Love grows in five cumulative (not disjunctive) stages," he writes, "each defined by its object: parents, animals, boys, girls and God."[58] It is obvious that the first awakening of affection is through relationship with one's parents. We have mentioned the place love of animals has in fostering affection. Here is what Senior writes about boy friendships: "Adolescents pair off in their way as in later life married couples do. And the fidelity of the latter depends on how well such bonds were fixed in the former because *dilectio* is false if not till death. Men who haven't got best friends, though their wives sometimes resent them, never measure up to having wives."[59] Senior has bold words concerning a boy's relationship with girls, deeming it at the top of the list of earthly friendships, leading to love of God: "The Kingdom of Heaven is the knowledge and love of God and we learn to bear the living flames of that love only through suffering the paler heats of human desire."[60]

High school, then, is the time for initiating a new type of relationship with girls. Risks are necessary, in Senior's view, not only in outdoor natural adventures, but also in this arena of girl-boy relationship. He warns against overprotecting the teenager and thus stunting his psychological

growth. Life is an adventure and a romance. We should not conduct it from a negative standpoint, that is, merely avoiding evil, but rather positively adhere to the good and learn to love:

> When a child hits twelve, he is ready for the adolescent experience and that means the explosion of physical aptitudes and the emotional responses to them—the call to dangerous adventures and to experiments in romance. . . . There are Catholic families who proudly send their eighteen-year-olds up to college carefully bound and wrapped at the emotional and spiritual age of twelve— good little boys and girls in cute dresses and panty-waists who never get into trouble or into knowledge and love. . . . Faith presupposes nature and cannot be efficacious in its atrophy. There is little point in keeping children out of Hell if you don't afford them the means of getting into Heaven.[61]

High school adolescents must be given a good formation so that they may understand moral principles and then, little by little, learn to live their own life and grapple with its challenges. Eventually, one has to throw them in the water. "So give them strong catechetics, strong preaching, good example, supervision in a general and determinate way but not in each particular and by all means permitting them the freedom of good, dangerous books as well as the dangerous games such as football or mountain climbing."[62]

Senior, of course, does not intend that boys and girls be thrown into near occasion of sin: "If first experiments begin between the sexes, the torch is put to an uncontrollable natural fire whose consequence is social disaster and personal sin."[63] When he recommends "dangerous" books, he does not mean unprincipled ones—his examples are *Romeo and Juliet* and *The Three Musketeers*. The first could indeed overexcite some youthful imaginations and emotions, but it contains some of the world's finest and purest lines regarding love. The second, while it does include some immoral attitudes that call for discernment, above all inspires generosity, courage and nobility. Literature such as this can impress upon

young folk insights into the human heart and personal human relationships, examples of refinement of sentiment, such as no other medium can convey.

A balanced, disciplined opportunity for this emotional development concerning girls would be had through the proximity of a sister school. The boys could thus begin, Senior writes, "the general love of beauty in girls, discovered in sports and plays, culminating at the Senior Waltz, with a prefiguration of the love of choice, in having their first 'date' and, walking home by moonlight, the first stir of emotion."[64] "General love," one that does not involve pairing off, but appreciating something beautiful in girls in general, can develop as boys watch them take part in sports. The boys, in their turn playing in front of girls, would be initiated in chivalry: "The first condition of the right relation of the sexes is that boys be heroes suffering for girls who watch and blush. Soccer is a high school joust."[65] Plays and dances would thus be an opportunity for boys and girls to interact, but they must be closely supervised. For stage plays, he enjoins: "Keep rehearsals strictly chaperoned and the company on stage so no two get alone."[66] And for the junior prom and the senior waltz: "Wise duennas make sure they change partners several times."[67]

While conservative parents and teachers might have a tendency to overprotect boys in the physical and emotional domains, in studies they usually do not protect them enough. Senior often warns against the harm done by bringing college-level work into this time of musical play. As we have seen, he insists that boys are not capable of diving into the conceptual domain: "Rational animals abstract universals from particulars at all ages, but boys can't handle strings of them without the concrete things in hand."[68] Furthermore, such an effort at abstract knowledge at this period would bypass knowledge of real things. The boys might learn the formulas, but would not actually know and love what they are talking about: "Liberal arts and sciences overload their brains, short circuit knowledge of particulars and turn out smart brats who argue about everything in a vacuum."[69] They would not have the delight and wonder that open the soul to great truths: "For the great majority [of boys], like too much liquid poured too fast into small cups, science spills out of brains and what is

taken actually retards understanding because it gives answers to questions not asked."[70] The boys, thus stuffed with "science," would in fact be incapable of fruitful college studies even when they reach the correct age for them: "The liberal arts . . . are college subjects that asphyxiate the arts themselves as well as boys if they are introduced too soon without the musical air they breathe."[71]

As high school is not the time for direct training of the intellect, neither is it the period for formal discipline of the will in virtues. Following Plato's and Aristotle's recommendation on musical education, the teacher should aid students in spontaneously directing their affections toward the good and the true. High school should, therefore, dispose students to virtue by attracting and inspiring rather than by laying down a number of rules. Senior observes: "In the gymnastic and musical modes, temperance is prefigured in stories, games and the lessons school life teaches in a general way about what is too little and too much . . . . Against bad habits, the school forms good ones in the daily routine, competitive games, emulation of fictional heroes and the good example of teachers."[72] Allan Bloom writes along the same lines: "Education is not sermonizing to children against their instincts and pleasures, but providing a natural continuity between what they feel and what they can and should be."[73] Let boys first experience the objective good—courtesy, generosity, courage—as attractive. Later they can reflect on virtues they have already recognized as beautiful, as well as directly exercise themselves in acquiring them.

High School Curriculum

For Senior, there should be two types of high school, according to a boy's aptitudes and interests: "At age thirteen, when . . . physical, mental and emotional distinctions occur, we need two schools: One offering a liberal, Latin education . . . and another practical and vernacular, in farming and the crafts."[74] He describes those whose talents incline them more toward the practical school: "It is reasonably clear in any eighth grade class that most prefer to work with their hands. Abstractions fail to interest and

literature bores them beyond distraction to revolt—they want real action ordered to the work they will do in the world."[75]

Discerning who may be of the intellectual bent and who may be inclined toward the practical is not always a simple thing. Some intellects develop later than others and acquire new interests. Nevertheless, the basic distinction does exist and there is a need for both types of school. In his writings Senior focuses mostly on the liberal school, but he does mention the basic format the vocational one should have: "Math and science are studied as tools for an apprenticeship in several occupations varying according to region, to which English, Music and History are subordinate but kept to the highest standards of popular culture"[76]—by which he means traditional, pre-Modernist songs and stories. Much of what he writes concerning schools that provide preparation for liberal professions could be applied to technical schools.

Senior outlines the curriculum for a liberal school: "Music is the formal light in which we see the seven material subjects: language, nature, corporal beauty, measure, the deeds of men, song and story."[77] He suggests the following schedule: at dawn, Lauds and Mass; at 8:00 a.m., Latin ("language"); 9:00 a.m., nature study; 10:00 a.m., calisthenics ("corporal beauty"); 11:00 a.m., mathematics ("measure"); 1:00 p.m., geography and history ("deeds of men"); 2:00 p.m., music ("song"); 3:00 p.m. to 5:00 p.m., sports and manual labor; 6:00 p.m., Vespers; and after supper, "story" in the form of a colloquium based on English literature and poetry. Compline and an examination of conscience complete the day.

Some important domains are missing from this list. It is remarkable that Senior prescribes English-language literature and poetry only for the colloquium. He probably has in mind the old days when Greek and Latin classics formed the core of literature studies. Senior gives the reason for other omissions: "There is no formal instruction in writing or drawing but plenty of both. Neither art nor composition is a subject in itself"[78]— they are accomplished in one of the subjects, such as drawing in nature study and composition in history. Also, although he foresaw a chaplain and an oratory with daily formal prayer and Holy Mass, he includes no class as such on religious instruction, perhaps because, as he said once,

"school is not a substitute for church." He doubtless presupposed a catechism class on Sundays. Nevertheless, for Senior, all studies should finally
aim at knowing and loving God: "Secular education is not only incomplete
but contrary to both God and nature; it is sacrilegious and unscientific. . . .
The ultimate formality of whatever subject studied [should be] the mind
of God as it is revealed in created things physical, mathematical and
ethical, and as it is imitated in things productive."[79] He is mainly emphasizing the fact that there should be no separation between the secular and
religious dimensions in history, literature, and nature study. In good
gymnastic and musical fashion, the Christian reference should be part of
everyday life: "Thomas Arnold said of Rugby [College] that its aim was
not so much to teach religion as to make the place religious. It must be so
with us."[80] Thus, he writes that at daily Mass "the homily sets the spiritual
theme of the day to be picked up in all the classes, work and play."[81]

Now we are prepared to examine a few of Senior's specific directives
on subjects and classes. Coming at eight o'clock, Latin is the first class
on the list. "Why Latin?" Senior asks. "Because it is the architectonic
language of Christian civilization."[82] He had taught Latin and had
definite ideas on language study. He urges immediate contact with the
language so that grammar will be learned through example rather than
rules. Abstract grammar is to be studied only after a certain fluency with
the language itself has been acquired. In addition, in order for a language
to become second nature to them, the boys must be immersed in it.
Senior, therefore, proposes that much of the day be spent conversing in
Latin. Thus nature study, history and music classes are to be conducted
in that language.

Furthermore, learning Latin should be, like other subjects, a playful
process. Most of the class is to consist of conversation about things and
events of everyday life, accompanied by gestures and pictures drawn on a
blackboard. The lesson should regularly involve a story: "Read aloud a
fable with good big illustrations, some tale the boys already know from
childhood so the meaning will be there before they have to think about
it."[83] The class should finish with memorization: "The last ten minutes
are spent memorizing the *Ave Maria* as the first step toward getting the

Rosary, Lauds and Vespers of the Little Office, the Ordinary of the Mass, *Catechismus Romanus pro Pueris* and several Scripture passages by heart."[84]

Then comes nature study at nine o'clock "to make suburbanites conscious of the rational content of the earth beneath their feet."[85] These classes should not be conducted as abstract science. Memories and imagination need to be formed by contact with real things—by looking at the stars and charting their movements; by observing frogs in their habitats rather than dissecting their corpses in a classroom:

> Popular science, spreading the habit of analysis outside the laboratory, confounds common sense. Boys have to start with the appearances of things—no telescopes, microscopes and dissections, but whole things as they are to us in ordinary life.[86]
>
> The classes go outdoors for Nature Study, taught from manuals like the Audubon Society's of birds, rocks, reptiles, plants and trees. No overloading brains with science, just the facts as the senses and emotions know them. This first contact with nature is indispensable for a right psychological growth in knowledge and is the only basis for higher studies at college. The freshman will learn by name every weed, bush, tree and vegetable and see how they take nourishment and reproduce. A nature study includes sketching and writing compositions about what is seen.[87]

Senior counsels the instructor to avoid talking much about God, lest words jump ahead of the experience of the students and hinder them from listening to God speaking through the book of creation:

> Don't intrude religion. Just let the world be there. Let God teach as He intends in the language of nature which He Himself invented for the purpose.... Wrestling in the dirt under a clean sky in the flat light of an October sun, licked by the fiery tongues of maple leaves as they roll in them, the cool indifferent pines observing—well, you don't have to say God made all this; it's in the excitation of their blood.[88]

Ten o'clock is to be the time for some physical exercise. "Calisthenics ('beautiful strength')," Senior writes, "is a set of exercises developing the body not for show but health. A boy should have the muscles that a boy should have. Beauty is the right relation of magnitude, proportion and splendor."[89] By these exercises along with manual work, "the physical seeds of rational control are planted in the muscles."[90]

At eleven o'clock, mathematics. As in grade school, they are to be taught as much as possible by "measuring, counting and figuring real things."[91] Algebra and geometry are to be learned by solving practical problems, in surveying, for example.

After lunch come history and geography. There should be a focus on facts and events, but for Senior, history is substantially "either rhetoric, where evidence is ordered persuasively toward the forming of opinion, or poetry, when persons and events are presented dramatically as if present."[92] We know which approach is appropriate for high school: "As in Nature Study, let the boys find out the Maker in the made. Tell stories of the great men of the past but don't theologize. The mode is poetry (story), not rhetoric (propaganda)."[93] Thus, these classes are to be composed, not of the study of economics and political systems, but rather of stories, by using literature, plays and songs. Stories will enable the student to appreciate and remember significant deeds:

> Tell stories of the great men of the past. . . . The Muses are daughters of memory and memory thinks in stories. . . . Alas, men now in their forties, taught nothing but scientific history, having nothing in their hearts but what they got outside of school from the muses of the Beatles and Rolling Stones whose collected works they remember—while none can tell you what the Seven, Thirty, or Hundred Years Wars were about or name the English Kings.[94]

At two o'clock, music. Singing is also learned naturally: "Each student discovers his voice the way he did his buoyancy swimming and his balance riding bikes. . . . Music is a matter of hearing and imitating sound."[95]

From three to five o'clock, the students are to practice sports and manual labor. Sports are, of course, an important feature of gymnastic. They also play a part in the musical mode, notably in beginning right relationships with girls, as we have seen. Senior suggests soccer in the fall, hockey in winter, and track in the spring. To illustrate how manual labor can contribute to the learning process, Senior points to Father Thomas Shields, first chair of the Department of Education at Catholic University, who, after having failed in school, discovered joy in intellectual life through farm work, as he reflected on real things, coming to questions and answers that grew out of his experience.[96] In high school a spirit of delight and wonder should inform the manual tasks: "Whatever the work, it must be something hard, spiritual, enjoyable and serious, not in the spirit of business, like work and sport today, but play."[97] Senior insists on the school supporting itself by honest, instructive labor: "The only honest endowment for a school is a self-sufficient farm, without machines, to feed a chaplain, four teachers, a cook and forty-eight boys who eat like hogs but also dig, hoe, chop, pitch hay and shovel dung." This work would also "keep teachers grounded in the things they teach"[98]—all the more as they would have to carry on alone during summer vacation.

The daily curriculum ends in the evening with a senior student or a teacher reading aloud to the boys from a classical book or helping them memorize poetry. The leader poses questions and guides relaxed and good-humored conversation about the text. Senior envisions these evening experiences as enjoyable and part of the boys' recreation, something akin to what he so highly recommends for family life. Leisurely oral reading in a group enhances appreciation of the text and provides a fitting learning framework for the boys: "In the . . . experience of reading aloud together, boys learn how each other feels; they acquire terms of reference for emotions words alone can't handle."[99]

The ideas and models in "The Restoration of Innocence" indicate what a gymnastic and musical education could be today for boys in home and school. Though Senior never taught at the grade or high school levels, his students have established schools where they have adopted his

major principles and implemented a number of his suggestions, with pronounced success for both boys and girls. These schools have helped cultivate, if not necessarily yet saints or scholars, teenagers who at least love to learn and are capable of friendships, with zest for life and hearts full of song.

Sources of Inspiration

*Without [the entry into the interior cellar], there is
no progress toward the Kingdom of Heaven, which
is the only goal of Christian life, whose only language is music. . . . To enter with Our Beloved Lord
into that prayer of quiet and to pray to Our Blessed
Lady that he might lead us there, we must learn to
speak that language too.*
—The Restoration of Christian Culture

HAVING surveyed Senior's thoughts on the education of boys
through high school, we now move on to his ideas regarding
the application of gymnastic and music at the college level. However, that
subject will be left for the last part of our book, where we will explore his
adventure at the University of Kansas. Here, to complete Part III, we will
present Senior's recommendations on from where the "dull, low places"
are to draw their Christian inspiration. Home, schools, the neighborhood,
work and everything else are to be ordered to man's final end, to his
supernatural good, namely, that he love God with all his heart, soul, mind
and strength, and his neighbor as himself for love of God. One can find
in Senior's writings three particular means of imbuing culture with the
Christian spirit, thus aiding man in attaining his goal: a worthy Mass,
contemplative houses and consecration to the Blessed Virgin Mary. All
three means are gymnastic and musical; they work through the senses,
imagination and emotions, marvelously linking body and soul, mind and

reality, nature and grace. Before examining each one, it would be useful to consider the personal, individual spiritual effort that lies at their base.

Be Ye Therefore Perfect

We must personally labor for the restoration of Christian culture. Senior states: "Civilization is not the creation of its outlaws [as Joyce said] but of men who have worked hard in the sweat of their brows building on the past."[1] He always called directly on his listener or reader. "Anyone, right now," he writes, "can live a better life if he wants to where he is. The answer lies where it always has, not in the laws of nations, which indeed determine the destinies of Sodom and Gomorrah; the answer lies in the laws of the Kingdom within us because there we make the choice."[2] Each one has a personal decision to make. Who will respond to the good and the beautiful, who will adhere to Christ if I do not? Nothing one does will be true and real if the heart is not.

Senior lays out some principles of the spiritual life in Chapter Four of *The Restoration of Christian Culture*, "The Catholic Agenda." Referring to exterior human action or work, he teaches that it has three goals: the immediate, the proximate and the final. We have reflected on certain aspects of the immediate purpose, which is to do a good job well in and of itself. For the proximate purpose, Senior explains that our work must be accomplished justly; that is, we must render to the other his due. Over and above that, work should tighten our bonds with one another. In other words, the second goal ultimately is fraternal charity, our communion together in Christ. "The proximate end of work," he writes, "is love of neighbor; work must make us friends."[3]

So that we do not confuse this Christian brotherly love with natural sentiments, Senior explains that charity is a supernatural activity, where one loves with God's love, letting Christ love in and through us. "The saints all say," he writes, "that Christian love, or charity, is a force which presupposes and makes use of affection as an instrument but is itself something else: Charity is not a human but a divine work accomplished through human work, with us as its voluntary instruments."[4] Consequently, our

main role lies in opening ourselves to God's action: "For our work to be efficacious in the order of love, we must first dispose ourselves to grace."[5] He identifies the essential obstacle to our being God's instrument: "The chief impediment to love of neighbor is love of self."[6] He concludes that "until we have crushed self-interest and become instruments of the only real agent of charity, every good work is vain."[7]

How do we go about crushing that self-interest, that is, our egoism, our disordered self-love that places ourselves at the center of perspectives? To that question, Senior replies that "the proximate end, perhaps surprisingly, is chiefly accomplished in prayer."[8] By prayer he means mainly solitary and silent recollection. We are usually poured out into the exterior world, wanting to see and be seen, worried about what people think of us, seeking sensible pleasures and so forth. In prayer, we turn away from the outward pull of so many sensible inputs and impulses; we collect our faculties in the direction of higher, supernatural realities.

Paraphrasing St. Catherine of Siena, Senior explains how it is that recollection can move us to fight our egoism. First, it permits us to examine our conscience and identify the egotistical impulses in our soul. He writes: "The practice of the proximate end of every work is achieved in what St. Catherine calls 'the cellar of self-knowledge,' where, in tears and penance, like St. Peter's, we find out what we are really like."[9] Second, by recalling Christ's Passion, we become aware of God's love for us in spite of our misery. Indeed, St. Peter was moved to tears because of Christ's gaze on him. Senior quotes St. Catherine, or God the Father speaking through her: "A man must persevere and remain in the cellar of self-knowledge in which he will learn My mercy, in the Blood of My only begotten Son."[10] Repentance emerges when we realize how far we are from responding properly to God's love. We are moved with "holy self-hatred," as St. Catherine called it, and at last resolve to take up mortification and the quest of virtues.

With this entry into the "cellar of self-knowledge" begins the process of removal of that major obstacle, which is self-love, thus enabling God's love to flow freely through us to others. Senior notes that recollection also provides a positive basis for fraternal charity: "Men come closer together

in quiet prayer than in any other way—come closer to each other because closer to Our Father in Heaven, because the Kingdom of Heaven is within the soul of each of us and insofar as we approach that Heaven inside ourselves we are just as much inside the souls of each other."[11]

Having entered into the depths of our own person, we reach the point where all men are alike. We share with each person in the mystery of God's call, and can learn to love all as ourselves.

This brings us to the third goal of our actions: "The final, or ultimate, purpose, the reason why we work and pray, is to know and love God as he is in himself, so far as that is possible."[12] Senior again indicates the means, namely, "imitating [God's] earthly life in Christ, the chief act of which was sacrifice."[13] This imitation does not consist in merely copying exterior actions. It flows from an interior participation in Christ's life. Through baptism, we have been grafted into Christ, and by our union with the Son we have been graciously elevated into a filial relationship with God as adopted children. We develop that filial relationship by giving ourselves over to Christ's influence, so as to be moved by His Spirit, the Spirit of sonship. Christ showed us how one lives as a son; His earthly existence reflected His eternal life as the Son. And since His "chief act" of filial love was His offering of Himself on the Cross, that is what we most need to imitate. We have to work our way back to the Father with and in Christ, and give ourselves as Christ did, in loving sacrifice. St. Paul wrote that we are "heirs of God and fellow heirs with Christ, provided we suffer with him."

In Chapter Nine we considered the importance of the poetic mode of knowledge for the spiritual life. While Senior does not speak about poetry or music in "The Catholic Agenda," elsewhere in the same book he forcefully maintains that it is needed in order for us to be drawn into the interior cellar, so as to cultivate love of God and of our neighbor. As the epigraph to this present chapter affirms, music is the language of the Kingdom of Heaven because it is the language of love. Senior explains that the ultimate objective of restoring music in the home is to learn that language:

Music really is the food of love and music in the wide sense is a specific sign of the civilized human species. Steeped in the ordinary pot of the Christian imagination, we will have learned to listen to that language by absorption, that mysterious music the Bridegroom [of the Song of Songs] speaks; and we will begin to love one another as he loves us.[14]

However, if the music of the home, of the neighborhood, of work and of school is to do its job correctly, it too must be nourished by music flowing from more supernatural sources.

The Holy Sacrifice of the Mass

Because religion is the first determinant of culture, public religious worship will be a culture's key activity: "Cult is the basis of culture,"[15] Senior writes. For Catholics, this cult consists principally in the Holy Sacrifice of the Mass, that way of our participating in Christ's offering, in His passage back to the Father. There, the individual and the community are oriented to the final end; there, members recognize and forge their deepest bonds around Christ.

Senior proclaims the paramount role Holy Mass has in culture with a sweeping, striking affirmation, as he was wont to do: "What is Christian culture? It is essentially the Mass." To demonstrate the truth of his statement he turns to facts, which was also his custom: "That is not my or anyone's opinion or theory or wish, but the central fact of two thousand years of history." Then he nuances and explains his proposition:

Christendom, what secularists call Western Civilization, is the Mass and the paraphernalia which protect and facilitate it. All architecture, art, political and social forms, economics, the way people live and feel and think, music, literature—all these things when they are right, are ways of fostering and protecting the Holy Sacrifice of the Mass.[16]

Thus, according to Senior, anything that is to be properly part of Christian culture should in some way shine forth from and lead back to Holy Mass. We have spoken of liturgy as being a work of art, and Senior has demonstrated how it also inspires art. In the Middle Ages, architecture was reborn to give a fitting home to the sacrifice of the Mass, sculpture and painting to adorn that home and point to the mysteries that take place therein, music and literature to celebrate and comment on those mysteries. One can readily understand, then, why those who were immersed in such a Christian environment lived, felt and thought together in reference to Christ and His Cross. Senior explains how political, social and economic forms in Christendom—the very structure of society, made up of farmer, craftsman, clerk and soldier—can be conceived as cultivating and protecting the Blessed Sacrament:

Around the church and garden . . . the caretakers live, the priests and religious whose work is prayer, who keep the Mystery of the Faith in its tabernacle of music and words in the Office of the Church; and around them, the faithful who gather to worship and divide the other work that must be done in order to make the perpetuation of the Sacrifice possible—to raise the food and make the clothes and build and keep the peace so that generations to come may live for him.[17]

Today's society is clearly far from being organized around Holy Mass. But even within the fabric of the Church, there have been departures from what can cultivate a sense for the higher things, for the spiritual. Being remiss about what surrounds Holy Mass, notably architecture, can have its consequences, affecting the celebration itself and thus our souls, as Senior writes: "If Sunday after Sunday congregations assist at the Holy Sacrifice of the Mass in a church built to the standards and specifications of Hamburger Heaven, it won't be long before the faithful have departed from the faith."[18]

Of greater import than addressing what surrounds it, as recent popes have made clear, it is the Mass itself that must be rehabilitated. In the

decades preceding Vatican II, celebration of Mass remained reverent and beautiful though the general culture of Western society was no longer prepared for such worship. In Father Frederick Faber's words, "the most beautiful thing this side of Heaven" had gradually become foreign to a noisy world that was increasingly insensitive to its meaningful signs. After Vatican II, the remedy to this situation often judged to be expedient was to lower the standards of liturgical celebration to the impoverished level of contemporary culture—using pop music instead of Gregorian chant, for example. With the introduction of a new rite of Holy Mass in 1969—the Novus Ordo Missae of Paul VI—the *status quo* was such that many took the opportunity to adopt further novelties taken from a cultural milieu that had essentially rejected God. This measure only hastened the debacle, because a Mass that is unworthily celebrated, that is not attractive and uplifting, does not cultivate a sense of the sacred nor the understanding of what is taking place; it cannot revitalize Christian culture. Confronted day by day with irreverence and inelegance, Senior lamented: "The norms for the celebration of the greatest act in the universe, the Holy Sacrifice of the Mass, are trifled with *ad libitum.*"[19]

Some orthodox Catholics, in trying to salvage things, have been too intellectual, focusing so intently on catechism and sound doctrine that they neglect the "music" that nourishes faith and love, that draws one into the mystery. They indeed tend to think that poetry is "silly stuff," as Senior once commented to be a tendency in some. Cardinal Ratzinger, by contrast, recognized the essential importance of the mysterious and the beautiful in experiencing our religion through liturgy: "The Church stands and falls with the liturgy. When the adoration of the Divine Trinity declines, when the faith no longer appears in its fullness in the liturgy of the Church, the faith will have lost the place where it is expressed and where it dwells. For this reason the true celebration of the liturgy is the center of any renewal of the Church whatsoever."[20] Both as cardinal and as pope, he often emphasized the importance of the beauty and the sensible dimension of the liturgy. For example, speaking of art in general but with reference to liturgy, Benedict XVI declared:

[There is a] need to involve, in the experience of faith, not only the mind and the heart, but also the senses through those other aspects of aesthetic taste and human sensitivity that lead man to benefit from the truth with his whole self, mind, body and soul. This is important; faith is not only thought but also touches the whole of our being.[21]

For Senior, the restoration of liturgy amounted to restoring the former rite:

From the cultural point of view, which I must insist is not a minor or accidental thing but indispensable to the ordinary means of salvation . . . the new Catholic Mass established in the US has been a disaster; and I must give public witness to my private petitions, with all due respect to the authorities, that its great predecessor—the most refined and brilliant work of art in the history of the world, the heart and soul and most powerful determining factor in Western Civilization, seedbed of saints— be restored.[22]

A very few years after this appeal by Senior, John Paul II reinstated Holy Mass according to the 1962 Missal; and in 2007 Benedict XVI, by recognizing that it had never been abrogated, reestablished its celebration as a regular part of Church life, calling it the "Extraordinary Form" of Mass alongside the "Ordinary Form," or the 1969 Missal. Benedict XVI knew that progress after such a collapse could only be slow and gradual. The faithful must come to rediscover the Extraordinary Form and experience its riches and beauty. He was convinced that its visible presence among us would also favorably influence the Ordinary Form, notably by inclining us toward a more reverential celebration. We all must work, pray and suffer to restore a liturgy that supports a living faith, where the sensible signs cultivate the interior life and renew a sense of the sacred and the invisible. Then liturgy can once again inspire culture.

Monastic Life

Senior insists on another factor as being essential to Christian culture and the restoration of a worthy Sacrifice of the Mass, ensuring its spreading influence throughout society: monastic life. Both his books about culture gradually build up toward a consideration of monasticism in their closing chapters. Monastic life epitomizes his ideas about Realism and Christian culture, being a central component of his practical projects. In developing this point, we will first consider his thoughts on what monastic life means for the monk himself, and then its importance for society.

In his life and writings, Senior was a veritable apostle of monasticism. He enjoined young Catholics to place it at the top of their list of possible professions:

> We must put this on our agenda: Encourage young men and women—particularly women, who have the greater aptitude—to do as Our Lord said, "be perfect." Of all the possible careers the young might consider and choose, they must put God's choice first and consider the possibility of a call to the contemplative life.[23]

Senior's strong advocacy stems from the fact that everything in monastic life is ordered to help the monk or nun enter into the cellar of knowledge of self and of God:

> The arguments and public martyrdoms are vain without the sacrifice of hearts. And what are the arguments and sacrifices for, except to bring us to the love of God? . . . The only way to Heaven is the Cross, whose straightest gate is a vocation to the religious life where as a monk or nun, formally under strict rule and direction, one commits himself entirely, in that burning furnace of charity, to God's love.[24]

Each religious order of the Church has its particular way of helping one commit oneself to God's love. Senior had a preference for the Benedictine way: "If I were a young man or woman seeking God today, I should

enter, if I could, a Benedictine monastery."[25] Comparing it to the Carthusian or Carmelite paths, he affirmed that "Benedict's is best understood as the spirituality of ordinary life."[26] By ordinary, he did not mean mediocre; he was referring to a spiritual path more readily accessible to all because more conformed to man's nature as incarnated spirit; a path where the sensible is largely used as a ladder to reach God. That is what particularly interests us here—to consider how monastic life forms an environment of truth through gymnastic and music, how it "touches the whole of our being," as Pope Benedict XVI desired.

As already noted, Senior once stated that all he had learned from philosophy and literature was summarized in the Benedictine *ora et labora*, which grounds the whole man in the soil while drawing him to the stars. Essentially, it is gymnastic and music at work, ordered toward allowing grace to operate in the soul:

> Through intimate intercourse with nature in manual work and the absorption of [God's] Presence in the Mass and by *lectio divina* of his Word, the singing of the Office and a life in integral conformity with it, the entire person of the monk, body and soul, is transformed in Christ . . . which is visible in the posture, attitude, grace of gait, gesture, speech of monks.[27]

Work, spiritual reading and liturgy are the three pillars supporting the Benedictine's gaze toward God and the divine mysteries. They are indeed "ordinary," the bread and butter of any fervent Christian life, but they can be developed in an ideal way in the monastic setting, in its healthy rhythm of alternation, each interpenetrating and influencing the other. Work in a monastery attains to the values we have mentioned, cultivating cooperation, responsibility, fraternal charity and obedience. Senior speaks of "intercourse with nature." Manual work provides the gymnastic contact with God's manifestation of Himself through His creation. While it is true that monks, like everyone else today, are implicated in mechanization, monasteries are usually in the country, often live off of agriculture, and nearly always practice at least some craft work,

thus being closer to natural things. The musical mode in a monastic setting can then fully operate, as the monk celebrates and meditates on God's Revelation and loving Presence through Scripture, Holy Mass and the Divine Office. There is nowhere like a Benedictine monastery to nurture prayerful, poetic reading and beautiful, reverential liturgy.

The expression "life in integral conformity" can be applied to the integration of the monk's entire environment and all his activities into his spiritual life, which accomplishes the desire St. Benedict expressed in his Rule: *Ut in omnibus glorificetur Deus* ("May God be glorified in all things"). In a Benedictine monastery everything is artfully arranged so that the monk can be nourished in natural and supernatural truth. There, all the "paraphernalia" Senior mentions concerning Holy Mass— architecture, art, music, social forms—radiate from and point to Christ and His mysteries.

Through contact with nature, through *lectio divina*, the liturgy and an artful environment of truth, a monk's memory and imagination are imbued with the good and the orderly, and he is attracted with delight and wonder to the beauty of the Christian mysteries. Blessed Newman's essay, *The Mission of St. Benedict*, proposes that the Benedictine life can be characterized by the poetic attitude: "To St. Benedict . . . let me assign, for his discriminating badge, the element of poetry."

After providing fifty pages demonstrating the poetry of Benedictine life and work, the future cardinal concludes that the poetic habit working through the things of this world renders the monk close to the other world, like a child: "We are told to be like little children; and where will we find a more striking instance than is here [in the Benedictine life] afforded us of that union of simplicity and reverence, that clear perception of the unseen, yet recognition of the mysterious, which is the characteristic of the first years of human existence."[28] As Newman would say, the monk's assent to religious objects is real not notional, particular not general, almost as if they were "objects of sight." Senior, in his turn, writes: "Monasticism is essentially the schooling of the personal experience of the Catholic Faith. To believe, one must taste and see."[29] The monk gradually acquires the ability, according to the ideal expressed in Senior's

poem, "Contemptus Mundi," to read this world like a book. He learns to gaze on the invisible through the visible. The monk lives naturally in the supernatural world. In *The Death of Christian Culture*, Senior quotes Carlyle on that author's experience of monks: "Religion lies over them like an all-embracing canopy, like an atmosphere and life-element, which is not spoken of, which in all this is presupposed without speech."[30]

For Senior, the contemplative life, the culture of holiness in the cloister, is an end in itself, it needs no justification. Nevertheless, he also appreciates monastic life as a necessary basis for a Christian society. He writes that "the simplest, most practical restoration of Christian culture will be the reestablishment of contemplative convents and monasteries."[31] To support that statement, he again refers to history. According to Senior, monastic life is "the central institution" of Christendom.[32] In the early Middle Ages, when, after the collapse of the Roman Empire, society had become unwoven and was losing sight of the great truths that guide human life, when ethical standards and law were breaking down, the West slowly regrouped itself around monasteries. Monasteries were closed gardens of Christian faith and life, little islands of light and warmth that enlightened and stimulated the world round about in a sort of process of osmosis. Senior envisions the possibility of contemplative monasteries, especially of the Benedictine order, fulfilling an analogous role today. Just plant them, he proposes, and they will renew the soil from which authentic Christian culture will spring up again.

The fundamental importance of monks and nuns to society lies in that, as Senior observes, "whatever we do in the political and social order, the indispensable foundation is prayer."[33] It is good for everyone that some be consecrated to prayer. Alluding to a scene in the Gospel according to Luke, of Mary of Bethany and her sister Martha—the traditional figures of the contemplative and active lives, respectively—Senior explains the indispensable role that contemplative religious orders play: "The greatest need in the Church today is the contemplative life of monks and nuns. There is the active life, but Mary chose the better part and everything that Martha does depends on her."[34] Senior sees the life of the contemplative, dedicated to prayer, as a total sacrifice in which other Christians can participate:

What is needed is the leaven of St. Benedict—that a significant number of the Church would sacrifice themselves to God as monks and nuns; and that a greater number among priests and laymen would participate in that sacrifice by nourishing the interior life insofar as that is possible in the midst of their active duties in the world.[35]

St. Thérèse of the Child Jesus taught that contemplatives are the "heart of the Church," energizing the members of Christ's Mystical Body.

The action of these front-line soldiers of the spiritual life takes place first of all invisibly in the communion of saints, where hidden bonds are woven that will be revealed only in Heaven. These bonds with monks are usually tighter for those who are spiritually linked to a monastery, and Senior counsels such an official association: "If I were called to the other vocations," Senior writes, "the secular priesthood or marriage, I should become an oblate of such a monastery or at least keep as close to it as I could consistent with my obligations."[36] An oblate is an individual who officially seeks God with the monks of a particular community, especially by praying some of the Divine Office and trying to apply the Holy Rule to his life, in communion with that monastery.

This spiritual proximity is the primary sense of Senior's affirmation that "in a well-ordered form of Christianity, we as simple Christians should live in the shadow of the Cassin Mountains,"[37] that is, of Monte Cassino, the monastery founded by St. Benedict, cradle of Benedictine life. Beyond that, it is, in fact, a good thing as well to actually live physically near a monastery or at least to visit one on a regular basis. Already, just by seeing a cloister on top of a hill one is reminded that man's destiny transcends this world. And encountering happy, healthy men or women who have nothing but God as their focus can be something of a proof of His existence, of His active care for human beings and of the fact that He can fill a man's heart.

Senior writes that the main witness of faith, after those who saw the risen Christ, was "the experience of persons who lived the Faith, chiefly under monastic rule, and saw for themselves—though in a glass darkly—that it is true."[38] In today's world of so much noise, talk and written material,

with arguments coming and going in all directions, the silent, living sign of the religious, of those who have had the "personal experience of the Catholic Faith,"[39] is all the more important and attractive.

This witness attests not only to the truth of our faith, but also to how we are to live it. We can reflect on this indirect teaching and preaching effected by the monks' lives in the framework of a text by Pope Paul VI. When he proclaimed St. Benedict "Patron of Europe," besides recognizing the patriarch's role in founding Christian Europe, the pope desired particularly to emphasize the need for that monastic foundation again today:

> The Church and the world, for different but converging reasons, need St. Benedict to go out from the ecclesial and social community and close himself up in an enclosure of solitude and silence, and from there to make us hear the enchanting tone of his calm and absorbed prayer, to win us over and call us to cross the threshold of his cloister; so to offer us the picture of a shop of divine service, of a little ideal society, where at last reign love, obedience, innocence, freedom in relation to things and the art of using them well, the preeminence of the spiritual, in a word: Peace, the Gospel.[40]

It might seem that being enclosed in solitude and silence would go against contributing to the common good, but the monk separates himself from natural society in order to concentrate on the one thing necessary and which is beneficial to all. Paul VI's words explain why. The monastery is "a shop of divine service," he says, using St. Benedict's own terms from the fourth chapter of his monastic *Rule*, where both monks and faithful learn to serve the Lord. In this passage, the pope speaks of prayer as attracting others to "come and see." This will eventually draw the faithful around the monastery to desire to enter themselves into the "cell of self-knowledge." Attending monastic services, they acquire a sense of the sacred, the ability to admire and adore; they learn to put the Holy Sacrifice of the Mass and worship at the heart of their life.

Even more than these purely supernatural and spiritual elements, Paul VI insists on natural values that are purified, regenerated, and lifted up in

the cloister, and which correspond to elements we have considered concerning the restoration of culture. In particular, he points out that the monastic community places before our eyes the "ideal society," the harmony of a family life in fraternal charity and obedience around the tender and firm paternal authority of the abbot, who represents Christ.

The pontiff also speaks of "freedom" and "art" in using things for the spiritual, for the ascent to God. For example—a point relevant to difficulties we have previously examined—the monk can help us learn how to use machines in a judicious, orderly way, respecting true human and spiritual values. The faithful are thus able to rediscover in a monastery the dignity of careful and generous labor for the common good, work that cultivates friendship and has for its end union with Christ. More generally, in "using things well" monks show how the environment and the whole course of the day are to be ordered. The monastery teaches the faithful how Christian gymnastic and music can be reestablished, so that they too can learn how to gaze through and beyond this world toward the invisible; to understand this world's relationship to the spiritual, so they too can become natural in the supernatural.

Thus, when all is in its proper place, the spiritual having primacy, and there is an awareness of the value of the sensible in its service, there ensues "Peace," as Paul VI concludes—which St. Augustine defined as the tranquility of order—as well as "the Gospel," which seems in this context to mean that the whole man and all his environment are evangelized. This Peace and this Gospel will radiate of themselves.

Senior experienced all this at the French Benedictine abbey of Fontgombault. It was, he said, "the closest place to Heaven that I have ever seen on earth."[41] He was thereby praising the monastery's liturgy and prayer-life, but also the order, the beauty and the simplicity of the more ordinary human activities—such as recreation, work, "manners"—joyfully and respectfully carried out in God's presence. Thus, while he had fond memories of drinking coffee with the cowboys in the rain as being "something near perfection," something as good, in its way, as a banquet in the *Odyssey*, he said that a meal at Fontgombault was part of "the life of perfection itself."[42]

It is well recognized that this orderly integration of the sensible and the natural into the spiritual was the key to Benedictine success in civilizing Europe, in forming the medieval synthesis of religion and life. Thus, John Paul II: "[St. Benedict] was a man who knew how to harmonize the soul and the body, nature and grace, the social and the spiritual, the old and the new; so that, maybe without foreseeing it, he created a new civilization."[43] Senior synthesizes the same thought in his own way, by describing the monastery's artful environment of truth as forming the soil of culture and disposing to God's grace those who come into contact with it:

> In the moral and spiritual order, we become what we wear as much as what we wear becomes us—and it is the same with how we eat and what we do. That is the secret of St. Benedict's Rule, which in the strict sense regulated monasteries and in the wider sense, through the influence and example of monasteries . . . civilized Europe. The habits of the monks, the bells, the ordered life, the "conversation," the music, gardens, prayer, hard work and walls— all these accidental and incidental forms conformed the moral and spiritual life of Christians to the love of Mary and her Son.[44]

He sees in the life of St. Thomas Aquinas, who lived in a Benedictine monastery as a lad before entering the Dominicans, an image of thirteenth-century philosophy and theology—of high medieval culture in general— growing out of Benedictine gymnastic and music: "St. Benedict, Patron of Europe, founded Monte Cassino in 529. St. Thomas as a little boy of five entered there to go to school around 1229—seven hundred years in the womb of Benedictine work and prayer and then you have St. Thomas! The seedbed of theology is the Benedictine life, without which no one has the prerequisites."[45]

The influence of Benedictine poetry contributed to yet another essential element in the formation of Christian culture. It led to the emergence of the Mother of God as Our Lady of the Middle Ages, its inspirer par excellence. For Christian culture to flourish in our day to the extent that

it could again produce something like the cathedral of Chartres or the *Summa Theologiae*, hearts must again be turned to her. Both of those great Christian works were dedicated to the Blessed Virgin Mary.

Consecration to the Blessed Virgin Mary

As mentioned, in the course of his two major books, Senior gradually progresses toward a consideration of the monastic life. In *Restoration of Christian Culture*, in particular, this progression culminates with the work's central thesis, as presented in its first chapter: "true devotion to Mary is now our only recourse."[46] The book closes with a chapter dedicated to the subject of consecration to the Blessed Virgin Mary. "Theology and popular piety agree," Senior writes, "that Christendom will be restored only when a determinate number of hearts are consecrated to the Immaculate Heart of Mary. . . . It is our first task, if we would work with [John Paul II] as Catholics for the restoration of the Church . . . to consecrate our homes, schools, parishes and hearts to her."[47] The book concludes: "All over the world at this very hour, Mary and her angels are moving among the human race. If we consecrate our hearts to hers we will be among those who make a difference."[48]

Senior reminds us that cult is the heart of culture. Cult in the strict sense of worship is reserved to God; but in the lesser sense of religious service, of devotion and honor given to someone, it can be applied to saints and angels, although in final reference to God: "God can be indirectly honored in his angels and saints because he is present in them by grace."[49] Now, it is obvious that among the saints Mary, the Mother of God, occupies first place and we owe to her a unique homage, as Senior writes: "By a large consensus of [ecclesiastical] doctors, councils and popes, as well as by the testimony of liturgy and common belief—the *sensus fidelium*—it would be rash and temerarious to deny that Mary is a special case."[50]

To support his affirmation, Senior first has recourse to theology, developing the theme of Mary's link with her Son in various ways. For example, he tells us that "Jesus owes honor and obedience to Mary in the debt of his nature as man to his natural mother. . . . Every cell of Christ's

body, each cell of the Eucharist, is a multiplied division of an original cell of hers still living on in these forms."[51] Jesus owes His human nature to her and we owe her Jesus. Thus theology teaches that the cult of Mary is intimately, inseparably tied to the cult of Christ. Consequently, for Christian culture to be well ordered, it must render Mary a special cult.

Senior also refers to the historical facts of the Middle Ages, as he does with the Holy Mass and with monastic life, beginning with a grand declaration: "Christian culture has been, in fact, nothing more nor less than the cult of the Blessed Virgin Mary."[52] He finds remarkable corroboration of his stance in Henry Adams's *Mont Saint-Michel and Chartres*, by the grandson of President John Quincy Adams, great-grandson of President John Adams: "When one of the best American historians (certainly the most reflective and philosophical)—not a Catholic, but a secular pessimist, Henry Adams wanted to sum up the difference between Christian culture and secular Humanism, he hit upon the famous contrast between the Virgin and the Dynamo."[53]

Paraphrasing Adams, Senior explains what that author meant by Dynamo and how it is the basis of modern culture: "In our time, in the reign of science and technology, Adams said, culture is nothing but the cult of dynamos—symbols of mindless, loveless, force," whereas "the entire culture of Christendom . . . was in fact simply the cult of Mary; it was all for her."[54]

Adams thus contrasted the cult of a person, a woman, a reality at once spiritual and warmly human, with modern man's cult of his own power and production. Another passage of his book is used by Senior to describe the astounding vitality that sprang forth from the medieval cult of Mary, far more vigorous than what issues from our worship of technology:

> At Chartres . . . was the highest energy ever known to man, the creator of four-fifths of his best art, exercising vastly more attraction over the human mind than all the steam-engines and dynamos ever dreamed of; and yet this energy was unknown to the American mind. . . . All the steam in the world could not, like the Virgin, build Chartres. Symbol or energy, the Virgin had acted as the greatest force the Western world had ever felt, and had drawn

men's activities to herself more strongly than any other power . . . had ever done.[55]

And Adams read well into the heart of the medieval man discerning the source of his inspiration:

[The cathedral of Chartres] is a child's fancy; a toy-house to please the Queen of Heaven—to please her so much that she would be happy in it, to charm her till she smiled. The Queen Mother was as majestic as you like . . . but she was still a woman, who loved grace, beauty, ornament . . . who considered the arrangements of her palace with attention, and liked both light and color.[56]

In *The Restoration of Christian Culture*, Senior speaks not only of devotion, but also of consecration to Mary. He recalls the request Our Lady made in Fatima that devotion to her Immaculate Heart be spread, and, specifically, that Russia be consecrated to her Immaculate Heart by the pope and bishops of the world. Pope John Paul II explained in a homily at Fatima how our own personal consecration relates to this: "Consecrating ourselves to Mary means accepting her help to offer ourselves and the whole of mankind to Him who is holy, infinitely holy."[57]

God alone is of himself sacred, holy. Something else is sacred, *consecrated*, when it belongs to Him. A consecrated chalice, for example, is one reserved for His use. To treat it like an ordinary cup would be a profanation. We are consecrated to God in Christ by our baptism. Our entire Christian life should develop that consecration, as we gradually submit to Christ all our powers, until we are truly, fully His. Consecration to Mary is intended to help that process. Jesus was all her life, she was totally consecrated to Him. By consecrating ourselves to Mary we enter, in a way, into her own consecration. Our imperfect, little offering is enveloped in her perfect, immaculate one. We are taken up in her movement toward God.

Both John Paul II and John Senior, in their discussion on the subject, had in mind the writings of St. Louis-Marie Grignon de Montfort,

the great apostle of consecration to God through Mary. To characterize that consecration St. Louis-Marie speaks in terms of living *in* Mary, that is, of being like a child in her presence; of living *by* her, which means relying on her help, as John Paul II mentioned, trusting in her; of living *with* Mary, taking her as model, accomplishing our actions with interior dispositions like her own; and of living *for* Mary, that is, striving to please her.

Senior elaborates on the last two points. Consecration "means not just the recitation of the words on a printed card, any more than fasting just means eating less, but a commitment to her interior life."[58] And in order to live for her, our intentions must be something akin to those of the builders of Chartres:

> So we must ask ourselves about our churches, our liturgies, our cities, our schools and homes, do they please the Blessed Queen of Heaven and earth, who is so sensitive to light and color and neglect, to disagreeable impressions and want of intelligence in her surroundings. And above all, within our hearts, what sort of rooms have we prepared for her where she might come and visit with her Son? Each article of clothing we wear, each game we play, each line we write, each experiment, conversation, business deal or vote is hers.[59]

In a way, one can say that Mary completes Jesus. We need a lady, a mother. The art historian Kenneth Clark reminds us in his *Civilisation* series that no religion without a feminine element ever produced great art. A man needs a lady for whom he desires to do beautiful things, who makes him more delicate and attentive to details. She inspires music in his soul and makes him a poet. Mary indeed represents a very "special," eminent case. This woman, who is Queen of Heaven and Earth, Mother of God and of Christians, breathes divine music into our souls. By striving to make all things beautiful for her, our home and its environment, our work, our schools, our liturgy, our monasteries, all our activity and culture will be more beautiful for her Son as well.

Holy liturgy refers to Mary as she who "has crushed all heresies."
Recognition that she is the Mother of God has always been a touchstone
to gauge whether someone has a sense of the Incarnation, of the fact that
Christ is at once true God and true man. The fundamental heresy of our
day is perhaps the denial of the natural order, of the very foundations of
culture. In the Virgin Mary there is a reclaiming of the value of the family, of the dignity of the mother, of love of children, of the nobility of
humble, hidden service. A culture that has devotion to Mary at its heart
knows that the human is not destroyed by God's presence, as the way
down and out of Orientalism would have it, but, instead, is perfected and
blossoms under the influence of the warm rays of grace. A culture inspired
by Mary will be full of energy for that ascent to the stars: "For a thousand
years there was a Christendom and its culture was the culture of Mary,
grounded in the humus of her humility, drawing us up."[60]

By way of conclusion to Part III, a few remarks are in order. Senior
was a man of back-to-the-beginnings, and became increasingly so as time
went on. He began his mission by trying to instruct his students in philosophy to form their intellect, but soon changed his focus to literature,
so as to form their imagination, and even, through a healthy contact with
natural things, to form their senses. He first worked to bring the ancient
classics back to the college reading list, and then applied himself rather
to promoting the "thousand good books," as he called them. Again,
although he was a college professor, he soon recognized the extent to
which his students lacked preparation and thus, the need to restore high
school education. Later, he went back even further, to concentrate on the
grade school and preschool levels. Finally, he perceived that it was the very
ground from which everything grows that had to be renewed, all our
cultural base, our environment itself—family and community life, our
work, our habitats, our clothes, our manners, our furniture, our songs and
stories. We must begin by restoring a Christian environment of truth in
the dull, low place within our reach.

Thus, according to our possibilities and the context of our day-to-day
existence, we need to bring reality and Christ back into our lives, in little
ways and small places. A culture formed by healthy gymnastic and

handsome music in the home, the community, school and workshop, inspired by a reverent and beautiful Holy Mass, by monastic life, and by the Blessed Virgin Mary, is the necessary foundation for a rich natural and Christian society, and will provide a soil well disposed for the seed of divine love in those immediately involved.

As a frame of reference for our time, Senior regularly points to the nineteenth century, that is, a period preceding the ascendancy of Modernism, of generalized Relativism and Positivism, prior to the dominance of industrialization. He considers it was the last period in which a normal human existence had been possible, when senses, imagination and emotion were still healthy and in contact with the land and things; when, in human-sized villages of craftsmen and farmers, a common music—literature, poetry, songs, stories—rose out of rich experience, cultivated bonds and encouraged generosity and fidelity.

More so, by far, than the good old cowboy days, Senior appreciates the Middle Ages, which were both more in harmony with the sensible world as well as more completely penetrated with poetry, with beautiful signs of the spiritual. Most important, the environment and the music of that period were Christian. For Senior the goal of culture is holiness, for which the Middle Ages provided a propitious soil. The very musical medieval Christian culture brought forth particularly gallant saints like St. Bernard of Clairvaux, St. Francis of Assisi, St. Louis of France, and St. Joan of Arc. After the Middle Ages, pernicious principles arising in the Renaissance and waxing in the Enlightenment progressively infected Western civilization, thus poisoning the soil needed for the cultivation of saints.

One can disagree with some of Senior's views regarding the Renaissance and the Enlightenment; it is plausible to maintain that certain true values were discovered, or at least brought to the surface, in those times. Neither is it evident that one should accept Senior's radical rejection of modern technology. However, we should be able to concur in his opposition to the germs of materialism, Empiricism and Rationalism of the Renaissance, as well as the secularism of the Enlightenment. And we must

recognize that technology, in fact, is increasingly becoming an overwhelming problem.

Senior, of course, knew that there can be no question of simply reproducing the Middle Ages. That too would be artificial—"Culture is a fact, not a new invention or a product,"[61] Senior writes. Witness to this is his acceptance of Protestant literature as part of our great English heritage. It is true that we must put aside much of our artificial environment and the fantasy art of our times. And we need references, models, principles, inspiration drawn from days that were healthier in many ways. We need a more natural milieu, and perhaps for that we can indeed refer to the nineteenth century and even to medieval times. And we need healthy music. We must nourish ourselves with the stories, songs, and drawings of days gone by to form our sensitivity, our hearts and our minds.

PART IV

May They Be Born in Wonder

Know, Sancho, I was born in this Iron Age to restore the Age of Gold.

—Don Quixote, quoted in the
Integrated Humanities Program booklet

John Senior, Greece, Christmas Break 1972-73 Academic year. Senior in foreground. Background: Frank Nelick, Dennis Quinn, Jim Brookes, and Suzanne Cupp. *Courtesy of Monica Sercer*

Features of the Integrated Humanities Program

In the dominance of science and technology, there
must remain some silent time and place, some quiet
grove among which a few at least may devote
themselves to nothing else but forever unpublished
knowledge and live in some little college-within-
the-college on the old Oxford plan.
—The Restoration of Christian Culture

THERE they were, modestly sitting in line, without a table before them or notes in their hands, facing 150 students in a near semicircle, Quinn in the middle as director, Nelick to his right as the elder professor, and Senior on the left. It was 1971. They were full of ardor and at the summit of their powers—Nelick was fifty-three, Senior forty-eight, and Quinn forty-four. Quinn was short and stocky, in good shape, with a full head of brown hair; Nelick was no taller, just as stocky, but beginning to fill out in the middle and carrying slightly sparse, gray hair. They made a contrast with Senior, slim and too tall for the classroom chairs. Quinn and Senior were in coat and tie, Nelick in a sweater. Quinn had a relatively high, quick, even nervous voice, Nelick a low, raspy one; Senior spoke slowly in a calm, soft tone. Quinn and Nelick gestured some as they spoke; Senior sat cross-legged and arms folded, without gestures but shifting position occasionally and putting two or three fingers on his lips when he reflected.

They were talking about the banquet at Menelaus's palace when Telemachus was seeking news of his father, Odysseus. The professors pointed out the undivided simple attention of the characters to their immediate experience. They spoke of the respect the ancient Greeks showed for the ordinary activities of eating and drinking, the careful attention they gave to the cup in their hand, to the furniture they were using, to the clothes they wore. The professors then pointed out how Homer wanted to contrast the grace and dignity of this civilized feast—its hospitality, prayer, story and song—with other feast scenes of the book, for example, that of the suitor's orgy and of the Cyclops gorging himself in his dark cave.

The conversation was relaxed and natural. Quinn and Senior carried the longer developments. Nelick, although at times absorbed in his cigar smoking, made poignant, often puzzling remarks, told a good story and interjected several humorous quips. The three spoke for about an hour and a half, with Senior bringing all to a climax, to a solemn, touching moment. Quinn had tears in his eyes.

As can be gathered, the IHP lecture was something to be experienced. It was a "conversation" that accomplished the etymological meaning of the word, that is, turning together—*con-versatio*—in this case, toward something beautiful that tugged at the students' hearts. They could not get enough of these classes. It was Senior's theory at work. Having considered his ideas on primary and secondary education, we can now turn to the Integrated Humanities Program, a realization of his principles in the context of today's college situation. After tracing the trajectory of Senior's thought, from the experiences of his boyhood to the fullness of his stature as person and professor, we have reached the culmination of our book, and are now prepared to understand the IHP in some depth. In the present chapter we will recount the program's beginnings, then introduce its orientation and lastly examine how its organization served that orientation.*

---

* The full story of IHP has yet to be written. Nevertheless, see Scott Bloch, "Prairie Fire," in *Sursum Corda* (Winter, 1996), 26–41; Robert Carlson, *Truth on Trial: Liberal Education Be Hanged* (Crisis Books, 1995); James Taylor, *Poetic Mode of Knowledge: The Recovery of Education* (State University of New York Press, 1998), Chapter Five; and William Wisner, *Whither the Postmodern Library? Library, Technology, and Education in the Information Age* (Jefferson, North Carolina: McFarland and Company, 2000), Chapter Three.

Beginnings

In the early summer of 1967, while serving on a committee established to choose a new president for the University of Wyoming, Senior admitted frankly and for grave reasons that, if a certain individual were chosen, he would leave the university. The choice indeed fell on the very man and Senior kept his word, to the great loss of the university.

Senior had written in a letter of the mid-1960s that he "missed home" and hoped to go back to the Northeast some day. Yet, in 1967 he chose Kansas. Later asked why, he replied, "Because the weather is so lousy and the people are so nice!" He doubtless continued to prefer having non–Ivy League, less cosmopolitan students. A former Cornell colleague who was in the English Department at the University of Kansas encouraged Senior to come there and recommended him to the administration. Senior was offered a job and invited to start a Comparative Literature graduate program like the one he had known at Columbia.

Thus, in the fall of 1967, at forty-four years of age and after seven good years in Wyoming, Senior joined the faculty at the University of Kansas. He had always been a member of the English Department at his previous positions, but, at KU, he was asked to switch to Classics so that the Comparative Literature program could function from that department in collaboration with various language groups. At Wyoming, he had taught what had become something of his specialty, namely, a class on Chaucer, which he brought to Kansas as well. One student who took that first Chaucer class described it as "one of the two most sublime experiences of my life—the other being Holy Mass at Fontgombault. Senior lifted up the whole class day after day. It was phenomenal!"

When Senior arrived at the University of Kansas, Frank Nelick had been teaching in the English Department for sixteen years and Dennis Quinn for eleven. The two had known each other before coming to Kansas. In 1950, during his undergraduate studies, Quinn had transferred to the University of Wisconsin because of its reputation for courses in Renaissance literature. Once there, he learned from colleagues that, while the faculty there were quite good, there was a particular graduate student who was "incredible." Thus, he enrolled in a class taught by Nelick.

The colorful, energetic teacher, who was working on his doctorate at the time, captured Quinn's admiration. A few years after Nelick had accepted a job at the University of Kansas, Quinn followed, in part because of his former teacher's presence. In the 1960s the two professors taught together a few times and, with Arvid Schulenberger, who had arrived at the University of Kansas in 1951, formed a controversial trio—controversial largely because their teaching affirmed the existence of truth at a time when Relativism was making sharp inroads in the academy.

It is interesting to note how much the educational views of Schulenberger, who in 1963 authored a slim volume entitled "The Orthodox Poetic: A Literary Catechism," would have resonated with those of John Senior. Schulenberger has this to say, for example, about Realism, citing Dante as his exemplar:

> Art imitates nature; the nature imitated, then, may in turn symbolize (imitate) the supernatural or the spiritual. Dante first renders or imitates a rose; the rose itself then becomes the symbol of an otherwise inexpressible reality. . . . Much of modern symbolist poetry [in contrast] represents the poets' attempts to slight or distort nature itself.[1]

Schulenberger died in a fatal car accident while returning home from teaching inmates at the federal penitentiary in Leavenworth, and so, sadly, he and Senior never overlapped at the University of Kansas.

After a short time, Senior contemplated leaving the University of Kansas: he had little in common with most of his fellow faculty, who seemed far more interested in trendy, eclectic subjects than in the Great Books and the perennial conversation they foster. Although he heard a few stories about Nelick, he did not meet him or Quinn for a time. On their side, neither of the two men was especially impressed by Senior's public inaugural lesson on Herrick, a poet they appreciated less than Senior did. Students, however, recognized the similarities in their outlooks and prompted an encounter. The three professors began conversing on literature, education and philosophy. Quinn

and Nelick found themselves in serene and effortless communion with the newcomer, notably concerning the fundamentals of Western civilization, the love of poetry, and the primacy of classroom teaching over research and being published. All three were traditional Christians as well—Quinn, although from a Catholic family, had not been baptized as a child and was a convert to Catholicism; Nelick was an Anglican at the time. Each was a brilliant, skilled, popular and award-winning professor.*

Building upon this common basis, the different temperaments, talents and backgrounds complemented each other nicely. Senior was a melancholic Northeasterner, a contemplative, a poet. Quinn was a sanguine and outgoing Midwesterner, practical, inventive, precise, an organizer. Nelick, also a Midwesterner, was a rough, somewhat gruff and choleric military man, but generous and good, with a plethora of personal anecdotes that revealed a wealth of concrete knowledge of men and things.† A common friend summarized their respective contributions to IHP with a formula that has some truth, although Senior would have strongly denied the part attributed to him: "Thanks to Nelick, the man of experience, the students realize there is a truth; getting to know Quinn, the just, virtuous man, they recognize there is a God; Senior, the spiritual and contemplative, converts 'em."

In 1966, the administration of KU, hoping to personalize the guidance of its underclassmen, inaugurated a college-within-the-college organization,

---

* In 1963 Nelick was awarded the H. Benjamin Fink "Outstanding Classroom Teacher of the Year," the only annual teaching award at KU at the time. Quinn won the same award in 1965. In 1969, Quinn was chosen by the senior class for the "Honor of the Progressive Educator" (HOPE) award. At the time he met the other two, Senior had recently been chosen by *Esquire* as one of the best teachers in the country. He would receive one of the three American Oil Company awards for classroom teaching in 1970 and the HOPE award in 1975.

† For intellectuals and university professors, Quinn and especially Senior had a rich store of experiences and activities, but Nelick's was amazing. He really did, for example, run off and join the circus as a boy. He helped his father tame wild mustangs during the Depression. He went to Canada to enlist when he was not yet of age for U.S. military service. As a navy pilot in World War II, he flew both in Europe and the Pacific. He was a captain and a brevetted commodore in the U.S. Navy and held all commands from squadron through unit to wing. While teaching at KU he found time to be advisor to athletes and foreign exchange students, serve on the university planning board, and be diocesan delegate for the International Anglican Congress, member and chairman of the Lawrence City Planning Commission and special agent to the Kansas attorney general. He was named commanding officer for the composite Fleet Squadron Cuban Missile Crisis.

with five subdivisions of the College of Liberal Arts, each with a certain measure of autonomy. Dean Waggoner proposed to Quinn that he direct one of them. When Quinn protested, the dean assured him that the position would not remove him from teaching, and told him that he would have pretty much a free hand to do what he wanted. Quinn thus accepted the deanship of Pearson College.

In 1969, the three professors detected in that college-within-the-college framework the opportunity to establish a program for underclassmen consonant with their views. The essential structure and direction of the program were drawn up quickly, for, as Senior observed, "Pearson College was a spontaneous fruit of what each one of us was doing on his own."[2] Quinn presented an outline of the project to the university administration and solicited the various subcommittees for necessary approvals. In the school year 1969–1970, while Nelick and Senior fulfilled previous teaching contracts, Quinn began teaching the projected class as a special version of the required English courses. In the fall of 1970, with all three professors, the Pearson Integrated Humanities Program (commonly called by Senior and others simply "IHP" rather than "the IHP") began in earnest. That first year they limited the number of students to twenty, selected by interview from about thirty honors-level applicants.

At the end of the first year, IHP classes were accorded the status of satisfying not only English, but most other liberal arts requirements as well. The program received for its second year a sum of $30,000 from a government grant (which the University of Kansas matched) to pay visiting speakers, graduate assistants, a secretary and other administrative needs. The professors distributed information to incoming freshmen, opening the program to all candidates of good will, not only honor students. They chose about 140 of the 250 or so candidates who came for interviews, a few of whom were upperclassmen. The main criterion for their selection was a willingness to learn—for example, without excessive preoccupation about grades. The interviews also served as the beginnings of a personal relationship between the professors and the students. The IHP adventure was under way. Even the professors could not have foreseen the explosion to come.

Restoring Liberal Education

In order to present the program's fundamental orientation, we can start by interpreting the three components of its name.* First, it would be *integrated.* Underclassmen at the university ordinarily enrolled in a jumble of courses and knew nothing of a common goal or a relation between the different disciplines, even between core classes. There was no such thing as a unified, cohesive faculty. "The freshman-sophomore curriculum is fragmented, incoherent and directionless,"[3] as the IHP brochure described the situation. Senior pointed out that, in fact, the little organization that did exist was established for the purpose of something other than learning: "A modern university is a collection of subjects loosely united by the demands of business and the professions of trained personnel and arranged for the convenience of its administrators."[4]

College education therefore was in sore need of an overarching perspective encompassing the various courses that would provide a sense of continuity and interconnection of ideas. The new college-within-the-college structure constituted a convenient base for regrouping the disparate strands of the freshman-sophomore liberal arts core curriculum into one two-year program. In this way literature, history, fine arts and philosophy could be presented as organic parts of a whole. As Senior wrote: "In an integrated program of studies every subject is seen in the light of each and all, and especially of the good, the true and the beautiful."[5]

With its two-year duration, the program also provided continuity; it gave leisure for the students to come to know the teachers' thought and for the teachers to form the students. This also allowed students in IHP to have a home and forge friendships in the classroom, in conformity with the university's intent regarding the college-within-the-college project. IHP, in the midst of a huge university, would have the advantages of a small liberal arts college. In a fragmented world, where the student was so often isolated and anonymous in his studies, having no one to talk to about his education, this community was a true haven.

---

* Pearson College was named after the building that housed its offices and a few classrooms, the building itself named after a KU benefactor.

Continuing our analysis based on the program's name, IHP would be a *humanities* class. Senior explained the objective: "The purpose of humanities is not knowledge but to humanize."[6] Studies such as this, that aim at forming the person rather than preparing him for a career, are at the heart of liberal education, and even beyond, at the heart of culture as defined in Chapter Ten. "It is . . . that growth of the person both in intellect and will," Senior wrote, "that transformation of his deepest life, which is the . . . reality of education. . . . The end of education is the perfection of each person."[7] Quinn specified how this requires forming not only the intellect but also the will and the emotions, the whole man: "We try to cultivate not just the mind or the heart, but both of these aspects of human experience. Not only to know, but also to develop the desire for knowledge. We want to humanize students and draw out their human responses in an integrated way."[8]

Humanities thus properly understood have been largely cast aside today for various reasons—economics, career building, a scientific mentality. Mathematics, science and technology dominate. Even in courses classified as humanities (because they do not deal with physical or social sciences), the approach is often mechanical and technical. Applications of a quantitative perspective to quality can be useful, but they do not lead directly to the goal, which is to humanize. Senior wrote:

Departments of Classics, Literature, Philosophy, History, Music, Arts and the like at universities are increasingly staffed with experts in the technical problems of editing texts, computerizing indexes and constructing linguistical, sociological, psychological hypotheses—all of which, whatever their value, is not human value; it is scientific research in the humanistic field; it is not itself humane.[9]

Senior underlined that the merely scientific approach disregards the goal of humanities. It forms cold machines rather than human beings:

Modern education has become increasingly suicidal in the encroachment of science on school and liberal arts colleges where

students traditionally have learned . . . poetry, music, history, nature—the love of these things not their dissection and analysis. . . . When that is lost, and the means take the place of the end, humanity destroys itself, a victim of its instruments.[10]

Consequently, IHP's objective would not be the acquisition of information. The program would not sidestep what an author wanted to communicate in order to classify themes and types he used or uncover his sources, all of which is like endlessly describing a banquet while dying of hunger. Senior said: "It is a matter as important as life and death of hearts not just to tabulate and classify but take and eat of the good, the beautiful and true."[11]

The word *program* in its name meant that IHP would be a synthesis of various classes. As to the program itself, in the sense of the plan for attaining to the goal of humanization, the professors judged that the most effective means to help students know and appreciate significant truth was simply to meditate with them on the great writings. Senior explained that IHP's aim was to allow participants to be led by the masters in the art of being human:

IHP is not a course, not the running through of a prescribed sequence (in the humanistic sciences such as literary and historical analysis), it is not an attempt to advance knowledge at all, but rather . . . to read what the greatest minds of all generations have thought about what must be done if each man's life is to be lived with intelligence and refinement.[12]

For Senior, the reigning cultural poverty largely resulted from ignorance of the classics, a fact intimately linked to the eclipse of the humanities and of liberal education. The classics focus on the deep, universal values in which everyone shares; they speak to everyone, they are, as it were, the consciousness of our civilization. As one IHP student put it: "[The great authors] participated with us in the study of things, and showed us a wonderful world, rich in beauty, sadness and triumph."[13]

The Integrated Humanities Program was to be a return to this centuries-old reflection.

The Great Books, Truth and the Poetic Mode

As we saw in Chapter Seven, other teachers and programs in the twentieth century had already returned to a liberal education through the classics. In the Great Books programs, students read the best books seeking to discern what the author said, rather than focusing on technical scholarship and historical research. These programs were integrated, with faculty and students learning together. Each professor in principle taught the ensemble of the various courses over the years, so that all, students and teachers, participated in the whole.

As implemented at secular colleges, however, these programs lacked intellectual, moral and spiritual direction. Indeed, the texts and the teachers were of various persuasions, or of none at all. The method was to present the Great Books of all sorts and then converse about them all together, students and faculty. How could an eighteen-year-old on his own find his way through such a pile of dense material brought together from all sides? "Good as reading the Great Books is," Senior wrote, "even the best Great Books will fail without a certain rule of truth by which conflicting ideas in the books can be judged true or false."[14] The negative effects of the lack of direction were aggravated, Senior believed, by use of the seminar setting, in which students discussed the books among themselves under the guidance of a teacher. He held that such a method taught students how to argue and win discussions rather than how to listen to truth.

In contrast to such programs, IHP's goal was not simply to offer a propitious forum for learning, but to lead students to discern the truth, as its brochure explained: "We aim at achieving a sound understanding of the central issues in Western Civilization and reaching valid, applicable conclusions."[15] In view of this, there were no structured discussion sessions among students.

IHP consisted substantially in, Senior wrote, "formal lectures to draw out not just the right questions, but the right answers."[16] We can sense

how revolutionary such an idea is in our times—unheard of especially in public schools—by the following little story. When the professors wrote their grant proposal, they described the philosophy of the program as seeing history under the light of one truth. When the representative of the National Endowment for Humanities met with the professors for drinks, she commented that the proposal was unique and interesting, but there was one small thing in the wording that needed to be changed. It was the part about teaching that there is a truth that can be seen under one aspect. The professors replied that they could not change that because it was the heart of the program. If it was going to be integrated, they could not teach from a disintegrated viewpoint. The woman seemed shocked.

There was a moment of silence. She gulped down the drink, but finally replied: "All right."

In the generation following the pioneers in the Great Books movement, there was interest in adopting the same outline among Catholic educational circles. In the fall of 1968, Senior attended a meeting in San Francisco with a dozen other professors to discuss the project of an envisioned college and its educational approach. The curriculum proposed for Thomas Aquinas College, in contrast to the status quo discussed above, would be unified and directed; it would be based on reading the Great Books in the light of the Perennial Philosophy. Senior thought he would probably join that faculty, as late as the summer of 1969. Nevertheless, he had a fundamental difference of opinion about the mode of teaching that was needed for students beginning college in our day.* He wrote to Van Doren about the meeting in San Francisco:

> My criticisms are chiefly not about the college proposed per se but about the impossibility of sending a young person to college without his having been to school. The liberal arts college begins with wonder and ends in wisdom. But the freshman has had wonder pretty much crushed out of him. . . . I think, therefore, the college must give all students a year, at least, of poetry, before the liberal

---

* Senior did become a member of Thomas Aquinas's Board of Visitors, mainly established as a list of noteworthy supporters.

arts properly begin—I should say <u>music</u>, in the sense of the things the <u>Muses</u> do. For example, it seems criminal to teach the liberal art of astronomy (the mathematical science) to someone who has never looked at the stars.[17]

This difference of opinion brings us to IHP's most distinctive feature and back to Senior's major theme. As we well know by now, modern eighteen-year-olds, according to Senior, have not had the normal, healthy experience and poetry of childhood and youth necessary for abstract initiation in ideas. One needs "years of training in gymnastics, music, poetry, art, history and in manners, morals and religion, which used to be supplied by Christian homes and school"[18] if high-level studies are to be fruitful.

This was all the more true in that in secular colleges like the University of Kansas, professors faced a student body of modern Hamlets and Descartes, skeptical and doubtful of the true, the good and the beautiful, of *being* itself. KU students had turned their backs on reality, as it were, and the first thing to do was to help them turn around again, to convert them, so that they could look with their eyes, mind and heart and see what was really there. Rather than a philosophical reflection on things already known and loved, IHP was a rediscovery of beauty, of friendship, of patriotism, as explained in its brochure: "[IHP] should be regarded as . . . a course for beginners, who look upon the primary things of the world, as it were, for the first time."[19] This fundamental orientation of IHP is echoed in the program's motto: *Nascantur in admiratione* ("Let them be born in wonder"). Thus, although its subjects were college students, IHP would operate substantially on the musical and—to a certain extent—gymnastic levels in order to relink students sensibly and emotionally to reality. As Senior observed: "IHP was a school occupying a college because the college wasn't doing its job and, since schools had been invaded by dialectic, we did the poetic work that was skipped."[20]

Nonetheless, since the professors were dealing with young adults whose intellects were beginning to think seriously about the fundamental human questions, IHP also initiated its students into ideas. It included some texts too difficult for high schoolers, and posed important questions

about the value of leisure and work, of authority and freedom, about the difference between civilization and barbarism, about vital issues such as love, the good life and authentic happiness. Yet, even when discussing fundamental values and presenting philosophical principles, the professors' teaching approach remained substantially within the poetic mode.

There was very little in the way of theoretical exposition. It was more by using stories and examples that they strove to lead the students to a sense of great truths, to a taste for the beauty and goodness of great values. Senior wrote: "I retired to Kansas, a rural state, to teach *philosophia perennis* by indirect means, forcing myself to rectify our students' imaginations by teaching . . . poetry."[21]

After two years of this remedying music, the professors foresaw that students would be able to go on to more scientific studies, as Senior explained: "[IHP was] a sort of preparatory program of knowledge in which meaning and spirituality find their fulfillment through the study of poetry and gymnastics (in the classical sense of the term)."[22] In fact, Nelick, Quinn and Senior hoped, once the two-year course was well established, to expand it to a full four-year college program, with the final two years of classes operating more in the mode of the seven liberal arts, in the strict sense—with higher mathematics, sciences, logic, and some philosophical reflection, much like the Great Books programs.

Classes and Activities

IHP was a composite but unified program, the elements of which worked together toward a gymnastic return to real things and a poetic discovery of their mysteries. The whole was substantially set up from the beginning, but with a few minor changes and additions over the years.

On Tuesdays and Thursdays, the three professors together would speak for about an hour and twenty minutes to the freshmen; then, after a short break, they would talk for an equal period of time to the sophomores. These team-taught lectures were the heart of IHP and we will come back to them. Once a week, freshmen gathered in groups of about twelve to ask questions of one or another of the professors. Two such

question-and-answer sessions a week, this time with all three professors, were available for sophomores who wished to come; most of them did so.

IHP's emphasis was on reading and comprehension rather than on composition; the students needed to have something in their head, to hold some convictions, before learning the particular skills of the writing trade. Nevertheless, graduate assistants taught small weekly rhetoric classes for the development of effective expression and writing, with exercises generally dealing with the current reading assignment in the program. A weekly drill session run by older students helped the class remember the facts and events of the books and master the geography, dates and names. At the end of the semester an eighty-minute class session was used for a test, which usually consisted of writing a paper on a given theme using the various readings of the semester.

Pearson students were encouraged to take classes in Latin, which were taught by Senior and assistants, with more advanced students leading exercises outside of class time. In passing, one can admire this eminent professor teaching two or three hours of beginner's Latin every day. It needed to be done, Senior believed, and so he did it. He taught by the oral method described in Chapter Twelve as a gymnastic and poetic mode. He used simple stories and the memorization of songs and poems, with no paradigms or lengthy grammar lessons. Teachers and students did Latin rather than study it, one might say. English was never spoken. After three semesters the students were capable to some degree of conversing in Latin. Senior would comment on and discuss with them such texts as St. Jerome's Vulgate translation of Scripture and St. Thomas Aquinas's commentary on the psalms. Because of Senior's engaging way of teaching, these enjoyable classes became an important component of the program. About half of the students took the course, making it one of the largest enrollments in college Latin in the United States at that time.

Especially during the 1971–1972 school year, when IHP had grant money, visiting lecturers gave talks and participated in the Tuesday and Thursday sessions. Occasionally other professors from KU lectured as well, to supplement the program with more specialized information and

additional perspectives. Sometimes an optional semester-long accredited class—one on Chaucer or Shakespeare, for example, a history or speech course, or one in drawing—taught by a KU professor outside the program, would be arranged for IHP students.

Forming the gymnastic and musical habit in the students required something beyond lectures and the class setting. To exercise the imagination, memory and emotions, each semester the students memorized ten exemplary, classical poems by the best English poets. They would meet twice a week in small groups, usually in a residence hall on campus, and a more senior student would read a poem out loud. The younger students did not follow the written text, but would learn the poem by heart, line by line, simply by listening to it. The IHP brochure made clear the objective: "Before attempting to think about poetry, we urge students to simply know and enjoy it as one knows and enjoys any song."[23] And Quinn explained why a premature analysis was carefully avoided: "[The scientific approach] poisons people's taste for poetry, music, art and philosophy, which the ordinary college student should enjoy. When students have to look deeply into the structure of a work, they lose the primary purpose of the literature: its emotional value."[24] An outgrowth of this poetic exercise was the practice of learning and singing a song before the start of the Tuesday and Thursday lectures.

It would be difficult to overestimate the importance of these poems and songs in nourishing the students' link to reality, in rousing their slumbering sensibilities and emotions to the beauty and variety of nature, to friendship, fidelity, love. We include here a sampling of such verses to convey a sense of what these eighteen- and nineteen-year-olds experienced. These young men and women were apt for love songs, of course, but they learned that their attractions could be refined and elevated to a higher and more fulfilling level. In the following, from a song by Ben Jonson, they encountered delicacy of sentiment:

Drink to me only with thine eyes,
And I will drink with mine
Or leave a kiss but in the cup
And I'll not look for wine.

Students acquired a sense of the meaning and beauty of honor reading about Richard Lovelace when he must leave his lady behind to fight for his king. Here is the last stanza of "To Lucasta, Going to the Wars":

Yet this inconsistency is such
As you too will adore;
I could not love thee, dear, so much,
Loved I not honor more.

A love for the homeland was awakened by lines of Sir Walter Scott's "Lay of the Last Minstrel":

Lives there a man with soul so dead,
Who never to himself hath said,
This is my own, my native land!
Whose heart hath ne'er within him burned
As home his footsteps he hath turn'd
From wandering on a foreign strand!

By coming to know such poems, the students began to perceive that man transcends material things. They were starting to be at home with mysteries. They were receiving rich images in their memory, things good and beautiful to think about and love. Alumni of the program agree that learning these poems was one of the most rewarding experiences in Pearson College. They understood and relished them more and more with the passage of time.

Weekly stargazing sessions were arranged for freshmen. They were taken to the darker skies outside city limits, and older students would point out constellations and recount the classical Greek myths pertinent to them. This humble, simple activity became a considerable factor in achieving a breakthrough to reality. Perhaps for the first time since childhood, these young adults felt free to respond emotionally and sensibly to the stars. In awe and admiration, they felt the call of beauty and realized that there is more to reality than quantity and technology.

Other activities were optional, but little coaxing was necessary. The professors recommended learning calligraphy so that students would acquire a taste for doing things well and beautifully. This proved a highly successful activity and became an avocation for a few. In subsequent years, there was some initiation in certain crafts for those who so chose. Stargazing was not officially part of the sophomore year, but the professors urged replacing that activity with visiting the elderly, those "even more beautiful stars," as Senior called them. Students found joy in giving of their time to people in need of affection and discovered something in their own souls deeper and more meaningful than egotistical quests.

In 1972 Quinn had another idea. During the 1972–73 Christmas break, the three professors directed a two-week trip to Greece, and the following year, during the winter break, freshmen traveled to Greece with Quinn, while sophomores went to Italy with Senior and Nelick. These countries were chosen because they provided the backdrop for many of the books read in class, allowing students to see and feel the physical features and climate, and visit the edifices where some of the events took place. The whole program spent the spring semester of 1976 in Ireland largely because the professors believed that their students needed to be immersed for a longer period of time in a culture that was similar to theirs, yet simpler, closer to nature. This outlook was exactly the opposite of the Modernist tendency to wander by pursuit of the different. Quinn explained:

> The purpose of living and studying in Europe is not to learn about "foreign" ways but rather to rediscover the roots of our own culture. . . . So dominant is modernization in America that college age students have almost no direct experience of traditional culture, with its slower pace, its love of a living past, its handcrafts, its unspoiled countryside. The consequence is not only that many young Americans do not know what Modernism is replacing, but also that they do not know what it means to be modern.[25]

A few students themselves initiated certain extracurricular events. In the fall of 1973 and for several consecutive years the program sponsored an

old-fashioned country fair, with games, square dancing, a pig roast and a large display of craftwork. In the spring of 1974, the students planned the first of several annual formal dances, where they happily practiced manners, courtesy and grace in the intricacies of the rhythm and steps of the Viennese waltz. Quinn said concerning these dances and their many rehearsals: "Although it would be premature to say that there is a new campus fad of decency, students are beginning to find that barbarism is a bore."[26]

Senior gave a toast at one of these balls in which he wryly pretended to be an old professor trying to tell the warm-blooded students out on the dance floor that Keats was right, that the painting on the Grecian urn freezing the present moment was superior to life. He alluded to Lucretius's assertion that all the love and joy of youth are simply the slightly swerving fall of atoms—although Senior's "swerve" also refers to the effects of the champagne, as he looks on the dancers through the glass cup:

Because you listen to a song unknown
to cold professors and their Grecian Urns,
but rather see the glitter now and here,
as guilty pulses jump and glances stir,
when girlish laughter shakes from loosened hair
and blushes rise on cheeks sweet music burns—
you hum! The dumb magister stands in awe,
a slightly swerved Lucretionist, absurd-
ly gazing at a hollow stem whose air
is sparkling atoms in a glassy void,
as love arising from the darkened world
upfalls like an intelligible tear
(this toast) reflecting in its crystal sphere
the waltzing constellations star by star.[27]

Thus, much vitality emanated from IHP. Healthy enjoyment entered into the students' pursuit of the true, the good and the beautiful. They realized that life and learning could go together. Friendships developed, and the program became a community with a common culture—which

not very long before had been everyone's culture—as the students came to appreciate values they had formerly misunderstood, or even scorned. Many of their acquaintances considered IHP activities and classes to be quite corny, but the students laughed at these opinions as they gazed on the stars, waltzed and sang. Don Quixote attacking the windmill became more or less of an official emblem of the program. The IHP brochure, boasting Quixote's figure on its cover, explained why:

> The spirit of the Pearson Program may be called Quixotic. Don Quixote has been both ridiculed and admired because he lived the chivalrous life when it was out of fashion . . . . Words like truth and faith and honor and love and courtesy and decency and simplicity and modesty are Quixotic, and the realities for which these words stand are, in this Iron Age, so Quixotic as to be positively despised by the sophisticated.[28]

Having considered the rich social and cultural atmosphere of IHP, we can now consider what and how the IHP professors taught.

Texts

For Senior, teaching was simple: "A teacher, student, a text—and talk."[29] The "text" in IHP was what it should be, a great thinker's instrument for helping readers see and love what he had to offer. The teaching, or "talk," was a second instrument, to help the texts do their job: "Good teachers," Senior wrote, "ignite the minds of their students when the virtual fire in texts is struck to actuality by sparks of their own will and wit."[30] Let us look first at the choice of texts.

The program's reading list was made up of complete primary works, as opposed to excerpts or manuals. Just as they moved the students away from city lights to see the stars in a natural way, so the professors eliminated intermediaries from the readings so that students could have direct contact with the great minds. Prefaces, introductions, footnotes and commentaries were omitted.

Why listen to mediocre modern critics when Plato or St. Augustine is speaking? As Senior observed, "Professional critics tell us what to think; their own works become substitutes for the books they explain; their opinions get into schoolbooks, encyclopedias and study guides, establishing a kind of intellectual bureaucracy between readers and real books."[31]

The books were chosen partly to sample different subjects, times, places and perspectives, partly to present decisive moments in Western history, and partly to set forth permanent and universal themes especially significant to the students. They were not grouped according to subjects, but rather presented in chronological order so as to acquaint the students with the movement of history and the development of ideas and culture. The Greeks were pored over in the first semester, the Romans and selections from the Old Testament in the second, parts of the New Testament and medieval authors in the third, and modern authors in the fourth. Such an organization was doubtless inspired by Mark Van Doren's Humanities Program at Columbia.

In the very first years of the program a couple of twentieth-century authors were included, but eventually the reading list stopped with the nineteenth century, as did the poems to be memorized. We have seen that for Senior, the imagination in the twentieth century was no longer properly and normally formed. Accordingly, works of our time were excluded as being improper for musical education at IHP. Moreover, students lacked knowledge of their own heritage, thus the focus on older books. The classics are the basis of our civilization. One of the major faults of modern education is the attempt to build upon a vacuum, as if we could reinvent everything.

Without knowing their past, students do not know who they are. They are not cognizant of what underlies the world around them and their own orientations. As Senior put it: "When a person says in all honesty, not just to be smart, but sincerely, that he cannot comprehend the past, he means that he cannot rightly comprehend anything at all."[32] Furthermore, according to the professors, the decisive debates had already taken place. Ideas put forth today were merely an outgrowth of what had been expressed more clearly and strongly in the past. Grounded in the principles gained

from older classics, the students would be enabled to read modern literature with better judgment.

To objections against this preference for older texts, Senior would simply reply, "Taste and see. Try them out; you will see for yourself." In the following lines from "Progress of Poetry," he encouraged a return to the Great Books by evoking a few scenes from Homer:

> How vainly men do sacralize
> sententious novelty
> and in ignorance disprize
> the Great Anthology.
> Take up the book and read again
> of Hector and Andromache,
> Achilles and his mother when
> they walked along the sounding sea,
> And Helen coming down the stairs
> who sees Odysseus
> in startled adolescent eyes—
> star-struck Telemachus.[33]

IHP students were able to sensibly and emotionally participate in most of the texts. A good third of the reading was poetry, strictly speaking—Homer, Virgil, *The Song of Roland*, Chaucer, Shakespeare—or poetic prose—*Ivanhoe* and *Don Quixote*, for example. Another third was made up of historical texts, still largely poetic in that they were narrated in story form and usually consisted of eyewitness accounts or autobiographies, a genre which tends to capture the reader's imagination—Herodotus's *Persian Wars*, Caesar's *Gallic Wars*, Cellini's *Autobiography*, Parkman's *Oregon Trail*.

The final third—philosophical and didactic texts—treated of important domains: political philosophy, for example, with works of Plato and Burke; education with Newman and Julian Huxley; religion with St. Augustine and Hume. A work of Aristotle had been assigned to IHP's pilot class and some reading in St. Thomas Aquinas had been planned

for the second year, but the professors soon found that these texts were too difficult for the students, or, at the least, not easily adaptable to IHP's poetic pedagogy. Therefore, they opted for more literary and imaginative texts that would lend themselves to an amateur philosophical reflection. This was the case with Boethius's *Consolation of Philosophy*. But the best example of poetic philosophy is found in Plato, who readily used myth and beauty to speak to the sensibility and emotions. Quinn explained the importance of reading Plato in a poetic manner so that one can appreciate the stories and absorb the whole experience of each scene:

> Most important and characteristic in the Socratic conversation is story-telling. Nothing more impoverishes and distorts the dialogues than a reading that attempts to distill the thought or ideas of argument, leaving aside as mere by products all of the non-philosophical elements, as if the conversation were merely a treatise put in a pleasant package. . . . The atmosphere of the dialogues, which is essential to what they actually effect is that . . . of the dinner table or sitting room.[34]

No doubt, it was this same atmosphere of conversation that Quinn, and his colleagues of the IHP, sought to create and successfully implemented in their own approach to teaching.

Conversational Teaching

For Senior, teachers learn together, while students eventually overhear their conversations and sit down to listen: "A faculty, studying the truth and conversing about it, are overheard by some who, though they don't know what it is, see something good, therefore desirable and, as such, urgent."[35] Something close to this ideal was taking place in IHP.

The eighty-minute team-taught class was not a lecture properly speaking, written out in advance and then read to the students. Nor was it a rehearsed presentation conducted by one of the three professors to then be analyzed or critiqued by the other two. Rather, it was an authentic

conversation, not even mentally prepared beforehand in any detail, as Quinn explained in an interview: "We didn't plan the lectures. We had lunch together before class started and on the way over to class I'd say, 'Well, what are we going to talk about?' and they'd say, 'I don't know. What book are we reading?'"[36]

This rather impromptu manner of teaching in IHP seemed especially suited to cultivating an understanding of the poetic mode. It is one thing to work things out alone in the office and then deliver the notated results in class, and another thing to talk to students while being attentive to their responses and difficulties. The conversational style allowed the teachers to follow more easily actual intuitions and insights brought up by students, so that the class could truly be a living meditation carried out in common, students ascending on the wings of the teacher. This was further enhanced by the fact that the professors had solid command of their subject and had no difficulty speaking extemporaneously about it. Even as individual teachers, they did not use notes in class; teaching together made this approach all the richer, the thoughts of one stimulating those of the other two.

Though Nelick and Quinn had been involved in experimentation with the conversational approach to teching earlier in the 1960s, they perfected it with Senior in the Integrated Humanities Program. The harmony was remarkable, with never a false note—no interruption, no impatience, not even noticeable disagreements. Here were three friends who enjoyed looking at beautiful things together and helping students discover them. The class was something like a Socratic dialogue in that it rose from the sensible to the spiritual, with each of the three men contributing his insights. Senior compared it to a jazz band improvising on familiar themes: "It's as if one of us were on clarinet and another on trumpet and another on piano. One of us starts to talk, the other picks up the tune and the other one gets the beat."[37] A fellow faculty member who attended the class a few times had this to say about it:

> The three professors complement one another without being repetitious or wayward. They possess a marvelous ability to

develop, explore, and refine upon the statements of another. . . . The students (and I) were participants in an *intellectual drama*, participants in the process by which the form and content of a great poem takes on a kind of life through the words of a teacher. . . . Only another teacher of literature can, I think, appreciate fully what happens—the amplitude, the range, the pleasing quality of the instruction in literature—when Professors Senior, Quinn and Nelick teach together.[38]

Students were not allowed to take notes. Note-taking was seen to hamper listening, reflecting and remembering, particularly as they were accustomed to jotting down phrases and key points with the sole purpose of reviewing them later for exams. As the program brochure stated: "The tendency is to fill up notebooks while leaving the mind empty."[39] In IHP these usually distracted young folks quickly learned to be totally present, with senses, heart and intellect. This was as it should be since, in this class, retaining exact formulas and information for future reference counted for less than glimpsing something beautiful here and now, feeling the appeal of wonderful truths. Students left the class enthralled, caught up in a vision. Instead of immediately turning to their little problems, as was often the case elsewhere, they lingered and mused among themselves on these great subjects.

Thus, the IHP class became an authentic, living meditation. And as would be normal in a lively, spontaneous, playful conversation about beautiful things, it was a lot of fun. In fact, mirth was an essential part of the classes because reality is at once grave and funny, great and little, as Senior knew so well. Describing what went on, a former student recalls that "merriment could suddenly turn into the deeply profound; a vision of things where sadness and joy lay down together in meaning."[40] This humor helped one adapt to the paradoxes and recognize the nuances in reality, and was, as another student remarked, "the best therapy for sick minds"[41] who take themselves too seriously.

Although the conversation was spontaneous, the professors had a rather set way of going about it. A session never began with abstractions

or generalizations. There was no preliminary survey of authors or periods, not even an introduction to the author of the book presently being studied.

Senior often enunciated the principle that since the essential goal of a literature class was to teach students how to read, class time should consist in reading a passage with them so they could learn how to read the rest by themselves. Thus, nearly always he or Quinn first read aloud a passage that threw light on the entire book or the fundamental views of the author, or presented a significant topic to address. The three would then enter into conversation, gently directing the students' imaginations and emotions to participate in the scene at hand and come to know its characters. The episode of Aeneas landing on the shores of Africa, or of St. Augustine stealing pears or Hamlet meditating in the graveyard, the personalities of Socrates, Caesar or Macbeth, all came alive when the professors described and discussed them.

They would point out key elements in the passage at hand, often pausing at a beautiful phrase or even an especially meaningful word. A graduate well remembers this aspect of the teaching:

> Details of the text could well turn out to be significant—the thong which latched a door in *The Odyssey*; the use of the word "jocond" in a poem by Thomas Gray and its etymological implications; a discussion of a seemingly minor character, like Palinurus in the *The Aeneid*, which we discovered, provoked from Virgil some of the most profound lines of poetry in the entire epic.[42]

At one point they would settle on a particular theme to be developed: in *The Odyssey*, for example, Penelope's fidelity to her husband; in Herodotus, his poetic style of history compared to the more studious and scientific approach taken by Thucydides; in discussing Plato, they expounded on the four types of government, on the respective natures of philosophy and poetry, on what it is to be a disciple; regarding Caesar, they conveyed a sense of what it is to be a great man; concerning Virgil, they spoke on the nature and reality of suffering; and with Roland, Gawain and Don Quixote, on chivalry and adventure. Once the conversation landed on a theme,

Senior would usually present a pertinent, traditional principle; the professors would tell an illustrative story, relate the theme to other readings and poetry, draw out examples from history and apply the theme to the present context and the students' lives.

In the course of the conversation, remarks might surface relevant to the historical background, or the perspectives of a time period, or to some notion governing the author's thought, but no effort was made to organize ideas into a system. The following class period would usually turn to a different, seemingly unrelated, passage and theme. After two or three such sessions on a given book, without an effort made to examine it in its entirety, the professors would go on to the next one.

Even with regard to the program as a whole, the professors were not systematic. They did not attempt, over a sequence of classes, to build up to a major affirmation, such as the immortality of the soul or God's existence. Rather, class by class, week by week, they meandered through various themes, ruminating at leisure and apparently going nowhere in particular. Their conversation resembled what Senior wrote about meditative reading:

> The student is like the bee gathering honey from several flowers—stuffed with sweetness, he forgets which ones were which—or like the worm who pushes forward blindly in the dark and then, accustomed to the place and knowing nothing of it save that he is there, pulls up his lower half: "This is a point of view," he says. "And though another may be greater and more splendid, none could be more true or ever quite the same!"—and pushes on again.[43]

Although it was not a cohesive edifice of ideas that emerged from the program, various themes did often recur under different aspects, and naturally converged. As the semesters went on, a few vital truths, certain basic values, such as the importance of the family, the permanence and transcendence of moral values, or the dignity and freedom of man, were particularly impressed on the minds and hearts of the students. Still more fundamentally, IHP aimed, first, at fixing the students upon the foundation

of the Perennial Philosophy—namely, that the real is really real, good, beautiful and wonderful—and, second, at engaging them in the great Western tradition.

Once these two goals were attained, IHP would have fulfilled its purpose. The students, then looking at reality with normal human eyes, imagination, mind and heart, and listening in delight and wonder to the great Western authors, could move forward for themselves. They could go on to higher, more abstract studies if they so chose. In any case, they would have a desire to learn. They would be prepared to seek the great truths and know where to look for them. They would be ready to undertake the adventure of human life.

A Fundamental Battle at the University of Kansas

In a university where the teaching of relatively trivial and even bizarre matters is tolerated under an inflated idea of academic freedom, it is stupid and indecent to suggest that the teaching of a magnificent, venerable, intellectually brilliant and spiritually splendid body of thought should be suppressed.

—Senior, letter to Howard Baumgartner

IT is time to investigate the controversy that raged around IHP. We will sketch the story, then reflect on the grievances brought against IHP and provide direct responses to these before examining what fundamentally underlay this opposition. As background for this analysis it will be helpful to first take a glimpse at Senior's life at KU, and especially at the joy he and his students took in the program.

Buzzes of Delight

Toward the end of his time in Wyoming, Senior had realized that the difficult and demanding work at the ranch was spreading him too thin. He needed to concentrate his energies more on his real profession—his work with students. In Kansas, therefore, Senior went back to his former choice of a simple home in the country. Even without ranch chores, however, he was a busy man. He drove into town early, recited the rosary

with students at the university chapel, attended Mass and then went to his morning classes—usually two or three hours of Latin and one or two hours of IHP question-and-answer sessions. After lunch, on Tuesdays and Thursdays, the two IHP lectures took three hours, after which he, Nelick and Quinn held a discussion session with the sophomore class. On other afternoons he taught at least one comparative literature class a week (on Dante, or St. Thomas Aquinas, Wordsworth, St. Augustine), instructed the IHP graduate assistants and attended committee or departmental meetings. As he wrote in a letter of 1971: "I have literally been teaching forty hours per week, am exhausted and happy."[1]

Senior had a right to be happy. He was no longer a maverick teaching a few students and only for a semester. He had a milieu where his poetic teaching could blossom, and with two good friends he was leisurely forming many docile pupils. A former student remarked how "within a few weeks, the entire class was welded to this new vision of teaching. One that none of us had ever experienced before."[2] Fruits were immediately palpable. Very quickly there was a shift among many or most students. Early on in the first semester, their hearts and minds came alive. They realized that they had been heading in the wrong direction, away from those beautiful values they were beginning to glimpse. They started putting aside their fantasy worlds and turning with interest to real things, hungry for what the professors and the great authors had to offer them.

They were becoming sensibly and emotionally linked to reality and learning to love the traditional Western cultural heritage as an inexhaustible fountain from which to draw.

A professor of the Great Books tradition who visited the University of Kansas to give a lecture at IHP noted in a letter to Quinn the extraordinary effect of their teaching, which he describes as a turning from Modernism to a beginning of the Perennial Philosophy:

Seldom in my more than twenty-five years within the academy have I felt among more congenial spirits. One really has to experience your program to believe it. Let me say that my satisfaction derived not only from what I learned from the subject-matters

being discussed but also from what I derived from the way in which your staff simply held your audience captive on tough but important subjects. In my judgment, your program is one of the most fascinating projects I am aware of in higher education. And it seems to be such a remarkable success. Where in an age of instantaneity, anti-historical and anti-rational bias and cult of the absurd could you find youngsters turning to tradition and finding it so richly supportive of the humanity that other programs seem to exploit rather than explain? Let me just say that you and your colleagues are doing a fabulous job and enjoying it, and I surely think your students ought to be envied.[3]

Part of the story is the initial disposition of the students, which helped make them receptive to the education offered at IHP. Especially in the first years of the program, toward the end of the hippie and anti–Vietnam War movements, the professors were dealing with students imbued with a spirit of rebelliousness. Like Senior in his youth, they had recognized that something was wrong with the world. In 1982, Senior wrote to one of the first alums, comparing the early students of IHP to those who had come a decade later, also having in mind his own youth and the Symbolists:

> The new generation is not like yours—yours was the worst and the best in extremes, sometimes mixed in the same person, but always extreme, seeking heaven or hell. This new one is more cautious, more like Dante's "trimmers" who don't want to take a chance on either heaven or hell. They are mostly looking for security, having been frightened by their older brothers.[4]

It was indeed rather the rebels who were most affected by the program. The more proper young men and women tended to be content enough with things as they were, and felt less inclined to seek something different. The desire for something better than the world they knew made the rebels more ready for a turnaround. It also disposed them to being responsive

to teachers who criticized many of the same wrongs of the contemporary world that they objected to as well—its greed, its spoiling of creation, its artificiality and complications, its emptiness of meaning. The professors were able to show them that they should not confuse all these blemishes with the traditional values of the West.

Attraction to these values was often facilitated, paradoxically, by a void in the general education and culture of the students. They were something like barbarians whom missionaries bring to the faith more easily than they can cultured pagans. Likewise, the students had few of the obstacles that an already developed but faulty human culture can erect against acceptance of truth. These unsophisticated Midwesterners were not dulled by already having heard and rejected superficially understood traditional formulas. On the contrary, they were struck by the obvious when the professors showed them, for example, that courage, fidelity and honor were in fact appealing ideals, well worth striving for. Also, since they had read little or no first-rate literature, when they were engagingly initiated into the works of Homer, Plato, Chaucer and Shakespeare, they were dazzled. Given the superficial life of paltry pleasures they were used to, the healthy, deeper enjoyments discovered in IHP—looking at the stars as if for the first time, learning poetry, singing Burns and Foster songs together and waltzing—were a revelation. All this goodness, beauty and truth presented to them by the professors was new and exciting.

Thus, far from being laborious, the IHP was great fun as professors and students were drawn together to beautiful things. An alum wrote: "The program demonstrated convincingly that [the] desire to know comes from the delight encountered in the knowing and this is what propels education at every level."[5] Senior speaks here of the joy experienced by the three professors in giving, and by the students in receiving:

Schools, because learning is a self-diffusive good, pour down love and knowledge on their pupils like voluntary rain. Ever since the Fall, men have worked in the sweat of their brows and women labored in pain. But schools (Puritans be damned!) are fun. Learning for its own sake calls them forth. The yachtsman hears the

wind and waves, the hunter the horn and hounds; zealous teachers and eager boys follow the buzz, as of bees in the brain, of sensitive, affective and intellectual delight.[6]

It seemed to many, or most, of the students that a whole new life was opening before them, a new world. They did not know at first where the buzzing was leading them to, but they sensed they were being guided by the professors to treasures that had real, perhaps ultimate meaning. There was something more to life than comfort and escapism. The students were baffled that no one had spoken to them of such obvious and good things before, but, rather, they had been fed with junk, in and out of their studies. No one had shown them healthy, nurturing literature, art, music, dance and games. They naively wondered how anyone could have turned away from such joyful activities and such deep, beautiful truths; how someone could have revolted against the great Western tradition; why the modern world had thrown such treasures away. And yet very soon, to their utter amazement, the magnificent Integrated Humanities Program itself would be viciously attacked.

IHP, RIP[*7]

By its third year, close to three hundred students were enrolled in IHP. It fulfilled nearly all the liberal arts requirements and constituted more than one-third of the credits of a normal freshman or sophomore load. If a student also took Latin and perhaps some other classes given by one of the professors, he could well be taking two-thirds or more of his classes in and around IHP. In the spring of 1974, a special major, Classical Antiquities, was created for students who had finished IHP and wanted to continue studying under the three professors' tutelage.† When conversions to Catholicism started to occur among the students, and some young men actually entered monastic life, the Integrated Humanities Program could

---

*   For a blow-by-blow account of this battle, see Carlson op. cit., chapters 4 through 6 and appendices.

†   Senior's Comparative Literature program never went far. He proved too controversial a figure for the necessary cooperation with other teachers and, in any case, became absorbed by his work with IHP.

no longer be ignored by the rest of the university and, eventually, even by the general public at large.

According to standard practice, a university committee was assigned to appraise the IHP during the 1971–72 school year. In the fall of 1972 its findings were presented to the College Assembly, the official deliberating body of the College of Liberal Arts and Sciences for requirements and courses, comprised of the faculty along with a few elected graduate assistants and students.

In the spring of 1973 the assembly held six rather tumultuous sessions concerning IHP. Although these were painful and tedious for the professors, Senior kept his humor. When an opponent prefaced his remarks with "To be perfectly honest . . .," he leaned over to his colleagues and said: "The last time I heard that phrase it was from a used car dealer." The debates ended with a majority vote ruling that the program would no longer fulfill requirements. It was decided that the administration should set up a permanent advisory committee for the program and that the professors would be prohibited from interviewing students for admission.

The fact that IHP could not fulfill requirements rendered it difficult for many students to find time for such a substantial elective class, but it maintained a high level of enrollment nonetheless and continued to prosper. The professors, in fact, kept to interviewing prospective participants, but without choosing among students for admission to the program. Some selection was accomplished by the very fact that taking IHP was no longer convenient—a student now had to positively desire this extra class purely for its own value. In May of 1974, Quinn obtained approval from the assembly for IHP to fulfill some humanities requirements. Over the coming months he also convinced the schools of journalism, engineering, business and architecture to accept IHP for English requirements. The University of Kansas senior class in the fall of 1974 elected Senior teacher of the year. He was quoted as saying: "The honor is not for me alone but for Pearson College and for Drs. Nelick and Quinn, who share the honor with me. We've been under attack for our 'innovative' ideas. This is a vote of confidence by students."[8]

The percentage of dropouts, however, was high since many students could not persevere through four semesters of elective classes. And the administrative embroilment continued. For example, the three professors' salaries were not in proportion to their academic exertion, the administration refused to endorse a semester abroad in France and an investigation was undertaken regarding "sexism" in IHP because the professors encouraged traditional roles. In 1974, the assembly disbanded the college-within-the-college structures, having found it difficult to coordinate them with university departments. This move might seem to have had little immediate effect on the program other than removing "Pearson" from its name—PIHP became IHP—and having offices moved from the Pearson building. But the program no longer had a home, the professors lost any last hope of expanding their program into a more complete college, and administrative justification for IHP as a rather autonomous program was less secure. The continual conflicts and attacks, compounded with their teaching load, created much strain on the professors. Quinn described it this way: "The three of us are burning ourselves out. Our lives are continual teaching and conference. I'm afraid the pressures are starting to get to us. We're running close to the edge all of the time and we receive absolutely no encouragement from anyone in the administration."[9]

About 150 students, the three professors and a few assistants went to Ireland for the entire spring semester of 1976. We have already referred to this trip and how it benefited the students through their contact with traditional village life. On the academic side, the semester also provided them continual interaction with their professors and a more integral learning experience. More conversions and religious vocations came from this group than any other. The "Irish pilgrims" also became the closest-knit group of any IHP generation, several marriages growing out of this time together. Deep tragedy also touched this semester abroad. Two students were stranded on a crag by an incoming tide and drowned in the cold sea. Yet even from this sad event good could be drawn. The loss of their two friends naturally touched the students' souls, moving them to meditate more deeply about life. It further bonded them to one another and to the

staff. They were also touched by the many tokens of sympathy received from all over Ireland.

This trip to the Emerald Isle was something of a summit of IHP's story, but it was also, in a way, the beginning of the end. News reached home of conversions and of visits to monasteries. It seemed to some people that IHP had gotten out of control. While the program was still abroad, the university administration determined that the professors could no longer distribute information about their classes, either through the mail or at information booths during the summer orientation. The rationale for the decree was that no other course did any recruiting and that it was not appropriate for courses to compete for students. Since IHP was not part of a department, it now had no means other than word of mouth to make itself known. In the fall of 1976, the number of freshmen enrolling dropped to fifty. Also there were only thirty-one students in the sophomore class, partly because relatively few freshmen had dared take a semester off for studies abroad the year before.

Following the sojourn in Ireland, there came criticisms and attacks, especially from outside the university, which openly bore upon the conversions and monastic vocations emerging from IHP. Various organizations put pressure on the university's administration and published articles to warn the public of IHP's "subversive" ways. They maintained that students of IHP fell into the pattern of people joining a cult—withdrawal from their family, turning their back on society, becoming sullen and secretive. In fact, students became more alert and more engaged with the society around them.

In December 1977, after about a year and a half of the increased pressure that followed the semester in Ireland, the dean of the College of Liberal Arts* ordered the Advisory Committee to not only advise, but also *supervise* IHP, and present a review of the program to the administration every semester. In its report for the spring 1978 semester, the committee raised questions about the desirability of IHP's presence at the University of Kansas and determined that an official investigation was necessary. By the fall of 1978, beginning enrollment in IHP was twenty-seven and only

---

*   Not Dean Waggoner.

nineteen students registered for the second-year class. The administration, therefore, saw fit to cut funding by three-fourths—from $16,000 to $4,000. As a result, the program had to reduce the number of its assistant teachers and could not rehire its faithful secretary, Suzanne Cupp, who had been with the professors from the first day. The Advisory Committee was assigned to conduct the investigation, for which it called on witnesses both for and against IHP. At this point Professor Nelick, exasperated with the ongoing harassment, left the program and returned to teaching on his own.

In January 1979, the Advisory Committee, in the official report following its investigation, concluded that IHP should no longer exist as a program because it was virtually under siege and had inadequate personnel, a low budget, lack of proper office space and a dwindling number of students. They proposed that another committee be organized to govern the interdepartmental humanities courses. This Humanities Committee would make decisions normally made by departments and thus hopefully solve the administrative, economic and information problems that plagued the isolated IHP. The Advisory Committee further recommended that another professor with different views be added to the IHP staff.

The dean acted quickly upon these recommendations, in fact, going well beyond them. In March, he instructed Quinn to transfer the IHP files and office key to the new Humanities Committee by June. The class was recast from a liberal arts program administered by Quinn and Senior into a sequence of four humanities courses under the direction of the committee. It was no longer a program, was no longer under the direction of the professors themselves and had no budget or office of its own. Quinn was offered a seat on the new Humanities Committee, which he declined. Senior was reported as saying that he would not serve if asked because "that would constitute bad faith about the work we've been doing. I won't participate in my own execution."[10] Neither Quinn nor Senior had yet decided if they would continue teaching what now would be simply a humanities course. "If someone is going to tell me how to teach, I'm not going to teach," Senior said.[11]

Some Favorable Witnesses

It seems that an objective evaluation of IHP should not have been difficult to conduct, dealing as it did with three well-qualified, experienced and reputable professors who were simply and magnificently accomplishing their appointed task, namely, arousing in their students an ardor for the great works and ideas of our civilization. Quinn proposed that an assessment of the program would take about a half hour:

> Nobody can spend fifteen minutes with any dozen of our students without discovering that they like the course, the books, and the teachers; that they have enthusiasm, <u>esprit de corps</u>; that they feel they are learning something important; that they take their study in PIHP seriously. No one could spend fifteen minutes with the books without discovering that this feeling is fully justified—Homer, Plato, Aristotle, Virgil, St. Augustine, St. Thomas, Chaucer, Shakespeare, Cervantes, Tolstoy.[12]

A number of people in a variety of roles—students, parents, professors, religious leaders—made favorable comments about the program at one point or another, contributing some general, commonsense assessment that will be useful to consider here.

Of course not all IHP *students* were won over to traditional Western ideas and values, to waltzing, reading old books, reciting poetry and looking at the stars. Even in the first years, when it was convenient to take the course as fulfillment of the liberal arts requirements, about one-fourth quit after a semester or two. Most all of those who remained, however, were ardent in their desire to study under the professors. Here are typical, general views, both from students who were not naïve freshmen. The first was a graduate student when he discovered IHP: "I don't know whether [the three professors] are right or wrong, but I know that I learned more in one semester in Pearson than in four years at the University of Kansas."[13] Another who followed the program as an upperclassman expressed what so many had experienced in IHP, in contrast to the emptiness they encountered elsewhere:

I drifted around the university for two years and found nobody offered any kind of education whatsoever. Then I found those three guys. Now they were really teachers. They weren't trying to aggrandize their positions through research. They weren't into getting their reports published in Psychology Today. They were just happy to teach and they were the best I've ever seen.[14]

A few *parents* of converts and of students who entered religious life were critical of IHP, but their testimonies often show that they had received false information. Also, there were instances where the students did not explain their new convictions well, or were impatient and abrupt when dealing with their parents' difficulties and misconceptions. The great majority of parents, however, even those of converts, heartily approved of IHP. Here are a couple of lines from one parent, a Phi Beta Kappa Columbia graduate, written to Quinn about his appreciation of the class itself: "My wife and I are greatly thrilled with what we have seen and heard concerning this program, which we consider to be most outstanding. I have never attended a lecture in my own college career which I considered more meaningful than the one I attended at Pearson last fall."[15] Another parent described what many others beheld suddenly emerging in their children: "In little more than one semester, we recognize in our son for very nearly the first time an awakening of exciting new interest, a zeal and genuine enthusiasm for learning."[16]

Some *professors* were vehement in their demand for IHP's suppression, but the majority of those who worked against it were content with chiseling the program down to the size of an ordinary class. A few faculty members admired and supported it. Several testified in favor of the class, at least concerning particular points. We have quoted above one professor's comments on the quality of the teaching. Here is one who contributed a realistic, commonsense assessment of the whole situation:

A number of [IHP students]—at least the ones with whom I have talked—are turned on . . . I am troubled by suggestions that somebody else should be teaching this group of students. Why? And

who? How many really think these freshmen and sophomores would be better off if this 24-hour program were chopped up into segments taught by grad students or by others. . . . Many of our students will leave KU without having had the stimulation of one fine teacher. . . . Here we have a gathering of young people who have 24 hours of Great Books from three of the finest teachers at the University.[17]

Another wrote on the influence IHP students had in other classes:

[IHP] students become deeply involved in the analysis and discussion of ideas, outside the classroom as well as inside. Such has been the overwhelming testimony of students in the Program . . . of parents . . . and of colleagues on the faculty whose classes enroll students in IHP. . . . Pearson students "transform a class" because they are truly interested in ideas.[18]

A handful of *religious leaders* joined in to attack the program, but there were those who spoke out to defend it. One Methodist pastor publicly registered his concern over a warning sent out by another minister of his denomination: "I feel that the case is overstated and tends to be inaccurate at several points . . . [IHP] has been a helpful and attractive program at KU and the testimony of students who have been in it (who are United Methodists) supports this kind of effort by a major university to explore the roots of our culture."[19] Another Protestant minister attended class and reported: "I have been in many courses. . . . It was the only class where I have felt so moved by my emotions. I have found myself enjoying the classics for the first time."[20] These ministers found nothing subversive in IHP, but simply a study of traditional Western culture.

Why, then, was the Program attacked? Why did smart, educated, often religious men and women conclude that IHP should no longer exist, or at least be greatly reduced and severely controlled? Opponents presenting objective reasons against IHP should now be examined.

Grievances and Responses

A summary statement in the 1978 report of the Advisory Committee encapsulates the criticism leveled at the IHP: "The Committee sees as major educational weaknesses of the Program a lack of tolerance for divergent points of view and the insularity of thought and staffing that has characterized the Program from its inception in 1970."[21]

The professors were certainly not "intolerant" in the ordinary sense of the word. No student is on record as having complained to an authority or the various examiners that he had been penalized for differing opinions. Witnesses attest that the professors respected the consciences of others, the right of each person to his own opinion, and that they were fair, forbearing and objective. Students were tested and graded on their knowledge of the material in the books and on their grasp of the ideas involved, not on conformity to the professors' thought.

Ordinarily "insularity of thought" consists in ignoring opposing information and arguments. Yet, through Lucretius, Descartes, Hume and others, the IHP professors presented what they sincerely considered to be the deepest and clearest of positions contrary to the Perennial Philosophy. The IHP brochure stated: "Challenges to the tradition are also studied in the Program, with a view to forming a just understanding of their force." Also, Plato, Virgil and Shakespeare are certainly not sectarian or even provincial or narrow. The great authors, made accessible by the professors' mediation, opened minds rather than closed them. They drew students out of their Modernist insularity, out of their ignorant and naïve belief in the self-sufficiency of modern fashions.

No doubt, it would be impossible for a two-year program intended for beginners to cover all grounds. IHP did not study Eastern thought or Immanuel Kant or, for that matter, Jacques Maritain. Nevertheless, as a comment from a colleague at KU illustrates, IHP's study of Western civilization largely sufficed to fulfill liberal arts requirements:

If, in 24 hours of course credits, PIHP really accomplishes its stated goal of fostering a first-hand acquaintance with the principal

classical authors of the ancient, medieval, and early modern world, this in itself will be a most notable achievement, bound to be reflected in a significantly richer appreciation and understanding by the student of the cultural, intellectual, political, social, and religious aspirations of mankind.[22]

As for "insularity of staff," adding a professor who did not share the philosophical and educational principles of IHP would contradict its very goal of providing a coherent formation in Western civilization. Because the professors were mainly speaking of elementary and first things, any difference would have had fundamental impact. Carrying on a team-taught class with a colleague who disagreed on basic points would turn the lectures into warfare. However interesting or useful debates may be in certain circumstances, in the context of the program they would do more to confuse than enlighten or instruct underclassmen.

Behind these grievances related by the Advisory Committee document was the central fear that IHP somehow "brainwashed" or indoctrinated its students, that is, lured them into irrationally adhering to the faculty's opinions. No observer, however, detected any brainwashing in the proper sense of methodical mental manipulation, intimidation, or stress. There was nothing secretive in positions or methods, as the professors explained: "Great pains were taken to inform students fully of the nature, content and methods of the Program."[23] They let everyone know in their brochure that they followed traditional Western values and Realist philosophy. They strove to inform parents about the program, inviting them to visit the class and holding symposia especially for them. The professors also pointed out when something in their teaching belonged to the general tradition or only to part of it, or rather was personal opinion.

Students certainly did not have the impression that they were being tricked or somehow violated. Here is an especially convincing testimony given by a student who did not adhere to the views of the three professors: "I love, honor and revere the teachers. But I haven't chosen their ideas, nor had them foisted upon me.... In PIHP there is no thievery of the student's freedom, but the teachers aren't afraid to give guidance when it is sought."[24]

In fact, students perceived that the professors had led them to the beginnings of critical discernment by providing references other than the day-to-day propaganda of modern culture and the media. They sensed that, for the first time, they would not be simply swayed with the wind but now had references for judgment and could begin to think for themselves.

One can ascertain by its fruits that IHP did not produce close-minded extremists. We have mentioned the intellectual awakening witnessed by parents and the students' interest in ideas as recognized by outside professors. While remaining enthusiastic about their formation in IHP, students went on to study successfully under other professors and in various fields. In 1978, Quinn mentioned that among former students twenty were then studying law, twelve in medicine, nine in nursing and fourteen in theology; thirty-three were in other graduate studies. In our Introduction, we referred to the bishops and religious superiors, the doctors and lawyers. Quinn added that "the graduates are influential, intelligent members of the community who still support IHP—not fanatics or crazy people."[25]

It is clear enough that none of the objections as formulated by the Advisory Committee held water. They were based on a perspective, an attitude, a choice that calls for further scrutiny.

Relativism versus Realism

Those who accused IHP of brainwashing or indoctrination of students in actuality confused those terms with advocacy teaching, that is, with arguing a particular case, something the professors certainly did. Thus, the chairman of the English Department testified to the Evaluation Committee in 1973: "In this Program the truth is taught by those who agree what the truth is in a framework of 'advocacy teaching.' To me this is a form of indoctrination or 'brainwashing.'"[26] Likewise, the chairman of the Western Civilization program proclaimed concerning IHP: "Advocacy teaching is only a euphemism for propaganda or indoctrination of one point of view."[27]

This identification of advocacy with brainwashing will lead us to the bottom line of the differences between the parties involved. For now we can

mention that Quinn responded, first of all, by pointing out that advocacy teaching was covered by the officially recognized academic freedom: "It must be asserted unequivocally that qualified teachers at Kansas have a right to teach the truth as they see it, provided they do not contravene the law and that they stick to their subjects."[28] He also brought forward how other teachers at KU championed particular doctrines without anyone raising objections. "It is well known," he wrote, "that everything from Zionism to Communism to Keynesianism to atheism to skepticism to population control is defended and advocated in this and in every other public university."[29] He concluded: "We have the same rights as our critics. They may advocate pluralism or skepticism or Eastern Thought or eclecticism or neutralism or scientism or Modernism and we can traditionalism."[30]

Thus, was an exception taken in regard to IHP? Quinn posed rhetorical questions to illustrate the fact: "How many students take more than 40 hours from professors who teach the scientific view of life? How many ethical relativists are there in the various social science departments, and how many students take large concentrations of classes with these teachers? Is there at KU a sort of unrecognized Women's movement faculty . . . with whom a significant number of students take a considerable number of hours?"[31]

A group of students who organized themselves to defend the program identified what they thought was the reason for the irregularity: "IHP takes a stand against many of the causes fashionable in the modern university: pornography, homosexuality, sexual promiscuity, zany new religions, communism, moral relativism, existentialism, the extremes of feminism and secularized Christianity."[32] As Quinn noted, there was very obvious advocacy in play among the promoters of these fads. Author and lecturer Alice von Hildebrand, who was kind enough to provide the foreword to this work, went to the philosophical heart of the matter when she described the IHP controversy as an "intellectual persecution waged upon those who defend the objectivity of truth, of moral values, of tradition and even of plain common sense. Academic freedom is the exclusive privilege of those whose educational aim is to debunk all objective values."[33] In other words, behind the onslaught was, at a minimum, a good

dose of some form of Relativism. The Western Civilization chairman put his objection to IHP in almost those very terms: "I am made extremely uneasy by the notion of 'truth' on which the whole program seems to be based. . . . Their 'truth' is one truth; and I am very much concerned lest other views and other truths not be given a fair hearing."[34]

For the Relativist, any affirmation of absolute truth, of anything beyond material facts and measures, seems intolerant and insular because it shuts the door on other ideas and possibilities. No advocacy can be legitimate, because one is only dealing with opinions. Consequently, in the mind of a relativist, vigorous convictions such as those arising among IHP students could only have been maneuvered by brainwashing. Relativism also could account for the strange animosity in the attack. We have seen how Senior pointed out the self-contradiction of a Liberalism that had become "dogmatic." He wrote of "an inquisitorial Liberalism ruthlessly exterminating everything that disagrees with it . . . in the name of freedom."[35] He also wrote:

> The currently established academic religion has as its first principle the axiom that no proposition may be held with such certitude as to exclude its contradictory. It is a doctrine dogmatically defined and adhered to with a ferocious emotional commitment, so that one is not opposed so much as anathematized if he steps outside its lines.[36]

This "ferocious emotional commitment" is due largely to the fact that Relativism is a fundamental choice that governs the rest of intellectual life. There is no dialogue with those on the other side of the divide—any opposite view must be countered by excommunication. Quinn was justified in turning the attack around:

> There has been a persistent effort to compel IHP to cease to teach according to the philosophy of its faculty and instead to teach according to the pluralistic philosophy widely held at the university. Now this *we* call intolerance and insularity; for the advocates

JOHN SENIOR AND THE RESTORATION OF REALISM

of this position are simply saying that a non-pluralistic approach will not be tolerated.[37]

Certainly not all those who criticized IHP formally professed Relativism, but most of them partook in the pervading Relativist perspective of modern academia. Quinn described the situation: "One may speak publicly in obscenities, one may chatter freely about sex of any kind and one may coolly debate the mires of homosexuality, cannibalism and abortion. But *veritas*—truth—is unmentionable, especially in that naked way, with no quotation marks of apology and without a thicket of qualifiers. It's a sort of metaphysical streaking."[38] Like bees in a hive, the faculty at KU reacted instinctively to IHP as a foreign element, and eliminated it.

Nevertheless, even in this relativistic atmosphere, IHP could perhaps have been left alone; the seemingly romantic and eccentric theories of these three sometimes cantankerous professors might have been tolerated, if the program had not produced such tangible results. Its amazing success represented a challenge to the assumptions and pretensions of modern professional education. Not only did IHP boys get their hair cut and girls start wearing skirts, but the students were also turning to Christ. It is remarkable that a few converts and vocations caused such an uproar, whereas thousands routinely lost their faith in Christ at the university, took up drugs and promiscuity, and went off on crazy fads and immorality with scarcely a raised eyebrow among the faculty. The fact is that the Relativism prevalent at the University of Kansas was of the Modernist type, which especially fought against traditional, Christian, Western values that used to be taught everywhere in former days. Senior's words provide an apt analysis:

> In the recent years of its establishment, this relativism has been imposed on everyone with all the inquisitorial force of a fanatic self-righteousness which . . . definitively excludes the realist view and especially its Christian expression. . . . Subtly and not so subtly relativism has established itself in the colleges where the Christian religion may be studied—provided that it is not believed.[39]

Most striking and troubling to opponents of IHP were the many conversions to the Catholic Church and the monastic vocations arising from the program. For the Modernist, the Catholic Church is the bastion of intolerance, insularity and brainwashing. As Senior put it: "Anti-Catholicism is the anti-Semitism of the Liberals."[40] A journalist writing about the "inquisition" of IHP identified the two points behind the debacle as being Relativism and the consequent "bigotry against the Catholic religion, which practically alone insists on another view of truth and history."[41]

The next chapter will consider the way in which the three professors advocated and truly educated without imposing conclusions upon their students. We will discover how it was that, by presenting Realism and the great Western tradition, they pointed toward the Catholic Church.

Dom Antoine Forgeot (Abbot of the Abbey Notre-Dame de Fontgombault), John Senior, the author, Lawrence, Kansas, 1998. *Courtesy of Annunciation Monastery of Clear Creak*

Realist Pedagogy
Taken Seriously

*We reject the idea that there are many truths in this
world from which to choose. We say there is one
truth, that it can be identified and that it can be
taught. That is the essence of PIHP.*

—Dennis Quinn

IN the reaction incited by the very existence of IHP—a little
enclave of the Perennial Philosophy in the midst of an established
Perennial Heresy—we find an archetypal conflict within the war that has
unceasingly raged between the two worldviews. From the fundamental
epistemological chasm between Realism and Relativism flow two opposed
understandings of education. Senior wrote: "What we are doing is very
controversial, but the reason it's controversial isn't religion. It deals with
the theory of education."[1] The question here is, what is it to teach? Can
one lead another to truth? This chapter will outline the principles of
Realist teaching and examine how they were applied by Quinn, Nelick
and Senior. Once this is established, we can proceed to present more
concretely how the three professors, by the very fact of leading them to
Realism and to the great West, helped their students open themselves up
to Christ and His Church.

Drawing Out the Right Answers

The relativistic mindset would hold that, because we cannot be sure of
anything beyond sense experience, beyond scientific data and techniques,

there are only two possible approaches to teaching. On one hand, there is totalitarianism, through which the teacher—operating on intolerance, insularity and brainwashing—imposes his opinions on the student. On the other hand is liberalism, which provides information and presents opinions without ever affirming, except as a personal opinion, that one position is true and another false. Confronted with this characterization, one would obviously opt for the latter. A KU professor of philosophy, in a statement directed against IHP, maintained that "the most important point of a liberal education is to offer a student as many intellectual options as possible."[2] And the chairman of the Western Civilization program compared the liberalist view of education with IHP's perspective:

> Adherence to [IHP's] idea of truth is only liberal in the sense of being non servile; it is not liberal in the sense of allowing young minds freedom of choice. It presents a "closed" vision of University educa-tion as opposed to the view that a University should be a "clearing house of ideas" where all ideas are sampled, studied and weighed and where each student can frame his own concept of truth, not one forced upon him by "advocacy teaching" (indoctrination).[3]

Before looking more closely at the Realist view of education informing IHP, we might immediately put forward three statements countering the Relativist standpoint. First, the concept of a liberal education as focused on freedom of choice is rather limited in the history of mankind, a novel idea that hardly knew existence before the twentieth century, that is, before Modernism. More traditionally, liberal education has been considered as effecting liberation from error, from slavery to senses and blind impulses. "Truth will make you free," said Our Lord. A man is truly free because he personally and lovingly adheres to the true, good and beautiful.

Second, concerning the secular Great Books programs, Senior clearly demonstrated that it is practically impossible for the unprepared student of our day to find his way through a mass of material without receiving direction. Such limitation aside, the Great Books programs at least did present the classic writings. One can infer from the comments above by

the two professors in the opposition that the ideal for them would be to present the greatest number of ideas possible—"all ideas," said one of them. Is the quantity of choices so of the essence that nothing can be left aside, that we should include all Eastern thought, medieval heresies, ancient Greek religions, modern cults, even overtly immoral or violent ideas? There must be some criterion, some measuring rod for the material even to make sense, and this is the role of the teacher to provide. It is obvious that quantity is not as important as quality. As the three professors used to ask rhetorically, is it better to have many television channels or one good one?

Third, neutrality is an impossibility. We have noted that very often the Relativist expressly advocates his own philosophy. Even a noncommittal presentation of ideas instills Relativism indirectly—a professor who excludes God from the conversation by that very fact teaches atheism or agnosticism. Quinn told a reporter: "We say what they are teaching is skepticism—that one side is as good as another."[4]

With these points in mind, we can now consider Realist education and how it was applied in the Integrated Humanities Program. Because it is possible to know permanent, universal and meaningful truths, a teacher should aim at leading students to see and love the true and good that he himself has seen and loved. As Quinn said, "To be honest with yourself and your students, you must teach what you can see with your intellect to be true and you must get the students to see that truth with their intellects."[5] When an individual discovers a truth, it would be dishonest to pretend not to see it, and selfish not to help others see it as well, particularly when the individual is in a teaching position.

This was the case with the three professors at IHP. They were convinced they had encountered beautiful and important truths, and they naturally desired to share them with those they were in charge of instructing. By this fact, their teaching was markedly different from what was found in other liberal arts classes. They taught "not like the scribes but with authority," as some students commented, spontaneously associating their teaching with that Scripture passage. The professors' earnestness called to mind the words of St. Paul: "I do not run aimlessly; I do not box

as one beating in the air." Nelick suggested this was the reason why youth flocked to IHP:

> Maybe the program is popular because we do have something to say. The students have found from experience elsewhere in the university that you can't teach about nothing. Well, I believe in advocacy teaching. Apparently the university feels that academic freedom means the freedom to teach nothing, not the freedom to teach something.[6]

An authentic Realist pedagogy may advocate an idea, but it does not "force" a "concept of truth" upon the student. We have earlier quoted Senior about drawing out the right answers, but in IHP there was no intention or effort to goad the students on to those answers. In fact, he was critical of the teaching at seminaries in the decades preceding Vatican II precisely because of its methodology of inculcating formulas. In his view, seminary professors tended to take St. Thomas Aquinas as the object of the study rather than as a guide for the necessary gaze on reality. They made of philosophy and theology a list of definitions and a fail-safe method to be applied, like a plastic-car instruction kit where all one needs to do is to follow the directions:

> Instead of the difficult task of using St. Thomas as an instrument in the study of theology, seminaries codified recensions of the *Summa* to be memorized, repeated by rote and sealed off from thought.[7]
>
> Priests were trained in disputation and knew the arguments—like high school children learning Euclid, they memorized axioms and worked proofs never having seen the truth but got the answers right![8]

This mechanistic type of fake teaching was diametrically opposed to IHP's ethos. Senior described learning as something eminently personal:

Every student studies himself. Leonardo da Vinci said Narcissus contemplating the reflection of his own beauty in the mirror of a pool was the perfect artist—the perfect student too, who sees in the mirror of language and nature a reflection of himself, discovering himself through what he thinks and feels. The anesthetic boy reflecting what the teacher says rather than his own sensitive, emotional, volitional and intellectual experience is as vain as the actor-teacher putting on an empty show.[9]

By these strong expressions, he was insisting on the point that students must see for themselves. The teacher is a guide to be followed, not a technician constructing an inanimate robot, or a programmer entering data into a computer. There is a middle ground between liberalism and totalitarianism. From our study of the poetic mode of learning, we recall how Senior emphasized the fact that the teacher is not the agent of the discovery of truth, but simply a discreet assistant of nature. A teacher helps the student in his own natural, personal activity of intellectual enlightenment, like a coach guides the athlete in running, or the mother bird coaxes its fledgling to fly, so that eventually the runner and the bird will be able to operate on their own.

In an interview, Senior explained this fundamental principle—how it is that the teacher assists the student, drawing out answers: "The truth within you is the only teacher. The only thing I do is prepare the way. I awaken the students and get them to recognize those things that are already part of their world."[10] Since a human being does not immediately see the essence of the object as the angel does, he can and needs to be assisted in drawing ideas out of his sensible experience and in relating images and ideas one to another. The good teacher points out what the student, in a way, already knows; he leads him to recognize what is contained in his "sensitive, emotional, volitional and intellectual experience." As Socrates expressed in his famous metaphor of the midwife, the teacher simply helps the student give birth to—or express to himself—what he has already received.

Employing the poetic mode seemed to be the most realistic, the most natural and fitting way to help the KU student of the 1970s to really see and love for himself. The IHP professors assisted the gradual learning process by slowly and patiently working through the sensible toward the spiritual, bringing out the spiritual present in the sensible. They underlined the splendor of truth shining through the sensible and cultivated the student's responsiveness to it. They nourished the student's connaturality with reality, so that the student could eventually grow into truth on his own.

Even having accepted IHP's Realist basis and use of the poetic mode, one could pose a searching question regarding the teaching approach and the environment of the program. The common assumption in the KU controversy was that, given three brilliant professors spending so much time with students over an extended period while strongly and unanimously advocating their views, and given a community of closely knit students pushing these same views, the pressure on eighteen- and nineteen-year-olds would prove overwhelming. Some critics of IHP, in fact, did believe that truth is one, adhered to Christ and even to the Catholic Church; but they still doubted whether students could lucidly judge for themselves in the midst of such imaginative, emotional and intellectual persuasion, even if there was no brainwashing properly speaking taking place. In that vein, a KU professor expressed her concerns:

> [IHP] involves a form of emotional commitment that families engender. When this also involves extensive contact with three good teachers who share a basic view of what the fundamental truths are and when the personal element is strong and exciting, the outcome can motivate students to adopt the ardent advocations [sic] of the teachers and the students around them under often subtle pressure with regard to a particular philosophical and religious view of truth.[11]

There are two aspects to the question: Should one assiduously follow a teacher? Is it good to be in the midst of enthusiastic students?

Concerning the first aspect, the student ordinarily should be docile, that is, should desire to learn and receive what is proposed with a welcoming, trusting mind and heart. No doubt there are cults, and there can be mindless and exaggerated devotion to a person; there are dangerous professors and even degenerate parents who distribute poison to youth. Such deviations, however, do not necessitate that students refrain from having a normal and natural attitude of soul when dealing with a competent, devoted and prudent teacher. This should especially be the case when the teacher presents not mere personal ideas, but rather the central and tested principles of Western tradition. And if the teacher is a master who can lead one more deeply into reality, helping one perceive its beauty and taste its goodness, if through him the student discovers meaning in life, then there is good reason for the student to place himself as a disciple at his feet and stick with him. Great teachers are rare. No teacher is infallible, but life has a way of sorting out errors, and one does not leave Socrates for Tom, Dick, or Harry simply in order to have more "options." Consequently, a filial relationship of trust and affection with such professors as found in IHP was healthy and normal, as was the desire to remain under their guidance.

As to the second aspect of the question, it is a normal thing, if not a necessary one, for students to have peers with whom they live, converse and play, who join, support and encourage them in their intellectual and moral pursuits. Such friendships are an integral element of a natural learning milieu and are appropriate for facilitating a love of truth and the good. In IHP, communion and affection resulted naturally and bonded the students in their joy of discovering and deepening beautiful truths together. In point of fact, Senior, in his usual fashion, strikingly stated that "the purpose of a university is . . . friendship."[12] A description of the environment at IHP by a student touches the point of the matter: "We had a real college experience for a few years. . . . Intellectual pursuits were real, play was real, faith was real, love and friendship were real. We experienced tradition as a living thing."[13]

Quinn characterized the IHP style of education as "home cooking." Instead of going out to eat at a cafeteria in order to have lots of choices,

IHP students joyfully received together a wholesome and tasty meal lovingly prepared for them by people who knew them and knew what nourishment they needed. This was not novel. Before the twentieth century, before Modernism and the triumph of Relativism, the normal liberal arts curriculum consisted of just such teaching of Western values, in a community setting, with students cordially gathered around their teachers.

The "proof" of the value of this Realist pedagogy in IHP could be had by attending the classes. For want of this possibility, we can attempt to convey a sense of how the professors, applying the poetic mode, helped students come to Realism, to the West and to Christ. Teaching at IHP was akin to gardening, the gardener helping his plant grow on its own. Knowing that the mind is made for truth, the three professors were confident that their students would respond to truth, goodness and beauty if only given the opportunity, through contact with good material and some orientation toward truth on their part. We will now examine how the IHP professors provided nourishment for their plants, tore out the weeds that would choke them, and worked the soil around them.

Rooting Students in Realism

The professors realized that the first step was to renew the students' normal trust in creation, especially human nature, to awaken them to the fact that reality is really real, that it is deep and beautiful, and that our faculties can perceive it. Though we have long dwelt on the professors' efforts at nurturing Realism, it will be helpful to consider a couple of specific points on their ways of going about it.

We have seen that the "food" provided for the students' nourishment was not something abstract like a theoretical treatise in epistemology, but rather included the concrete occupations of stargazing, waltzing and poetic literature—activities that united their imagination and emotions to reality. The first book on the IHP reading list was Homer's *Odyssey*, which is at once gymnastic and poetic, concrete and beautiful, with its boats and sea, its banquets and tales. Senior observed that already by

their reaction to this book one could tell which students were going to turn around.

Thus it was mainly by immersing the students in reality, delightful and wonderful, that their sick imaginations and weak mental habits were purified, and Realist convictions fostered. Nevertheless, in order to help awaken in them the natural response to reality's appeal, now and then the professors would directly attack the weeds of the various forms of Relativism and subjectivism. The readings provided ample opportunities for this—in the Sophists' promotion of Relativism against Socrates, in Lucretius's materialism, Descartes's doubting of the senses, Hume's skepticism, Julian Huxley's scientism. The professors would briefly and simply draw attention to the obvious, through unsophisticated, commonsense arguments that anyone could grasp—for example, that it is an obvious contradiction to hold as true that there is no truth, to affirm that an affirmation is impossible; it is absurd to want proof of sensible evidence, that is, of what provides the very basis of all proof. In this vein, Nelick recalled an incident from the life of Samuel Johnson. Asked by a foppish young philosopher how he could know that a thing really existed, the old realist kicked a chair—"That's how I know!"—Nelick replicating the gesture. More particularly, contrary to scientific reductionism and our quantitative mentality—both of which lead, as we have seen, to disrealization and the psychologizing of knowledge—the professors pointed out, for example, that the theory of refraction of light does not explain away the mystery and beauty of rainbows.

The professors' interventions, however, were primarily of a positive order, working the good soil. Rather than directly counter Relativism or advocate Realism, they let poetry, literature and the stars do their work. The professors emphasized those aspects that would bring the students to sense the richness and depths of *being* and thus become interested in reality. They did this in a poetic way, not so much by abstracting concepts from the text at hand as by getting the students involved in the subject matter: in the banquet of the *Odyssey*—by speaking of the wine, the clothes, the furniture—or in the friendship between David and Jonathan,

in Gawain's chastity, in Ivanhoe's chivalrous courage. They brought into relief the mystery and beauty of these realities and values. Listening to and participating in their professors' poetic meditation, the students were naturally caught up in it; the beauty of the subject swept them beyond their pseudoscientific imagination. They soon realized that there is more to reality, more within the human soul, than any microscope can ever uncover. Little by little, they acquired the habit of a poetic gaze on the world and began spontaneously delighting in reality and wondering on their own about its mysteries.

Thus it was that IHP students were formed in Realism—not by definitions and syllogisms. Even if they scarcely knew what the word Realism meant, even if they were incapable of successfully arguing for it in a debate with skeptics, nothing could eradicate what they had seen and tasted. They knew that they had hold of something real. No nihilistic argument, however clever, can stand up against the splendor of the stars, or obliterate the nobility of a generous human action. The students viscerally knew that these things were beautiful, good and true, and that their souls were in correspondence to them.

Opening Hearts to the Great Western Tradition

To achieve its goal of holistic education, IHP had to restore the students' confidence not only in reality and in their own faculties, but also in their own heritage and past, in the Christian West. Here again the nourishment consisted simply of the great writings that dealt, not so much with Western civilization as such, but with particular themes—family, honor, courage, chivalry, education. The beautiful expression of these values kindled in the students a love for the authors. Senior expressed it in this way:

> The student who opens his heart to Homer, Plato, St. Augustine, the author of the Song of Roland, Dante, Chaucer and Shakespeare . . . learns to love these authors whose Beauty, Truth and Good shine through the dark divine and human matter of their

works like swarms of stars in the honey-combed night of time; he gazes on them with the thrilled fear we call "awe" or "wonder," the way a lover gazes upon his beloved.[14]

The students grew to treasure the civilization to which these authors and their writings belonged. As Senior commented: "If you get someone . . . into Plato or Newton or Shakespeare, he will see for himself why men have fought and died for civilization."[15] Thus, IHP's main task in leading students to traditional Western culture was to help them open their hearts to its great authors and the timeless themes they explored. Senior used to say that he was simply a porter who ushered students into the palace of great Western classics.

However, there were weeds to be contended with that hampered this genial contact with the classics. A notable impediment consisted in prejudices held against the old authors. At the beginning of the course, the students would spontaneously react according to the modern tendency to disdain antiquated texts, written when nothing was known of molecules and the subconscious, when one purportedly so naively received traditional stories and glorified heroes.

They took it for granted that the ancients had long ago been largely surpassed. To counter this state of affairs, there was a constant and resolute effort at IHP to fight the *a priori* critical, condescending attitude that would not trust enough to listen to what the author had to say. As Senior wrote, "Such a critical intelligence, whatever its use in the marketplace, is prophylactic of the beautiful, the good and true."[16]

We have mentioned that the professors eschewed introductions and commentaries that reflected a disparaging stance since they would have inevitably colored the students' reading. Furthermore, they would bring into focus the bias of critics who dismissed what the authors wrote whenever their statements went beyond what modern experimental science could explain or analyze. The teachers showed that, for instance, there was no reason to suppose that St. Augustine's belief in miracles was due to an unenlightened backwardness in his time, or that Herodotus was a simpleton because he thought events were pregnant with meaning. A text from

Quinn concerning Herodotus illustrates how the professors showed that perspectives of former times, in fact, were not stupid:

> Since the subject matter of history is dark, Herodotus' standard of accuracy differs from that of the modern "scientific" historian. The Greek, who does not demand unrelieved Cartesian clarity, is comfortable with the "rule of thumb," approximation—as are most of us in most human affairs, knowing that precision in such matters is impossible and that efforts at precision in qualitative things are always reductive—as if "life," for example, were only a sequence of squiggles on a brain scan screen.[17]

More generally, the professors cultivated an atmosphere of trust and receptivity toward the past, which helped to counterbalance the tendencies of the cynical eighteen-year-olds with whom they were dealing. For example, they seemed to take for granted the veracity of the old stories—of Odysseus's voyage, or Aeneas's landing in Italy. What Senior stated about learning dates in high school history applies well to the approach adopted in IHP: "The dates are decisive, but scholars by no means decisive about date. Some are legendary. Let the boys learn them and face the disputes in graduate school, if they get there."[18] In this first poetic education, what mattered was to listen and receive, to learn the tales, to grasp the general line of history, to delight and wonder. Scholarly historical research and arguments could come later.

In fact, rarely was an opportunity to emphasize the worth of times past lost in IHP. It was easy to show their obvious superiority in the areas of painting, sculpture, literature, architecture, music, or even in ordinary things such as clothes, dishes and furniture, but the course also communicated an appreciation for old-fashioned ways of doing things—for the nobility and meaning of manners, for ceremonies and customs. Waltzing and learning calligraphy brought home to students the worthiness and grace of old forms. Through all these means, the professors led their students to discover that civilization is not synonymous with technology, that authentic civilization—harmony between the spiritual and the material, esteem for

family life, for virtue and rule of law—was much more present in the past than in our technologically advanced society. Nevertheless, they also liked to point out in detail how pre-industrial civilizations often managed quite well even in technical areas, such as in the construction of aqueducts, and the installation of plumbing or central heating.

Trust and docility toward the Western past were especially cultivated through their teachers' veneration for the great writings. It was through the students' classroom experience—observing their professors' oral ponderings as they pointed out and illuminated treasure after treasure in the texts under discussion—that the students recognized the profound insights, the moral, spiritual and philosophical strengths of the old classics. They also learned a little humility as the professors, especially Nelick, helped them realize that, although the current generation could look up information in an encyclopedia and push buttons on machines, it knew next to nothing about real things, knew much less history than its ancestors, and had almost none of the literary, moral and philosophical culture of the past.

Such discoveries broke through the students' incredibly naïve and self-sufficient narrowness. They emerged from their Modernist shell and quickly shed the major prejudices they had about the value of bygone authors. These young folk who had once considered the old classics to be dusty, irrelevant volumes, the pastime of a few scholars, discovered them to be altogether enlivening and pertinent to the deep questions in their own hearts. After their professors' meditation, students would virtually run home to plunge into the book in question.

However, the West has undergone significant cultural changes. As the readings advanced, two divergent and incompatible philosophical currents emerged. The professors demonstrated how Plato, Cicero, St. Augustine and Boethius had confidence in the true, the good and the beautiful, and let these values, as found in the sensible world, lead their minds and hearts to the spiritual and the Absolute. In other words, the professors unearthed a great tradition that adhered to the basic tenets of the Perennial Philosophy, whatever differences and disputes there might be on particular, although sometimes important, points. On the other hand, the Sophists, Lucretius, Descartes and Hume represented an attitude that rejected the

call of a reality that is universally experienced. These authors held positions reflective of some form of the Perennial Heresy, opposed to the great values the students had begun to appreciate. The students were able to discern between Realism and Anti-Realism, and thus entered into the fundamental theme of the course.

The students also recognized, with the help of Nelick, Quinn and Senior, that these two foundational and opposing views applied not only to philosophers, but to cultures in general. The professors showed that a basic Realist wisdom and practice passed from the Greeks by way of the Romans to the Christian West. They especially enjoyed speaking about the robust attitude prevalent in the simple harmony of medieval life, so earthly in many ways yet pointing to the stars. Discussing the Renaissance, during which the common outlook began shifting toward disrealization, the professors traced this revolution less by use of philosophical formulas than by citing examples of the waning wonder for mysteries, linked to a growing curiosity for resolving technical problems. Students in IHP also read some post-Renaissance representatives of the great tradition, but these were identified as increasingly isolated as the tide of modernity rose. Of course, there had been achievements since the Renaissance, but, according to the professors, these positive developments had generally been built upon some fissure and were thus not usually as robust as their Realist forebears.

The professors often brought into relief how some or even many elements of the Perennial Philosophy had been rather common in our culture until fairly recently. They helped students identify in their own familial past—in their grandparents' generation, for example—a more human, moral and noble perspective of life. Senior observed that he had simply gotten the youth to recognize what was already part of their world. IHP students thus understood that they had but to dig a little under the surface of contemporary culture to find a more beautiful America and Europe. They realized that the professors had led them back to their real home, which they had never really known before except superficially, namely, the great Western, Christian tradition. In following this tradition, they knew they were walking on a well-trodden and sure path.

Many went further, as we know, all the way into the Catholic Church. This fact raises a last question about IHP's pedagogy. Why did so many conversions and vocations arise from this course?

A Poetic Reserve

The IHP reading list contained nourishment for religious exploration, in particular for the traditional Christian faith, and even to some extent for Catholicism. This was inevitable, since the West until modern times was, in fact, religious, and for centuries Christian and Catholic.

The classes never involved any polemic against non-Christian religions, much less against Protestantism. If there was any weeding, it was not on the religious front, but rather in the removal of obstacles that prevented the students from being open to the true, good and beautiful, and therefore, eventually to God. The effort was mainly directed to doing battle against Anti-Realism and the general *a priori* critical spirit of the youth.

Throughout the IHP course, there was never even an objective presentation of Christian doctrine. The course did not treat of God, or of Revelation, or of how Christ saved us on the Cross. Professors did not ponder Christ's nativity or His death and resurrection. There was nothing of what is commonly thought of as apologetics, such as demonstrating how Christ fulfilled the Old Testament prophecies, or presenting the proofs of His resurrection, or His founding of a Church.

The professors approached even the most overtly religious texts in ways anyone of good will would do. The themes brought into light in Christian books were of the same order as those underlined in Homer, Plato and Virgil. In treating the Old Testament, for example, the professors dwelled on the very first verse—"In the beginning God created Heaven and earth"—and tackled in a poetic way the rather philosophical subject of what is a beginning and what is time. They dedicated a class or so to reviewing the nature of stories through the Samson tales and the account of the duel between David and Goliath. Another class period pondered the "valiant woman" described by the Book of Proverbs. Concerning the

Confessions, they commented on St. Augustine's analysis of his stealing pears as a boy just for the pleasure of crime. They described how St. Francis lived and thought in the poetic mode.

Non-Catholics, who made up a majority of the class, felt at ease and often studied under the professors outside of IHP. Even the few who did not have a Christian background did well. The Advisory Committee, in its 1979 verdict, had to admit that the IHP faculty did not evangelize in class; that is, they did not directly promote the Christian faith: "In the face of charges of religious indoctrination and proselytizing, the committee has found no evidence that the professors of the Program have engaged in such activities in the classroom."[19]

Nevertheless, since the Integrated Humanities Program was a quest for significant truths, it did touch on religious ideas, at least by dint of the impact religion had in history. Quinn put this into perspective: "We encourage students to become deeply involved with Plato, Homer, poetry and philosophy, and we say the same thing about religion. You have to take it seriously."[20] Furthermore, the professors did not hide their own beliefs, as if ashamed of them. The class was conducted assuming general presuppositions of traditional Christianity, as was customary in public education still in the 1950s when references were largely Christian, even if Christ Himself was rarely mentioned. Just as the three professors did not first give an account of epistemology, modern science or critical history in order to look at reality and read the great authors, likewise they did not feel obliged to prove views still rather common to our civilization. They considered it acceptable, when speaking to students in a Christian society, to presume that God exists and to allude occasionally to Christ with reverence and faith.

When the professors did mention something properly religious, it was not as if they were seeking an excuse to bring in religion; the point was raised only when it was relevant to the day's subject and when their musings naturally led to it. In this case, usually they simply posed a rhetorical question, in order to stimulate the students toward private reflection and investigation. As Senior told a journalist: "If you read Virgil, who says you have to make a commitment, it turns out to affect you personally. Some people

have accused us of trying to decide what those commitments ought to be for our students, and that just isn't true. But it is true that we raise the question."[21] And questions raised concerned God and religion in general, rather than specifically the figure of Christ. For example, when discussing in Plato's works the view that all things have an end, Senior raised the question of man's end, without providing or expecting an answer. Interestingly, such questions were never specific to the Catholic Church.

Although the professors did not intimate in class that one could come see them privately about religion, students often did go to them with more personal queries, which indeed sometimes turned to that vital subject. Even in these private conversations, however, the professors were far from pushing their students to conversion. One graduate of the IHP Program commented:

> I recall when I decided, on my own, without anyone remotely suggesting I should convert. And I went to Mr. Senior after hours. I said that I had read Augustine and something had hit me. I wanted the beauty and the majesty of the Catholic Church.... To my surprise, he told me, "If it is real, it will wait. Just ride out the wave, see if it is real. You might also consider saying a prayer to Our Lady, the Hail Mary, or the Our Father, just for guidance."[22]

Why such discretion? Senior once said about his teaching: "The subject is always the same, only the occasions are different." Among the metaphors for teaching and learning he would evoke, in addition to the bee seeking after various treasures or the worm dealing with what is right in front of it, Senior also referred to the eagle circling around the sun, the one central truth. He was always thinking or speaking indirectly about Christ in one way or another, but he, as well as Nelick and Quinn, knew very well that in the supernatural order, more than in any other, it is impossible for a teacher to impose truth. One cannot steer a person to the faith, because it is not the result of human effort; the virtue of faith is caused by God intervening supernaturally, enlightening the mind and attracting the heart. Nonetheless, because the Lord desires to use human

instruments to eliminate obstacles and dispose the heart for grace, a teacher can play a role in the process. In this regard, the three professors accomplished what they considered appropriate according to their office in a public university, with students of all types, though usually having some measure of a culturally Christian background.

When asked "how IHP did it," Senior always directed attention first and foremost to prayer. He responded to an interviewer: "Regarding conversions to Catholicism . . . the seeds of which, of course, are planted by efficacious grace, a miracle that the Catholic students in our program asked for in their prayers while singing Lauds and Vespers from the Little Office of the Holy Virgin and by attending (when a priest could celebrate it) the Latin Mass of our Fathers."[23]

Nevertheless, he recognized that the course prepared a favorable soil for receiving that seed of grace. In the same interview, after describing IHP's work at rectifying the students' imagination by the experience of physical realities and of great literature, he stated: "I will say that truth, whose glorious manifestation on earth is faith, grows naturally in minds who are thus disposed."[24]

In other words, the professors perceived their task in helping students come to Christ simply as directing and attuning them to reality and Western literature, which in their turn pointed toward God and Christ. We know of Senior's recommendation to high school teachers that they not "theologize," but "let the boys find out the Maker in the made." Likewise, the IHP professors had simply to keep to their leisurely meditation on what the great authors were saying, following each theme for itself and letting it eventually lead on its own in the direction of Christ. The very pagans pointed higher and forward, as Virgil steered Dante on the path to a paradise that the Roman poet himself could not enter. "Grace attaches to nature," Senior wrote. "Students were converted as much by reading Plato as by Augustine. . . . When we taught the beauty of a poem or Homer's *Odyssey*, we were not faking it, or trying to imbue the text with some phony Catholic gloss. The truth is always the truth and if it is really true, it will lead you to the transcendent truth."[25]

Indeed, it was not necessary to refer to Catholic dogma at any time or in any way, for there was something providential in Greek and Roman civilization as preparation for the faith. Senior wrote, "Classical culture was and is the *præparatio fidei*, its philosophy and literature the Egyptian gold and silver Christendom has taken on its pilgrimage."[26] The professors did not even have to invent or impose an order of discovery, for it was already there. The learning process thus developed gradually, much as Western thought had done. It followed the historical path that had opened up the West to Christian truth and then to the blossoming of that truth in a full Christian environment. "Western tradition," he wrote again, "taking all that was the best of the Greco-Roman world into itself, has given us a culture in which the Faith properly grows."[27]

The professors had simply to dispose the students to the readings and let the West do its work, indicating here and there how the beautiful truths they were discovering beckoned farther.

As a last point for our reflection on the Integrated Humanities Program, we will survey the four semesters of the course in order to obtain a sense of how the wholesome nourishment of classical texts, read in chronological order, with a little hoeing and weeding along the way, helped students experience the West as pointing toward Christ.

Præparatio Fidei

There was indeed something providential, first of all, in the delight the Greeks took in reality and in their openness to mystery. Already when reading Homer in the first semester, the students had an inkling that they were at the threshold of an unknown world of beauty. Homer, and the Greeks in general, also recognized spiritual presences; they spoke of the gods, which the professors seemed to take seriously. Another major author read during that semester was Plato, who directly reflected on spiritual values and, in his dialogues, rose toward an Absolute beyond this world.

During the second semester, the professors pointed out, for example, that the Romans had a less childlike attitude toward reality than the

Greeks did and that this more mature disposition also played a role in Western development. Thus, Virgil recognized the mystery of the *lacrimae rerum*—"the tears of things." Previously, in the first semester, the professors had posed the question whether Odysseus, now home at last, could in fact be satisfied with Ithaca as the final goal of his life. In the second semester, they remarked that Virgil looked farther than Homer when he has Aeneas follow a mysterious call to continue forward; somehow home lay before him in the future, not behind him in the past in Troy.

After pondering reality with the Greeks and the Romans, the students were ready for the Old Testament at the end of the second semester. Perhaps even more so than with other works, the professors let the Bible speak for itself. They acknowledged that, in this case, they were before something of a different order. The truths and values that the Greeks and Romans groped toward by reasoning and philosophy were presented in Holy Scripture as simply having been given from above to the Hebrews, this little nomadic people. The students were able to realize of themselves that the knowledge of a loving, personal Creator was something far beyond the pagan myths and even what the old philosophers had envisioned, and that the Ten Commandments synthetically brought out the best of, and more than, what the Greeks and Romans had discerned about the moral life. The pagans, for all their brilliance, knew neither the source nor the end of human life, nor the why of its actual state of pain and sorrow: Where did we come from, where are we going, why is there evil and pain? Without the professors arguing the point, it emerged that the Old Testament provided at least a beginning of a response to these questions: Man came from God, but fell away and had to labor to return to Him. Yet it was obvious that the Old Testament itself begged completion. The full, ultimate answers had not been uncovered, the story not yet finished. Peace and abundance in the Holy Land could not, any more than in Ithaca, be man's ultimate destiny. The Old Testament explicitly aimed farther than itself, to a messianic era and a new covenant.

In the beginning of the third semester, with the reading of a portion of the New Testament, the professors had little work to do in order for the students to recognize Christ as a unique figure. Compared to Him,

what were Odysseus, Caesar or Charlemagne, these great men whom the professors had praised? And His revelation transcended even that of the Old Testament, as He spoke with such ease and so concretely of the intimate secrets of the Father, of things previously unknown yet which corresponded to the deepest, mysterious yearnings of the human soul. The students read and even memorized part of the Sermon on the Mount and had no difficulty in perceiving on their own how much it fulfilled, intensified and deepened the Ten Commandments.

Discreet comments, nevertheless, helped the students recognize the fulfillment of all things in Christ. The professors pointed out, for instance, how the whole Bible in its entirety made up a perfect story. It began in the peace of paradise, as the stories of Odysseus and of Aeneas had begun in the peace of hearth and family. But the Fall, like the Trojan War, brought on an adventure that reached its climax in Christ's Death and Resurrection—an apex far more sublime than Odysseus's killing of the suitors of Penelope or Aeneas's landing in Italy. And the story of the Bible closed with something like a "return to the beginning," like Odysseus to Ithaca, as well as a "going forward," like Aeneas to something greater. But in this case, the return and the going forward were in relation to our final home, a kingdom greater than the Roman Empire, to a communion with God superior even to that of the Garden of Eden.

An especially important book in the third semester was St. Augustine's *Confessions*. As in a paradigm, students perceived in St. Augustine's homecoming to God, to Christ and to the Church, the passage from the Greco-Roman pagan civilization to the new, Christian world. This work was a breakthrough for many students as, with St. Augustine, they lived their own personal movement away from darkness and evil, and their turning toward Christ. In the medieval writings of that semester they experienced a flourishing of newly discovered great truths and beauty, in the warm sunlight of Christ. They perceived, as it were, an incarnation of the psalms in St. Francis's poetic expression and profound realization that all things are God's gifts. They found in the Christian chivalry of Roland and of St. Louis of France something far superior to the cunning of Odysseus or the wrath of Achilles.

The larger number of representatives of the Perennial Heresy in the fourth-semester readings confirmed in a negative, contrasting way the nobility of the Christian views the students had come to know. Reading these modern authors, they easily realized that, as the Western world steadily immersed itself more and more in disrealization, idle curiosity, greed and materialism, it became less Christian. The professors helped them recognize that the healthier minds that arose in the latter periods—Shakespeare, Cervantes, Scott, Newman—drew from better, more Christian days.

Thus, while the professors focused their work on the natural level, pulling out weeds and preparing the soil, the students grew toward the stars. Nearly every individual who attended IHP for the two full years of the course concluded that there must be Someone behind the beauty and order of this wonderful world—that there is a God. And anyone who followed the classes somewhat earnestly was deeply impressed by Christ's beauty and goodness, as well as by the Christian culture He inspired. It is no surprise, then, that the large majority of IHP students came or returned to Christ, or at least deepened their faith in Him.

Three factors stimulated in some of them a desire to investigate the Catholic Faith. First was the course material itself. The period of the Middle Ages, with all its charm, was obviously Catholic, and the students recognized that there was something particularly special about St. Augustine, Chaucer and Newman. Second was the fact that Senior and Quinn, and eventually Nelick as well—these fascinating teachers, these wise and good men—were Catholic. The professors acknowledged their role in this: "Although the IHP faculty never denies that as Catholics they influenced students in a religious way, such influence was indirect, largely through example."[28]

One student gave this witness about his own, rather typical, case: "All the professors did was provide the seeds of thought. Anytime you run into someone you respect, you try to find out what inspires them to be the way they are. I never talked to them about becoming a Catholic. I just decided one day to attend an inquiry class at church."[29] The third factor was the snowball effect triggered by experiencing the conviction and joy of the students who had become Catholics.

With the aid of some personal reflection and private research, many students recognized that the beautiful truths they were discovering blossomed and were at home especially in Catholicism. They realized that, at the heart of the Western tradition and splendid civilization they were falling in love with stood, not mere Christian inspiration or thought, but the concrete Catholic Church herself. A journalist wrote: "[IHP is simply] the presentation of reality as explained by great minds and the position of such thought in the center of a history that indisputably and without contradiction involved Catholicism as the main transcendent reality. That conversions might follow was not the result of anything improper—but the very opposite, the presentation of truth at its proper place."[30] Becoming aware of the Catholic Church's role in Western culture does not yet constitute faith, of course, but it can be a major element in disposing one to grace.

In the first years of IHP, students who desired to learn about Catholic doctrine were normally instructed by the local parish priest, Fr. Michael Moriarty. This Irishman's deep Christian roots and down-to-earth good sense were a perfect complement to the professors' teaching and a solid anchor for the young students' enthusiasm. As Senior remarked: "Students saw [Fr. Moriarty's] humor and the reality of the Faith in him and they said, 'I want that.' You can't have conversions from an idea. It has to come from seeing the thing itself."* [31] While Fr. Moriarty was pastor, Senior taught catechism on Sundays and in later years sometimes assisted with the instruction for reception in the Church.

Probably about ten or fifteen percent of IHP students converted—and others reverted—to Catholicism. Sometimes this came years after completing the program, after years of reflection, prayer and maturation of ideas. In fact, this adventure touched all involved, as Senior wrote: "Our single aim in teaching is to join with the faculty and students in discovery and love of truth."[32] Nearly all of the graduate assistants eventually converted. Professor Nelick himself entered the Catholic Church in the spring of 1973, during the third year of the program.

---

* Senior penned a poem about Fr. Moriarty and his brother, a priest in a nearby town: "The Moriartys." See *Pale Horse*, 58.

As for the vocations that came out of IHP, they too, of course, were a gift from God, but, no doubt, facilitated by the program in some ways. Writing about the study of older Christian works in the positive atmosphere of IHP, Senior alluded to Elijah hearing God's soft voice on Mount Horeb: "Students have the right to learn and therefore to try these texts and methods on their own and not their enemy's grounds. Given such an opportunity, not at all compelled or pressured, some will hear that whistling of a gentle air and find vocations."[33] The very fact of conversion, the sudden, overwhelming discovery of God and Christ, can often lead to a vocation. And since, in order to become Catholic the converts had to cast aside most of their very Modernist pasts, they sometimes had few bonds holding them back, making it a rather simple thing to leave all behind and turn totally toward the Lord as priests or religious. Also, through the culture of the poetic mode at IHP, the students learned to look on things as good and beautiful, but most of all as signs and figures of the absolute Good and Beauty. So why stop at the signs, however beautiful they might be?

References to monastic life might have surfaced a couple of times in class in the course of the program's two years. Senior was not the least apologetic about this, as he explained to a reporter: "When you study Western civilization you'll discover, among other things, that one of the great strands of the rope is monasticism. It's bound to come up—it's one of the central things human beings do."[34] It was not difficult for students to see how well monastic life corresponded to the poetic ideal put forth by IHP. A monastery, today, is a unique place where mystery is part of one's milieu; it is something medieval and musical, a contrasting relief to our dry, scientific times. As mentioned previously, Senior individually encouraged sojourns to the Abbey of Fontgombault, and even organized some himself. Those who went there were deeply moved by this incarnation of the faith, where the supernatural was almost tangible. These visits to the venerable Benedictine abbey had a decisive role in awakening vocations, including for those who followed the call to religious life elsewhere or became secular priests.

By 1973, the hopes entertained for developing and extending IHP into a four-year program had already been stifled, and especially after the

autumn semester of 1976, the program's work was much hindered. Although these words of Senior were not about the program's termination, they do sum up the attitude with which he faced it: "I should rather cheer us up with the neat old truth that we are not meant to succeed in this world anyway, but rather to do the job in front of us as best we can, because our Hope is in the next."[35] Yet, what was an axiom with him, that "it can't be done and we must do it anyway," was eminently true of IHP. The three professors did indeed accomplish the seemingly impossible. Against all odds, they turned hundreds and hundreds of young, disconnected men and women around, opening these deprived souls to undreamed of vistas, to a world of beautiful mysteries, to the real world, and provided the wholesome foundation upon which they could build a fulfilling life. The three could have addressed to their students the same words St. Paul wrote to the Corinthians: "You yourselves are our letter of recommendation, written on your hearts, to be known and read by all men." What Senior modestly said in a letter to a monk can be applied to countless former students in other spheres of life: "You monks are like an orchard whose trees are bearing a nutritious and delicious fruit. It was our privilege to be the workers in the orchard for a while for some of you when as young saplings we could prune a twig now and then and mulch the soil over your tender roots. And now there you are, straight and strong."[36]

The main issue at KU was not that brainwashing was taking place at IHP, and its students being tricked into the Catholic Church, as the accusations leveled against the program would have it. Rather, the issue was that the truths these students were learning had been forgotten—or rejected—by the faculty at KU locally, by Western academia, and even by Western culture in general. This was largely because of an unfounded belief that man cannot know universal truths. Such prejudice keeps one even from seeking truth or believing that it can be taught. It could be said that the IHP experience was like the stargazing it promoted. The professors simply got these city kids away from urban streetlights out under the night sky and pointed, and the students saw that the stars were real and beautiful. As Quinn said in a public meeting with the Advisory Committee: "We don't dictate what is true—it is there to be seen."[37]

Nothing is perfect here below. In the 1990s, looking back on the IHP experience, Senior actually asked himself if the emphasis on poetry had not been excessive:

> I fear IHP ism-ized poetry . . . in order to resist the encroachment of dialectic in the school. . . . We had our reasons, but in isolating "murder to dissect" . . . we gave the impression that anatomy itself is wrong, and in resisting a false, dialectical rhetoric, paid scant attention to the ethical and political order, the province of genuine rhetoric. Adolescents ain't for virtue, that's for sure—will presupposes sensible appetite. But in celebrating sense we tended to disparage virtues as impersonal and cold.[38]

In countering an analytic approach to literature and poetry, and to life in general, the professors perhaps neglected to give analysis a proper place. And, while stimulating emotions and combating Puritanism, they did not say much about virtuous discipline. Nonetheless, their teaching approach had to focus on gymnastic and music because of the neglect, scorn and misunderstanding with which the poetic mode is met in our materialist, positivist, Freudian culture. When that basic mode of knowledge is left aside, students are deprived of the necessary foundation for education. Given the encroachment of the methods and perspectives of experimental science, it was necessary that the elemental approach to reality—with awe, wonder, desire, respect for mystery—be first restored. The professors had to stimulate some passion in these youthful but already often burnt out, sometimes despairing, souls. They had to attract them to beauty, show them that values really existed, that joy was possible; they sought to give them a taste for life. There can be nothing truly fruitful in studies, or, for that matter, in life, without delight, *eros* and wonder. As when guiding a sailboat, the professors leaned to one side to restore the balance.

CHAPTER SEVENTEEN

Love Stronger Than Death

Praise death
that Sahara,
barren as Sarah
or Elizabeth.

—"Lauds," from Pale Horse, Easy Rider

OUR study of Senior's thought and his efforts to restore Realism in society has come to a close. It remains now to relate the story of his final years, as he approached death and eternity beyond. As the lines above reflect, while death is an unknown desert, a dark night that all must pass through, it will not be sterile when one is prepared by the water and light of God's grace.

Last Years at the University of Kansas and Two Books

Following the suppression of IHP, rather than moaning about the injustice done to them, Quinn and Senior simply went about their work of teaching. They conducted their humanities course as before, without any real control by the Humanities Committee. The class had substantially the same reading list as IHP and most of the accompanying activities, notably memorization of poetry. The family atmosphere also remained. There were differences, however. Nelick, who had left the IHP in 1978 to teach on his own, was irreplaceable. After his departure, the "flavor of practical, hard reality was not as pronounced,"[1] as a student

commented. And a sequence of four courses at three credits each had neither the continuity nor quite the scope of IHP. In addition, the professors turned the discussion sessions over to a graduate student; there was no rhetoric class, and Senior's Latin classes were phased out.*

At first, the number of students enrolled in the beginning semester of the sequence was only about twenty, with fewer than ten completing the four semesters. However, that number quickly grew with a marked resurgence in 1981 when 150 individuals enrolled, largely due to the efforts of a group of students who privately published a brochure on the class, distributing it to incoming freshmen. Conversions and vocations also began anew. Things were looking up.

Senior's two main books came out during these years. *The Death of Christian Culture*, composed of talks and articles penned during Senior's days at both Wyoming University and KU, was published in 1978. The book brought Senior some notoriety and he was occasionally asked to speak around the country in the course of the next few years. These later public lectures constituted the bulk of his second book, *The Restoration of Christian Culture*, published in 1983.

The two works are similar: both unearth the wayward principles underlying the miseries of the present culture and provide some practical remedies for them. In fact, Senior had originally intended to give the latter title, "The Restoration of Christian Culture," to the first book. Yet, as indicated by the wording, *Death* focused more on the miseries and *Restoration* on its remedies.

In *Restoration* Senior seems to acknowledge the validity of some criticism of the title of the 1978 book: "This is to be a positive book, a program for the Restoration of Christian Culture. Indeed I believe it is imprudent to document the disaster quite so much as some of us have."[2] Furthermore, *Death of Christian Culture*, addressed to a university audience, is more philosophical, more literary, and more scholarly than *Resto-*

---

* There had always been difficulties among the members of the Classics Department concerning Senior's lack of standard methodology in class and his use of ecclesiastical pronunciation; in the late 1970s the number of students had declined. Members said, however, that the decisive issue was Senior's extensive reliance on student instruction.

ration, where Senior speaks mostly to families and the ordinary man. Also, by the time he published *Restoration,* Senior probably had realized that patching up at the university level was not nearly enough, and that efforts should be focused upon pre-university education and the family.

His two books were read and appreciated in conservative Catholic circles, but this acclaim found no echo in academia. Among the few reviews triggered by their publication, there were a couple of favorable accounts in minor journals written by friends. But brief notices from others outside Senior's circle harshly criticized him, for reasons which were all too superficial. One of the detractors summarized his impression of *The Death of Christian Culture*: "Senior is too often guilty of the worst sort of pedantic scribbling, endlessly making literary allusions—often pointlessly, always tendentiously." Another wrote about the same book: "The numerous quotations have scant or no bibliographical references. Frequent excursions into semantics and etymology add little to the discussion. Coupled with the book's verbosity, they rather serve to distract the reader. . . . Not recommended."[3] It would seem that these critics simply skimmed through the book!

Translations of his books published in France, one in the early and the other in the mid-1990s, were surprisingly more successful, generating higher sales. The two works in their French versions also provoked wider commentary and discussion. One well-known French magazine, *La Nef,* hailed the appearance of *Death* as "the literary event of the year in Catholic publications."[4] The major conservative Catholic journals gave the books important and favorable reviews, a couple of which were cited in our introduction. A few, however, offered particular criticisms that were of greater substance than those of the Americans, dealing as they did with Senior's rejection of modern technology and of the general principles of modern finances, as well as his negative views on the possibility of understanding St. Thomas today.

At about the time the French editions came out, there was a renewal of interest in Senior's writings in the United States, notably among the younger generation. *The Restoration of Christian Culture* was reprinted in the mid-1990s, *The Death of Christian Culture* in the early 2000s. One

reviewer at that time rejoiced in his discovery of *The Death of Christian Culture*: "It's hard to believe this book was published in 1979 [*sic*]—it is a throwback to a time when culture meant something other than the latest dress featured on 'Sex and the City.' This cranky book . . . has a little bit of everything. . . . Be warned: this is hard-core Catholic writing that has the old take-no-prisoners tang to it. A delight to read. Highly recommended."[5] In 2008, both books were re-edited by IHS Press.*

Retirement and Two Booklets

The post-IHP period of teaching extended only for four years. In the early 1970s Senior had been forced to reduce his teaching hours because of fatigue, but he had no particular health problem in the years following, although stress and pressure from the battles over IHP certainly took their toll. Then, one day in July 1983 he felt some chest pain while on a walk. Blockages were found and a cardiac bypass was performed. In our day, cardiac surgery and the application of stents are routine; patients recover and return home quickly. But at the time this was a new procedure and not all was in place. Senior seemed to be recovering normally and resumed his teaching in the fall. However, one of his heart vessels closed again and he was rushed in for another bypass. Following the procedure, there were bleeding complications; as his daughter put it, the whole affair was "pretty horrendous."

For a while the dream remained that Senior might return to teaching, but hopes of that soon vanished. In June 1984 he wrote in a letter, referring to his body—as did St. Francis of Assisi and others—as the "donkey," and alluding to the scene of the talking donkey in the Book of Judges: "The doctors have insisted—and the old donkey speaks too in his way if not as Balaam's—that I must quit teaching, so my days are left for prayer, and of

---

* One may regret that Senior's beautiful dedications and acknowledgments were omitted in the 2008 editions and a newly composed dedication inserted in their stead, without any reference to the fact that it was not his. Also, some references were added without indication that they had not been in the original.

course that's a blessing. I must walk—which I always loved to do—and rest—which I have loved too much—and may read as much as I want."[6]

For Senior's students, both old and new, the effect of this unexpected, sudden silence of the master at the early age of sixty was comparable to what was said when Newman retired from St. Mary's of Oxford: it was as if the bells of Big Ben were no longer heard. Quinn carried on alone with the humanities class for a few years and then went back to teaching various literature courses, until his retirement at the close of the spring semester of 2006, at age seventy-nine.

Senior settled into his new life. After some time he did regain enough strength to be able to carry out some activity. On a few occasions, he met with Quinn's students as a group, and Quinn regularly brought promising students to see his retired colleague. Also, in the late 1980s an alumnus, then a religious novice-master, asked Quinn and Senior to record a condensed version of the IHP classes for his novitiate. That went well, so that the two old friends over a period of years made about ten sets of twelve tapes each—on Plato, Shakespeare, lyric poetry, children's literature, St. Gregory the Great's commentary on Job. The two would sit around Senior's dining room table, chatting in a relaxed and cordial atmosphere, interrupted once in a while by the roaring commotion of Mrs. Senior's Afghan hounds! Unfortunately the technical quality of the recordings was too poor for general broadcast, it being regularly difficult or impossible to discern what was being said. Perhaps they will eventually be ameliorated.

The retired professor still maintained some sporadic public activity, giving a few talks over the years to small, familiar groups, and penning a handful of short, rather circumstantial articles. For a while he took up listening to a Christian radio station. Also, in later years he and his wife were given a video player, and they enjoyed watching a film from time to time. Senior, that anti-machine man, amusingly called those sessions "a delicious hypocrisy." He too was a human being . . .

Most especially, he returned to his lifelong predilection. He said in passing once, in about 1990, that all he liked to read then was poetry. As late as 1998, one year prior to his death, he commented in a letter

that he was reading Virgil's *Georgics* several hours a day! He also wrote more poetry during those years of retirement. In 1992, he published *Pale Horse, Easy Rider*, a compilation of his verses from the early 1960s on, that is, postdating his conversion. Unfortunately, the publishing company was very small, so that the book to this day is little known. This is to be regretted, as the poetry is rich and layered. Here is how Senior characterized his own style: "Some poems, the best (Shakespeare's songs for example), are mysterious in import but clear in meaning. . . . Other poems (most of these) are more like puzzles; the mystery is in the grammar and expression. The difference is like that between beer and tea. You drink the healthful draught right off but, for the stimulant, must stir the pot several times to bring the flavor out."[7] Some have been surprised by certain lines of his poetry, which, without being sensual or erotic, humorously evoke some common human foibles in the sensible domain.

Although religion does emerge from time to time, one might have expected a more openly religious tone. Just as in his teaching, Senior probably perceived his role more as restoring a healthy natural order. Modesty was also a factor. He did not feel the inclination to make public what was always so intimately present to him. Someone who is living the faith can radiate a healthy Christian spirit without preaching.

Senior remained keenly interested in what was going on—in his family, of course, in his students and what they were doing, in Church life, and in political affairs. He continued to be in contact with a few friends on the faculty at KU and with many former students, regularly meeting one or another for lunch at a restaurant, sometimes reading and discussing his latest poetic effort.

Former students would telephone him day and night to discuss Plato, or their dissertation, or the crisis in the Church, or to ask advice about homeschooling, or perhaps what to do with a recalcitrant son. Or they might drop by. On these occasions, he would stop what he was doing, sit down with them and offer them a beer. He might even join in, saying: "I'm not supposed to drink any alcohol, but maybe I should for charity's sake, right?" Once he was found reciting the Breviary and pointed to the

text he was meditating on—about hellfire and worms. He said: "I think maybe I could handle the fire, but those worms, ooh!" Once the old man sincerely declared that, in fact, he had always wanted to be a cowboy. The visitors then heard Mrs. Senior's voice coming from the kitchen: "Now, John, you always wanted to be a teacher too."

Senior faithfully kept up correspondence as well. In this time of e-mail and telegraphic style, he remained attentive to the art of letter writing. His letters were usually brief, but always good literature, with a little story and a couple of interesting and uplifting remarks. His affection here came out more than in face-to-face meetings. If someone had a serious question, he took the time to reply more fully. One should hope that a collection of his letters will be published some day.

Senior did group into book form a series of letters of the early 1990s addressed to five former students who hoped to establish a high school, and titled the manuscript "The Restoration of Innocence: An Idea of a School" (yet unpublished). These letters form a compendium of his thoughts on education. Who would have imagined that this old college professor would reflect on such details as to where to place the latrines, or what is the most economic, handsome, simple and functional architectural design for a school, or how to help fourteen-year-old boys sing on pitch? However, his feet were not always on the ground. It is doubtful that teachers, who themselves could probably scarcely speak Latin, would be capable, as Senior suggests, of holding teenage boys accountable for conversing in Cicero's language several hours a day, including at the time of recreation. And it is impossible to crowd into one day all that he prescribed, especially as he intended the boys to take care of the school's pigs and cows. We have spoken in Chapter Thirteen of the Spartan conditions he proposed. Senior himself acknowledged that he might be a little too idealistic, commenting on the education efforts, including the establishment of schools, by former students of his: "Mine was a talent for ideas most of which will never be realized—and those that have been are transformed and made much more in action."[8] The particular school envisioned in "Restoration of Innocence" never came to be, but the manuscript of the book—typed on a computer by himself!—which

Senior handed to a few friends, was largely disseminated and used in various educational endeavors. This book and the accompanying article, "History and the School" (likewise unpublished), form something of an educational testament. It seems he wanted to cram into them everything he was musing about in those days, even some elements only loosely related to the topic of the book and the article. These last writings are still quite vigorous; some say they are his best.

Former students and friends of IHP found a way to carry on their poetic conversation by forming what they named "The Belloc Society." Usually a member would give a talk that would then be discussed over a few drinks. At first Senior declined the invitation to attend because of his health, but with good spirits:

"On the Splendid Invitation to the Belloc Society"

Regretfully I must renege
(pardon the defection);
my friendly pharmacist (the prig)
compounded a prescription
contra-indicating booze
What! will wastrels go
and medicate the tankless Muse
sipping H2O?

He did occasionally attend, and thoroughly enjoyed himself. He described these meetings in a letter to a monk, again with the old allusion to the banquet as a figure of the day to come. This extract gives a good taste of his letter-style:

Some students several years ago started a series of monthly festivals in honor of "Old Thunder" as Belloc's parents called him.... The hundred or so survivors of Pearson College within driving distance converge on the Castle Tea Room (a Bellocian structure you might remember built by a half-mad ex-Confederate colonel

who wanted to live like a medieval duke). We drink and, contrary to your rule, talk too loud and laugh too much, but the notion is to celebrate the coming dawn (which is already here!) at the end of this night in which we have dreamed our lives. Well, we love one another, despite our deplorable manners, and talk of nothing else but all the true, good and beautiful things that come from Him, the One in whom we live, (and love) and have our being.[9]

Thus, the old professor kept himself occupied. Everyone who had any contact with him then bears witness that he was as sharp as ever. Yet, he no longer was on the front line of the intellectual and cultural war. As he observed in a letter to a former student: "It is time for you and your generation to fight the good fight. If anything still depends on me—well, that's a failure in teaching I refuse to face!"[10] Senior felt out of the fray and enjoyed his retreat and the role of elder counselor. He was also exercising spiritual detachment. He actually discarded his books—all but about twenty, he said. He went to Mass, prayed the rosary, recited the Benedictine Office, and read the saints. And he was learning about suffering and death.

In "The Restoration of Innocence," Senior referred to "the school of suffering" as beginning at about the age of sixty, and "the school of death," at about seventy. As his heart attack occurred when he was sixty, he was right on time, one might say, for the first of those two ultimate periods of education. A poem written soon after his retirement provides a glimpse into how he was beginning to feel. "The Loveliest of Trees" alluded to Housman's poem of the same title about a youth sadly pondering that he would have too few springs to enjoy the cherry blossom. Senior compared himself to an old cherry tree. The young keep him alive, he said, by their affection and need of his counsel:

Another Winter on my head,
I gaze out at the storm with dread
. . .
The young behind me at the fire
. . .

How could they understand the fear
that, take or leave a crumb or year,
there won't be more than four or five,
that they are keeping me alive,
as freezing age, wind, ice and snow
break the brittle cherry bough.[11]

Beyond Senior's fragile health, his later years were assailed by distress of a more fundamental nature. Long before the "school of suffering" began officially, as he would have it, when he turned sixty in 1983 with the breakdown of his health, he already grieved over the collapse of civilization and the crisis in the Church. One can discern an ever increasing dismay over the years. In the first part of *The Death of Christian Culture*, written in the 1960s, he sets forth the classics of antiquity as being the key to the restoration of culture. Given the decline he perceived in the preparation and capability of his students in the following years, he scarcely mentioned the old classics in *The Restoration of Christian Culture*, but encouraged family reading of the best English works, the "thousand good books" instead. He affirmed, in fact, in the same book, that "Mary is now our only recourse."[12] "I used to say to turn to Virgil," he said, in a conversation in the mid-1970s, "now I say 'Let's pray the rosary.'" Though his trust in Our Lady did not waver, by the 1990s he looked upon the *status quo* with fatalistic eyes. He wrote at that time: "Since World War II, the public thing (*res publica*) has been destroyed. Beyond recovery. [America] will never be the greatest modern nation of my childhood even if it survives anarchy or invasion."[13]

In an interview also in the 1990s, he said, concerning Christian culture: "The crisis is over; we have lost."[14] Intimately linked to this cultural collapse was what Senior called the "Dark Night of the Church," a crisis that was at the heart of Senior's preoccupations.

A Dark Night

At the time of his conversion, Senior believed he had found in the Catholic Church the haven against Modernism. It did not take very long,

however, for him to discern the Perennial Heresy manifesting itself there as well. He had entered Noah's ark, but soon discovered, as all converts do, that he could not simply sit back as a spectator and enjoy the voyage. He had to man the pumps. "Once I had embarked safe and sound on the ship of the Church," he wrote, "I was dismayed to see it headed straight towards the shipwreck that I had just escaped. A worldly Church and a world without the Church on the edges of the abyss."[15]

We have mentioned how Senior's gaze of faith on the tremendous reality of Holy Mass made him agonize when confronted with the so common scandalous irreverence of the day. He wrote in a poem:

The possibility of prayer
persists upon the dentist's chair;
not even instruments that drill
banish all that's beautiful.
God is everywhere we seek
save this Hour every week,
when all that's crackpot, cruel and crass
celebrates *itself* at mass.[16]

This crisis in the Church did not concern the Mass alone. Here is how Senior described it in the 1970s, when some of its aspects were perhaps at their worst: "There is little comfort in the visible Church now. The liturgy, set upon by thieves, is lying in the ditch; contemplatives are mouthing political slogans in the streets; nuns have lost their habits along with their virtues, virgins their virginity, confessors their consciences, theologians their minds."[17]

Fleeing such things, in his retirement years Senior attended the Masses of the Society of St. Pius X. It would be a grave omission not to bring up a matter of such importance. Yet, we must proceed carefully so as not to give a distorted impression, and begin by recalling the story of Archbishop Marcel Lefebvre and the SSPX.

Retired from missionary work in Africa—where, as Superior General of the Holy Ghost Fathers, he had helped establish several dioceses,

becoming the first archbishop of the diocese of Dakar, Senegal—Lefebvre was approached in the later 1960s by several seminarians to help them sort things out and make provision for them somehow, in the midst of the confusion and agitation that arose in the wake of the Second Vatican Council. In 1970 he launched the Society of St. Pius X and its seminary in Ecône, Switzerland. Both quickly flourished while elsewhere religious houses and seminaries were generally languishing. Tensions soon developed with authorities, however, especially since the Society continued to celebrate Holy Mass according to the rite prior to the 1969 Novus Ordo. At one point the archbishop made some declarations against the validity of Vatican II's teaching and the reforms that followed, which eventually led to the Roman decision in 1975 to close the seminary and suppress the Society. This put the archbishop in a tragic dilemma. When almost everything was apparently falling apart in the Church, he and his followers were striving to uphold Catholic doctrine, discipline, Sacraments, and culture. He chose not to submit. The Holy See then suspended him and the Society priests from their priestly functions. The archbishop and his priests nevertheless continued operating as before.

The situation remained at a deadlock until 1988, when Archbishop Lefebvre signed a protocol with the Holy See whereby he could ordain a bishop chosen by the pope from among the members of the SSPX, thus reestablishing the society and assuring its continuation after the archbishop's death. Lefebvre, however, was wary and ultimately pulled back from the agreement. Against the express command of the pope, on June 30, 1988, he ordained, on his own authority, four SSPX priests as bishops. This illicit ordination, as gravely attacking the unity of the Church, brought on automatic excommunication of all the bishops involved. The archbishop died in 1991, still excommunicate, but the Society carried on.

Roman ecclesiastical authorities acknowledge that they are in the presence of a special case. In 1988 then-Cardinal Ratzinger, speaking about the large following of Archbishop Lefebvre, told some bishops: "There is no doubt whatever that a phenomenon of this sort would be inconceivable unless there were good elements at work here, which in general do not find sufficient opportunity to live within the Church of

today."[18] And he went on to mention three important and common errors that the Society of St. Pius X was fighting: desacralization of the liturgy, treating Vatican II as an absolute beginning without taking previous Magisterium teaching and tradition into account, and relativization of truth notably in ecumenism and interreligious dialogue. In 2000 Cardinal Castrillon Hoyos (then head of the Pontifical Commission Ecclesia Dei, established to assist "traditionalist" groups, as they are called) wrote in an open letter to Bishop Bernard Fellay, the Superior of the SSPX, that he "noted neither the scent of heresy nor the will to incur a formal schism on your part, but only the desire to contribute to the good of the universal Church."[19] The Holy See treats with respect communities affiliated with the Lefebvre movement and receives them and individuals back with open arms. A case in point is the Apostolic Administration of St. John-Marie Vianney, founded in Campos, Brazil, by Bishop Castro Mayer, who collaborated with Archbishop Lefebvre in the ordinations of 1988. When it returned to full communion in 2002 after the death of its founder, this association was granted permission to have a bishop of its own exercising episcopal jurisdiction over its members. The same offer was made to the Society of St. Pius X. In 2009, Benedict XVI lifted the excommunications of the illicitly ordained bishops and initiated an official dialogue between the Holy See and representatives of the Society. Discussions did not lead to a solution during that pontificate. The Society still does not legally exist, and all its priests and bishops remain suspended.

As for the faithful who go to SSPX Masses, the then-secretary of Ecclesia Dei wrote in 2002 that, although he could not recommend this, one could fulfill one's Sunday obligation by attending a Mass offered by a priest of the Society, and could even justifiably contribute to the Sunday offering, adding that "if your primary reason for attending were to manifest your desire to separate yourself from communion with the Roman Pontiff and those in communion with him, it would be a sin. If your intention is simply to participate in a Mass according to the 1962 Missal for the sake of devotion, this would not be a sin."[20]

Now to Senior's case. In the early 1970s, he obtained from a university chaplain not connected with the Society the legitimate, daily celebration

of the pre-1969 Latin Mass for him and his students. However, after two years the same priest decided to discontinue this. During the following few years Senior commonly went to Masses of the 1969 rite. In the spring of 1975 he visited Archbishop Lefebvre at his seminary in Ecône, but was not convinced at the time by the reasons the archbishop furnished him for disobeying. He decided that Ecône was not a solution for his students who were interested in pursuing a priestly vocation.

Nevertheless, in the early 1980s Senior began slipping off to SSPX Masses from time to time. In 1983, in the hospital recovering from a heart attack, scandalized by a remark of the Catholic chaplain, he called on a priest of the Society for Holy Communion. Senior concluded that priests who take this much trouble to bring him the Blessed Sacrament in such a worthy way were the ones for him.* From that point on, he would attend Masses of the Society, and even became somewhat involved for a while with the parish, giving a few talks there. Some of his students, as well, taught at the same parish for a while. Senior did at one point, however, try out the "Indult Mass"—that is, the 1962 rite of the Mass under the authority of the diocesan bishop—but found it unsatisfactory, because of the modernist architecture of the church building and the celebrant's lack of familiarity with the older rite.

Fundamentally, Senior's approach was that of an elderly man in retirement. Everywhere else he looked, Church life was rather a mess, whereas he knew his spiritual needs would be taken care of by priests of the SSPX. A friend, recalling a leisurely conversation with him about the subject, described his attitude: "Senior knew that the Society would take care of him in sickness and in death—in the manner that he wished *and* that he thought worthy of almighty God. He was absolutely sure that they would remain constant and that he could depend on them. . . . There were never any surprises with the SSPX—irritations, problems, yes, but the treasure of the Church's liturgical life would remain intact and preserved."[21] As Senior expressed himself to a journalist, "When the ship

---

* Senior's poem "Compline" mentions this Holy Communion. See *Pale Horse*, 12.

goes down, there's a point at which the captain says, 'Every man for himself.' You grab what you can get."[22]

However, Senior's view of the Society was by no means utopian. The same journalist commented: "He disagrees with some of [the Society's] positions and admits to being both troubled and confused by the issues surrounding them."[23] Senior told him that this was somewhat inevitable: "Sure, they have their problems—any splinter group does. When you lose the pope you lose the principle of unity."[24] In conversations with friends, he spoke of the Society's shortcomings in seminary training and education, not having enough liberal arts and poetry and, therefore, not turning out well-rounded priests and lay people. He discerned Jansenist tendencies in clergy and laity alike, with too much of a focus on the Christian life being made up of a list of rules and repressions rather than leading on to good by the attraction of beauty. He always feared that those associated with the Society were closing in on themselves in a sectarian way.

Senior remained in warm contact with friends who did not follow Archbishop Lefebvre, without making an effort to win them over to the Society. He showed humble respect for priests who used the 1969 ritual. Quite significantly, witnesses tell us that Senior went to confession to priests in obedience to Rome. This clearly suggests that these confessors did not judge him to be sinning by attending Society Masses.

To Senior, the differences between conservative Catholics resembled a lover's quarrel and were analogous to the Great Schism at the end of the Middle Ages, when St. Vincent Ferrer adhered to one supposed pope, while St. Catherine of Siena followed another. He had this in mind when he wrote: "There will be saints on both sides of this dispute."[25] He would therefore, for the most part, stay out of debates on the subject while waiting for better days: "We are at the point of Newman's great hymn 'Lead, kindly light, the night is dark and I am far from home.' Newman's advice in times like these is silence and prayerful expectation."[26]

In spite of that general orientation, Senior was not afraid to speak out when he thought he had a duty. We have from him two substantial writings in the early period following the 1988 episcopal ordinations. The first is an article entitled "The Glass Confessional." Senior's old friend Walter

Matt, the editor of the *Remnant*, prevailed upon him to write on the question of what followers of the archbishop should do, where they now should go to Holy Mass. Senior began: "These hasty notes document a state of mind (in anguish) in the days between the consecrations at Ecône, the threat of excommunication hanging over us who attend Mass at Society of Pius X Chapel and the Sunday coming up."[27]

Leaving canonical and theological questions to experts, Senior put the case in categories we are familiar with: "[Obvious facts and first principles of reason] stand prior to argument, have nothing to do with expertise, their best custodian is the man in the street. . . . We are not talking about arguments, but the grounds of argument. . . . Obvious fact is not scientific conclusion but common sense evidence everyone (honest and in his right mind) can see." There is no argument against evidence. Senior therefore maintained that "no authority, supreme court, king, pope or angel from heaven can compel against obvious facts in clear and present danger." He applied this assertion to the situation in the Catholic Church today:

> It is an axiom of obedience that you cannot set up private judg-ment against authority. In Ecclesiastical matters this means that the pope is the supreme court of all disputes in faith and morals. But [we are] not talking about private or any kind of judg-ment. . . . No helmsman follows orders to steam full ahead into an iceberg. . . . Anyone can see the Church is steering straight into the looming ice of unbelief.

In the 1970s, to illustrate why he did not follow Lefebvre and why we must obey the Holy See even when its commands seem to go against the good, Senior would say that if you were steering a boat and the captain told you to go full steam ahead toward an iceberg, you should follow the order. "It's better to lose a ship than destroy the navy by disobedience," he said. In this article he used the same image but did a turnabout, coming to the archbishop's conclusion. Senior held that it was obvious that the Church was running toward apostasy and even the pope could not com-mand against this evidence.

To lay out the obvious fact of the "shipwreck of the Catholic Church," Senior vigorously enumerated some woes: "I mean a new Mass, a new catechism, a new morality, a flagrantly mistranslated Bible, an architecture and music which constitute a thoroughly orchestrated and rehearsed attack on Catholic doctrine and practice." He elaborated a bit further on how the Mass was leading to the iceberg of unbelief:

A well instructed man can shut his eyes and ears at a Novus Ordo Mass and teach himself from memory that this action is the self-same sacrifice at Calvary offered under the un-bloody appearances of bread and wine, but it is not possible for ordinary people, and especially children who have no memory of such things, to keep the faith in the face of an assault on the senses, emotions and intelligence.

Senior weighed the gravity of disobeying the pope. Soon after the *Remnant* article, he wrote in a private letter: "The metaphor [of the iceberg] is inexact. Change it to this: you are driving around a blind curve on a narrow road when suddenly a 20-ton truck comes straight at you. You swerve—and smash into a tree! To avoid one danger Mgr. Lefebvre has smashed into another."[28] This is all the more true in that in Senior's view the choice facing Archbishop Lefebvre was between disobedience on the one hand, and on the other, the abolishment of all his work, altogether losing the celebration of Holy Mass according to the 1962 rite. Thus he wrote three years later in a letter to the editor: "There are some . . . who have bent to authority . . . choosing what they believe to be the lesser evil to serve the greater good. There are others like Archbishop Lefebvre who have resisted even to disobedience because they think there is no greater good than the propitiatory sacrifice of Christ in the Mass."[29]

However, we have seen, in fact, that the Holy See intended to reestablish the Society by giving it a young bishop at the side of the archbishop, in order for it to carry on. After Archbishop Lefebvre's decision to ordain bishops of his own choice, many of the scattered faithful either followed the archbishop or found no 1962 Mass nearby. This was the case with Senior.

But he always maintained that in this situation one was in the realm of opinion and had to decide according to prudential judgments given varying circumstances. At the close of a public letter, he offered his perplexity to the Lord and Our Lady: "Our agony (if nothing else) is pleasing to God and the Blessed Mother. These are not just difficult but impossible times and Their hearts are surely moved by all Their little ones who really don't know what to do but do the best we can, loving them and each other."[30]

In "The Glass Confessional," Senior put forward by name three prominent laymen and one religious superior who could be looked upon as references for one's own personal decision. In point of fact, immediately after the consecrations each and every one of the four cited people publicly declared his intention to no longer follow Archbishop Lefebvre. Senior himself, however, did not go along with them. A few years later when priests of the Fraternity of St. Peter—a community in union with Rome that celebrates Holy Mass according to the 1962 ritual—moved near enough to his home, he did not switch over. He feared the Fraternity and the indult would not last, and that if he were to start attending Mass there he would not be able to go back to Mass at the Society.

In fact, all of Senior's arguments bear heavily on the side of the choice of Archbishop Lefebvre and the SSPX. After *so many* disappointments, he had lost his trust in the hierarchy and even in the Holy See. Regarding *Ecclesia Dei adflicta*, the papal document through which John Paul II extended the possibility of celebrating Mass according to the 1962 ritual, he wrote in "The Glass Confessional": "Read the papal statement ten times if you can. You don't need arguments; it constitutes in itself a proof of its own radical insincerity." He very much feared that this permission for the use of the 1962 Missal aimed at drawing conservatives into a trap; that it was, on the part of the Vatican, "a Masonic tactic like Lenin's 'one step backward, two steps forward.'"[31]

In "Lost at Sea," the other important document Senior wrote at the time, based on a talk given on the subject, he brought out more clearly how the highest authorities were responsible for the shipwreck. He commented that at the Second Vatican Council there were "heretical intrusions such as 'collegiality' and 'religious liberty.'"[32] The popes too are guilty

of the shipwreck: "By ambiguity, innuendo and omission, the Conciliar popes have taught error, encouraged immorality and permitted, if not promulgated, liturgies harmful to the faith."[33] Senior thought the Church was being run by Modernists who refuse the principle of contradiction: "[the pope and his advisors are phenomenologists who] think all truth, both notional and real, including dogma and the facts, evolves—in a word that there is neither dogma nor fact (no 'things'), that everything becomes and nothing is."[34] He concluded that "to ordain bishops without papal consent does not incur excommunication if it is necessary to save the sacraments from the mafia in Rome"[35] and "if you obey the pope and even if under the Indult you do not participate, you tacitly accept heresy, immorality and sacrilege."[36]

Those are inflammatory statements, but Senior continued to have some qualms about his practical decision. A couple of years later he went so far as to say: "I really don't have a position. That's why I don't write anymore."[37] To the end, he went back and forth on what to do, as one of his sons said. In 1998, sick in the hospital and knowing he was probably in the last months of his life, he discussed the issue anxiously and at length with the chaplain. He resolved to begin attending the Masses at the Fraternity of St. Peter. A priest linked to the Fraternity brought him Holy Communion in the hospital and remarked how grateful the old professor was. When Senior got out of the hospital he indeed went to Fraternity Masses a few times but soon returned to the familiar Society Masses. A friend said Senior was disappointed because the Fraternity Mass was not as good as what he was used to at the Society—not as many women wore veils, the singing was not up to par, the church building was modernist. It was difficult after all this time to leave the church he was used to and that had become a home for him; to leave these priests and faithful he knew and admired for their tenacity. His basic outlook had probably not changed, and he so desired a beautiful, reverent Requiem Mass. A family member had already bought a burial plot for him in a cemetery owned by the SSPX and he would eventually be buried by a priest of the Society.

Although Senior saw better and more deeply than most the presence of Modernism in Church life, he erred at least in defending the

episcopal consecrations of 1988, in his decision to attend Society masses when he could have gone to Holy Mass celebrated by priests of the Fraternity of St. Peter, and in pretty much giving up, turning his back on the pope and on the legitimate pastors of the Catholic Church. Senior's participation in the Society was not limited to the type of attendance at Mass foreseen by the secretary of Ecclesia Dei. It is one thing to uphold and defend the Holy Mass according to the 1962 ritual, quite another to inveigh against the Holy See and the Second Vatican Council. For Senior, the Church had collapsed and all we could do was flee to our little group of conservatives until the hierarchy would come to its senses, until a new pope would set things right. He wrote in a public letter: "It is an irony that experts get so involved in arguments they often fail to see the fact (I speak of men much wiser than myself, learned in theology and canon law who can't admit the times are such that rules don't hold)."[38]

It is not our task here to argue out in detail these subjects, but a few remarks are in order. Firstly, concerning Pope John Paul II. This now-canonized saint was certainly not insincere in offering the possibility to celebrate Holy Mass and other Sacraments according to the 1962 liturgical books. Nor did he deny the principle of contradiction. No one who knew John Paul II could possibly hold that this priest who was so devoted to the Blessed Eucharist and the Holy Sacrifice was secretly working toward a Mass "accommodating all the people and creeds of the world."[39] Even if he went as far as he thought he could in ecumenism and interreligious dialogue, promoting any common ground, he was careful not to violate Catholic doctrine. In his talks he clearly made the necessary distinctions.

An illustration of Senior's impulsive judgment in this case might be an irate article he wrote regarding John Paul II's reception of Mikhail Gorbachev, then head of the Soviet Union, where he jumped the gun, likening it to the pope's kissing his visitor's ring.[40] In fact, it was just the contrary: Gorbachev was recognizing his defeat before the "highest moral authority on earth," as he called the pope.[41] He was, rather, morally kissing the pope's ring. John Paul II knew what he was doing. His fight against

Communism through truth and moral values had a major role in the collapse of the Soviet Union.[*]

Beyond the defense of a particular pontiff, we must affirm that, while it is true that one can to a certain extent flee corrupt modern culture as proposed by Senior, it remains that one does not have the right to flee the Holy Church. And there is no Catholic Church without bishops who have jurisdictional authority, and without the pope, the visible head of the Church, whom God gave us to lead and teach us. We cannot say rules don't hold when they come directly from a divine institution, an institution essential to the Church. To disobey the pope is more than a question of human laws. We cannot deny the evils we see in the Church, nor, for that matter, the positive good in many of the SSPX's positions and efforts, but neither should we disobey Christ's vicar. Besides the obvious facts of the crisis of the Church and the first principles of reason, there are the articles of the Creed, one of which is that the gates of hell shall never prevail against the Church led by her head, Christ's vicar. This means that Christ promised that a pope will not lead us into an iceberg of apostasy. Peter's boat may leak but there will be no shipwreck; it will not sink.

In the thirteenth century, faced with a scandalous, comfortable clergy, several groups returned to evangelical poverty, but some of them left the Church to do so, caused disorder and eventually disappeared, while St. Francis remained faithful to Rome and bore permanent fruit. Outside of the communion with Peter one might well hold on to some important but largely forgotten truths. It is, however, almost inevitable that one's views and heart become narrower, because one is cut off from living contact with the earthly head of Christ's Mystical Body. The Church is our Mother who carries us.

In the present crisis, we must trust God and so accept, with humble and even docile submission, authorities who represent Him in the measure that they authentically teach and command in union with the pope. The Apostolic Association of St. John-Marie Vianney, although it still

---

[*] See the last part of George Weigel's *Witness to Hope: The Biography of Pope John Paul II* (New York: HarperCollins Publishers, 1999) for a good study on objections to certain actions and statements of John Paul II.

had difficulties with certain teachings of ecclesiastical authorities, recognized the necessity of communion with Rome and therefore returned to obedience, while continuing to discuss problems and waiting for light. We must hold on to what is sure, listen and try to learn, and understand current Church teachings in continuity with tradition. In a discourse to the Roman Curia, Benedict XVI addressed the apparent contradictions, and thus difficulties, in seemingly new Church orientations of our times: "It is clear that in all these sectors [relationship between faith and modern science, between the Church and the modern State, and between the Christian faith and world religions] . . . a discontinuity had been revealed, but in which, after the various distinctions between concrete historical situations and their requirements had been made, the continuity of principle proved not to have been abandoned. It is easy to miss this at first glance."[42] He went on to examine as an example the council's teaching on religious liberty.*

Senior's errors in this realm do not derogate from the integrity of his soul, to which everyone who knew him in those final years still witness. It was his very faith and love that made him recoil so strongly against sacrilege, profanation and the bad doctrine he was faced with. He was searching to love God and men as he judged best in the darkness of our times. He certainly used rash and harsh words in the two articles we considered here. One can feel more than twenty years of pent-up frustration and anger coming out, accentuating further Senior's rhetorical tendency of extreme, sometimes rather impulsive, statements. We might apply to our dear professor what Pope Benedict XV wrote of Dante, who also had difficulties with Rome: "One must pity a man, so battered by fate, if sometimes, with ulcerated mind, he broke into invectives which exceeded [all] limits." The pope went on to point out that never for an instant did the poet call into question the supreme power of the keys entrusted to the Supreme Pontiff.[43] Senior would have gladly shed all his blood in witness to the dogma of papal supremacy and infallibility, to the One, Holy, Catholic and Apostolic Church.

---

* On this subject, one might recommend *Vatican II: Renewal within Tradition*, ed. Matthew Lamb and Matthew Levering, Oxford Press, 2009.

School of Death

Senior's last public appearance was in 1995, at a reunion arranged by former students for the twenty-fifth anniversary of the Pearson Integrated Humanities Program. The two-day event, attended by about 150 alumni, included poetry recitation, singing, a waltz and a talk by the three old professors. The audience was in hushed expectation before the talk. Then Senior began, as he had so often, "As we were saying last time . . ."—met with a roar of laughter. He then established the theme of the talk: "Love ye one another." He was thinking not only of Our Lord's line in his farewell discourse to his Apostles, but also of his own patron saint, the Evangelist St. John, who, according to St. Jerome, in his old age rarely said anything else to his disciples. Nelick was in what turned out to be the last year of his life, and Senior helped the ailing old man enter into the conversation by telling a story about Nelick and his father. The students thus once again experienced in Senior, this man now twelve years into retirement and seventy-two years of age, the same wonderful and witty teacher they had known and admired in class, with the delicate charity he had always shown.

Senior wrote a little poem for the occasion that conveys a sense of the mutual affection that existed among IHP students and teachers, who continued to share a common gaze, fixed on the beautiful, the good and the true. That springtime of discovery had proved itself to be genuine; its life had not withered.

> This April neither fades nor feints
> where we at Beauty's Truth first kissed,
> like the communion of all saints
> whose lips touch in the Eucharist.[44]

After this reunion, Senior spoke publicly no more. To a former student who implored him to continue the recordings of conversations with Quinn, he responded with an amusing letter telling how the modern world was becoming more foreign to him every day. In the extract below, the quotation is from Keats's "Ode to a Grecian Urn," conflated with "Ode to a Nightingale."

Phil Rizzuto had just quit baseball broadcasting for the Yankees after more than forty years:

Like Phil Rizzuto, "I'm no longer on top of the game." . . . The nightingale's song remains in "the midst of other woe," but the old woes of my generation no longer make sense to students who haven't the same habits as mine. Television and rock records didn't exist [in my youth]. Women didn't work back then. They had only got the right to vote three years before I was born and most of them hadn't learned to exercise it![45]

Not only was he feeling outstripped by a world that was moving on, but his physical weakness was also becoming more pronounced. He had to have a pacemaker inserted in 1995. At about this time, his brother began to notice that in their monthly telephone conversations John had less to say. In a way similar to St. Paul's line, "Though our outer nature is wasting away, our inner nature is being renewed every day." Senior described his ebbing stamina:

Physically and, I fear, mentally weaker week by week and month by month, be assured that as physical hearts and minds fail the will and spirit are stronger than ever. The best thing about old age is its stupidity and weakness. It is the best college of senectude that teaches directly in the flesh, will and intelligence that we don't do and know very much. This is something I know by study and believe in faith but now see face to face.[46]

He was learning not only about old age and weakness. Now in his seventies, Senior was attending the "school of death." Just as he had suffered before formally entering the school of suffering, so he had been reflecting about death and the afterlife long before 1993, when he turned seventy. He had sometimes recalled in his talks that "as Socrates said . . . all philosophy is a meditation on death. Revelation repeats the philosophic truth: Man, know that thou art dust and to dust thou shalt return."[47] There

was nothing morbid in this, but simply a facing up to a grave, essential fact in human existence. We must prepare to leave the world of the relative for that of the absolute.

Senior's meditation certainly became more intense when he had his brush with death in 1983 from his heart complications, and then was told that the transplanted vessels might be rejected within five years. He went a decade beyond those five years, but the continual proximity of the angel of death during his retirement helped him focus on the "one thing necessary." Perhaps his poetry, permeated with the thought of death, allows us to overhear some of his inner thoughts. In a couple of stanzas of "A Parliament of Birds" he cast a nostalgic glance toward the beautiful world that charmed his sensitive soul all the more that he knew he would not see it for much longer:

> A parliament of birds convenes
> outside the sickroom window,
> unanimous as Spring returns
> to take us under.
> The judases with red blossoms
> celebrate the season.
> O fresh, young world!—nothing becomes
> you so much as the leaving.[48]

He did not often write of Heaven, but it could not have been far from his mind in those days. In the first two stanzas of "Contemptus Mundi" he evoked the future life as transcending the varieties and riches of nature that he was still so attached to:

> How great the joys of heaven are
> that need no April to recover
> or surprise, no lilacs nor
> the pumpkins of October!
> There they need no sun and rain-
> bows are of emerald.

Why must we burn in heart and brain
by flaming fickleness enthralled?[49]

In the beginning of 1998 Senior received the news that an object of
much yearning and effort was soon to become reality: Fontgombault
Abbey was to found a monastery in the United States, in nearby Oklahoma.* Senior had extolled the monastic life as one of the foundations
from which would spring the restoration of Christian culture. Now, some
of his former students who had heard the call and left all to follow it in
France, would be returning to establish the same contemplative mode of
life not far from their former professor, the original source of their inspiration. But, a few months after receiving the happy news, the knell began
to toll. Losing weight and feeling unwell, he went to see a doctor. His
blood count was down; cancer was discovered. The surgery to remove the
tumor was a relatively simple procedure; he should have been in the hospital not more than ten days. Surgery trauma, however, troubled his
already weakened heart, and soon other organs started failing. Another
operation was necessary, so that he had to remain in the hospital, in the
end, for a total of five weeks.

A nurse related that Senior took the ordeal with good cheer, serenity
and patience; he was very grateful for anything one might do for him and
never made big demands. The old professor put himself in God's hands
and, although feeling some anxiety, kept a substantial serenity. The same
nurse added that Senior spoke of the KU Humanities Program without
ever making the slightest allusion to any persecution. Interestingly, the nurse
was a fallen-away Catholic, trying out some sort of Buddhism in those days.
The two spoke of many things—of T. S. Eliot, Hinduism, Marxism.... The
born teacher did it one more time: the nurse returned to the Faith of his
childhood under the persuasive poetic influence of his patient.

After those long weeks in the hospital, it took Senior a couple of
months to recover sufficiently in order to withstand the prescribed chemotherapy. His daughter wrote about that period: "Physically, Dad was

---

* Our Lady of Clear Creek Abbey; seven of the thirteen founding monks were IHP alumni, five of
whom were converts.

very tired. The chemotherapy made him feel ill most of the time and exhausted. He kept up a very brave front, though. He joked about things even though we knew certain symptoms worried him." After six months of chemo sessions, the results were unpromising: the scan showed that the cancer was still there. Senior could have tried a desperate second series of treatments, but he decided to desist. This decision was made known right before Christmas 1998, which was a sad one in the Senior household.

As he desired, Senior was able to stay home for his remaining days. His wife, who had become a nurse in the early 1970s to look after Senior's health, took strict care of him, with a hospice worker checking up on him on a regular basis. His daughter, Penny, and his elder son, Matthew, lived out of state but came home as much as they could. His younger son, Andrew, lived nearby and was with him much of the time. Senior had perked up somewhat after the chemo sessions were over. He regained his appetite, and was still occasionally getting out of the house in February. There were good days when he was sometimes even "chipper," Matthew said. He wrote letters and read, and spoke briefly with students and friends on the phone. A few were allowed to stop by for a moment and pray a rosary with him and Mrs. Senior. Dr. Quinn, that colleague in a unique collaboration of close to thirty years, came with his wife for a memorable goodbye visit. Most important, Senior did his "schoolwork." He had already been praying the penitential psalms over and over again for quite some time, and in these last months he added to his prayers a daily recitation of the Litanies of St. Joseph, patron saint of the dying.

Senior had once written: "What will it be for us when we say the Hail Mary for the last time, when 'Now' *is* the 'hour of our death,' and we must say, 'Amen'?"[50] On April 8, 1999, at the age of seventy-six, he was peacefully praying the rosary with his wife. At one point, he told her to recite the next decade without him as he was too tired. Having finished it, she looked up and saw that his soul was gone. Thus, as one former student remarked, he died praying with the woman he most loved on earth to the woman he most loved in Heaven.

Valediction

The orderly had stopped the cart
for us to say goodbye,
the agony about my heart
pausing to comply.

. . .

You spoke the final words, so close
I only heard a breath
between them saying something else,
something strong as death.[51]

A Risk of Certainty

There is a risk in certainty
no merest chance affords
the consequence is amnesty
forever afterwards,
the odds, zero to infinite,
loss impossible,
like playing Russian roulette
with all the chambers full.

—"Le Pari," from Pale Horse, Easy Rider

THE present work has endeavored to explore, in some depth, Senior's writings on education and culture by drawing upon his experiences and philosophical principles, by surveying authors who influenced him as well as other influences, and by contrasting and comparing him with others. Senior tended to carry things to extremes, but one can maintain that his basic doctrine is of vital importance today. Within a rather general trend among various groups that were seeking a return to something more natural in the midst of our artificial world, Senior had recourse to metaphysical and epistemological foundations and, as a teacher, focused on the learning process. Building especially on Plato, Aristotle, St. Thomas and Newman, drawing insights from literature and poetry, and learning from his experiences in the last breaths of cowboy life, as well as in Modernist nihilism, Senior came to some solid contributions that can be broadly grouped around the notion of Realism.

Senior, in fact, developed a robust and comprehensive approach to conveying Realism, in which the whole man—senses, imagination, emotion, will and intellect—are involved. He recognized the urgency of reestablishing man's sensible and emotional connection to reality. With this in view, he articulated the Realism, naturalness and dynamism found in the natural progression of education as perhaps no one ever has. Concentrating on the first steps of education, he acquired new insights into the poetic mode of knowledge, as well as into the necessity of incarnating gymnastic and music throughout our lives.

In concluding this work, a brief recapitulation is in order—not by way of repetition, but to underline Senior's ultimate purpose by elaborating on these contributions. Bearing in mind the title and epigraph of this book, then, let us examine how Realism, nourishment of the soil and ascent to the stars are intertwined.

For Senior, the objective of education was not merely scholarly and historical information, but "as Socrates said, 'the entire conduct of life.'"[1] Senior always called upon his auditors to lift their gaze above immediate gratification, projects and advantages, to the authentic adventure of human life, as reflected in this passage from his address to the KU graduating class of 1975:

> In the pursuit of happiness, in marriage or friendship, in vocations, recreation, politics and just plain jobs—in the long run—we have to ask what the whole thing is: What are all those activities and commitments parts of? . . . If a student forgets everything he learned at school or college, he had best remember this one question. It will be on the very final examination that his own conscience will make at the last hour of his life: In the pursuit of horizons—of horizontal things—have you failed to raise your eyes and mind and heart up to the stars, to the reason for things, and beyond, as Dante says at the top of the tower of his poem:
>
> > To the love which moves the sun
> > And all the other stars?[2]

Senior himself had always sought the stars. He was at least seeking adventure, something beyond comfort and security, when as a scrawny thirteen-year-old New Yorker he ran off to become a cowboy. He was reacting against immediate pleasure and egotistical pursuits, he was seeking some sort of absolute, when he desired to help establish the earthly paradise of Marxism or when he turned to the spiritual world with Plato, Symbolist poetry and Eastern thought. He one day ascertained, however, that his journey was leading nowhere, finding nothing; the stars seemed to be fading. He feared that life had no meaning, that it was not an adventure after all. Providence eventually led him to St. Thomas Aquinas and to a path out of the dark labyrinth. He perceived the stars once more, felt a renewal of their call and soon had the presentiment of a love whispering to him through their beauty. He grasped that the meaning of man's life was to seek Someone who was already seeking him.

Thus, he discovered where lies the real human adventure. Chapter Eight of *The Death of Christian Culture*, entitled "The Risk of Certainty," contrasted the aimless descent of Modernist Relativism with the adventure of the way up to truth and faith:

> We expire in the lazy, utterly helpless drift, the spongy warmth of an absolute uncertainty. Where nothing is ever true, or right or wrong, there are no problems; where life is meaningless we are free from responsibility, the way a slave or scavenger is free. Futility breeds carelessness, against which stands the stark alternative: against the radical uncertainty by which modern man has lived—as in a game of Russian roulette, stifled in the careless "now" between the click and the explosion, living by the dull grace of empty chambers—the risk of certainty.[3]

One might think it would be uncertainty that involves problems and cares, whereas certainty would remove them. It was quite the contrary, however, as Senior discerned in his analysis. In his Chapter Eight, he used the example of loveless, sterile sex to show that radical uncertainty is careless because where "nothing is ever true," nothing matters. Where

all is meaningless, there is no risk, no problem, no adventure, because there is nothing to live for, nothing to seek, nothing to lose. One is then "free from responsibility," because there is no value to respond for, no one to respond to. Such a life is indeed similar to Russian roulette, that sardonic game that carries the absurdity of the world to a dramatic paroxysm—to be or not to be, who cares?*

Certainty, by contrast, involves risks because when there is a truth, things do matter. Then there is a right and a wrong, something to seek and something that can be lost. In that case, our actions are meaningful and we are responsible for our choices. There is the possibility of adventure, which Senior explains as "putting oneself forward to meet the unexpected, the risking of what we have in favor of what we might have, the known in favor of the unknown, staking something on the future."[4] There is something to love, and something to risk for that love.

This idea of adventurous risk is eminently true for the Christian who deals with, not simply a truth, but Absolute Truth, Truth in person. Senior paraphrased the core of a sermon by Newman:

> Christian life is a real adventure and the call to it a question: as if you were a businessman who put his savings in a merchant ship, you must ask, "Suppose the ship goes down? How much have I ventured that I might lose if Christianity were false? . . . Or have I prudently invested in the world as well, so that if heaven fails, at least I will have had a successful time below?"[5]

Human life is not a drift or a stroll, but a pilgrimage with an objective, and one must leave things behind in order to attain it. Senior proclaimed that we are to sacrifice all things: "Christ says you must not just give something of yourself but everything."[6] Indeed, Christ told us we must prefer His love to our family, to our possessions, and of course to ourselves—we

---

* Senior referred several times to the theme of Russian roulette and the moment of suicide in the context of Modernism. See, before his conversion, *The Way Down and Out*, 142–143; and, after his conversion, a poem on Hemingway, "Death in the Afternoon," in *Pale Horse*, 22, as well as the poem quoted in the epigraph of this chapter, from *Pale Horse*, 16.

"must risk the death of love."[7] A faithful Christian life seems to be a risk, a gamble—a *pari* or wager as he states in the epigraph above, referring to Pascal's famous text. We have to grope toward something we do not see, go beyond all we can directly enjoy, experience or know.

Senior, like everyone else, felt the risk, but he knew it was "the risk of certainty," as he expressed it in the poem, with "amnesty forever afterwards" and "loss impossible." In this world, especially in the natural order, we can lose; but with Christ, in the supernatural order, there really is no risk of loss because we rely, not on "chance" or "*dull* grace," but on *divine* grace. God has proved His love by the gift of His Son. Christ's death on the Cross was the opposite of suicide by the game of Russian roulette, played out of disgust or hate for a meaningless world. Christ gave Himself all the way to death in order to save the world, for love of the world. Now it is up to us to respond to His initiative during this "dark, though very beautiful night," as Senior called this life.[8] In this context, continuing his discussion in "The Risk of Certainty," he quoted two of his favorite authors, the first speaking of trusting in the dark, the second of the hundredfold already received here below in return for that trust, for our sacrifices:

"Lead kindly light," Newman had written:

> Lead, kindly light, amid the encircling gloom,
> Lead thou me on.
> The night is dark and I am far from home,
> Lead thou me on.
> Keep thou my feet; I do not ask to see
> The distant scene—one step enough for me.

"On a dark night, kindled in love with yearnings—O happy chance!" said St. John of the Cross.[9]

Understandably, then, Senior desired to lead his students to the great truths, and ultimately stir them up to the adventure of seeking God. From the standpoint of this adventure, there were three basic attitudes among

the students. In terms Senior might have used around 1960, there were those who, like Baudelaire and the Symbolists—and Senior in the 1950s—were ready for a risk in order to find some meaning in life; others, like Sartre and the Existentialists, had despairingly given up the quest, and perhaps in revolt against everything and everyone; finally, there were trimmers who were not interested in looking up to the stars, but simply hoped to find repose in "the spongy warmth" of this world.

The epigraph to our book stands well as a commentary to this situation: "There is something destructive—destructive of the human itself—in cutting us off from the earth whence we come and the stars, the angels and God himself to whom we go." Senior's text continues: "John Donne said, 'Be more than man, or thou art less than an ant.' And a Catholic would add the complementary truth: Admit that you are less than angels or you will think yourself more than God."[10]

The Existentialist types of student felt condemned and the trimmers were reconciled to being cut off from the stars, closed up in this world like ants. They became even less than ants, as they groveled in disorders, sensual pleasure, comfort and riches. The Symbolist type indeed tried to be more than man. But he supposed that the only way to attain to this was by cutting himself off from the earth, bypassing sensible and reasonable knowledge like a pure spirit, an angel. Along with the Symbolist, the poor college student ready for a risk tried to jump directly to the stars. Senior observes here that this angelic pretension leads one to consider oneself "more than God"—in reference to the Hindu effort to go beyond all reality and therefore even beyond God, to look on reality from a higher vantage point than God Himself! As we know, the Symbolist, like the college student, having found nothing, usually fell back into the sensual. As Paschal explained long ago: *Qui veut fair l'ange fait la bête.**

The choice between ant and angel has failed. A middle road exists, however, that is in fact something of a crest between two downward slopes. Senior writes:

---

* Whoever wants to play at being an angel will act like a beast.

The Greek word for man is *anthropos*, a combination of *ana*, meaning "upward," and *tropos*, meaning "turn"; man is the upward-turning animal who walks erect, whose head is fixed in such a way that he can see the sun and the stars. . . . St. Isidore of Seville . . . comments: "Man walks erect and sees the heavens in order to serve God, not seeking to satisfy himself on earth like the animals whom God made by nature prone and obedient to their belly. Man is duplex interior and exterior." . . . So anthropos, the upward-turning beast, is the intelligent humus, this little piece of earth into which God breathed a living likeness of Himself.[11]

Man is not an ant, unable to look upward. He is more than an ant because he is intelligent, because God has breathed His likeness into him. This intelligence and likeness open him up to "more than man." He is not made simply to receive information about the world and figure out how things work. He emerges from this world to reach upward; he is made for the stars. Plato had grasped something true when he said that man has, as it were, a memory of the spiritual world that this sensible world evokes and reminds him of. On the other hand, man is not an angel who naturally flies among the stars. He is less than an angel because he is humus. He is neither purely material nor purely spiritual, but a body with a spiritual depth. We must rectify Plato, who envisioned man as receiving ideas directly from above. Our intellect does not have innate ideas but simply a light, an inclination. It aims for the stars, but it must use this world to actually go beyond it. Our intellectual light needs something to shine on.

St. Thomas elucidates this tendency in man. We recall his describing that the intellect looks on all things as *being*, as the ear hears sound and the eye sees colors. We can thus characterize more precisely our intellectual light as a sense of *being*. Its activity of recognizing essences, of forming ideas, is in fact a measuring of degrees of *being*. The mind is made for *being*, it seeks *being*, that is, ultimately, God, but it requires the experience of things, of various beings, in order to understand to some extent what *being* is and so climb toward absolute Being, toward He Who Is. That is why, in fact, we either go up or go down. When we gaze on the

world, we look for Being, for the absolute, for the infinite, for God, whether we realize it or not. If we try to stop at things of this world, we endeavor to stretch them into something infinite. We then go down by making idols out of limited things; we indeed grovel before them like ants.

With the help of Aristotle and St. Thomas especially, Senior recognized that the three types of attitude his students held were rooted in one philosophical error. All three derived from the Perennial Heresy, from Modernism, fundamentally from the refusal of *being*, of our fundamental orientation to *being*. Behind Baudelaire, Sartre, and even the trimmer, were imaginative figures like Hamlet and living philosophers like Descartes, doubting "to be." The prejudice dictating that sure rational knowledge, presented as perhaps the only reality, consisted in the quantitative and mechanical world of modern science, diverted the students from a more natural and deeper gaze. The sole escape from this dreary vision without depth, beauty or goodness seemed to be the irrational—drugs, sex, wild music—whether at first in some hope of something better as with the Symbolists, or in suicidal despondency with the Existentialists, or simply to avoid thought, like the trimmers. It was because many of Senior's students thus restrained their gaze to a superficial level of reality and otherwise lived in fantasy that their quest did not lead to real stars, to the true and the good, to God; or that they gave up on, or were not even attracted to, the adventure. The world was made to lead them to God, but for this they first had to look at it in a full way, and listen to its messages. They had to accept not just the measurable surface, but the *being* of things, which would then draw them more and more deeply into reality. Reality itself would then stimulate the desire for more than this world; it would point and launch them toward the stars.

Senior therefore saw that his task was to reconnect his students to reality—beyond the mathematical schemas of modern science—with *being*, with the existence of things. The obstacle to this was not only the pseudoscientific, materialist imagination with which they were imbued, whereby quantity is the only reality. Just as fundamental was the artificial and sensational world the students lived in. Their senses first had to be connected to reality before the remainder of their faculties could delve

into it. A full sensible connection to reality would not be accomplished by some sort of Positivism that severs sensation from the rest of one's powers. It would only be achieved in a normal, human, integral way, where what is sensed reverberates in our whole being, where sense, memory, imagination, emotions, mind and will function together. Senior, therefore, cultivated the sensitivity of the human person, with its natural dynamic ordered to the spiritual, to *being*.

Senior thus focused on the first two steps in education—on gymnastic, and on music and the poetic mode of knowledge. He encouraged delightful experience, and cultivated, through wonderful music, what experience his students might have. Through a poetic type of knowledge, he helped them recognize in an experiential way that things were really real, that they had substance and depth. Even though the students could not grasp the fact clearly in thought, or prove it in a syllogism, they perceived their own communion with things, their correspondence to them as they tasted the sweetness of beautiful mysteries that touched their souls. They discovered that, somehow, they were part of a whole, that they participated in something greater than themselves. Thus fixing their roots in the soil, they were also stimulated to an ascent to the stars.

Senior worked toward this vigorous Realism through the great works of Western literature—Homer, Virgil, Chaucer, Dickenson—with their love of concrete things, their appreciation for beauty and the individual qualities of things that bring out rich human values—friendship, fidelity, courage, compassion, love of family, attachment to a particular place. Students awakened to the fact that there are realities worth giving themselves for, worth sacrifices and risks. They were inspired to launch themselves into the adventure of truth, goodness and beauty. Without comprehending it in metaphysical terms, they knew they were connected with *being*; they tasted the beauty of things that they knew as a participation in absolute Beauty.

The Western literature Senior utilized for his work was of course largely Christian, and communicated some experience of Christian values, of Christ Himself and His mysteries. He nevertheless focused on the natural level in his teaching, fertilizing the soil, stimulating the desires of

his students, helping them discern their aim, being certain that nature, traditional Western culture and, with God's grace, supernature would do the rest. And he knew as well that the habit of the poetic mode would continue to serve them under God's grace, because, as Christians, they would have to go beyond the law and live as generous, free, trusting children of the Father. It would enable those who dared to walk forward into the obscure night with a firm, confident, cheerful step, to risk all for the All.

Senior in fact especially sought and found in poetry the culture of that something extra, something beyond duty, which calculating reason cannot explain; something chivalrous, generous, gratuitous, audacious. He took these Hamlets who hesitated about getting out of bed in the morning for fear that the floor might not be there, and endeavored to transform them into rough, courageous cowboys who scorned bruises, who rode forth with abandon in quest of adventure. Even more so, he strived to inspire knights in service of weak and little ones, performing heroic deeds in honor of their lady. However, for him both the cowboy and the knight were but images of and stepping stones toward the ultimate, most audacious adventure—accepting the challenge of responding to God's love.

A last word from this extraordinary professor leaves us with a lively picture of his secret desire for himself and his students. Senior hoped to kindle in himself and in others the generous abandon characteristic of St. Teresa of Avila, keeping Christ company on the Royal Road of the Cross, or of Roland and Olivier, giving their lives for their king, their country and their God. Such a risk of certainty is the fine flower of gymnastic and poetry. That is the stuff of which saints are made:

> The Camino Real of Christ is a chivalric way, romantic, full of fire and passion, riding on the pure, high-spirited horses of the self with their glad, high-stepping knees and flaring nostrils and us with jingling spurs. . . . The one thing needed, the *unum necessarium* of the Kingdom, is to love as he loves us, which is the love of joy, of suffering and sacrifice, like Roland and Olivier charging into battle to their death defending those they love as they cry "mon joie," that's the music of Christian Culture.[12]

Endnotes

Dictatorial Relativism

1. *The Man Who Was Thursday*, 43.
2. *The Abolition of Man*, 24.
3. Ibid.

Introduction

1. Allan Bloom, *The Closing of the American Mind* (New York: Simon and Schuster, 1987), 25.
2. See Senior, *The Death of Christian Culture* (New Rochelle, New York: Arlington House, 1978), 22–23.
3. Senior, *The Restoration of Christian Culture* (San Francisco, California: Ignatius, 1983), 181.
4. *Death of CC*, 132.
5. C. S. Dessein and Thomas Gorwall eds., *Letters and Diaries of John Henry Newman*, vol. 30 (Oxford: The Clarendon Press, 1973), 159.
6. *Restoration of CC*, 11.
7. Marcel Clément, *L'Homme Nouveau*, review of *The Death of Christian Culture*, January 2, 1996, "Culture." The translation is mine.
8. R. L. Bruckberger, *La Pensee Catholic*, review of *The Restoration of Christian Culture*, November–December 1991, "Les Livres." The translation is mine.
9. "Le Secret de Natalia Sanmartin," interview by Philippe Maxence, *L'Homme Nouveau*, April 12, 2014, p. 19.
10. *Restoration of CC*, 124.
11. Ibid., 139.
12. Ibid., 13.

Chapter 1

1. *Restoration of CC*, 59–60.

2. Robert Carlson, "A Tribute to John Senior, Shepherd of Souls," *The Wanderer*, May 20, 1999.

3. Senior, *Pale Horse, Easy Rider* (Lawrence: Shakespeherian Rag Press 1992), 38–39.

4. Senior, "The Restoration of Innocence: An Idea of a School" (mss 1994), 73.

5. Kempton Lindquist, "Professor Senior," *University Daily Kansan*, August 21, 1974, p. 2.

6. *Restoration of CC*, 8. This acknowledgment is not included in the posthumous IHS Press edition.

7. Senior, *The Remnants: The Final Essays of John Senior* (Forest Lake, MN: The Remnant Press, 2012), 128. This is a posthumous collection of some of Senior's writings.

8. Mark Van Doren, *The Autobiography of Mark Van Doren* (New York: Greenwood Press, 1958), 202.

9. Thomas Merton, *The Seven Storey Mountain* (New York: Harcourt, Brace and Co., 1948), 139.

10. *Pale Horse*, 27.

11. Lindquist, "Professor Senior," 2.

12. Ibid.

13. Ibid.

14. James McConkley, letter to Francis Bethel, October 27, 2005.

15. *Restoration of CC*, 127.

16. *Final Essays*, 134. Taken from Philip Maxence, "Des Leçons à Méditer. Entretien avec John Senior," *La Nef*, May 1995. Senior set down his answers in English in this interview, but these were not available from the publisher. Subsequently the interview was published in English in *The Remnants*.

17. Ibid., 133.

18. Ibid., 134.

19. *Death of CC*, 96.

20. Lindquist, "Professor Senior," 2.

21. Van Doren, *Autobiography*, 340.

22. *Final Essays*, 134-5.

23. Ibid., 127.

24. Dennis Quinn, *Iris in Exile: A Synoptic History of Wonder* (Lanham, Maryland: University Press of America, 2002), 307 n.1.

25. See Leon Surette, *The Birth of Modernism* (Montreal: McGill-Queen's University Press, 1993), 237–238.

Chapter 2

1. Senior, *The Way Down and Out: The Occult in Symbolist Literature* (Ithaca, New York: Cornell University Press, 1959), xxiii.
2. Ibid.
3. Ibid., xix.
4. Senior, letter to Richard Harp, August 19, 1996.
5. *The Way Down and Out*, xxi.
6. Ibid., 39.
7. Ibid., 30. The scholar is A. O. Lovejoy in his book *The Great Chain of Being* (Cambridge, Mass., 1936).
8. Ibid., 16.
9. Ibid., 31.
10. Ibid., 39.
11. Ibid.
12. Ibid., 15.
13. Ibid., 54, quoting Northrup Frye, *Fearful Symmetry: A Study of William Blake* (Princeton, 1947), 431.
14. Ibid., 40.
15. Ibid.
16. Ibid., xix.
17. Quoted in "The Perennial Philosophy," *Sunrise* magazine, April 1984.
18. Aldous Huxley, Introduction, *Bhagavad-Gita* (New York: Barnes and Noble, 1995), xi.
19. *The Way Down and Out*, xxi.
20. Ibid., 51.
21. Ibid., 59.
22. Ibid., xix.
23. Ibid., 82.
24. Ibid.
25. Ibid., 50.
26. Ibid., 51.
27. Ibid., 62.
28. Ibid., 53.
29. Ibid., 94. The translation is mine.

30. Ibid., 143.
31. Ibid., xxv.
32. Ibid., 46.
33. Ibid,. 31.
34. Ibid., 57.
35. Ibid., 95.
36. Ibid., 43.
37. Ibid., 96.
38. Ibid., 17.
39. Ibid., 200.
40. Ibid., 31.
41. Ibid., 95.
42. Ibid., 13.
43. Ibid., 203.
44. Mostly found in Rimbaud's "voyant" manifesto as outlined in letters to his teacher Georges Izambard (May 13, 1871) and his friend Paul Demeny (May 15, 1871).
45. Ibid., 108.
46. Ibid., 66.
47. Ibid., 97.
48. Ibid, 92.
49. Ibid., 93.
50. Ibid., 63.
51. Ibid., 200.
52. Ibid., xx and 200.
53. *Death of CC*, 58.
54. *The Way Down and Out*, xviii.
55. Ibid., 11.
56. Ibid., 21.
57. Ibid., xix.
58. Ibid., 126.
59. Ibid., 201.
60. Ibid.
61. Ibid., 203–204.
62. Ibid., 203.
63. Ibid., 204.
64. Ibid., 44.
65. Ibid., 49.

66. Ibid., 95–96.
67. Ibid., 203.
68. Ibid., 63.
69. Ibid., 203–204.
70. Bev Sandberg, "Super Prof," *Branding Iron*, September 23, 1966, p. 8.
71. *Death of CC*, 53.
72. Ibid., 66.

Chapter 3

1. *Death of CC*, 34.
2. Ibid., 58.
3. *The Way Down and Out*, vii.
4. René Guénon, *Introduction to the Study of the Hindu Doctrines*, trans. Marco Pallis (New Dehli: Munshirem Manoharla, 2000), 281.
5. Ananda Coomaraswamy, *Hinduism and Buddhism* (New York Philosophical Library, nd.), 11.
6. *Death of CC*, 60.
7. Ibid.
8. Ibid.
9. Ibid.
10. Ibid., 60–61.
11. Guénon, *Introduction*, 157.
12. Ibid., 281.
13. *Death of CC*, 58.
14. *Final Essays*, 128.
15. Ibid., 135.
16. See St. Thomas Aquinas, *Summa Theologiae*, I, q.28, a.4, 5m. All translations from St. Thomas are my own.
17. *Final Essays*, 128–129.
18. Aristotle, *Physics*, 3.3.202b18.
19. *Final Essays*, 135.
20. Aquinas, *Summa*, I, q.16, a.1 and q.21, a.2.
21. *Death of CC*, 21.
22. Ibid., 22.
23. Aquinas, *Summa*, I, q.11, a.2, 4m.
24. Chesterton, *St. Thomas Aquinas* (New York: Image Books, 1956), 165–166.
25. Aquinas, *Summa*, I, q.11, a.2, 4m.

26.   Ibid., I-II, q.94, a.2. See also St. Thomas's *Commentary on Aristotle's Metaphysics*, #605.

27.   Aristotle, *Metaphysics* 4.4.1006a29, quoted in *Death of CC*, 21–22.

28.   *Death of CC*, 22.

29.   *Final Essays*, 128.

30.   *Death of CC*, 34–35.

31.   Ibid., 61.

32.   Ibid., 35.

33.   Ibid., 21.

34.   Pope Pius XII, *Humani Generis*, para. 29. All translations of papal documents are from the Vatican Press.

35.   Jacques Maritain, *An Introduction to Philosophy*, trans. E. I. Watkin (New York: Sheed and Ward, 1937), 99.

36.   *Restoration of CC*, 179.

37.   Heraclitus, fragment 38.

38.   *Death of CC*, 45.

39.   Ibid., 65.

40.   Chesterton, *St. Thomas Aquinas*, 179.

41.   *Restoration of CC*, 10.

Chapter 4

1.   *Death of CC.* 68.

2.   Ibid., 67.

3.   Ibid., 61.

4.   Ibid.

5.   Ibid., 67.

6.   Ibid., 62.

7.   St. Augustine, *Selected Sermons*, ed. Q. Howe Jr (New York: Holt, Rinehard and Winston, 1966), 102–103.

8.   Letter to Francis Bethel, December 4, 1974.

9.   *Restoration of CC*, 184.

10.   See for example Aquinas, *Summa*, I, q.3, a.4.

11.   Vatican I, *Dei Filius*, para. 1.

12.   Ibid., para. 2.

13.   Aquinas, *Super Librum De Causis Expositio*, lesson 6.

14.   *Death of CC*, 17.

15. Ibid., 51.
16. *Final Essays*, 14.
17. *Death of CC*, 17.
18. Letter to Francis Bethel, December 4, 1974.
19. Ibid., 65.
20. Ibid., 49–50.
21. Ibid., 67.
22. *Final Essays*, 17.
23. *Death of CC*, 140.
24. Ibid.
25. Ibid., 135.
26. Letter to Francis Bethel, December 4, 1974.
27. *Final Essays*, 139.
28. *Restoration of CC*, 165.
29. *Death of CC.*, 142.
30. Ibid., 137.
31. Ibid., 141.
32. Lindquist, "Professor Senior," 2.

Chapter 5

1. *Final Essays*, 132–133.
2. *Death of CC*, 55.
3. Ibid., 26.
4. *Restoration of CC*, 211.
5. Ibid., 233.
6. *Final Essays*, 119.
7. *Death of CC*, 29.
8. *Restoration of CC*, 211.
9. *Death of CC*, 25.
10. Ibid., 29.
11. Ibid., 25.
12. *Restoration of CC*, 211–212.
13. Ibid., 195.
14. *Death of CC*, 30.
15. Ibid., 27.
16. Ibid., 42.

17.   Ibid., 41.
18.   Ibid., 41.
19.   Ibid., 61.
20.   Ibid., 46.
21.   Ibid., 32.
22.   St. Pius X, *Pascendi Dominici Gregis*, September 8, 1907, para. 6.
23.   *Death of CC*, 20.
24.   Ibid., 33.
25.   Ibid., 42.
26.   *Death of CC*, 20.
27.   Ibid.
28.   "History and the School," 10.
29.   Ibid., 4.
30.   *Death of CC*, 20.
31.   Ibid., 126–127.
32.   *Restoration of CC*, 179.
33.   *Death of CC*, 56.
34.   Ibid., 20.
35.   Ibid., 25.
36.   *Restoration of CC*, 153.
37.   *Death of CC*, 25.
38.   Ibid., 27.
39.   Ibid., 23–24.
40.   Ibid., 48.
41.   Ibid., 39.
42.   Ibid., 28.
43.   Ibid., 32.
44.   Ibid., 41.
45.   Ibid.
46.   *Restoration of CC*, 49.
47.   *Death of CC*, 24.
48.   Ibid., 29.
49.   Ibid., 24–25.
50.   Ibid., 34.
51.   Ibid.
52.   Ibid., 25–26.
53.   Herbert Read, *The Philosophy of Modern Art* (Greenwich, Conn: Fawcett Publications, 1967), 19–20.

54. *Death of CC*, 98.

55. Ibid., 51.

56. Ibid., 30.

57. Ibid., 22.

58. Chesterton, *Chaucer* (New York: Farrar and Rinehart, 1932), 28.

59. *Death of CC*, 43.

60. Ibid., 22.

61. Ibid., 23.

62. Ibid., 26.

63. *Restoration of CC*, 84.

64. *Death of CC*, 23.

65. Ibid., 49.

66. Ibid., 25.

67. Ibid., 36.

68. Ibid., 5.

69. Ibid., 35.

70. Ibid., 35–36.

71. *Restoration of CC*, 199.

Chapter 6

1. Nancy Kuemmerlein, letter to Francis Bethel, February12, 2005.

2. Penny Fonfara, letter to Francis Bethel, August 3, 2005.

3. "Restoration of Innocence," 28.

4. Fonfara, letter.

5. Robert Butler, "Teachers Put Faith in 'Medieval Spirit,'" *Kansas City Times*, April 1, 1977, 14A.

6. *Death of CC*, 15.

7. Ibid., 153.

8. "Restoration of Innocence," 29.

9. *Restoration of CC*, 22.

10. "Restoration of Innocence," 25.

11. *Restoration of CC*, 108.

12. Ibid., 215.

13. Ibid., 108.

14. "Wassail," *Pale Horse*, 61.

15. "Restoration of Innocence," 44.

16. *Restoration of CC*, 89.

17. See *The Way Down and Out*, 97.

18. Senior, "In the Time of the Breaking of Nations," *The Remnant*, October 15, 1989, p. 10.

19. Whittaker Chambers, *Witness* (Washington, D.C.: Gateway Publishing, 1980.)

20. *Restoration of CC*, 100.

21. *Death of CC*, 64.

22. Senior, letter to Richard Harp, August 19, 1996.

23. *Restoration of Christian Culture*, 155.

24. "Restoration of Innocence," 86.

25. *Death of CC*, 95.

26. Ibid., 172.

27. "Restoration of Innocence," 17.

28. Ibid., 25.

29. Carlson, "Tribute."

30. Ibid.

31. *Death of CC*, 93.

32. *Restoration of CC*, 155–156.

33. "Restoration of Innocence," 17.

34. Joseph Fessio, e-mail to James Conley, April 9, 2009.

35. "Restoration of Innocence," 14.

36. *Pale Horse*, 64.

37. *Death of CC*, 95.

Chapter 7

1. *Restoration of CC*, 76.

2. Senior, letter to Mark Van Doren, July 14, 1967.

3. Charles Taylor, letter to Francis Bethel, March 24, 2005.

4. Ibid.

5. Fonfara, letter.

6. Ibid.

7. *Death of CC*, 134–135.

8. *Restoration of CC*, 186–187.

9. Aquinas, *Summa*, I, q.85, a.1.

10. Ibid., q.84, a.7.

11. Ibid.

12. *Restoration of CC*, 187.

13. "Restoration of Innocence," 79.

14. See Aquinas, *Summa*, I, q.85, a.1.

15. "Restoration of Innocence," 79.

16. *Final Essays*, 136.

17. *Death of CC*, 137.

18. Ibid., 7.

19. Ibid.

20. *Final Essays*, 132.

21. *Restoration of CC*, 135.

22. William Wordsworth, "The World Is Too Much With Us."

23. *Pale Horse*, 49.

24. "History and the School," 13.

25. *Restoration of CC*, 136.

26. Ibid.

27. See Plato, *Timaeus*, 47a; Aristotle, *Metaphysics*, 1.2.982b; and St. Thomas, *In Duodecim Libros Metaphysicorum Expositio*, I, lesson 3.

28. *Restoration of CC*, 189.

29. Ibid., 28.

30. Ibid., 29.

31. *Final Essays*, 138.

32. "Restoration of Innocence," 78.

33. *Final Essays*, 137.

34. *Restoration of CC*, 138.

35. Plato, *The Republic*, trans. Paul Shorey, 4.441e–442a.

36. Ibid., 7.525c.

37. Mark Mitchell "Truth Within Is the Only Teacher," *University Daily Kansan*, September 25, 1974.

38. *Restoration of CC*, 204–205.

39. Robert Frost, *Collected Poems and Plays* (New York: Literary Classics, 1995), 777.

40. See Aristotle, *Metaphysics*, I, 2, 982b, 12–13; and Plato, *Theaetetus*, 155.

41. See *Death of CC*, 44; and "The Uses of Education," *Wyoming University News*, June 1967, p. 2.

42. "Restoration of Innocence," 13.

43. Ibid.

44. Ibid.

45. Ibid.

46. Senior, "The Thousand Good Books, or, What Everyone Should Have Read," appendix added to The Roman Catholic Books reprinting of *Death of CC*, 179.

47. Wordsworth, "My Heart Leaps Up."

Chapter 8

1. *Restoration of CC*, 135.

2. "Restoration of Innocence," 88.

3. *Final Essays*, 129.

4. *Death of CC*, 43.

5. Ibid., 44.

6. *Restoration of CC*, 27.

7. Ibid., 188.

8. Van Doren, *Liberal Education* (Boston: Beacon Press, 1959), 89.

9. *Death of CC*, 44.

10. Van Doren, *Liberal Education*, 94–95.

11. Mitchell, "Truth Within," 13.

12. Senior and Georgia Dunbar eds., *Poems for Study* (1951), 147.

13. "Restoration of Innocence," 23–24.

14. Jean Leclercq, *The Love of Learning and the Desire for God: A Study of Monastic Culture* (New York: Fordham University Press, 1982), 75.

15. Benedict XVI, *Deus Caritas Est*, December 25, 2005, para. 5.

16. Bloom, *Closing*, 71–72.

17. "Restoration of Innocence," 24.

18. "History and the School," 8.

19. *Final Essays*, 118.

20. *Restoration of CC*, 9.

21. See Aristotle, *Nicomachaen Ethics*, 3.5.1114a32 to 1114b25.

22. See Plato, *Republic*, 7.518c and following.

23. "Restoration of Innocence," 19.

24. Ibid., 24.

25. See Aquinas, *Summa*, II–II, q.180, a.3, 3m.

26. Plato, *Theaetetus*, trans. F. M. Cornford, 155d.

27. Ibid., *Phaedrus*, trans. R. Hackforth, 251a–b.

28. See the allegory of the cave in *Republic*, 7.514 and following.

29. See Aquinas, *ST*, I–II, q.32 a 8.

30. *Restoration of CC*, 153.

31. Plato, *Republic*, 3.403a and c.

32. *Death of CC*, 144.
33. "Restoration of Innocence," 29.
34. Plato, *Republic*, 3.411d.
35. *Poems for Study*, 150.
36. Ibid., Introduction.
37. "In the Time of the Breaking of Nations," 10.
38. Aristotle, *Poetics*, trans. Ingram Bywater, 1451b5.
39. "Restoration of Innocence," 24.
40. *Restoration of CC*, 33.
41. *Restoration of Innocence*, 14.
42. Chesterton, *The Defendant*, (London: J. M. D. and Sons, 1901), 26.
43. "Restoration of Innocence," 85.
44. *Final Essays*, 118.
45. *Restoration of CC*, 13.
46. Plato, *Republic*, 3.401d.
47. "Know Thyself," *Pale Horse*, 46.
48. Bloom, *Closing*, 133–134.
49. Ibid., 133.
50. See "Restoration of Innocence," 88.
51. Ibid.

Chapter 9

1. *Restoration of CC*, 194.
2. "Restoration of Innocence," 28.
3. "History and the School," 2.
4. Aristotle, *Nicomachean Ethics*, trans. W. D. Ross, 1.3.1095a.
5. "History and the School," 2.
6. Ibid.
7. Ibid.
8. Ibid.
9. "Restoration of Innocence," 28.
10. Plato, *Republic*, VI, 511.
11. "Apologia Poetica," *The Remnant*, September 30, 1990, 10.
12. Aquinas, *In Libros Posteriorum Analyticorum Expositio*, lesson 1.
13. "History and the School," 2.
14. "Restoration of Innocence," 28.

15. See Aristotle, *Metaphysics*, 1.1.980a and following.

16. See "Restoration of Innocence," 15.

17. "Restoration of Innocence," 13.

18. *Restoration of CC*, 194.

19. Ibid.

20. "History and the School," 2.

21. "Restoration of Innocence," 13.

22. Taylor, *Poetic Knowledge*, 83.

23. Aquinas, *Summa*, I–II, q.45, a.2.

24. Jacques and Raissa Maritain, *The Situation of Poetry* (New York: Philosophical Library, 1955), 51.

25. Ibid., 64.

26. Maritain, *Creative Intuition in Art and Poetry* (New York: Pantheon Books, 1953), 21.

27. Ibid., 23–24.

28. "History and the School," 2.

29. "Restoration of Innocence," 29.

30. Ibid., 27.

31. See Aquinas, *Summa*, q.1, a.9.

32. Aquinas, *Summa*, I, q.2, a.2, and II–II, q.27, a.4.

33. Senior, letter, *The Remnant*, August 15, 1991.

34. Newman, *Historical Sketches* II (London: Longman, Green and Co., 1888), 386–387.

35. "Restoration of Innocence," 28.

36. Chesterton, *Uses of Diversity* (London: Methuen and Co., 1920), 13.

37. See Aristotle, *Metaphysics* 2.1.993b, and Aquinas, *Commentary of Aristotle's Metaphysics*, II, lesson 2.

38. Aquinas, *Summa*, I, q. 5, a. 5, 1m.

39. "Restoration of Innocence," 24.

40. Chesterton, *Orthodoxy* (Garden City, New York: Image Books), 17–18.

41. Newman, *Sketches* II, 387.

42. Taylor, *Poetic Knowledge*, 82.

43. Etienne Gilson, *The Christian Philosophy of St. Thomas Aquinas* (New York: Random House, 1956), 368.

44. Joseph Rassam, *La Métaphysique de S. Thomas* (Paris: Presses Universitaires de France, 1968), 13–14. The translation is mine.

45. "Restoration of Innocence," 29.

46. Ibid.

47. "History and the School," 7.

48. Aquinas, *Summa*, II-II, q.1, a.4.

49. Newman, *University Sermons: Fifteen Sermons Preached before the University of Oxford* (London: Rivingtons, 1872), 225.

50. Ibid., 235–236.

51. See Aquinas, *Summa*, I, q.1, a.6,3m and I-II, q.45, a.2.

52. *Restoration of Innocence*, 29.

53. Letter to David Whalen, May 26, 1995.

54. "Apologia Poetica," 10.

55. "Restoration of Innocence," 87.

56. See Joseph Pearce, *C. S. Lewis and the Catholic Church* (San Francisco: Ignatius Press, 2003), 37–39.

57. Erasmo Leiva-Merikakis, *Fire of Mercy* (San Francisco: Ignatius Press, 1996), 45.

58. Eugene of the Child Jesus, quoted in Leclercq, *The Love of Learning*, 216.

Chapter 10

1. *Restoration of CC*, 217.

2. "Restoration of Innocence," 23.

3. *Restoration of CC*, 233.

4. John Paul II, address given to UNESCO, June 2, 1979 in *France, Message of Peace, Trust, Love and Faith* (Boston: St. Paul Editions, 1980), 189.

5. Joseph Ratzinger, *Truth and Tolerance, Christian Belief and World Religions* (San Francisco: Ignatius Press, 2004), 60.

6. *Restoration of CC*, 12.

7. Ibid., 222.

8. "History and the School," 1.

9. Coomaraswamy, *Christian and Oriental Philosophy of Art* (New York: Dover Publications, 1956), 92.

10. *Restoration of Christian Culture*, 222.

11. *Death of CC*, 8.

12. *Restoration of CC*, 12.

13. Ibid., 161.

14. Ratzinger, *Truth*, 61.

15. "History and the School," 1.

16. *Restoration of CC*, 234.

17. Newman, *An Essay in Aid of a Grammar of Assent* (Notre Dame, Indiana: University of Notre Dame Press, 1979), 62.
18. *Restoration of CC*, 121.
19. Ibid., 233.
20. *Death of CC*, 133.
21. *Restoration of CC*, 180.
22. *Death of CC*, 138.
23. Ibid., 132.
24. "Restoration of Innocence," 92.
25. *Death of CC*, 132.
26. *Final Essays*, 19.
27. *Death of CC*, 143.
28. Paul VI, *Evangelii Nuntiandi*, 8 Dec. 1975, para 20.
29. *Death of CC*, 107.
30. Ibid., 132.
31. *Restoration of CC*, 124.
32. *Death of CC*, 70.
33. Ibid., 103.
34. Ibid., 101.
35. Ibid., 142.
36. Pius XII, May 16, 1947, Homily for the canonization of St. Nicholas of Fluc, Documentation Catholique, XXIV col 777. The translation from the French version is mine. For the original, see Acta Apostolicae Sedis, XXXIX, 210.
37. John Paul II, *Evangelium Vitae*, March 25, 1995, para. 20.
38. Ibid., para. 23.
39. Ibid., para. 12.
40. "Restoration of Innocence," 2.
41. *Restoration of CC*, 143.
42. Ibid., 15.

Chapter 11

1. "Restoration of Innocence," 92.
2. *Restoration of CC*, 73.
3. Ibid., 207.
4. "History and the School," 21.
5. *Final Essays*, 129.
6. *Restoration of CC*, 20.

7.   "Restoration of Innocence," 29.

8.   Letter to Whalen.

9.   *Death of CC*, 7.

10. Ibid., 6–7.

11. *Restoration of CC*, 74.

12. Ibid., 102.

13. Ibid., 28.

14. "The Uses of Education," 2.

15. "Restoration of Innocence," 7.

16. *Death of CC*, 95–96.

17. *Restoration of CC*, 30.

18. Ibid., 24.

19. Ibid., 25.

20. Ibid., 42.

21. Ibid., 25.

22. Ibid., 72.

23. Ibid., 73.

24. Ibid., 78.

25. Ibid.

26. "Restoration of Innocence," 91.

27. Ibid., 90.

28. *Final Essays*, 105.

29. Letter to Mark Van Doren, April 16, 1970.

30. Letter to his brother, Hereward, nd.

31. *Final Essays*, 112.

32. John Paul II, *Laborem Exercens*, September 14, 1981, para. 19.

33. *Restoration of CC*, 63.

34. Ibid., 67–69.

35. Ibid, 75–76.

36. *The Awakening of Miss Prim*, Natalia Sanmartin Fenollera, trans. Sonia Soto (New York: Simon and Schuster, 2014), 4.

37. Ibid., 64.

38. Ibid., 23–24.

39. *Death of CC*, 96.

40. "Apologia Poetica," 10.

41. *Restoration of CC*, 32.

42. "The Thousand Good Books," from the Roman Catholic Books reprinting of *The Death of Christian Culture*, 179.

43.   Ibid., 180.

44.   *Restoration of CC*, 34.

45.   "Restoration of Innocence," 34.

46.   *Restoration of CC*, 34.

47.   Ibid., 33.

48.   Ibid., 35.

49.   Ibid., 40.

50.   Ibid.

51.   Ibid., 35.

52.   Ibid., 32.

53.   Ibid., 222.

54.   Ibid., 83-84.

55.   "History and the School," 1.

56.   *Final Essays*, 138.

57.   Douglas Van Steere, *Work and Contemplation* (New York: Harper and Brothers, 1957), 93.

58.   "Restoration of Innocence," 91.

59.   *Restoration of CC*, 221.

60.   Ibid., 100.

61.   Ibid., 84.

62.   "History and the School," 7.

63.   Ibid., 10.

64.   *Restoration of CC*, 63.

65.   "History and the School," 1.

66.   *Restoration of CC*, 92.

67.   See Leo XIII, *Rerum Novarum*, May 15, 1891, para 7–23; see also Pius XI, *Quadragesimus Annus*, May 15, 1931, para. 44–5; and John Paul II, *Centesimus Annus*, May 1, 1991, para. 13.

68.   See Pontifical Council for Justice and Peace, *Compendium of the Social Doctrine of the Church*, April 2, 2004, para. 335.

69.   *Restoration of CC*, 70.

70.   Quoted in Van Steere, *Work and Contemplation*, 62–63.

71.   *Restoration of CC*, 93–94.

72.   Fessio, e-mail.

73.   *Restoration of CC*, 52–53.

74.   "History and the School," 13.

75.   Maxence, "Leçons," 18.

76. John Paul II, *Laborem Exercens*, para. 5

77. Benedict XVI, *Caritas in Veritate*, June 29, 2009, para. 14 and 69.

78. Alicia Van Hecke, "The Restoration of Christian Culture," http://www.love-2learn.net/node/923, July 8, 2000 (accessed February 26, 2006).

79. *Restoration of CC*, 62.

80. Ibid.

81. Eric Brende, *Better Off: Flipping the Switch on Technology* (New York: Harper Collins, 2004), 233.

Chapter 12

1. "History and the School," 8.

2. "Restoration of Innocence," 47.

3. Ibid., 86.

4. Ibid., 19–20.

5. Ibid., 91.

6. Ibid., 33.

7. Ibid., 5.

8. Ibid., 33.

9. Ibid., 5.

10. Ibid.

11. Ibid., 33.

12. Ibid., 49.

13. "The Uses of Education," 2.

14. "Restoration of Innocence," 47.

15. Ibid., 33.

16. Ibid.

17. Ibid.

18. *Restoration of CC*, 32.

19. "Restoration of Innocence," 41.

20. Ibid., 5.

21. Ibid., 35.

22. Ibid., 36.

23. Ibid., 37.

24. Ibid.

25. Ibid.

26.   Chesterton, *Orthodoxy*, 54.
27.   "Restoration of Innocence," 60.
28.   "The Uses of Education," 2.
29.   "Restoration of Innocence," 35–36.
30.   *Restoration of CC*, 30–31.
31.   "Restoration of Innocence," 5.
32.   Ibid., 3.
33.   Ibid.
34.   "History and the School," 7.
35.   "Restoration of Innocence," 47.
36.   Ibid.
37.   Ibid., 8.
38.   Ibid., 48.
39.   Ibid.
40.   Ibid., 54.
41.   Ibid., 22.
42.   Ibid., 5.
43.   Ibid.
44.   Ibid.
45.   Ibid., 3.
46.   Ibid, 5.
47.   Ibid., 14.
48.   Ibid., 4.
49.   Ibid., 22.
50.   Ibid., 23.
51.   Ibid., 18.
52.   Ibid., 6.
53.   Taylor, *Poetic Knowledge*, 177.
54.   "Restoration of Innocence," 85.
55.   Ibid., 48.
56.   Ibid., 60.
57.   Ibid., 48.
58.   Ibid., 89.
59.   Ibid., 88.
60.   *Restoration of CC*, 41.
61.   Ibid.
62.   Ibid., 41–42.

63. Ibid.
64. "Restoration of Innocence," 91.
65. Ibid.
66. Ibid.
67. Ibid.
68. Ibid., 27.
69. Ibid.
70. Ibid., 8.
71. Ibid., 85.
72. Ibid., 26.
73. Bloom, *Closing*, 80.
74. "History and the School," 8.
75. Ibid.
76. Ibid.
77. "Restoration of Innocence," 71.
78. Ibid., 8.
79. *Restoration of CC*, 204.
80. "Restoration of Innocence," 8.
81. Ibid.
82. Ibid., 72.
83. Ibid., 76.
84. Ibid., 77.
85. Ibid., 19.
86. Ibid., 23.
87. Ibid., 8.
88. Ibid., 79
89. Ibid., 19.
90. Ibid.
91. Ibid., 9.
92. "History and the School," 3.
93. "Restoration of Innocence," 80.
94. Ibid.
95. Ibid., 9.
96. Ibid., 8.
97. Ibid., 9.
98. Ibid., 10.
99. Ibid., 60.

Chapter 13

1. *Death of CC*, 79.
2. Ibid., 71.
3. *Restoration of CC*, 85.
4. Ibid.
5. Ibid., 86.
6. Ibid., 87.
7. Ibid., 88.
8. Ibid., 82.
9. Ibid., 87.
10. Ibid., 86.
11. Ibid., 103.
12. Ibid., 82.
13. Ibid.
14. Ibid., 43.
15. Ibid., 226.
16. Ibid., 15–16.
17. Ibid., 16.
18. Ibid., 224.
19. Ibid., 240.
20. *Looking Again at the Question of the Liturgy with Cardinal Ratzinger, Proceedings of the July 2001 Fontgombault Liturgical Conference*, ed. Alcuin Reid (Farnborough: Saint Michael's Abbey Press), 9.
21. Benedict XVI, General Audience of Wednesday, June 3, 2009, *Osservatore Romano*, weekly edition in English, June 10, 2009, 15.
22. *Restoration of CC*, 38.
23. Ibid., 98.
24. *Death of CC*, 160.
25. *Restoration of CC*, 143.
26. Ibid., 161.
27. Ibid., 162.
28. Newman, *Historical Sketches II*, 426.
29. *Death of CC*, 147.
30. Ibid., 56.
31. Ibid., 97.
32. *Death of CC*, 164.
33. *Restoration of CC*, 15.
34. *Death of CC*, 160.

35. Ibid., 148.
36. *Restoration of CC*, 143.
37. *Final Essays*, 140.
38. *Death of CC*, 146.
39. Ibid., 147.
40. Paul VI, homily for the consecration of the basilica of Monte Cassino, *Documentation Catholique*, t. 61, November 15, 1964, 1436. The translation is mine.
41. *Final Essays*, 140.
42. *Restoration of CC*, 169.
43. John Paul II, Allocution to the Mayor of Subiaco, September 28, 1980, *Le Pape Parle de St. Benoit* (Paris: Tequi, 1980), 128. The translation is mine.
44. *Restoration of CC*, 222–23.
45. Ibid., 142.
46. Ibid., 10.
47. Ibid., 239.
48. Ibid., 244.
49. Ibid., 227–228.
50. Ibid., 228.
51. Ibid., 230.
52. Ibid., 233.
53. Ibid., 233–34.
54. Ibid., 234.
55. Ibid., 236–37.
56. Ibid., 237–38.
57. Antonio Martins, *Fatima and Our Salvation* (Chulmleigh, Devon: Augustine Publishing Company, 1985), 73.
58. *Restoration of CC*, 18.
59. Ibid., 238–239.
60. Ibid., 233.
61. "Restoration of Innocence," 34.

Chapter 14

1. Arvid Schulenberger, "The Orthodox Poetic: A Literary Catechism," self-published mimeograph, 1963, pp. 2–3.
2. Mark Mitchell, "Truth Within," 13.
3. Quinn, *Nascantur*, 5.

4. Senior, "Integrated Humanities Program: A Definition," *The Integration of Knowledge: Discourses on Education*, ed. Dennis Quinn (Lawrence: IHP, 1979), 3.

5. Ibid.

6. Ibid., 4.

7. *Death of CC*, 95.

8. Deb Riechmann and David Reeder, "In Search of the Good Guys," *Kansas Alumni*, April 1979, p. 1.

9. *Restoration of CC,* 49-50.

10. "Integrated Humanities Program: A Definition," 4.

11. *Restoration of CC*, 153.

12. "Integrated Humanities Program: A Definition," 4.

13. Bloch, letter to Robert Carlson, November 30, 1993.

14. *Restoration of CC*, 185.

15. Quinn, *The Pearson Humanities Program, an Announcement and an Invitation* (Lawrence: PIHP, nd), 2.

16. *Restoration of CC*, 193.

17. Letter to Mark Van Doren, July 26, 1969.

18. *Restoration of CC*, 193–194.

19. Quinn, *Nascantur*, inside cover.

20. Letter to Whalen.

21. *Final Essays*, 134.

22. Ibid., 133.

23. Quinn, *An Announcement*, 3.

24. Candy Nieman, "No Notes," *University Daily Kansan*, October 29, 1988.

25. Quinn, *Nascantur*, 8.

26. "Pearson Students Revive Waltz," *Kansas Alumni*, May 1974, p. 5.

27. "At the Pearson College Waltz," *Pale Horse*, 31.

28. Quinn, *Nascantur*, 10.

29. "History and the School," 20.

30. *Restoration of CC*, 197.

31. "Gorbachev's Ring," *The Remnant*, December 15, 1989.

32. "Uses of Education," 2.

33. "The Progress of Poetry," *Pale Horse*, 34.

34. Quinn, *Iris in Exile*, 85.

35. "Restoration of Innocence," 3.

36. Dana Lorelle, "When Wonder Cultivated Catholicity," *National Catholic Register*, March 6, 2005, culture section.

37. Mitchell, "Truth Within," 13.
38. Peter Cassegrande, letter to Howard Baumgartel, chairman of Educational Policies and Procedures Committee, April 27, 1972.
39. Quinn, *Nascantur*, 13.
40. William Wisner, *Whither the Postmodern Library? Libraries, Technology, and Education in the Information Age* (Jefferson, North Carolina: McFarland and Co., 2000), 66.
41. Bloch, letter.
42. Wisner, *Whither*, 65.
43. *Death of CC*, 175.

Chapter 15

1. Letter to Mark Van Doren, December 28, 1971.
2. Wisner, *Whither*, 66.
3. Vincent Smith, letter to Dennis Quinn, January 14, 1972.
4. Letter to Philip Anderson, nd.
5. Wisner, *Whither*, 66.
6. "Restoration of Innocence," 86.
7. Title taken from a cartoon in the *University Daily Kansan* of April 17, 1979.
8. "Senior wins '74 HOPE," *University Daily Kansan*, 21 Oct. 1974. "KU's Outstanding Educator Picked," *Topeka Capitol Journal*, 20 Oct. 1974.
9. Bill Hoch, "PIHP Methods, Content Generate Criticism," *University Daily Kansan*, January 27, 1975.
10. "College Assembly Votes to Do Away with IHP," *Kansas Alumni Magazine*, June 1979.
11. Ibid.
12. Quinn, letter to Dean Wagonner, March 2, 1974.
13. Sesto Prete, letter to Howard Baumgartel, April 24, 1972.
14. Butler, "Medieval Spirit," 14A.
15. Quinn, "Visitors' Responses to PIHP" (Lawrence: PIHP, nd), 1.
16. Ibid., 2.
17. Calder M. Pickett, "24 Hours That Should Be Kept," *University Daily Kansan*, March 2, 1973.
18. Walter Crockett, "Statement on Pearson Integrated Humanities Program."
19. Richard Johnson, letter, *Interchange*, January 24, 1977.
20. Deb Riechmann, "Merits of IHP Stated at Forum," *University Daily Kansan*, November 22, 1978.

21. "Report of the Integrated Humanities Program Advisory Committee to the Committee on Undergraduate Studies and Advising," May 16, 1978.

22. Albert Burgstahler, "Some Reflexions on the Report of the Committee on the Evaluation and Advancement of Instruction Concerning the Pearson Integrated Humanities Program," April 23, 1972.

23. Dennis Quinn, Frank Nelick, and John Senior, "To Purchasers of Cults, Sects and the New Age," letter mailed to subscribers by *Our Sunday Visitor*, nd.

24. Michael Flynn, "PIHP Defended," letter, *University Daily Kansan*, February 3, 1974.

25. Deb Riechmann, "Faculty Defends IHP," *University Daily Kansan*, December 4, 1978.

26. George Worth, letter to Baley Price, chairman of the Subcommittee for Evaluation of Innovative Courses and Programs, November 26, 1971.

27. James Seaver, "Statement to G. B. Price Committee," October 12, 1972.

28. Quinn, letter to Dean George Waggoner, March 2, 1972.

29. Ibid.

30. Carlson, *Truth on Trial: Liberal Education Be Hanged* (South Bend: Crisis Books, 1995) 72.

31. Quinn, "To Members of the Pearson Program Advisory Committee," January 10, 1975.

32. "KU Humanities Defenders Organize," *Lawrence Journal World*, July 22, 1977.

33. Alice von Hildebrand, "Foreword," *Truth on Trial* by Robert Carlson, ix.

34. Seaver, "Statement."

35. *Death of CC*, 177.

36. Ibid., 125.

37. Quinn, letter to Wil Linkugel, chairman of the PIHP Advisory Committee, November 13, 1978.

38. Quinn, "Higher Education: The Pluralist Monopoly," *The University Bookman*, vol. 28, n.1, 1988, p. 3.

39. *Restoration of CC*, 179–180.

40. *Death of CC*, 177.

41. Frank Morriss, "Why Do They Fear Truth?" *The Wanderer*, February 2, 1979, p. 1.

Chapter 16

1. Chuck Alexander, "Prof Defends Students' Entry into Monastery," *Wichita Eagle*, April 10, 1977.

2. Robert Butler, "Teaching Issue Splits KU," *Kansas City Times*, March 29, 1973, 16A.

3. Seaver, "Statement."

4. Jerry Seib, "Opinions, Emotions Vary on Humanities Program," *University Daily Kansan*, November 18, 1976.

5. Butler, "Teaching Issue," 1A.

6. Butler, "Medieval Spirit," 14A.

7. *Restoration of CC*, 131.

8. "History and the School," 6.

9. "Restoration of Innocence," 71.

10. Mitchell, "Truth Within."

11. Frances Horowitz, "Remarks to the College Assembly," February 20, 1973.

12. *Restoration of CC*, 155.

13. Bloch, letter.

14. "Integrated Humanities Program, a Special Course" (Lawrence: Friends of the Humanities, nd).

15. *Death of CC*, 105.

16. *Restoration of CC*, 154.

17. Quinn, *Iris*, 66.

18. "Restoration of Innocence," 82.

19. "Report of the Integrated Humanities Program Advisory Committee to College Committee on Undergraduate Studies and Advising," January 20, 1979, p. 13.

20. Riechmann and Reeder, "In Search," 3.

21. Ibid.

22. Scott Bloch, "Prairie Fire," *Sursum Corda*, Winter 1996, p. 33.

23. *Final Essays*, 134.

24. Ibid.

25. Bloch, "Prairie Fire," 28.

26. *Death of CC*, 8.

27. *Restoration of CC*, 31.

28. Senior, Quinn, and Nelick, "Purchasers."

29. Butler, "Medieval Spirit," 14A.

30. Morriss, "Why Do They Fear Truth?," 1.

31. Bloch, "Praire Fire," 34.

32. Senior, letter to Howard Baumgartel.

33. *Death of CC*, 177–178.

34. Reichmann and Reeder, "In Search," 3.

35. *Restoration of CC*, 121.

36.   Letter to Francis Bethel.

37.   Reichmann, "Faculty Defends IHP."

38.   Letter to David Whalen.

Chapter 17

1.   Bloch, letter.

2.   *Restoration of CC*, 15.

3.   David Pietrusza, "Books in Brief," review of *The Death of Christian Culture*, *National Review*, January 1979, p. 111; and Norman Desmarais, "Education," review of the same, *Library Journal*, November 1978, p. 2235.

4.   Maxence, «L'Amour de la Sagesse,» *La Nef,* October 1996.

5.   Patrick Odaniel, "The Kraken Awakens," review of *The Death of Christian Culture*, Amazon.com, http/www.amazon.com/review/R7RG9949HEWCL, August 12, 2003 (accessed 2006).

6.   Senior, letter to Phillip Anderson, June 11, 1984.

7.   *Pale Horse*, 64.

8.   Letter to Robert Carlson, January 30, 1995.

9.   Senior, letter to Francis Bethel, nd.

10.   Carlson, "A Tribute."

11.   "The Loveliest of Trees," *Pale Horse*, 55–56.

12.   *Restoration of CC*, 10.

13.   "Restoration of Innocence," 92.

14.   *Final Essays*, 140.

15.   Ibid., 135.

16.   "The Sacrifice of Fools," *Pale Horse*, 59.

17.   *Death of CC*, 159.

18.   Joseph Cardinal Ratzinger, "Card. Ratzinger's 1988 Remarks to the Bishops of Chile," *Una Voce America*, http//www.unavoce.org/cardinal_ratzinger_htm (accessed February 26, 2006).

19.   "Letter of Cardinal Castrillon Hoyos to Mgr. Fellay," *Una Voce Magazine*, http//www.unavoce.org/castrillon_hoyos_to_fellay.htm (accessed February 26, 2006).

20.   John Vennari, "Vatican Admits Society of St. Pius X Masses Fulfill Sunday Obligation," *Catholic Family News*, July 2003, referring to a letter of September 27, 2002, by Msgr. Camille Perl, Ecclesia Dei secretary.

21.   Alison Reavis, letter to Francis Bethel, nd.

22.   Jeffrey Rubin, "Reviving Christendom," *Latin Mass Magazine*, July–August 1993, p. 19.

23. Ibid.

24. Ibid.

25. *Final Essays*, 88. The original appeared in *The Remnant*, July 15, 1988, p. 4. I quote here according to the original article. The text in *Final Essays* says, "there may be saints...."

26. Letter to Philip Anderson, January 8, 1989.

27. *Remnants*, 79.

28. Letter to Philip Anderson, January 8, 1989.

29. Letter, *The Remnant*, August 15, 1991.

30. Ibid.

31. Ibid.

32. *Final Essays*, 95.

33. Ibid., 92.

34. Ibid., 94–95.

35. Ibid., 93.

36. Ibid., 92.

37. Letter, *The Remnant*, July 15, 1991.

38. Ibid.

39. *Final Essays*, 95.

40. See "Gorbachev's Ring."

41. George Weigel, *The End and the Beginning* (New York: Doubleday, 2010), 177.

42. Benedict XVI, address to the Roman Curia, December 22, 2005, *Osservatore romano*.

43. Walter Peters, *Life of Benedict XV* (Milwaukee, Wisconsin: Bruce Publishing Co., 1959), 263.

44. John Senior, "I.H.P. Reunion," quoted in Bloch, "Prairie Fire," 39.

45. Carlson, "A Tribute."

46. Letter to Philip Anderson, April 14, 1997.

47. *Restoration of CC*, 90.

48. *Pale Horse*, 56.

49. "Contemptus Mundi," *Pale Horse*, 55.

50. *Restoration of CC*, 81.

51. *Pale Horse*, 62.

Conclusion

1. *Death of CC*, 167.

2. See ibid., 93.
3. Ibid., 128–29.
4. Ibid., 128.
5. Ibid.
6. Ibid., 153.
7. Ibid., 159.
8. Ibid., 178.
9. Ibid., 159–160.
10. *Restoration of CC*, 214.
11. Ibid., 216–217.
12. Ibid., 17–18.

Bibliography

This bibliography contains those works referred to more than once in the text.

Aquinas, Thomas. *Summa Theologiae.*

Aristotle. *The Basic Works of Aristotle*, ed. Richard McKeon. New York: Random House, 1941.

——————. *Caritas in Veritate.* June 29, 2009.

Benedict XVI. *Deus Caritas Est.* December 25, 2005.

——————. Letter to Robert Carlson, November 30, 1993.

Bloch, Scott. "Prairie Fire." *Sursum Corda.* Winter 1966.

Bloom, Allan. *The Closing of the American Mind.* New York: Simon and Schuster, 1987.

——————. "Teachers Put Faith in 'Medieval Spirit." *Kansas City Times*, April 1, 1977, 1A and 14A

Butler, Robert. "Teaching Issue Splits KU." *Kansas City Times*, 29 March 1973, 1A and 16A.

——————. "A Tribute to John Senior, Shepherd of Souls." *The Wanderer*, May 20, 1999.

Carlson, Robert. *Truth on Trial: Let Liberal Education Be Hanged.* South Bend, Indiana: Crisis Books, 1995.

——————————. *Orthodoxy.* Garden City, New York: Image Books, 1959.

Chesterton, G. K. *St. Thomas Aquinas.* New York: Image Books, 1956.

Fessio, Joseph. E-mail to James Conley. April 9, 2009.

Fonfara, Penny. Letter to Francis Bethel. August 3, 2005.

Guénon, René. *Introduction to the Study of the Hindu Doctrines,* trans. Marco Pallis. New Dehli: Munshirem Manoharla, 2000.

——————————. *Centesimus Annus*, May 1, 1991.

——————————. *Evangelium Vitae*, March 25, 1995.

John Paul II. *Laborem Exercens*, September 14, 1981.

Leclercq, Jean. *The Love of Learning and the Desire for God: A Study of Monastic Culture.* New York: Fordham University Press, 1982.

Lindquist, Kempton. "Professor Senior." *University Daily Kansan*, August 21, 1974.

Maritain, Jacques. *Creative Intuition in Art and Poetry.* New York: Pantheon Book, 1953.

——————————. With Raissa Maritain. *The Situation of Poetry.* New York: Philosophical Library, 1955.

Maxence, Philippe. "Des Leçons á méditer. Entretien avec John Senior." *La Nef,* May 1995.

Mitchell, Mark. "Truth Within Is the only Teacher." *University Daily Kansan,* September 25, 1974.

Morriss, Frank. "Why Do They Fear Truth?" *The Wanderer,* February 2, 1979.

Newman, John Henry. *Historical Sketches II.* London: Longman, Green and Co., 1888. Pontifical Council for Justice and Peace. *Compendium of the Social Doctrine of the Church.* April 2, 2004.

Plato. *The Collected Dialogues,* eds. Edith Hamilton and Huntingdon Cairns. Princeton, New Jersey: Princeton University Press, 1973.

Quinn, Dennis. *Iris in Exile: A Synoptic History of Wonder.* Lanham, Maryland: University Press of America, 2002.

——————. *The Pearson Humanities Program: An Anouncement and An Invitation.* Lawrence: PIHP, nd.

——————. *The Pearson Humanities Program, Nascantur in admiratione.* Lawrence: PIHP, nd.

Ratzinger, Joseph. *Truth and Tolerance: Christian Belief and World Religions.* San Francisco: Ignatius Press, 2004.

Reichmann, Deb. "Faculty Defends IHP." *University Daily Kansan,* December 4, 1978.

——————. With David Reeder. "In Search of the Good Guys." *Kansas Alumni,* April 1979.

Rubin, Jeffrey. "Reviving Christendom." *Latin Mass Magazine,* July–August 1993.

Seaver, James. "Statement to G. B. Price Committee." October 12, 1972.

Senior, John. Ed. with Gloria Dunbar. *Poems for Study.* 1951.

——————. *The Way Down and Out: The Occult in Symbolist Literature.* Ithaca, New York: Cornell University Press, 1959.

——————. "The Uses of Education." *Wyoming University News,* June 1967.

——————. Letter to Mark Van Doren. July 14, 1967.

—————————. Letter to Howard Baumgartel, April 25, 1975.

—————————. Letter to Francis Bethel. December 4, 1974.

—————————. *The Death of Christian Culture.* New Rochelle, New York: Arlington House, 1978.

—————————. *The Restoration of Christian Culture.* San Francisco: Ignatius Press, 1983.

—————————. "The Glass Confessional." *The Remnant.* July 15, 1988.

—————————. "In the Time of the Breaking of Nations." *The Remnant,* October 15, 1989.

—————————. "Gorbachev's Ring." *The Remnant.* December 15, 1989.

—————————. "Apologia Poetica," *The Remnant,* September 30, 1990.

—————————. Letter to *The Remnant.* August 15, 1991.

—————————. *Pale Horse, Easy Rider.* Lawrence, Kansas: Shakespeherian Rag Press, 1992.

—————————. "The Restoration of Innocence: An Idea of a School." Mss., 1994.

—————————. "History and the School." Mss., 1995.

—————————. Letter to David Whalen. May 26, 1995.

—————————. *The Remnants: The Final Essays of John Senior.* Forest Lake, Minnesota: The Remnant Press, 2012.

—————————. With Dennis Quinn and Frank Nelick, "To Purchasers of Cults, Sects and the New Age." letter mailed to subscribers by *Our Sunday Visitor,* nd.

—————————. Letter to Hereward Senior, nd.

——————. "The Thousand Good Books, or, What Everyone Should Have Read." Mss. nd, partly available in the appendix of the Roman Catholic Books reprinting and the IHS edition of *The Death of Christian Culture.*

Taylor, Charles. Letter to Francis Bethel, March 24, 2005.

Van Doren, Mark. *Liberal Education.* Boston: Henry Holt and Co., 1943.

——————. *The Autobiography of Mark Van Doren.* New York: Greenwood Press, 1958.

Van Steere, Douglas. *Work and Contemplation.* New York: Harper and Brothers, 1957.

Index